Boko Haram

▷▷▷▷▷▷▷▷▷▷▷▷▷▷▷▷▷▷

PRINCETON STUDIES IN MUSLIM POLITICS

Dale F. Eickelman and Augustus Richard Norton, Series Editors

A list of titles
in this series
can be found at the
back of the book.

Boko Haram

THE HISTORY OF AN
AFRICAN JIHADIST MOVEMENT

▶▶▶▶▶▶▶▶▶▶▶▶▶▶▶▶▶▶▶▶▶▶▶▶▶▶▶▶▶▶▶▶▶▶▶▶▶▶

Alexander Thurston

Princeton University Press

Princeton and Oxford

Copyright © 2018 by Princeton University Press

Published by Princeton University Press, 41 William Street, Princeton, New Jersey 08540

In the United Kingdom: Princeton University Press, 6 Oxford Street, Woodstock, Oxfordshire OX20 1TR

press.princeton.edu

Jacket design by Kathleen Lynch

Maps produced by Miles Irving, University College London. www.Milesmap.co.uk.

Library of Congress Cataloging-in-Publication Data

Names: Thurston, Alexander, author.
Title: Boko Haram : the history of an African jihadist movement /
    Alexander Thurston.
Other titles: Princeton studies in Muslim politics.
Description: Princeton : Princeton University Press, 2018. | Series: Princeton
    studies in Muslim politics | Includes bibliographical references and index.
Identifiers: LCCN 2017013034 | ISBN 9780691172248 (hardcover : alk. paper)
Subjects: LCSH: Boko Haram. | Terrorist organizations—Nigeria. |
    Terrorism—Nigeria—Religious aspects—Islam. | Islamic fundamentalism—
    Nigeria. | Jihad. | Islam and politics—Nigeria.
Classification: LCC HV6433.N62 B68 2018 | DDC 363.3250966923 LC record
    available at https://lccn.loc.gov/2017013034

British Library Cataloging-in-Publication Data is available

This book has been composed in Minion Pro and ITC Avant Garde Gothic Std

Printed on acid-free paper. ∞

Printed in the United States of America

1 2 3 4 5 6 7 8 9 10

Contents

▶▶▶▶▶▶▶▶▶▶▶

Acknowledgments

▶▶▶▶▶▶▶▶▶▶▶▶▶▶▶▶▶▶▶▶▶▶▶▶▶

Given the bleak nature of its subject matter, this book was sometimes difficult to write, intellectually and at times emotionally. I have incurred a number of debts along the way. First, I thank Fred Appel and Princeton University Press for commissioning the book. I am grateful to Thalia Leaf and Stephanie Rojas of the press for their help. Three anonymous reviewers for the press provided suggestions and feedback that strengthened the book. I also thank William McCants and Shadi Hamid of the Brookings Institution's Project on U.S. Relations with the Islamic World for commissioning the paper "'The Disease Is Unbelief': Boko Haram's Religious and Political Worldview," on which part of this book is based. Anne Peckham of Brookings provided invaluable editorial and technical assistance for that project. Some portions of the paper appear verbatim in chapters 2, 3, 4, and 5, while other portions have been modified and updated.

Second, I would like to express gratitude to the community of scholars and thinkers who work on the grim topic of Boko Haram. I have benefited tremendously from exchanges with Marc-Antoine Pérouse de Montclos, Adam Higazi, Hilary Matfess, Andrea Brigaglia, Carmen McCain, Paul Lubeck, Murray Last, Freedom Onuoha, Abdulbasit Kassim, and Ambassador John Campbell. I owe special thanks to Brandon Kendhammer for sharing several key sources with me. I have also leaned heavily on the work of scholars whom I have not met, including Kyari Mohammed and Abdul Raufu Mustapha, and of scholars whom I met briefly long ago, such as Ahmad Murtada. I owe major intellectual debts to the community of scholars and practitioners who study Nigeria more broadly, including Muhammad Sani Umar, Roman Loimeier, John Paden, Peter Lewis, Carl LeVan, and Matt Page. I am also indebted to scholars who study jihadism, especially Aaron Zelin—without his meticulous efforts to collect and preserve jihadist primary sources, this book could not exist in its present form. All errors of fact or interpretation in the book are mine alone, of course.

Third, I thank colleagues at Georgetown University, my academic home since 2014. Scott Taylor, Lahra Smith, and Ken Opalo of the African Studies Program are wonderful and supportive colleagues. I also value the ongoing mentorship I receive from John Voll and Jonathan Brown. Early research related to this book was presented at Georgetown's Prince Alwaleed bin Talal Center for Muslim-Christian Understanding in October 2014, and I am grateful for that opportunity.

Finally, I thank my family and friends. My wife, Ann Wainscott, spent long hours with me patiently discussing the material, ideas, and arguments that have gone into the book. Her love and support mean a great deal to me. I also appreciate the encouragement I received from my parents, Robert Thurston and Margaret Ziolkowski; my sister, Lara Thurston; and my grandparents Theodore and Yetta Ziolkowski, all of whom carefully followed the book's progress. My son, Jack, made for delightful company during the final revisions of the book. It is my hope that by the time he reaches adulthood, our world will be less turbulent and violent.

This book is dedicated to all the victims of the Boko Haram crisis, especially the innocent but also those who, through their recklessness, have wronged themselves and others.

Boko Haram

▶▶▶▶▶▶▶▶▶▶▶▶▶▶▶▶

Introduction

▶▶▶▶▶▶▶▶▶▶▶▶▶▶▶▶▶

Boko Haram, a movement claiming to act in the name of Islam, has killed tens of thousands of people in Nigeria and the neighboring countries of Niger, Chad, and Cameroon.[1] Tens of thousands more have died amid the broader crisis that Boko Haram precipitated. Civilians, Muslims and Christians alike, have fallen victim to hunger and disease, and millions in the region now face precarity. Others have been killed by the Nigerian security forces, whose heavy-handed response to Boko Haram has exacerbated the conflict. Boko Haram is one of the deadliest jihadist groups in the world, and the crisis surrounding it is one of the globe's worst.

Boko Haram took shape in the northeastern Nigerian city of Maiduguri in the early 2000s. The group became notorious—but also attracted support—for its contention that Western-style education (in the Hausa language, *boko*) was legally prohibited by Islam (in Arabic and Hausa, *haram*). In Boko Haram's eyes,

---

[1] Figures for the death toll are disputed and inexact. Some totals do not distinguish between the violence Boko Haram commits and the deaths inflicted by security forces and civilian vigilantes. Most databases rely on press reports, meaning that casualty counts can be too high or, more likely, too low. Some violence is never reported at all—journalists' access to combat zones and especially to rural northeastern Nigeria has often been blocked by both Boko Haram and the Nigerian government. Institutions tracking violence include the Council on Foreign Relations (http://www.cfr.org/nigeria/nigeria-security-tracker/p29483), John Hopkins University School of Advanced International Studies (http://www.connectsaisafrica.org/research/african-studies-publications/social-violence-nigeria/), and the Armed Conflict Location and Event Data Project (http://www.crisis.acleddata.com/category/boko-haram/).

Western-style education belonged to a larger, evil system. That system included multiparty democracy, secular government, constitutionalism, and "man-made laws." For Boko Haram, all these institutions are not just un-Islamic but anti-Islamic.

Over time, Boko Haram has preserved core elements of its message. But Boko Haram has also periodically shifted its strategies, tactics, and self-presentation. This book reconstructs the movement's history, paying attention to how its doctrine interacted with the changing environment around it.

The book is organized chronologically, dividing Boko Haram's career into five phases. First, there was the movement's prehistory: the decades from the 1970s to the 1990s, when its future founders grew up amid political uncertainty, disruptive urbanization, interreligious violence, and widespread debate about the relationship between Islam and politics. Second, from approximately 2001 to 2009, there was a phase of open preaching. One portion of Boko Haram attacked local authorities in 2003–4, but the group's decisive turn to violence occurred in 2009, when the sect launched an uprising across several northern Nigerian states. This rebellion was crushed, and Boko Haram's founder, Muhammad Yusuf, was killed by police. A third phase, from 2010 to 2013, centered on terrorism. Led by Yusuf's companion Abubakar Shekau, Boko Haram bombed major targets, including in the capital, Abuja, and perpetrated regular assassinations and raids in the northeast.

During a fourth phase, from 2013 to 2015, Boko Haram controlled territory in northeastern Nigeria. The group offered civilians a stark choice: embrace Boko Haram's brand of Islam, or face violence. It was in this phase that Boko Haram's most infamous attack occurred: the kidnapping of 276 schoolgirls in the town of Chibok in April 2014. The fifth phase began when Boko Haram's "state" largely fell to the militaries of Nigeria and its neighbors. Boko Haram then resumed its clandestine existence and intensified its terrorism. As part of its latest incarnation, Boko Haram declared its affiliation to the Islamic State, also known as ISIS and ISIL, in March 2015—a move that soon brought schisms within the group. With a host of actors now involved in the conflict, Boko Haram remains deadly.

Central Arguments

This book argues that Boko Haram represents the outcome of dynamic, locally grounded interactions between religion and politics. I stress the *dynamism* of these interactions because Boko Haram is reactive and adaptable. The group has sometimes subtly shifted its core doctrine in response to external events. I stress the *local* aspect of interactions between religion and politics because most of the key moments in Boko Haram's history occurred in Maiduguri and northeastern Nigeria. The group's trajectory reflects decisions taken by individuals, decisions shaped by the contingencies of their locality. A hyperlocal view is necessary if one is to answer the question of why Boko Haram emerged in Maiduguri and not in Kano or Sokoto, or in any of the other numerous Nigerian and Sahelian cities where one can find poverty, corruption, and radical preachers. Only by closely examining Boko Haram's history in northeastern Nigeria does it become possible to identify critical junctures in the movement's trajectory.

This approach breaks with two prevailing explanations for Boko Haram's emergence. One explanation holds that Boko Haram is best understood as an extension or even a puppet of the global jihadist movement—casting Boko Haram as a kind of "Nigerian al-Qaedaism," and claiming that foreign backers, especially Algerians, long pulled Boko Haram's strings.[2] A second explanation depicts Boko Haram as the product of a collision between poverty, "poor governance," and economic disparities between northern and southern Nigeria.[3]

These explanations fail because each emphasizes one factor as a master explanation for Boko Haram, either transnational jihadism or "relative deprivation." But as William McCants has written, efforts to identify a single cause that drives jihadist movements are problematic. McCants has proposed a broader framework:

> To my mind, the most salient [causes] are these: a religious heritage that lauds fighting abroad to establish states and to protect one's fellow Muslims; ultraconservative religious ideas and networks exploited by militant recruiters; peer pressure (if you know someone involved, you're more likely to get involved); fear of religious persecution; poor governance (not

---

[2] Jacob Zenn, "Nigerian al-Qaedaism," *Current Trends in Islamist Ideology*, 14 March 2014, http://www.hudson.org/research/10172-nigerian-al-qaedaism-. Zenn has written prolifically about ties between Boko Haram, the Boko Haram splinter group Ansar al-Muslimin, and al-Qa'ida in the Islamic Maghreb, but much of his work is driven by an alarmist agenda involving a highly selective use of evidence. Zenn's overall integrity, moreover, is decisively undermined by his 2014 report for the lobbying firm the Bow Group, in which he links the U.S. Democratic Party to Boko Haram, casts the Nigerian political party the All Progressives Congress as an Islamist organization, and accuses Emir of Kano Muhammadu Sanusi II—a target of Boko Haram—of supporting the sect. See Jacob Zenn, "Exposing and Defeating Boko Haram: Why the West Must Unite to Help Nigeria Defeat Terrorism," Bow Group, 2014, https://www.bowgroup.org/sites/bowgroup.uat.pleasetest.co.uk/files/Jacob%20Zenn%20Bow%20Group%20Report%20for%2022.7.14.pdf. Another, more credible but ultimately derivative work that emphasizes global jihadism and Boko Haram's ties to other jihadist actors is Caroline Varin, *Boko Haram and the War on Terror* (Santa Barbara, CA: Praeger, 2016).

[3] See, for example, Seth Kaplan, "How Inequality Fuels Boko Haram," *Foreign Affairs*, 5 February 2015, https://www.foreignaffairs.com/articles/africa/2015-02-05/how-inequality-fuels-boko-haram.

type of government); youth unemployment or underemployment in large cities; and civil war.[4]

To the list, I would add politics, in the sense that jihadist movements are political actors and in the additional sense that political developments can enable or constrain their activities. In this book, I adapt Abdul Raufu Mustapha's "empirically based multidimensional approach" for analyzing Boko Haram, which highlights five factors: religious doctrines, poverty and inequality, post-1999 politics, youth agency, and geography.[5] But to avoid a "kitchen sink" problem where anything and everything is proposed an explanation for Boko Haram, I focus on interactions between religion and politics, and I flesh out the role of agency.

Going further, I would emphasize again that the next challenge is to localize such factors—not just at the level of a country, but at the level of a city, Maiduguri, and a few states. After all, jihadist movements are diverse. Jihadist ideology is not a one-size-fits-all package of bad ideas. Rather, organizations like Boko Haram—even if they are in dialogue with global jihadist trends—develop localized doctrines that evolve through interactions with their surroundings. Additionally, Boko Haram merits a different kind of analytical treatment than that typically given to jihadist groups that began as small, clandestine militant cells. Almost uniquely among contemporary jihadist movements,

[4] William McCants, "Trump's Misdiagnosis of the Jihadist Threat," Brookings Institution Markaz Blog, 11 November 2016, https://www.brookings.edu/blog/markaz/2016/11/11/trumps-misdiagnosis-of-the-jihadist-threat/.

[5] Abdul Raufu Mustapha has proposed one such framework for understanding Boko Haram, which is close to mine. See Mustapha, "Understanding Boko Haram," in *Sects and Social Disorder: Muslim Identities and Conflict in Northern Nigeria,* edited by Abdul Raufu Mustapha, 147–98 (Suffolk: James Currey, 2014); in a way, the present book tries to localize Mustapha's approach and to more deeply investigate his category of "agency."

it began as a mass religious movement before transitioning to armed struggle. And to an unusual degree among peer movements, it stresses Western-style education as an enemy.

This study builds on excellent academic studies of Boko Haram's doctrine,[6] operations, and career.[7] Journalists have provided valuable perspectives on the movement's violence,[8] as well as on the atmosphere of corruption and contentious politics in Nigeria.[9] Other studies address topics that this book cannot, for reasons of space, cover, especially Boko Haram's treatment of women.[10]

---

[6] Anonymous, "The Popular Discourses of Salafi Radicalism and Salafi Counter-radicalism in Nigeria: A Case Study of Boko Haram," *Journal of Religion in Africa* 42:2 (2012): 118–44; Ahmad Murtada, "Jama'at 'Boko Haram': Nash'atuha wa-Mabadi'uha wa-A'maluha fi Nayjiriya," *Qira'at Ifriqiyya*, 13 November 2012; Kyari Mohammed (Muhammad Kyari), "The Message and Methods of Boko Haram," in *Boko Haram: Islamism, Politics, Security and the State in Nigeria,* edited by Marc-Antoine Pérouse de Montclos, 9–32 (Ibadan, Nigeria: French Institute for Research in Africa, 2014); and Abdulbasit Kassim, "Defining and Understanding the Religious Philosophy of Jihadi Salafism and the Ideology of Boko Haram," *Journal of Politics, Religion and Ideology* 16:2–3 (2015): 173–200.

[7] International Crisis Group, "Curbing Violence in Nigeria (II): The Boko Haram Insurgency," 3 April 2014, http://www.crisisgroup.org/~/media/Files/africa/west-africa/nigeria/216-curbing-violence-in-nigeria-ii-the-boko-haram-insurgency.pdf; Marc-Antoine Pérouse de Montclos, "Nigeria's Interminable Insurgency: Addressing the Boko Haram Crisis," Chatham House, September 2014, https://www.chathamhouse.org/sites/files/chathamhouse/field/field_document/20140901BokoHaramPerousede Montclos_0.pdf; and Adam Higazi, "Mobilisation into and against Boko Haram in North-East Nigeria," in *Collective Mobilisations in Africa,* edited by Kadya Tall, Marie-Emmanuelle Pommerolle, and Michel Cahen, 305–58 (Leiden: Brill, 2015). Virginia Comolli's *Boko Haram: Nigeria's Islamist Insurgency* (London: Hurst, 2015) provides an informative overview of the sect's career but has little sustained analysis.

[8] Mike Smith's *Boko Haram: Inside Nigeria's Unholy War* (London: I. B. Tauris, 2015) has a particularly compelling account of Boko Haram's 2011 bombing at the United Nations headquarters in Abuja.

[9] Andrew Walker, *"Eat the Heart of the Infidel": The Harrowing of Nigeria and the Rise of Boko Haram* (London: Hurst, 2016).

[10] As this book went to press, Hilary Matfess was completing a book on Boko Haram and women, of which I have read only parts, but which promises to be a strong contribution. See also Mia Bloom and Hilary Matfess, "Women as Symbols and Swords in Boko Haram's Terror," *PRISM* 6:1 (March 2016), http://cco.ndu.edu

This book's contribution lies in clarifying how ideas and environments interacted to produce and sustain Boko Haram. The book is not an ethnography, but rather a documentary history. Drawing on underutilized documents and sources, ranging from long-forgotten government reports to religious texts and propaganda videos in Arabic and Hausa, the book reveals the dynamism of Boko Haram's doctrines and illuminates the political and social foundations of the localized niche that the movement came to occupy.

Religion, Politics, and Boko Haram

Religion and politics, as analytical categories, are highly contested. Here I adopt functional definitions suited to the task of analyzing Boko Haram. For my purposes, religion has two dimensions. First, it is a mode of speaking that lays claim to the values of a religious tradition, in this case Islam.[11] Second, religion is a field of social interaction where actors and institutions present themselves as representatives of a religious tradition. In

---

/Portals/96/Documents/prism/prism_6-1/Women%20as%20Symbols%20and%20 Swords.pdf; and International Crisis Group, "Nigeria: Women and the Boko Haram Insurgency," 5 December 2016, https://d2071andvip0wj.cloudfront.net/242-nigeria -women-and-the-boko-haram%20Insurgency.pdf. See also Dionne Searcey, "Boko Haram Turns Female Captives into Terrorists," *New York Times*, 7 April 2016, http:// www.nytimes.com/2016/04/08/world/africa/boko-haram-suicide-bombers.html; and Obi Anyadike, "Coerced or Committed? Boko Haram's Female Suicide Bombers," IRIN, 19 April 2016, https://www.irinnews.org/analysis/2016/04/19/coerced-or -committed-boko-haram%E2%80%99s-female-suicide-bombers-0.

[11] This definition is akin to Talal Asad's famous notion of Islam as a "discursive tradition." See "The Idea of an Anthropology of Islam," Georgetown University Center for Contemporary Arab Studies, Occasional Papers Series, 1986. If the definition sounds tautological, that is because it is—perhaps what makes a discourse religious is the speaker's self-conscious intention that he or she be understood as religious according to the conventions of a given tradition.

the religious field, "social capital" has to do with matters such as one's perceived piety, knowledge, and charisma.[12]

Many analysts, skeptical of the explanatory power of "religion" and conceiving of "religion" in terms of individual conviction and faith, dismiss any effort to examine the religious content of jihadist movements; others are keen to disassociate jihadism from Islam. It is impossible to say whether Boko Haram's leaders, members, and sympathizers really "believe" in the group's messages. But Boko Haram's leaders and followers appear to care a lot about religious ideas. Boko Haram emerged in a context where religious study circles were widespread and where, whether out of piety or ambition, many young men assiduously sought religious knowledge. Some of the youth who joined Boko Haram were keenly interested in understanding theological issues. One early Boko Haram video shows Muhammad Yusuf answering detailed questions from the audience regarding Islam's internal theological and sectarian divisions.[13] Religious ideas also became a bitter source of conflict for Boko Haram: between Muhammad Yusuf and even more hardline voices within the early movement; between the movement and its closest religious peers; and between the movement and the wider society.

Boko Haram members, even the movement's leaders, made sacrifices for those ideas. If leaders had simply sought power or had been "rational actors" motivated entirely by greed, one would have expected Yusuf not to have launched an ill-planned uprising against one of the most powerful governments in Africa. Moreover, one would not have expected Yusuf to remain defiant in custody when he must have sensed that his execu-

---

[12] Pierre Bourdieu, "Genesis and Structure of the Religious Field," *Comparative Social Research* 13 (1991): 1–43.

[13] Boko Haram, untitled video called simply "Film.3gp," undated, https://www.youtube.com/watch?v=xthVNq9OKD0.

tion at policemen's hands was a distinct possibility. Indeed, the Boko Haram conflict has been marked by so many twists and turns, so much violence and hatred between people who knew one another personally, and so much contingency that it seems absurd to treat the participants as rational actors who could leisurely weigh the costs and benefits of their actions. It seems especially absurd to treat all participants in the crisis as secular rational actors who believe they inhabit a purely material universe.

Caring about religion is a part of jihadism generally. As Shadi Hamid has remarked in the case of the Islamic State, "religion matters a great deal" to jihadists: "It inspires supporters to action; it affects the willingness to die (and, in the case of ISIS, the willingness to kill); it influences strategic calculations and even battlefield decisions."[14] As one study of jihadists in Pakistan has found, "religious ideals . . . can influence individual and collective choices" when those ideals have "moral or practical appeal for the believer" and "when the prescribed beliefs were repeatedly seen to help address the everyday realities of life."[15] My findings are similar, and they parallel a recent study of recruitment into Boko Haram. That study's authors found that "religion was a thread running through many stories of youth choosing to join," but they also found that recruitment was a complex affair involving financial incentives, social pressures, and varying degrees of coercion.[16] Taking religion's role

[14] Shadi Hamid, "Does ISIS Really Have Nothing to Do with Islam? Islamic Apologetics Carry Serious Risks," *Washington Post*, 18 November 2015, https://www .washingtonpost.com/news/acts-of-faith/wp/2015/11/18/does-isis-really-have-nothing -to-do-with-islam-islamic-apologetics-carry-serious-risks/.

[15] Masooda Bano, *The Rational Believer: Choices and Decisions in the Madrasas of Pakistan* (Ithaca, NY: Cornell University Press, 2012), 8–9.

[16] Mercy Corps, "Motivations and Empty Promises: Voices of Former Boko Haram Combatants and Nigerian Youth," April 2016, 14, https://www.mercycorps.org/sites /default/files/Motivations%20and%20Empty%20Promises_Mercy%20Corps_Full %20Report.pdf.

seriously, not just as it informs jihadist rhetoric but also as it shapes jihadist action, does not have to mean saying that the Islamic State or Boko Haram represent Islam's "center of gravity."[17] Nor does it have to mean discounting other, political and socioeconomic explanations.

Even if religion was simply ideological cover for Boko Haram's ambitions, its religious messages would be worth studying. Far from being the ravings of madmen, its leaders' sermons and videos are structured speeches. Religion, or what Boko Haram considers religion, is part of that structure. By paying attention to what Boko Haram actually says, one can learn a great deal about the movement—not only about how it understands jihad, but also about how it frames events in religious terms.

Moreover, "religion" does not necessarily refer to individual belief. Paying attention to the "religious field" can also shed new light on jihadism. In northern Nigeria's religious field, Boko Haram occupies a complicated niche: the movement benefited from existing infrastructures but also took advantage of important vacuums. Building on one classic study of "the fragmentation of sacred authority" in northern Nigeria,[18] I trace religious fragmentation in Maiduguri and northeastern Nigeria between the 1970s and the 2000s, showing how this atmosphere contributed to Boko Haram's emergence. One consequence of that approach is, for me, an uncomfortable but necessary observation: Boko Haram's early messages were less marginal, in the context of northern Nigeria, than is often assumed. As one study of a Saudi Arabian dissident movement found, "fringe" movements sometimes start out with support from mainstream religious au-

---

[17] Juan Cole, "Today's Top 7 Myths about Daesh/ISIL," Informed Comment, 17 February 2015, http://www.juancole.com/2015/02/todays-about-daesh.html.

[18] Ousmane Kane, *Muslim Modernity in Postcolonial Nigeria: A Study of the Society for the Removal of Innovation and Reinstatement of Tradition* (Leiden: Brill, 2003).

thorities. Dissidents can experience the loss of mainstream support as a critical juncture on the road to violence.[19] This trend fits Boko Haram as well: it first sought to co-opt more mainstream religious rhetoric and then reacted violently when mainstream voices denounced it.

Reading through the historical record, I found many postcolonial northern Nigerian elites—university intellectuals, members of the hereditary ruling class, politicians, and others—espousing antipathy toward Western-style education and secular government. Few of these figures advocated armed jihad in the 1980s and 1990s. Those who are still living have all denounced Boko Haram. Nevertheless, it is important to show that Boko Haram's ideas did not come out of thin air. The movement tried to harness and amplify certain ideas that were already circulating in the religious field, particularly during the period between 1999 and 2003, when northern Nigerian states were intensively implementing Islamic law (shari'a)[20]—a development that is indispensable to understanding Boko Haram's emergence.

Politics, for this book's purposes, has two aspects. On one level, politics involves a struggle to control resources, resource flows, and decision making—a struggle over "who gets what, when, how."[21] This kind of politics necessarily involves an effort to build coalitions and marginalize opponents. Boko Haram has often been portrayed in analytical literature as the result of impersonal, abstract forces like economic deprivation, regional

[19] Thomas Hegghammer and Stéphane Lacroix, "Rejectionist Islamism in Saudi Arabia: The Story of Juhayman al-'Utaybi Revisited," *International Journal of Middle East Studies* 39:1 (February 2007): 103–22.

[20] For an analysis of shari'a implementation, see Paul Lubeck, "Nigeria: Mapping a Shari'a Restorationist Movement," in *Shari'a Politics: Islamic Law and Society in the Modern World*, edited by Robert Hefner, 244–79 (Bloomington: Indiana University Press, 2011).

[21] Harold Lasswell, *Politics: Who Gets What, When, How* (New York: Whittlesey House, 1936).

disparities, unemployment, corruption, poor governance, and educational backwardness. In Nigeria's "do or die" politics, however, these forces operate in intensely political and personal terms. The politics that helped birth (and sustain) Boko Haram had to do with stark questions of who wins and loses, who uses whom, and whose expectations are raised only to be met with bitter disappointment later. A focus on the politics of "who gets what" illuminates critical features of life in northeastern Nigeria from the 1970s to the present. The combination of ferocious political competition and unaccountable politicians translated into bitterness among Boko Haram's core constituencies.

On another level, politics is a struggle to define a community's values,[22] to make or unmake a consensus. In this sense, politics and religion are intimately related: religious blueprints for reorganizing society are inevitably political projects as well. Boko Haram's leaders are political figures not just because they seek to control people and territory, but also because they want to redefine what it means to live in the Lake Chad region and what it means to be a Muslim there. The struggle to define values often plays out in the arena of symbols, and the Boko Haram crisis is no different—Boko Haram has sought to appropriate not only the Qur'an and the Sunna (model) of the Prophet Muhammad, but also figures from northern Nigeria's past.[23] Boko Haram's leaders have repeatedly rejected central symbols of Nigerian national identity—the constitution, the pledge of allegiance, the national anthem—and have proposed countersymbols, including the "strange flags" flown by Boko

---

[22] David Easton, *A Framework for Political Analysis* (Upper Saddle River, NJ: Prentice Hall, 1965), 50.

[23] On Boko Haram's use of history, see Atta Barkindo, "How Boko Haram Exploits History and Memory," Africa Research Institute, 4 October 2016, http://www.africa researchinstitute.org/newsite/publications/boko-haram-exploits-history-memory/. Barkindo's contention that Boko Haram was peaceful until 2009, however, is inaccurate.

Haram since 2003.[24] Boko Haram has fixated on politics in the narrow sense of disrupting elections and challenging politicians, but also in the broader sense of trying to remake the symbolic landscape of Nigeria and its neighbors.

There are significant gaps in what can be known about Boko Haram at present. Even basic facts, such as whether its official leader, Abubakar Shekau, is alive or dead, are contested. The group's leadership structure, financial operations, internal culture, and recruitment strategies remain largely opaque. Various conspiracy theories, most of which depict Boko Haram as a front for other actors, have distorted analysis of the group.[25] At the same time, there is a dangerous temptation to depoliticize movements like Boko Haram, and to erase the histories of backroom deals, impunity, and state violence that can drive jihadism. While unequivocally condemning Boko Haram, this book also contends that just as politics was part of the cause of the violence, so must politics—including controversial decisions about who wins and loses in the aftermath of the crisis—be part of the solution.

Boko Haram: What's in a Name?

As a movement, Boko Haram has been known by many names.[26] Parts of the movement have been labeled "Yusufiyya," after its founder. The "Nigerian Taliban" label stuck for a time

[24] The quotation is from Goodluck Jonathan, "Jonathan Declares State of Emergency in Borno, Yobe, Adamawa States," Channels Television, 14 May 2013, https://www.youtube.com/watch?v=3GglRw0urlw.

[25] See Mustapha, "Understanding Boko Haram," for an adept rebuttal of various conspiracy theories.

[26] This section is a modified and updated version of my blog post "Boko Haram: What's in a Name?," which appeared on Sahel Blog on January 7, 2013, https://sahelblog.wordpress.com/2013/01/07/boko-haram-whats-in-a-name/.

after the 2003–4 uprising. The phrase "Boko Haram" is itself a nickname given by outsiders. One sect member has said:

> This appellation appeared first among the general public. On one side, that was a result of their difficulties in pronouncing the true name, and from another side it is an appellation derived from what our scholars frequently mentioned in order to counsel people, especially parents and the students of institutions and universities, and the rest of those concerned with education. . . . In any case we are dissatisfied with this appellation and we do not call ourselves by it. Calling us by it is a form of derisive nicknaming.

In the sect's early days, the member continued, Yusuf "did not name the society by any name." Even the group's official Arabic name came only when Shekau took power.[27]

"Boko Haram" is often rendered in English as "Western education is forbidden." That translation, however, sacrifices some nuance and depth. *Haram* is an Islamic legal term designating a forbidden act. Yusuf argued that Islam itself forbid Western-style education: "These foreign, global, colonialist schools have embraced matters that violate Islamic law, and it is forbidden to operate them, support them, study and teach in them."[28] Yusuf's invocation of colonialism was deliberate—he saw total continuity between northern Nigerian Muslims' experience of subjugation to Britain from 1900 to 1960 and their position in postcolonial Nigeria. Muslims, Yusuf felt, needed to protect the purity of Islam from any other systems that might corrupt it. Hence Yusuf claimed that declaring Western-style educa-

---

[27] "Wali Gharb Ifriqiya: Al-Shaykh Abu Mus'ab al-Barnawi," *Al-Naba'* 41 (2 August 2016): 8–9, https://azelin.files.wordpress.com/2016/08/the-islamic-state-e2809cal-nabacc84_-newsletter-4122.pdf.

[28] Muhammad Yusuf, *Hadhihi 'Aqidatuna wa-Manhaj Da'watina* (Maiduguri: Maktabat al-Ghuraba', likely 2009), 84.

tion haram was an obligatory religious act, rather than merely his personal opinion. Boko Haram has repeatedly resorted to the claim that it is merely implementing what Islam enjoins, rather than placing new demands on anyone.

Boko is a tricky word to translate. One false etymology holds that the word is a corruption of the English "book." Linguists, however, believe that *boko* is an indigenous Hausa word. Originally, it meant "fraud," "sham," or "inauthentic."[29] It could be used as a verb meaning "doing anything to create [an] impression that one is better off, or that [something] is of better quality or larger in amount than is the case." *Boko-boko* could mean "hoodwinking."[30] During British colonial rule in northern Nigeria, this original meaning of *boko* as "fraud" was attached to Western-style schooling and to the Romanized script for writing Hausa, known as Hausar Boko. Calling Western-style education *boko* connoted a feeling that colonial schools could mislead Muslims into accepting false knowledge. In present-day northern Nigeria, some Muslims feel deep ambivalence toward Western-style education: such schooling is sometimes viewed with suspicion, but it is also recognized as a path to worldly success.

More than just education is bound up in the word *boko*. The phrase *'yan boko*, where *'yan* means "people," could be translated as "representatives of Western education"—people who have graduated from Western-style schools. But the phrase can have a broader connotation—"people who operate within Western-style frameworks and institutions" or "representatives of Western culture" or even "Westernized people." *'Yan boko*

[29] Paul Newman, "The Etymology of Hausa *Boko*," Mega-Chad Research Network, 2013, http://www.megatchad.net/publications/Newman-2013-Etymology-of-Hausa -boko.pdf.

[30] G. P. Bargery, *A Hausa-English Dictionary and English-Hausa Vocabulary*, 2nd impression (London: Oxford University Press, 1951 [1934]), 117–18.

are elites, who hold power because they can navigate Western-style institutions. And just as Western-style education itself can simultaneously evoke suspicion and aspiration, so too can its products be both despised and admired.

Put all these ideas together, and "Boko Haram" means something like "Western culture is forbidden by Islam" or "the Westernized elites and their way of doing things contradict Islam"—not just in schools but also in politics and society. As the sect itself said in one statement:

> Boko Haram does not in any way mean "Western Education is a sin" as the infidel media continue to portray us. Boko Haram actually means "Western Civilisation" is forbidden. The difference is that while the first gives the impression that we are opposed to formal education coming from the West, that is Europe, which is not true, the second affirms our believe [*sic*] in the supremacy of Islamic culture (not Education), for culture is broader, it includes education but not determined by Western Education. In this case we are talking of Western Ways of life which include: constitutional provision as if relates to, for instance the rights and privileges of Women, the idea of homosexualism, lesbianism, sanctions in cases of terrible crimes like drug trafficking, rape of infants, multi-party democracy in an overwhelmingly Islamic country like Nigeria, blue films, prostitution, drinking beer and alcohol and many others that are opposed to Islamic civilisation.[31]

The word *boko* stood in for a system of ideas and institutions that the group not only rejected, but also considered diametrically opposed to the countersystem represented by its version of Islam.

---

[31] "Boko Haram Resurrects, Declares Total Jihad," *Vanguard*, August 14, 2009, http://www.vanguardngr.com/2009/08/boko-haram-ressurects-declares-total-jihad/.

Under Shekau, the group adopted the official Arabic name "Ahl al-Sunna li-l-Da'wa wa-l-Jihad."[32] The widespread translation "People Committed to the Propagation of the Prophet's Teachings and Jihad" conveys the basic meaning but misses a few nuances.

First, it is important to examine the notion of *ahl al-sunna*, short for *ahl al-sunna wa-l-jama'a*, meaning "the people of the Prophet's model and the Muslim community." *Al-jama'a* conveys the notion of consensus within the community. To claim the title *ahl al-sunna* is to claim the right to dictate who is and is not a true Muslim. The idea of *ahl al-sunna* is particularly important for Salafi Muslims, a movement I discuss below. For Salafis, the phrase *ahl al-sunna* functions to suggest that there should be no difference between being a Sunni and being a Salafi. Salafis claim not just that they "propagate" the Prophet's teachings, but that they alone embody them.

Nevertheless, spreading the message is important—hence the idea of *da'wa*, "calling people to Islam." Many Salafis consider da'wa their core duty. The call extends to non-Muslims, but it also involves enjoining other Muslims to bring their own practices and beliefs in line with Salafis' understanding of Islam. By emphasizing da'wa, Boko Haram sought to convince itself, other Salafis, and other Muslims that it had not abandoned global Salafism's missionary goal. But adding "jihad" to the group's name conveyed a readiness to fight. The full Arabic name might be translated "Salafis for Preaching and Jihad," or even "Orthodox Muslims Who Call People to True Islam and Who Engage in Holy War"—again, "True Islam" according to Boko Haram.

With its affiliation to the Islamic State in 2015, Boko Haram's official name became Wilayat Gharb Ifriqiya, or "Islamic State

[32] Often rendered in clumsy, partly phonetic transliterations.

West Africa Province." This name positioned Boko Haram as an administrative unit within the Islamic State's "Caliphate." As with other "provinces," the name intentionally ignored internationally recognized boundaries—after all, Boko Haram did not become the Islamic State's "Nigeria Province."[33] When it accepted Boko Haram's allegiance, the Islamic State emphasized the way its provinces were redrawing maps: "It was the rejection of nationalism that drove the mujahidin (fighters) in Nigeria to give bay'ah (fealty) to the Islamic State and wage war against the Nigerian murtaddin (apostates) fighting for the Nigerian taghut (idolatrous tyrant)."[34] The Islamic State and its new affiliate sought to depict the conflict in Nigeria entirely in religious terms: all actors were judged to be genuine Muslims, "crusader" Christians, or "apostates."[35]

Religious Ideologies: Salafism, Jihadism, and Salafi-Jihadism

To understand Boko Haram's worldview and place the sect in its global, national, and local contexts, three terms are critical: *Salafism*, *jihadism*, and *Salafi-jihadism*. These terms are widely used but seldom precisely defined.

"Salafism" derives from the Arabic *salaf*, meaning "predecessors." The phrase *al-salaf al-salih* or "pious predecessors"

---

[33] Yet neither did the name hearken back to historical, pre-colonial names for this region, such as *bilad al-sudan*, "The Lands of the Blacks." That geographical designation was used by an offshoot of Boko Haram, Ansar al-Muslimin fi Bilad al-Sudan, "The Defenders of Muslims in the Lands of the Blacks." Such rhetorical choices, however, can be overemphasized: the main point is that Boko Haram, as of 2015, treated itself as a loose part of the Islamic State and as an entity that would ignore national boundaries.

[34] "Foreword," *Dabiq* 8 (Jumada II 1437/April 2015): 3–6; 5.

[35] "The Bay'ah from West Africa," *Dabiq* 8 (Jumada II 1437/April 2015): 14–16.

has special resonance in Sunni Muslim communities, referring to the earliest Muslims, whom contemporary Muslims
see as pure. Salafis strive to emulate those early Muslims, but
like other Muslims, they make choices about which aspects of
the early community to highlight, and which to downplay.
Theologically, Salafis emphasize a literalist understanding of
the Qur'an and the Sunna (tradition or model) represented
by the Prophet Muhammad. Salafis narrowly interpret the Islamic injunction to worship one God, and they try to "purify"
other Muslims of alleged deviations in belief and practice.[36]
Historically, Salafism in its present form dates to the twentieth
century, when the Kingdom of Saudi Arabia began to act both
as a hub, attracting Salafis to the kingdom from elsewhere, and
a transmitter, disseminating Salafism to new areas.[37] By the
closing decades of the twentieth century, Salafism had spread
throughout the world—but it had also become "localized" in
various nations,[38] including Nigeria.

"Salafi-jihadism" is one major branch of the Salafi movement,[39] but jihadism's origins are different than those of Salafism. In Islamic history, jihad (meaning "to strive") has encom-
passed both military and nonmilitary meanings. Jihad was
the subject of intensive legal debate that restricted its scope and

[36] Bernard Haykel, "On the Nature of Salafi Thought and Action," in *Global Salafism: Islam's New Religious Movement*, edited by Roel Meijer, 33–57 (New York: Columbia University Press, 2009).

[37] Stéphane Lacroix, "Between Revolution and Apoliticism: Nasir al-Din al-
Albani and His Impact on the Shaping of Contemporary Salafism," in *Global Salafism*, 58–80; and Alex Thurston, *Salafism in Nigeria: Islam, Preaching and Politics*
(Cambridge: Cambridge University Press, 2016). Henri Lauzière has argued that the
words "Salafi" and "Salafiyya" did not acquire their contemporary connotations until
the twentieth century. See *The Making of Salafism: Islamic Reform in the Twentieth
Century* (New York: Columbia University Press, 2015).

[38] Terje Østebø, *Localising Salafism: Religious Change among Oromo Muslims in
Bale, Ethiopia* (Leiden: Brill, 2012).

[39] Quintan Wiktorowicz, "Anatomy of the Salafi Movement," *Studies in Conflict
and Terrorism* 29:3 (2006): 207–39.

imposed conditions for who could lead a jihad.[40] "Jihadism," in contrast, refers to an ideology that took shape between the 1960s and the 1990s, initially among radicals inspired by the Muslim Brotherhood's Sayyid Qutb (1906–66). During these decades, jihadists took a complex legal and spiritual concept, reduced it to military action and ideological extremism, and oriented it toward new enemies. Few of the original jihadists were fluent in the theological world of Salafism.

For jihadists, many Muslim rulers are Muslim in name only. In jihadists' eyes, these rulers' reliance on "man-made laws," their repression of Muslim activists, and their alliances with the West expose them as infidels. Some jihadists identify the West—particularly the United States and Israel—as the "far enemy" or ultimate target, believing that Muslim societies cannot be purified so long as the United States maintains its global hegemony. "Salafi-jihadism," then, refers to the combination of Salafi theology with jihadist ideology, a hybridization that solidified in the 1990s. For groups like Boko Haram, one consequence of that fusion has been a pronounced willingness to commit violence against Muslim civilians. If Salafis view non-Salafi Muslims as being at risk of deviation, and if jihadists view most Muslim rulers as infidels who merit death, then Salafi-jihadists treat ordinary Muslims as needing violent correction. And even if one views the Salafi-jihadist ideology as a mere cover for jihadists' material ambitions, the ideology is nonetheless important to understand in that it becomes a

[40] John Renard, "Al-Jihad al-Akbar: Notes on a Theme in Islamic Spirituality," *Muslim World* 78:3–4 (October 1988): 225–42; Ayesha Jalal, *Partisans of Allah: Jihad in South Asia* (Cambridge, MA: Harvard University Press, 2010); Paul Heck, "*Jihad* Revisited," *Journal of Religious Ethics* 32:1 (March 2004): 95–128; Asma Afsaruddin, *Striving in the Path of God: Jihad and Martyrdom in Islamic Thought* (Oxford: Oxford University Press, 2013); and Michael Bonner, *Jihad in Islamic History: Doctrines and Practice* (Princeton, NJ: Princeton University Press, 2006).

key way such groups attempt to communicate with the rest of the world.

Patterns of Islamic Authority and Dissent in Northern Nigeria

To situate Boko Haram in its religious context, it is helpful to understand the major players in northern Nigeria's Muslim religious field. First, there are hereditary Muslim rulers or "emirs." The emirs are descendants of families that came to prominence during the nineteenth century. In northwestern Nigeria, the foremost hereditary ruler is the Sultan of Sokoto, descended from Uthman dan Fodio (1754–1817). Dan Fodio established the Sokoto Caliphate, a Muslim empire, in the early nineteenth century, defeating local Hausa kings and uniting their territory under a system where his lieutenants ruled different emirates.

Precolonial northeastern Nigeria, meanwhile, became the eventual epicenter of the Bornu empire, another Muslim polity. In the nineteenth century, Bornu became a target of dan Fodio's jihad. The empire turned to a Muslim scholar, Muhammad al-Amin al-Kanemi (1776–1837), for military help and religious legitimacy. After Bornu successfully resisted the jihad, al-Kanemi's descendants displaced the ruling dynasty. The present Shehu of Borno, considered northern Nigeria's second-most senior hereditary ruler after the Sultan of Sokoto, is a descendant of al-Kanemi.

Second, there are Sufi orders. Sufism offers spiritual disciplines that aim to bring the believer into closer contact with God and the Prophet. In Nigeria as elsewhere, most Sufis are organized into orders that involve hierarchies of *shaykhs*.

Northern Nigeria's most prominent orders are the Tijaniyya, which was founded in North Africa in the late eighteenth century by Ahmad al-Tijani (1737–1815), and the Qadiriyya, which traces its lineage to the Persian mystic Abd al-Qadir al-Jilani (1077–1166). In Nigeria, Sufism was a relatively elite phenomenon until the mid-twentieth century, when Sufi reformers transformed the Tijaniyya and Qadiriyya into mass-based organizations.[41] Sufism now shapes the spiritual life of many Muslim communities in the north.

Long-standing links between the emirs and Sufi shaykhs make these groups a "Muslim establishment" for northern Nigeria. Groups that oppose the Muslim establishment of emirs and Sufis often find themselves marginalized. Sometimes, the status quo has been destabilized. For example, on the eve of the colonial conquest, a warlord from present-day Sudan named Rabih al-Zubayr conquered and ruled Bornu between 1893 and 1900, when the French killed him in battle. The combination of Rabih's adventuring and the colonial conquest fundamentally disrupted life and politics throughout the empire. This turbulence affected Bornu's subsequent integration into British and French colonies, with both colonial powers openly manipulating succession within the ruling family of Bornu. But as an establishment, the emirs and the Sufi shaykhs survived the disruptions of both the late precolonial period and colonialism itself.

British colonialism preserved, but also fundamentally altered, the position of the emirs in northern society. For the first time, the emirs were subjected to the authority of non-Muslim outsiders, which altered the social contract between

---

[41] John Paden, *Religion and Political Culture in Kano* (Berkeley: University of California Press, 1973).

the emirs and their subjects. In the postcolonial period, civilian politicians and military administrators sometimes openly challenged or manipulated the emirs. Many northern Muslims continue to respect their hereditary rulers. But some Muslims have come to see these rulers as creatures of the true political authorities, be they British colonialists in the past or Nigeria's elected politicians in the present.

Third, there is the Salafi movement. Northern Nigerian Salafism originated with Abubakar Gumi (1924–92). Educated in colonial schools, Gumi served as northern Nigeria's senior Muslim judge after independence. After 1966, when Gumi's political patron was killed in a military coup, Gumi shed his official roles and became an anti-Sufi polemicist.[42] In 1978, his followers founded Jama'at Izalat al-Bid'a wa-Iqamat al-Sunna (the Society for the Removal of Heretical Innovation and the Establishment of the Prophet's Model). Known as Izala, this mass organization spread anti-Sufism throughout northern Nigeria,[43] including to Maiduguri, where Boko Haram originated. Izala's activism provoked bitter debates between Sufis and Salafis.

In the 1990s, generational change evoked intra-Salafi competition. Young Izala preachers like Ja'far Mahmud Adam (1961/2–2007) studied at Saudi Arabia's Islamic University of Medina in the 1990s. They returned home to find Izala divided after Gumi's death. Drawing on the prestige of their education, the Medina graduates built a following outside Izala,

---

[42] Abubakar Gumi, *Al-'Aqida al-Sahiha bi-Muwafaqat al-Shari'a* (Beirut: Dar al-'Arabiyya, 1972).

[43] Roman Loimeier, *Islamic Reform and Political Change in Northern Nigeria* (Evanston, IL: Northwestern University Press, 1997); Kane, *Muslim Modernity*; and Ramzi Ben Amara, "The Izala Movement in Nigeria: Its Split, Relationship to Sufis and Perception of Shari'a Re-implementation," Ph.D. dissertation, Bayreuth University, 2011.

teaching texts they had studied overseas.[44] They also recruited young preachers into their network. One of these recruits was Muhammad Yusuf, the founder of Boko Haram, although he soon became too controversial for the mainstream Salafi movement. Adam and Yusuf's break was a major milestone on Boko Haram's road to jihadism. Today, most Nigerian Salafis, including Izala and the Medina graduates, bitterly oppose Boko Haram.

Throughout the history of present-day northern Nigeria—indeed, throughout centuries of history in northwest Africa as a whole—Islamic movements have arisen and demanded that the surrounding societies purify themselves, embrace Islamic law, and throw off the domination of outsiders. Uthman dan Fodio's jihad began with such a purifying impulse. Other historical rebellions have included various "Mahdist" uprisings, led by men who claimed to be the Mahdi, a figure some Muslims believe will appear near the end of time. Postcolonial Nigeria has seen its share of uprisings as well, most infamously the millenarian "Maitatsine" group that I discuss in chapter 1. Maitatsine followers wreaked havoc in northern cities off and on from 1980 to 1985.

Boko Haram has strategically drawn on some of the styles of previous movements, sometimes working to claim the mantle of dan Fodio.[45] In a compelling study, Murray Last has compared movements of religious dissent in northern Nigeria. Such movements, Last found, typically first withdraw from the surrounding society to preach purification. Only after conflicts with authorities have the dissenting movements launched up-

---

[44] See Thurston, *Salafism in Nigeria*, for a more detailed discussion of this history, and for a more technical definition of Salafism that classifies Gumi and parts of Izala as only partly Salafi. See also Andrea Brigaglia, "A Contribution to the History of the Wahhabi Da'wa in West Africa: The Career and the Murder of Shaykh Ja'far Mahmoud Adam (Daura, ca. 1961/1962—Kano 2007)," *Islamic Africa* 3:1 (Spring 2012): 1–23.

[45] Kassim, "Defining and Understanding."

risings. Last has shown that over the past two centuries, authorities have often pursued one of two responses to dissent: ignoring it or crushing it.[46] Boko Haram fits many of these patterns.

Other analysts, less subtle than Last, have portrayed Boko Haram as the second coming of dan Fodio, Rabih,[47] or Maitatsine.[48] There are problems with such approaches. For one thing, both Maitatsine and Boko Haram originated in an urban setting, breaking with the rural character of previous uprisings. Additionally, Boko Haram is theologically distinct from dan Fodio (a committed Qadiri Sufi), Rabih (a Mahdist sympathizer), and Maitatsine (whose founder developed idiosyncratic readings of the Qur'an and claimed to be a prophet). Understanding Boko Haram requires attention not just to past religious uprisings, but also to the context in which Boko Haram emerged, including Nigerian politics at the turn of the twenty-first century.

Nigeria's Contentious Politics

Nigeria is one of the most important countries in the world. It has, by far, Africa's largest population, 180 million or more people. By 2050, Nigeria may have 400 million people.[49]

[46] Murray Last, "From Dissent to Dissidence: The Genesis and Development of Reformist Islamic Groups in Northern Nigeria," in *Sects and Social Disorder*, 18–53.

[47] John Neville Hare, "How Northern Nigeria's Violent History Explains Boko Haram," *National Geographic*, 14 March 2015, http://news.nationalgeographic.com /2015/03/150314-boko-haram-nigeria-borno-rabih-abubakar-shekau/.

[48] Abimbola O. Adesoji," Between Maitatsine and Boko Haram: Islamic Fundamentalism and the Response of the Nigerian State," *Africa Today* 57:4 (Summer 2011): 99–119.

[49] United Nations Department of Economic and Social Affairs/Population Division, "World Population Prospects: The 2015 Revision, Key Findings and Advance

Analysts often portray Nigeria as a prisoner to the legacies of colonialism. It is true that British rule—which formally began in the south in 1861, and in the north in 1900—brought together diverse peoples. It is also true that the colonial government administered northern and southern Nigeria in different ways, even after the "amalgamation" of the two territories in 1914. The north experienced "Indirect Rule" through the emirs. Indirect Rule left a multifaceted legacy with two prominent negative aspects: first, the imposition of Muslim rule over some non-Muslim populations, which fostered lasting bitterness and contributed to postcolonial religious violence in the north;[50] and second, a low level of educational and economic development for northern communities. The south developed a more vibrant economy, more progressive politics, and better infrastructure.

These colonial differences generated postcolonial disparities, with greater economic opportunity in the south. But it would be a mistake to stereotype Nigeria as an African state doomed to perpetual conflict because of "artificial borders." Even when outsiders have been at their most pessimistic about Nigeria's prospects, the country has surprised them: witness Nigeria's historic transfer of power from one civilian party to another with the election of President Muhammadu Buhari in 2015. Nigeria, with as many as 550 linguistic groups[51] and with grim legacies of intercommunal violence, will likely never eliminate the challenges of managing diversity and building

---

Tables," 2015, 21, http://esa.un.org/unpd/wpp/Publications/Files/Key_Findings_WPP _2015.pdf.

[50] Moses Ochonu, *Colonialism by Proxy: Hausa Imperial Agents and Middle Belt Consciousness in Nigeria* (Bloomington: Indiana University Press, 2014).

[51] Roger Blench, "An Atlas of Nigerian Languages," 3rd ed. (Cambridge: Roger Blench, 3 December 2012), vi, http://www.rogerblench.info/Language/Africa/Nigeria /Atlas%20of%20Nigerian%20Languages-%20ed%20III.pdf.

national unity. Those challenges, however, have occasioned creativity as well as conflict.

Following its independence from Britain in 1960, Nigeria underwent tremendous political fluctuations: a civilian-led parliamentary system from 1960 to 1966, a succession of military rulers and failed democratic transitions from 1966 to 1999, and a period of unbroken multiparty civilian rule from 1999 to the present (the Fourth Republic). Nigeria's 1999 constitution established a strong presidency, a bicameral legislature, and a federal system comprising thirty-six states. The president and the country's powerful governors are limited to two terms in office. Elections for national and state offices are held every four years. Democratization has amplified ordinary people's demands for better and less corrupt government—even if those demands are seldom met.[52]

For understanding Boko Haram, four aspects of Nigerian politics are relevant: cutthroat elections; pervasive corruption; severe inequality; and the violence and impunity that surround approaches to conflict management. Subsequent chapters detail how these trends operated at the level of the northeast, but for now a more general overview is in order.

Nigeria's elections are highly contested but sometimes blatantly fraudulent. From 1999 to 2015, the People's Democratic Party (PDP) held the presidency and often controlled a majority of legislative seats and state governments. But politics remained competitive. Around the country, gubernatorial elections were and are often hard fought. In addition to pouring vast sums of money into these elections,[53] governors

[52] Daniel Jordan Smith, *A Culture of Corruption: Everyday Deception and Popular Discontent in Nigeria* (Princeton, NJ: Princeton University Press, 2006).

[53] Benjamin Aluko, "Political Finance-Related Corruption and Its Implication for Governance and Peace-Building in Nigeria," Wilson Center Africa Program Research Paper no. 16 (February 2017), https://www.wilsoncenter.org/sites/default/files /aluko_research_paper.pdf.

and other political "godfathers" sometimes recruit youth and criminals to harass rivals and voters. The 2003 gubernatorial election in Borno State, a key event in the empowerment of Muhammad Yusuf, was part of a larger trend where godfathers recruited unsavory actors to help them take power, and then later turned on these allies.

Corruption is widely seen by Nigerians as their country's biggest problem. Corruption afflicts the highest levels of government. In 2006, the head of Nigeria's Economic and Financial Crimes Commission estimated that some $380 billion had been "stolen or wasted" since independence.[54] A decade later, Nigeria's minister of information alleged that $9 billion had been lost to corruption just during the 2010–25 tenure of President Goodluck Jonathan, including $2.1 billion purportedly stolen from funds allocated for fighting Boko Haram.[55] Corruption is not just at the top: it pervades everyday life. Police officers systematically extort citizens.[56] There are off-the-books fees for many bureaucratic processes.[57] Corruption creates resentment among many citizens and weakens the state's ability to respond to insecurity.

In terms of inequality, Nigeria's economy is usually one of the fastest growing in the world. In 2014, Nigeria became, temporarily, Africa's largest economy and the world's twenty-sixth largest economy, with a gross domestic product of nearly $510 billion. Yet population growth—from 89 million in

[54] "Nigerian Leaders 'Stole' $380 Billion," BBC, 20 October 2006, http://news.bbc.co.uk/2/hi/africa/6069230.stm.

[55] Michelle Faul, "Nigeria: Minister Alleges $9 Billion Stolen from Economy," Associated Press, 18 January 2016, http://bigstory.ap.org/article/6665615f06fe4b04b1d719d5e551876b/nigeria-minister-alleges-9-billion-stolen-economy.

[56] Human Rights Watch, "'Everyone's in on the Game': Corruption and Human Rights Abuses by the Nigeria Police Force," August 2010, https://www.hrw.org/sites/default/files/reports/nigeria0810webwcover.pdf.

[57] D. Smith, *Culture of Corruption*.

1991 to over 140 million in 2006, to more than 180 million in 2016—has outpaced economic growth. As of 2016, 43 percent of the population was under the age of fifteen years; another 19 percent was under the age of twenty-five.[58] Economic growth has been mostly jobless. Under the Fourth Republic, government economic policies featured "limited focus on poverty reduction, jobs creation and income generation."[59] The result is that most Nigerians are poor. More than 60 percent live on less than a dollar per day.[60] Official unemployment stood at 24 percent in 2011,[61] and it is likely far higher.

If Nigeria's economy looks deeply unfair at the national level, it looks even worse in the north. In the postcolonial period, northern agriculture—the region's key employer—weakened amid dependence on oil and greater centralization of power and wealth at the federal level.[62] When economic recession hit Nigeria after the oil boom of the 1970s, the north lost ground. Between 1980 and 2006, the poverty rate in the North East zone rose from 35.6 percent to 72.4 percent—making it the second poorest zone in the Nigerian federation after the North West (79.2 percent). Poverty rates in Nigeria's three southern zones rose through the same period, reaching between 55.9 percent and 63.1 percent in 2006, but have remained lower than in

[58] United States Central Intelligence Agency, "The World Factbook—Nigeria," https://www.cia.gov/library/publications/the-world-factbook/geos/ni.html.

[59] Zainab Usman, "The Successes and Failures of Economic Reform in Nigeria's Post-military Political Settlement," University of Oxford Global Economic Governance Programme Working Paper 115 (March 2016), 45, http://www.globaleconomic governance.org/sites/geg/files/GEG%20WP_115%20The%20Successes%20and%20 Failures%20of%20Economic%20Reform%20in%20Nigeria%E2%80%99s%20Post -Military%20Political%20Settlement%20-%20Zainab%20Usman.pdf.

[60] "Nigerians Living in Poverty Rise to Nearly 61%," BBC, 13 February 2012, http://www.bbc.com/news/world-africa-17015873.

[61] National Bureau of Statistics (Nigeria), *2011 Annual Socio-economic Report* (2011), 10–11.

[62] Michael Watts, *Silent Violence: Food, Famine and Peasantry in Northern Nigeria* (Athens: University of Georgia Press, 2013 [1983]), 470.

the northern zones.[63] Meanwhile, birthrates in 2008 were 7.3 children per woman in the North West and 7.2 children per woman in the North East, well above southern zones' rates of fewer than five children per woman.[64] As chapter 1 describes, the period from the 1970s to the 1990s saw massive dislocation and ad hoc urbanization in northern cities like Maiduguri. Many youth were struggling or jobless at precisely the time when hereditary Muslim rulers were losing their longstanding powers of surveillance and control.

Meanwhile, Nigeria has a de facto system of violence and impunity when it comes to rebellions and riots. When rebellions occur, Nigerian authorities pursue a straightforward process to restore order: first, deploy force (usually soldiers rather than police) to stop or slow the disturbance; second, make gestures of reconciliation, such as granting amnesty to combatants or releasing prisoners back into normal life; and third, exhort all parties to move on in a spirit of unity. Authorities seldom make systematic efforts to hold perpetrators of violence accountable.

Over the long term, this approach to conflict has left grievances unaddressed. And when the playbook does not work, politicians and security forces have difficulty adapting. Boko Haram arose partly because of the Nigerian government's failure to effectively resolve past incidents of inter-religious violence, and the prolongation of the Boko Haram conflict owes much to the widespread human rights abuses committed by

[63] T.K.O. Aluko, "An Evaluation of the Effects of the National Economic Empowerment and Development Strategy (Needs) on Poverty Reduction in Nigeria," in *Nigeria's Democratic Experience in the Fourth Republic since 1999: Policies and Politics*, edited by A. Sat Obiyan and Kunle Amuwo (Lanham, MD: University Press of America, 2013), 360–79.

[64] National Population Commission of Nigeria, "Nigeria 2008 Demographic and Health Survey: Key Findings," 2009, http://dhsprogram.com/pubs/pdf/SR173/SR173.pdf.

the security forces against actual and suspected sect members. Conflict management strategies from Nigeria's past have not helped end the threat posed by a movement that questions the fundamentals of Nigeria's existence, including the secularity of the state, the possibility that Muslims and Christians can live together in peace, the prospects for multiparty elections to ensure good governance, and the idea that the past can be forgotten. President Jonathan, in office for the most severe portions of the insurgency, made halfhearted efforts to talk to Boko Haram, but his administration's overall approach emphasized repression. President Buhari has shown more flexibility, but the Nigerian military continues to speak and act as though body counts and territorial control are the main metrics of success.

In sum, Nigeria's contentious politics, economic inequality, endemic corruption, and counterproductive conflict management strategies are part of the environment that contributed to Boko Haram's rise. This book shows how environmental factors influenced the decisions of local actors. But Boko Haram's emergence was not inevitable, and the sect has interacted dynamically with the political dysfunction and economic malaise that surround it.

The Structure of the Book

Chapter 1, "The Lifeworld of Muhammad Yusuf," examines interactions between religion and politics in Nigeria during the first three decades of Yusuf's life (1970–99). Despite government-led efforts to build national unity in the wake of Nigeria's 1967–70 civil war, religion became more prominent in elite debates over policies and institutions, as well as in local, intercommunal clashes. Such clashes were seldom followed by serious efforts to hold perpetrators accountable. At the same time, a host of new Muslim voices arose in northern Nigeria, where they competed for influence, sometimes by voicing strident opinions on politics.

Chapter 2, "Preaching Exclusivism, Playing Politics," reconstructs Boko Haram's activities and messages between its emergence in the early 2000s and its disastrous mass uprising in 2009. Yusuf and his companions defined Salafi Muslim identity narrowly and exclusively. At the same time, Boko Haram dynamically responded to fluctuations in the sect's political position. The movement also reacted to internal debates among its leaders and to disputes between Yusuf and other Salafis.

Chapter 3, " 'Chaos Is Worse Than Killing,' " examines Boko Haram's initial resurgence under Abubakar Shekau. From 2010 to 2013, the sect adopted terrorist tactics and brought its violence into new parts of northern Nigeria. Shekau presented violence as the only theologically legitimate option left for Boko Haram. Yet amid ideological justifications, the group pursued score settling and predation. Chapter 3 also reviews the story of Boko Haram's loose relationship with al-Qaʻida and its affiliates.

Chapter 4, "Total War in Northeastern Nigeria," recounts the transformation of the conflict, starting in 2013, from guerrilla warfare to broader forms of violence and contestation. Boko Haram's approach evolved in response to the crackdown by Nigeria's security forces and the emergence of the Civilian Joint Task Force, a government-backed vigilante movement in northeastern Nigeria. The pursuit of total war by both sides is critical context for understanding some of Boko Haram's most brutal actions, including its kidnapping of the Chibok girls.

Chapter 5, "Same War, New Actors," discusses the increasing involvement of external actors. These actors include Nigeria's neighbors—especially Niger, Cameroon, and Chad—and a wider range of international players, from the United States and France to the Islamic State. As with the mutually reinforcing violence of Boko Haram and Nigerian security forces, the involvement of Nigeria's neighbors and outside actors has further intensified the conflict. Amid Boko Haram's military defeats and its increasing violence against Muslim civilians, prominent voices within the group increasingly questioned Shekau's leadership in 2016. These dissidents sought to soften the group's message and reduce its insularity, refocusing its enmity on the state and Christians.

At the time of writing, Boko Haram remains a serious security threat for Nigeria. In 2015, the new administration of President Buhari promised to defeat the sect by the end of that year. In December, Buhari proclaimed the "technical" defeat of the group.[65] A year later, Buhari announced the "final crushing" of Boko Haram.[66] But it was clear that Boko Haram would continue to trouble Nigeria for some time to come. Even once the sect is defeated, the crisis will have long-term humanitarian, political, and religious repercussions. If Boko Haram is partly a result of the failure of past efforts to resolve conflict through violence, then it will be vital for Nigerian authorities and citizens—and their partners in Africa and beyond—to address the aftereffects of the crisis in a way that reduces, rather than increases, the prospects for renewed conflict in the future.

[65] "Nigeria Boko Haram: Militants 'Technically' Defeated—Buhari," BBC, 24 December 2015, http://www.bbc.com/news/world-africa-35173618.

[66] Michelle Faul, "Nigeria: Boko Haram Is Crushed, Forced Out of Last Enclave," Associated Press, 24 December 2016, http://bigstory.ap.org/article/bee6467 7ffbf4d968b05692a0d86d877/nigeria-boko-haram-crushed-forced-out-last-enclave.

1

The Lifeworld of Muhammad Yusuf

It is grimly ironic that Muhammad Yusuf, one of the most divisive figures in Nigerian history, was born at the start of a decade when Nigeria's government undertook a quest to rebuild national unity. Yusuf was born in 1970,[1] and his future companion Abubakar Shekau was born around 1969.[2] In those years, Nigeria's civil war was ending, and an oil boom was approaching.

Yet for many Nigerians, the promise of the early 1970s gave way to disappointment. Inequality widened. Corruption worsened. Religion became increasingly politicized. The 1980s and 1990s witnessed repeated instances of mass intercommunal violence. Authorities, urging citizens to look to the future and forget the past, chronically failed to enforce accountability. This chapter shows how, after living through these troubled decades, Yusuf and Shekau could come to make statements like "the government of Nigeria has not been built to do justice. . . . It has been built to attack Islam and kill Muslims."[3]

---

[1] Taye Obateru, Kingsley Omonobi, Lawani Mikairu, and Daniel Idonor, "Boko Haram Leader, Yusuf, Killed," *Vanguard*, 30 July 2009, http://www.vanguardngr.com /2009/07/boko-haram-leader-yusuf-killed/. One official Boko Haram account gives Yusuf's birth date as 1967 but is unique in doing so. See Abu Muhammad ibn Muhammad ibn Yusuf, "Nabtha Mukhtasira Jiddan 'an 'Hayat Muhammad ibn Yusuf al-Barnawi,'" in Muhammad Yusuf, *Majmu'at Khutab li-l-Imam Abi Yusuf Muhammad bin Yusuf al-Maydughari*, Mu'assasat al-'Urwa al-Wuthqa li-l-Intaj al-'Ilmi (2015), 4.

[2] United Nations Security Council, "Security Council al-Qaida Sanctions Committee Adds Abubakar Mohammed Shekau, Ansaru to Its Sanctions List," 26 June 2014, http://www.un.org/press/en/2014/sc11455.doc.htm.

[3] Muhammad Yusuf, "Open Letter to the Federal Government of Nigeria," 12 June 2009, https://www.youtube.com/watch?v=f89PvcpWSRg.

Sources on the early lives of Yusuf and Shekau are thin. One hagiographical account of Yusuf's early years, purportedly by one of his sons, says that Yusuf first studied Islam under his own father, memorizing the Qur'an by the time he was fifteen years old. "Then he traveled and went around the country seeking knowledge. He was, may Allah have mercy on him, open-hearted and deeply acquainted with books, and just as he employed all his time in seeking knowledge, so he employed it also in spreading it."[4] Whether or not this account is true, what seems clear is that both Yusuf and Shekau were born in rural settings, but then they became mobile as young men, developing a growing political and religious consciousness.

[4] Ibn Yusuf, "Nabtha Mukhtasira Jiddan," 4.

We can tell some of the developments from this period that marked them. First, in their preaching, they would bitterly recall the Muslim-Christian violence that occurred at Kafanchan in 1987 and Zangon-Kataf in 1992. These two towns were far from their homes in geographic terms but close in emotional ones. Yusuf said later that he had been horrified by authorities' handling of those incidents and others.[5] Second, both men would be absorbed, by the eve of the new millennium, by the Salafi current that gained force beginning in the late 1970s. Finally, both men would seize on the deeply felt ambivalence toward Western-style education in northern Nigeria. That ambivalence found voice even in the north's Western-style universities, where Yusuf may have attracted his first followers.

What we know about Boko Haram's social base is also limited, but we do know that in early postcolonial northern Nigerian Muslim society, various trends—political, economic, and social—were intertwining with shifts in Muslim identity and politics. What it meant to be a northern Muslim was increasingly up for grabs. This uncertainty, combined with rapid urbanization, altered relationships between elders and youth, patrons and clients, and people and their neighbors.[6] These trends were particularly disruptive in the northeast, including in Maiduguri, where Boko Haram later emerged. Young migrants to the city—such as Yusuf and Shekau, who likely arrived in the early 1990s—often encountered poverty and inequality. The poor and the young increasingly drifted beyond the control of the classical poles of religious and political authority: the emirs,

---

[5] Muhammad Yusuf, "Tarihin Musulmai," undated (likely 2009), https://www.youtube.com/watch?v=eUQYNucjqUE.

[6] Ousmane Kane, *Muslim Modernity in Postcolonial Nigeria: A Study of the Society for the Removal of Innovation and Reinstatement of Tradition* (Brill: Leiden, 2003), chapter 1.

the Sufi shaykhs, and the politicians. As part of showing how religion and politics interacted to shape Boko Haram, this chapter argues that Yusuf and Shekau's revolutionary understanding of Islam reflected the context of political failures, religious fragmentation, and dashed expectations in northeastern Nigeria.

Dashed expectations were acute when it came to education. Successive administrations, regional, state, and national, cultivated false hope about education even as many Muslims remained skeptical about the moral orientation of Western-style schooling. Muslim activists—even many who would later express horror over Boko Haram, and who never promoted violence—increasingly criticized Western-style education starting in the 1970s. In this atmosphere, a rising generation of Muslims was primed to view government and Western-style education with mistrust and even hatred.

A Quest for Unity amid Division

Optimism at Nigeria's independence in 1960 gave way to tragedy. In the political system of the time, based around three (later four), regions, prominent politicians in the Western and Eastern Regions of Nigeria chafed under the domination of the Northern Region, whose conservative politicians had been closer to the British colonial administration than their more radical southern counterparts. Politics became a winner-take-all affair. The federal government imposed a state of emergency in the Western Region in 1962, targeting opposition politicians there. After the North and its allies swept the elections of 1964–65, they marginalized the major parties of the West and East. In January 1966, junior officers from the Igbo, the largest ethnic group in the East, led a coup. They killed prominent northern Nigerian politicians and sought to undo the northern-dominated political system.

The new military government's Unification Decree abrogated Nigerian federalism, sparking fears in the north that Igbo domination would follow. Pogroms broke out in northern cities against the Igbo, and northern officers led a successful countercoup. In 1967, civil war broke out. The Igbo-dominated Eastern Region—rebaptized the Republic of Biafra by its leaders—attempted to secede. During the 1967–70 civil war, Biafra was reintegrated into Nigeria at tremendous cost: in addition to military casualties, over a million civilians died of starvation and disease during a blockade.[7] Although most of these events occurred far from where Yusuf and Shekau were growing up, the boys' lives would be shaped in multiple ways by postwar policies.

Authorities' handling of postwar reconstruction reinforced what was to become a deep-seated pattern in Nigerian political culture: the idea that after collective trauma, looking forward was preferable to looking back. At the war's end in January 1970, military head of state Yakubu Gowon proclaimed the "dawn of national reconciliation"[8] and a policy of "no victor, no vanquished."[9] The civil war was to be forgotten, as were the events that precipitated it. A 1968 pamphlet from the government of North Eastern State, where Yusuf and Shekau grew up, put an optimistic spin on the violent elections, coups, and pogroms of the 1960s: "The events we witnessed prior to and

---

[7] Toyin Falola and Matthew M. Heaton, *A History of Nigeria* (Cambridge: Cambridge University Press, 2008), chapter 7.

[8] Yakubu Gowon, "The Dawn of National Reconciliation," speech broadcast 15 January 1970. Full text available at https://maxsiollun.wordpress.com/great-speeches-in-nigerias-history/.

[9] Max Siollun, *Oil, Politics and Violence: Nigeria's Military Coup Culture (1966–1976)* (New York: Algora, 2009), 167.

after 1966 can be said to be part of a process in the evolution of an acceptable system of government to our people."[10] This pattern of avoiding accountability, when it was applied to Muslim-Christian intercommunal conflicts in the 1980s and 1990s, would contribute to Yusuf and Shekau's conviction that the Nigerian state was incapable of doing justice. Yusuf would later express contempt for some of the signature unity-building initiatives of the 1970s, such as the National Youth Service Corps, which assigned college graduates to do service projects outside their home states. Nigeria's authorities and their Western backers had hoped such initiatives would build "brotherhood ['yan'uwantaka]," Yusuf said. But, he continued, "God, Glory to Him, the Most High, did not agree, because He had His [own] goal"—replacing the "school of democracy" with Islam.[11]

In the 1970s, alongside high-flown rhetoric about Nigeria's "federal character," there were recurring signals that the country remained profoundly uncertain about what form its government should take. Gowon was deposed in the bloodless coup of 1975, after his promises to restore civilian control had worn thin. Under Murtala Mohammed (1975–76) and Olusegun Obasanjo (1976–79), the military organized a transfer of power back to civilians. Soon, however, the civilian-led Second Republic of 1979–83 collapsed amid regional antagonisms, corruption, recession, and electoral fraud.[12] The military regime of Muhammadu Buhari (1983–85) was initially hailed for its effort to restore "discipline," but it soon lost favor: the economy sputtered under austerity, and Buhari proved

---

[10]North Eastern State of Nigeria, *The North Eastern State of Nigeria* (Zaria: Gaskiya, 1968), 3.

[11]Yusuf, "Tarihin Musulmai."

[12]Richard Joseph, *Democracy and Prebendal Politics in Nigeria: The Rise and Fall of the Second Republic* (Cambridge: Cambridge University Press, 1987).

authoritarian. Buhari was removed by another general, Ibrahim Babangida. He ruled from 1985 to 1993, manipulating and dividing key constituencies while enriching himself and his circle. Although Babangida initiated a transition of sorts in 1993, the short-lived, nominal Third Republic soon fell prey to General Sani Abacha, who ruled until his death in 1998. Abacha instituted new levels of political repression.[13]

Nearly all the heads of state from 1960 to 1999 were from the north, but the region's political dominance did not translate into prosperity or security for ordinary northerners. Amid the many coups and transitions, configurations of power shifted among Nigeria's elites.[14] Yet the system remained an oligarchy.[15]

Uncertainty and predation also characterized local politics. During Yusuf and Shekau's youth, Nigeria's internal boundaries were repeatedly redrawn. Yusuf was born in Jakusko Local Government Area (LGA),[16] likely in a village called Girgir.[17] His future deputy was born in Tarmuwa LGA, in a village named Shekau—making his name effectively "Abubakar from Shekau." Until 1967, Jakusko and Shekau villages were part of the Northern Region, but in the military's administrative reorganization they became part of the newly created North Eastern State. In 1976, another reorganization broke North Eastern

---

[13] Peter Lewis, "From Prebendalism to Predation: The Political Economy of Decline in Nigeria," *Journal of Modern African Studies* 34:1 (March 1996): 79–103.

[14] Carl LeVan, *Dictators and Democracy in African Development: The Political Economy of Good Governance in Nigeria* (Cambridge: Cambridge University Press, 2014).

[15] Shehu Othman, "Classes, Crises, and Coup: The Demise of Shagari's Regime," *African Affairs* 83:333 (October 1984): 441–61; Lewis, "Prebendalism to Predation."

[16] This was the answer Yusuf gave in his police interrogation on 30 July 2009. See the English translation at https://maxsiollun.wordpress.com/2009/08/03/videos-of-boko-haram-suspects-being-interrogated-and-executed/, and the video at https://www.youtube.com/watch?v=ePpUvfTXY7w.

[17] Obateru et al., "Boko Haram Leader."

State into three smaller units. One of these was Borno State, which at the time contained Jakusko. When Yusuf was twenty-one, a new state, Yobe, was carved out of the old Borno State; Jakusko and Shekau now fell inside Yobe. These repeated administrative reorganizations helped to make local politics more cutthroat.

The recurring pressures for new state creation between the 1960s and the 1990s illustrate a core tension in Nigerian politics: authorities felt that the only way to keep Nigeria united was to further divide it.[18] State creation exercises were meant to give greater political representation to constituencies that felt stifled by the major ethnic groups—the Hausa, Yoruba, and Igbo. In this way, authorities hoped to weaken smaller groups' calls for autonomy and secession.[19] In practice, however, the new states became "arena[s] of exploitation" for local elites. Corruption thrived at multiple levels of the federal system.[20] State governments were supposed to rely on internal tax revenue, but most states depend on federal revenue allocations for 80 percent or more of their operating budgets.[21] This political and financial structure made state governors powerful and wealthy. Elections became "do-or-die" not just at the national level, but also in gubernatorial contests. As the next chapter discusses, the fierce nature of state-level politics would contribute to Boko Haram's rise.

[18] Henry Alapiki, "State Creation in Nigeria: Failed Approaches to National Integration and Local Autonomy," *African Studies Review* 48:3 (December 2005): 49–65; 50.

[19] Rotimi Suberu, "The Struggle for New States in Nigeria, 1976–1990," *African Affairs* 90:361 (October 1991): 499–522; 501.

[20] Othman, "Classes, Crises, and Coup," 443.

[21] Paul Adams, "State(s) of Crisis: Sub-national Government in Nigeria," Africa Research Institute Briefing Note 1602 (March 2016), http://www.africaresearchinstitute.org/newsite/wp-content/uploads/2016/03/ARI_Nigeria_BN_final.pdf.

For the first three decades of Yusuf's lifetime, Nigeria seemed doomed to political failure. Military dictatorships bred repression. Civilian rule, whether parliamentary or presidential, bred strife. Governments leaned left or right, but economic crisis worsened. By the mid-1980s, some Nigerian Muslims felt that their country had tried all the major secular forms of government (military, parliamentary, presidential) as well as capitalism and a bit of socialism. Yet nothing seemed to work.

The political uncertainty paralleled and spurred a growth in Muslim political and social activism in the north. As the Nigerian nation was repeatedly reimagined, the idea that Nigeria was directionless fed into forms of Islamism—projects aimed at suffusing state policies with Islamic values and rulings. Some activists' language foreshadowed claims that Boko Haram would make later. "Islam," one northern intellectual wrote in 1988, "stands out clearly from man-made ideologies as the only lasting hope for mankind."[22]

In 1999, when Yusuf and Shekau were on the threshold of their thirties, Nigeria returned to civilian rule. This time, the integrity of the political system held. The Fourth Republic has withstood severe tests: disputed elections, the unexpected death of President Umaru Yar'Adua in 2010, and the transfer of power from one party to another in 2015. Yet when the initial transition occurred, there were reasons for disaffected young northern Muslims to feel cynical and angry. The presidency rotated to the south, to the former military ruler and born-again Christian Olusegun Obasanjo. Corruption showed no sign of abating, even as multiparty politics allowed the public

---

[22] Abdullahi Mustapha, "Introduction," in *On the Political Future of Nigeria*, edited by Ibraheem Sulaiman and Siraj Abdulkarim (Zaria: Hudahuda, 1988), ix.

more space to express anger about financial crimes.[23] Poverty increased, including in the north. Nigeria secured $18 billion in debt relief in 2005, but many ordinary Nigerians remained unemployed. From the perspective of down-and-out youth in urban northeastern Nigeria, who had grown up witnessing a string of failed transitions, the notions of "democracy" and "economic liberalization" may have seemed abstract, meaningless, or even sinister.

Disruptive Urbanization

Yusuf and Shekau spent their childhoods in Yobe, one of the most rural and isolated states in the north. As young men they came to Maiduguri, the largest city in northeastern Nigeria. It is not known when Yusuf settled in Maiduguri, but he was prominent there by 2001, suggesting that he arrived by the mid-1990s at the latest. Shekau reportedly moved to Maiduguri in 1990, to the Mafoni Ward.[24] In Maiduguri, Yusuf and Shekau joined thousands of other immigrants from surrounding regions.

Urbanization brought massive social change to a region that had previously been isolated from the rest of Nigeria and even from other parts of the north. Politically and culturally, precolonial Maiduguri belonged to a different world, more oriented to the Lake Chad basin than to Hausaland. For perspective, Maiduguri lies approximately 250 kilometers from Chad's

[23] Daniel Jordan Smith, *A Culture of Corruption: Everyday Deception and Popular Discontent in Nigeria* (Princeton, NJ: Princeton University Press, 2006).

[24] International Crisis Group, "Curbing Violence in Nigeria (II): The Boko Haram Insurgency," 3 April 2014, 19, http://www.crisisgroup.org/~/media/Files/africa/west-africa/nigeria/216-curbing-violence-in-nigeria-ii-the-boko-haram-insurgency.pdf.

capital, N'Djamena, but nearly 600 kilometers from either Kano or Jos, the two nearest Nigerian cities of greater size.

British colonialism had a profound impact on Maiduguri. British administrators turned Maiduguri from a site "empty of life save on the weekly market day"[25] into the capital of Borno Province in 1907. Maiduguri grew rapidly, from an estimated population of 10,000 in 1910 to 60,000–80,000 people by independence.[26] At the same time, linguistic and infrastructural barriers marginalized Borno Province.[27] Colonial administrators paid only intermittent attention to Kanuri, the province's main language.[28] Meanwhile, the railway did not reach Maiduguri until 1964, whereas Kano had been connected to Southern Nigeria in 1911. Even present-day Yobe State, far to Maiduguri's west, had joined the rail network in 1930.[29] As one Maiduguri resident put it to me, in a quasi-metaphorical sense Borno has five "borders"—one each with Chad, Niger, and Cameroon, one with the rest of Africa, and one with the rest of Nigeria.[30]

If Borno was isolated from the rest of the north, Maiduguri was nevertheless a magnet for the surrounding countryside. As one account put it, with a bit of exaggeration, "From the 1940s on Maiduguri was rapidly swept from a remote provin-

---

[25] Boyd Alexander, *From the Niger to the Nile* (New York: Longmans, Green, 1907), 1:267.

[26] Jonathan Owens, *Neighborhood and Ancestry: Variation in the Spoken Arabic of Maiduguri, Nigeria* (Philadelphia: J. Benjamins, 1998), 117–20.

[27] *Annual Report for Northern Nigeria*, 1907–8, 43.

[28] Norbert Cyffer, "Maiduguri and the Kanuri Language," in *From Bulamari to Yerwa to Metropolitan Maiduguri: Interdisciplinary Studies on the Capital of Borno State, Nigeria*, edited by Rupert Kawka (Köln: Rüdiger Köppe Verlag, 2002).

[29] Shehu Tijjani Yusuf, "Stealing from the Railways: Blacksmiths, Colonialism, and Innovation in Northern Nigeria," in *Transforming Innovations in Africa: Explorative Studies on Appropriation in African Societies*, edited by Jan-Bart Gewald, André Leliveld, and Iva Peša (Leiden: Brill, 2012), 275–96.

[30] Skype interview with Ahmed Bolori, 9 January 2017.

cial town steeped in traditional ways that had hardly changed for hundreds of years into a thriving town with all the urban equipment and responsibilities of the twentieth century."[31]

In the late twentieth century, there was much to drive northeastern Nigerian villagers toward towns. When Yusuf and Shekau were growing up, the North Eastern State was poor and heavily agricultural. As of 1968, the Maiduguri Oil Mills was "the only industry of any importance" in its massive territory.[32] Already in the 1950s and 1960s, an American anthropologist working in northern Borno found that many people "said . . . that they farm because they can do nothing else."[33] Around Gwoza, southern Borno, villagers in the hills lived in households with an average size of ten persons. These villagers faced an environment with scarce water, little arable land, and pervasive theft of livestock.[34] Some of Boko Haram's recruits later came from the Gwoza Hills.

By the late 1960s, northeastern cities faced an influx of migrants, mostly from elsewhere in the north. For example, the population of Potiskum, present-day Yobe State, doubled from 31,000 in 1963 to nearly 60,000 in 1976.[35] Many migrants had jobs awaiting them, facilitating their integration into the city. Many migrants did not. The Max Lock Group, a British firm hired by the North Eastern State government to conduct planning and household surveys in seven cities from 1972 to 1976, found that between a third and a half, or more, of migrants

[31] Max Lock Group Nigeria, *Maiduguri: Surveys and Planning Reports for Borno, Bauchi and Gongola State Government* (Max Lock Group Nigeria, 1976), 6.1.6.

[32] North Eastern State of Nigeria, *North Eastern State of Nigeria*, 56.

[33] Ronald Cohen, *The Kanuri of Bornu* (New York: Holt, Rinehart, and Winston, 1967), 79.

[34] *The Resettlement of Gwoza Hill Peoples* (Maiduguri: Department of Geography, Borno State Advanced Teachers College), appendix A (November 1982), 4–7.

[35] Max Lock Group Nigeria, *Potiskum: Surveys and Planning Reports* (Max Lock Group Nigeria, 1976), 5.1.1.

were job hunting in the northeast's largest cities.[36] These migrants were largely unskilled: in Maiduguri, only 3.3 percent of all workers had administrative, professional, or managerial occupations, only 1.4 percent were "business or trades merchants," and only 7.9 percent were in "skilled services" or "building trades."[37] Many migrants found only low-status work. As one study of people from the Gwoza Hills commented, "Lacking in education and marketable skills, the bulk of those immigrants are absorbed as daily paid manual labourers in such fields like road construction, and building."[38] The lack of skilled workers, the Max Lock Group's planners wrote, "will not stop Maiduguri developing. . . . But the standard of living, comfort and health of its future citizens will depend on the skills available now and in the immediate future."[39]

During the 1970s, "Maiduguri was transformed completely" owing to unplanned sprawl.[40] By the mid-1970s, nearly half of the city's population had been born somewhere else.[41] New urban arrivals found themselves vulnerable. In rural Kanuri society in the 1950s and 1960s, one's mother's relatives were a key source of social and financial support, and one's father's relatives were even more important. As an American anthropologist observed, "A man with no agnates [male relatives on his father's side] is not just unfortunate—he is a social outcast. He has no group to stand up for him as a result of his birth into society; he has no legal right to a father's inheritance, he is thought of as an outcast, he must rely solely on his wits, and

[36] Max Lock Group Nigeria, *Potiskum*, 5.2.3.

[37] Max Lock Group Nigeria, *Potiskum*, 5.5.1

[38] *Resettlement of Gwoza Hill Peoples*, appendix A, 8.

[39] Max Lock Group Nigeria, *Maiduguri*, 5.5.1.

[40] Rupert Kawka, "The Physiognomic Structure of Maiduguri," in *From Bulamari to Yerwa*, 50.

[41] Max Lock Group Nigeria, *Maiduguri*, 4.2.9.

he cannot easily be trusted."[42] This was the position in which some Kanuri immigrants to Maiduguri found themselves in the 1970s and after.

Meanwhile, non-Kanuri immigrants like those from around Gwoza found themselves outsiders in a classically Kanuri city. In rural areas, conversion to Islam had facilitated entry into Kanuri society for non-Kanuri up through the middle of the century.[43] In late twentieth-century Borno, new converts to Islam found fewer economic opportunities. Many were left adrift.[44]

Urban sprawl in Maiduguri resulted not only from the sheer volume of immigrants, who were coming at a rate of nearly 10,000 a year, but also from administrative confusion. Across the north, local governments were adjusting to new state and federal powers. Maiduguri faced an additional, unusual administrative challenge: rival local government structures. In 1972, authorities established a Maiduguri Township Authority, whose functions largely overlapped with the preexisting Local Authority. Although technically responsible for different geographic areas, in practice the two municipal governments competed—meaning that responsibility for regulating development often fell through the cracks.[45] The result was not only unplanned sprawl, with a host of associated health and development problems, but also a breakdown in hereditary religious authorities' mechanisms of surveillance and control.

Across Nigeria, local government was often the primary theater of political experimentation during the 1970s, 1980s, and

---

[42] Cohen, *Kanuri*, 35.

[43] Cohen, *Kanuri*, 65.

[44] Thomas Mösch, "Why Has Borno Become a Stronghold of Terror in Nigeria?," Deutsche Welle, 15 July 2014, http://www.dw.com/en/why-has-borno-become-a-stronghold-of-terror-in-nigeria/a-17788683.

[45] Max Lock Group Nigeria, *Maiduguri*, 6.1.6.

1990s. In the transitions to the Second and Third Republics, local government elections came first in the sequence of elections (1976 and 1991, respectively). For local governments, expectations could be daunting: after the 1976 elections, the newly reformed Borno State local governments were charged with managing everything from "control of vermin" to "control of hoardings, advertisements, use of loudspeakers in or near public places."[46] These wide-ranging responsibilities proved impossible to fulfill, creating resentment among ordinary people.

Within Maiduguri, many wards were not only increasingly diverse, but also poor and vulnerable, reflecting the intersection of immigration, unplanned urban sprawl, inadequate infrastructural development, and rising social tensions. In a southern neighborhood of Bulabulin, one of the poorest areas of the city, the Max Lock Group observed in the mid-1970s that

> this is a notoriously squalid area, overcrowded, with leaking buildings and poor or non-existent ventilation, mosquito-ridden, badly drained, swampy, and liable to flooding in the rain season, bad sanitary conditions, foul air—generally an unpleasant environment in which to live, and condemned as such by the inhabitants. Our interviewers found that there were many complaints, that a lot of people expressed strong dislike for the area and considered that rents were high in relation to conditions. . . . Many also expressed concern at the amount of drunkenness and violence, and most of our interviewers were loathe to go into the area after dark.[47]

---

[46] Borno State Government, *Local Govt. Reforms and You* (Maiduguri: Information Division, Military Governor's Office; printed by Baraka Press Limited, 1977), 22.
[47] Max Lock Group Nigeria, *Maiduguri*, 4.2.5.

Such was the environment in which many of Boko Haram's future followers were growing up.

In the 1980s, serious problems of youth criminality emerged in Borno. One Sufi leader from Maiduguri recalls,

> A glut of youths who were deprived of either or both western and Islamic education as a result of parental negligence or absence of government programs (such as lack of employment) began organizing themselves into groups or gangs. They began committing heinous crimes including robbery, rape and murder within the community.[48]

The criminality elicited a response from the military administration. "Operation Damusa" or "Operation Zaki" sought to break the power of gangs in Borno. The gangs appear to have recruited among not just Borno indigenes but also Chadians, suggesting that crime was already attracting those migrants who could not find gainful employment in Borno.[49] The Sufi leader quoted above argues that this early wave of criminality was a forerunner of Boko Haram.

The military response demonstrated the state's failure to seriously address youth violence and criminality: across Nigeria, various antirobbery operations in the 1980s and 1990s were criticized for being involved in criminality of their own.[50] One commentator from Borno has written,

---

[48] Khalifa Aliyu Ahmed Abulfathi, "The Metamorphosis of Boko Haram: A Local's Perspective" (Maiduguri: Sheikh Ahmed Abulfathi Foundation, 2016), http://sheikhahmadabulfathi.org/content/metamorphosis-boko-haram-0.

[49] Jonathan Owens, *Neighborhood and Ancestry*, 364 n. 185.

[50] Tekena Tamuno, "The Nigeria Police Force and Public Security and Safety," in *Security, Crime and Segregation in West African Cities since the 19th Century*, edited by Laurent Fouchard and Isaac Albert, 119–40 (Paris: Karthala, 2003), 136.

By the time the soldiers relinquished power, Operation Zaki had become a monster that had to be tamed by the succeeding civilian regimes. The soldiers who gave the squad its fearsome monstrous garb and the fire power were withdrawn and an all police anti robbery unit . . . was formed to, first of all eliminate the increasing acts of extra judicial killings as well as the high level extortion that were prevalent in the previous squad.[51]

Youth criminality and state criminality, in other words, sometimes fed one another.

By the 1990s and 2000s, Maiduguri was a large, cosmopolitan city. The 1991 census, probably undercounting, showed that Maiduguri LGA had some 621,000 inhabitants.[52] By the mid-1990s, the city may have hosted as many as 850,000 residents.[53] On one level, the city was thriving:

Maiduguri's age-old commercial centre used to be on Babban Layi, which simply means "a wide street." It used to be a shoppers' paradise for textile, electronics, clothing, and household items. Lebanese and Chadian merchants jostled alongside low-tech con men and pickpockets—all hoping to get a slice of the bulging sacks of money freely freighted around on wheelbarrows. Overloaded trucks, known locally as *giwa-giwa*, transported goods from Babban Layi to neighbouring countries such as Chad and Cameroon, and even to distant places like Sudan and the Central African Republic.[54]

---

[51] Bukar Ahmed, "Borno Police and Its Squad of Extortionists," *Daily Trust*, 30 June 2007, http://allafrica.com/stories/200707130678.html.

[52] Paul Francis et al., *State, Community and Local Development in Nigeria* (Washington, DC: World Bank, 1996), 40.

[53] Kawka, "Physiognomic Structure."

[54] Jimeh Saleh, "How Boko Haram Attacks Have Changed the Maiduguri Where I Grew Up," BBC, 30 April 2012, http://www.bbc.com/news/world-africa-17847718.

Yet on another level, the city was full of poor migrants fleeing failing farms, overstretched households, and drought-ridden Niger and Chad.[55] For young arrivals like Yusuf and Shekau, the contrasts must have been staggering: they could worship at the Muhammad Indimi Mosque, built by one of Nigeria's richest men; but they would also have seen clear evidence of the failures of Nigeria's federal and state governments to make life better for ordinary people. A 1996 World Bank report described two wards in Maiduguri, Bulabulin and Zajiri. In the former, "unemployment [was] general (especially among school leavers), and prostitution widespread"; in the latter, a village consumed by city sprawl, "the ward [was] unplanned, lacking infrastructure and services. . . . There is a high incidence of endemic diseases, including measles, whooping cough, typhoid and diarrhea. The government provides few amenities in Zajiri, and there is little in the way of community initiatives to compensate for this."[56] Whether out of conviction or opportunism, Yusuf and Shekau would soon attempt to build an antigovernment movement in Maiduguri and beyond.

Intra-Muslim Struggles

Compounding Maiduguri's social tensions was a "fragmentation of sacred authority." Around the world, such fragmentation has involved the rise of new kinds of Muslim leaders as well as an increasingly vigorous competition to speak for

[55] Muhammad Nur Alkali, Abubakar Kawu Monguno, and Ballama Shettima Mustafa, "Overview of Islamic Actors in Northeastern Nigeria," Nigeria Research Network Working Paper no. 2 (January 2012), 4. Available at http://www3.qeh.ox.ac.uk/pdf/nrn/WP2Alkali.pdf; accessed October 2014.

[56] Paul Francis et al., *State, Community and Local Development in Nigeria*, 41.

Islam.[57] In northern Nigeria, fragmentation has taken three forms: challenges to the emirs' independence and authority; Sufi-Salafi conflict; and the rise of minority, dissident sects.

Under colonialism, northern Nigeria's emirs were arguably at the height of their power, except for a few emirs who were deposed for angering the British. But those who got along with the British found their powers solidified. Systems of surveillance helped to maintain law and order under the emirs. In Borno, the Shehu presided (and still presides) over a hierarchy that extended through district heads (*ajia*) and their subordinates, known as *lawan* and *bulama*. The district head had a "pivotal" office, as "the person to whom all attention in the capital turns if something goes wrong." The Shehu and the British often transferred and dismissed district heads, indicating a considerable degree of centralized control. District heads, meanwhile, maintained substantial networks of informants and assistants.[58]

The emirs successfully navigated the transition to independence, with all its political complexities. At that time, the northern elite was remarkably unified in ruling the region and attempting to shape its religious identity. After withstanding challenges from young reformers who wanted to curtail emirs' powers, the hereditary rulers struck compromises with the emerging political class. The northern premier, Ahmadu Bello (1910–66), was both a member of the emirate class (as a descendant of Uthman dan Fodio) and a Western-educated politician who attracted the support of many younger, Western-educated northerners. The emirs supported Bello's Northern People's Congress (NPC), the ruling party in the north and

[57] Kane, *Muslim Modernity*, 69; Dale Eickelman and James Piscatori, *Muslim Politics*, 2nd ed. (Princeton, NJ: Princeton University Press, 2004), 70.

[58] Ronald Cohen, "The Analysis of Conflict in Hierarchical Systems: An Example from Kanuri Political Organization," *Anthropologica* 4:1 (1962): 87–120; 96.

the dominant party in national politics.[59] In Borno, the emirs demanded voters' support for the NPC, equating support for the party with support for "the traditional political structure of the society, and . . . the moral order that holds it together."[60] Much of the north, including Borno, functioned at times as a one-party state.

Starting in the 1970s, however, emirs' systems of control began to weaken, especially in cities where most residents no longer knew all their neighbors. The influx of strangers and the decline in social cohesion fed a rising sense among northern Muslims that formerly secure spaces—the home, the town, and the entire Muslim north—were becoming vulnerable, physically and spiritually.[61] In Maiduguri, the Shehu of Borno and his hierarchy of district, ward, and village heads were initially able to supervise the city's transformation and its internal affairs during the late colonial and early postcolonial periods.[62] But over time, Maiduguri's new, ethnically diverse urban periphery slipped outside the Shehu's control:

> A gradient can be traced from the Shehu's palace to the urban fringe. The central wards are religiously—and culturally— more homogeneous, and the people there stuck closer to Kanuri traditions. Farther away from the palace towards the urban fringe, the culture was less pure Islamic and less typically Kanuri, as more non-Moslems and thus more non-Kanuri lived there.[63]

[59] Mahmood Yakubu, *An Aristocracy in Political Crisis: The End of Indirect Rule and the Emergence of Party Politics in the Emirates of Northern Nigeria* (Aldershot, UK: Avebury, 1996).

[60] Cohen, *Kanuri*, 109.

[61] Murray Last, "The Search for Security in Muslim Northern Nigeria," *Africa* 78:1 (February 2008): 41–63.

[62] Max Lock Group Nigeria, *Maiduguri*, 6.1.6.

[63] Rupert Kawka, "Social Status and Urban Structure in Yerwa" in *From Bulamari to Yerwa*, 159–187; 169.

By the mid-1970s, many wards remained majority Kanuri—such as Limanti, Gambaru, and Fezzan—but many other wards, such as Mafoni and Bulabulin, were home to thousands of Hausa, Fulani, Shuwa Arabs, and other ethnic groups from Borno and nearby Chad.[64] It is worth noting that later, Yusuf established himself not in Maiduguri's Kanuri core, but in a newer area, Railway Quarters.

During the 1970s and after, it became clear that emirs were losing some prestige—not so much that they lost mass support, but enough that they suffered visible setbacks. Emirs lost even more of their independence from politicians, and they lost even more of their ability to rein in Muslim radicals. Popular expectations and government rhetoric emphasized the democratically elected, responsive nature of local government—a trend that further compartmentalized the role of hereditary Muslim rulers. When a Borno State commission recommended strengthening the law enforcement powers of hereditary rulers in the wake of a 1982 religious crisis (see below), the state's civilian-run government defended the 1976 local government reforms. The recommendation to reempower the emirs, the government said, went "against the spirit of the [1979] Constitution."[65]

Emirs' subordination to politicians was not complete. Elected politicians who attempted to discipline emirs often lost out—in Kano, the leftist governor Abubakar Rimi (served 1979–83) suspended the emir and curtailed his powers but backtracked after the emir's supporters rioted in 1981.[66] But some emirs

---

[64] Max Lock Group Nigeria, *Maiduguri*, 7.3.17–7.3.20.

[65] Borno State Government, *Government White Papers on the Report of the Commission of Inquiry into the Religious Disturbances in Bulum-Kutu Area of Maiduguri between the 26th–29th October, 1982* (Maiduguri: Borno State Government, 1982), 10.

[66] Olufemi Vaughan, *Nigerian Chiefs: Traditional Power in Modern Politics, 1890s–1990s* (Rochester, NY: University of Rochester Press, 2006), 173–74.

ended up appearing to be tools of politicians. In 1988, Ibrahim Dasuki, a business associate of Ibrahim Babangida, was appointed as Sultan of Sokoto. He was summarily removed in 1996 at the whim of a new military dictator, Sani Abacha.[67] Meanwhile, many of the younger emirs became indistinguishable, in terms of educational and professional makeup, from other members of Nigeria's elite. Their backgrounds are in the military, business, or the civil service, rather than in Islamic studies. Reluctant to defy politicians and little different from them in background, the emirs have lost significant independence.

Such trends operated in the northeast as well. In the 1970s, a single military governor—Brigadier Musa Usman—was in office long enough to appoint two of the Shehus of Borno, including Mustapha ibn Umar al-Kanemi, who ruled 1974–2009.[68] Growing up, Yusuf and Shekau would have witnessed emirs' political subordination in Yobe. Following the 1991 gubernatorial elections, Yobe's new governor, Bukar Abba Ibrahim, divided the state's four Islamic emirates into thirteen. Military rulers soon reversed the decision, but when Ibrahim reclaimed the governorship in the 1999 elections, he again implemented the plan. The state's most prominent emir, Muhammadu Ambali of Fika, challenged him in court but lost.[69] The governor had the final say.

Although Yusuf and Shekau celebrated the memory of Uthman dan Fodio, the historical source of many contemporary emirs' authority, they saw the political weakness of emirs in their own time. This trend may have reinforced the young

[67] William Reno, *Warlord Politics and African States* (Boulder: Lynne Rienner, 1999), 188–202.
[68] Baba Gana Kachalla Ali, *A History of Yerwa since 1907*, vol. 1 (Maiduguri: n.p., 2005), 11.
[69] Ola Amupitan, "Potiskum's Resistance to Damaturu as State Capital," *This Day*, 21 August 2002, http://allafrica.com/stories/200208210417.html.

men's sentiment that Nigerian secularism was destroying Islam—and their feeling that the emirs had no moral authority over them. Nigeria's Salafi movement, discussed below, became increasingly confrontational toward hereditary rulers during the 1990s and 2000s, the period when Boko Haram was emerging. Ja'far Adam, Yusuf's onetime mentor, publicly argued that the emirs—"our leaders with turbans," he dismissively called them—had squandered their prestige and power, and had failed to discharge their core duties of spreading Islam and preserving the Muslim community's moral order.[70]

Amid a wider, nationwide feeling that "the trouble with Nigeria is simply and squarely a failure of leadership,"[71] Nigerian Salafis gave an edge to the broader critique of leaders. Salafis charged that what was missing—even from Muslim heads of state, Sufi shaykhs, and Muslim emirs—was a genuine commitment to Islam. Yusuf, by the end of his life, was attacking the historical foundation of the Shehu of Borno's legitimacy. Yusuf argued that Muhammad al-Amin al-Kanemi (1776–1837), founder of the ruling dynasty in Borno, had supplanted what Yusuf saw as the genuinely Islamic dynasty that preceded him. "It wasn't al-Kanemi who brought Islam to this area," Yusuf told his followers. "He destroyed it."[72] Yusuf's attack clearly extended to al-Kanimi's descendants.

When Boko Haram began its campaign of violence, it initially refrained from targeting hereditary rulers, but by 2012 it was directing violence at rulers in the northeast: in 2012, the Emir of Fika barely escaped an attempt on his life by Boko Haram. For one commentator, the image of that emir "stum-

---

[70] Ja'far Mahmud Adam, "Siyasa a Nigeria" (recorded lecture), 2003.

[71] Chinua Achebe, *The Trouble with Nigeria* (Oxford: Heinemann, 1983), 1.

[72] Muhammad Yusuf, "Tarihin Musulmai," undated, https://www.youtube.com /watch?v=eUQYNucjqUE. The lecture likely dates from early 2009, given that in it Yusuf references his arrest by Nigeria's intelligence service, which occurred in November 2008.

bling over his traditional robes, his turban flailing behind him as he fled for safety," symbolized a broader change that had taken place within the lifetime of Yusuf and Shekau: "Not too long ago, refusal to remove your shoes in the presence of district heads, not to talk of an emir, could be interpreted as a rebellion, and in some places, punishable . . . [but now] a new boldness is in place," and Muslims were increasingly defying the emirs.[73]

Other poles of religious authority have also been challenged. In the 1950s and 1960s, there was relative unity among northern Nigeria's Muslim elites: Ahmadu Bello welcomed Islamic modernists and anti-Sufi reformers into his circle but remained positively disposed toward Sufism. He encouraged Sufis and their critics to work together under the banner of Jama'at Nasr al-Islam (the Society for Victory of Islam). Some divisions occurred, of course: A leftist party challenged Bello, including on religious grounds;[74] conflicts occurred between the Qadiriyya and Tijaniyya Sufi orders;[75] and Bello had battles of wills with certain emirs. Yet the divisions that burst forth in the late 1960s and 1970s, after Bello and other northern elites were killed in the coup of 1966, were sharper.

In the 1970s, Sufi shaykhs faced a major theological offensive from the emerging Salafi current. In 1972, Abubakar Gumi (1924–92), the emerging leader of the Salafi camp, published the anti-Sufi tract Al-'Aqida al-Sahiha bi-Muwafaqat al-Shari'a (The Correct Creed in Accordance with Islamic Law). He accused

[73] Salisu Suleiman, "Northern Traditional Institutions and the Crises of Legitimacy," Sahara Reporters, 24 September 2012, http://saharareporters.com/2012/09/24/northern-traditional-institutions-and-crises-legitimacy-salisu-suleiman.

[74] Jonathan Reynolds, The Time of Politics (Zaminin Siyasa): Islam and the Politics of Legitimacy in Northern Nigeria, 1950–1966 (Bethesda, MD: International Scholars, 1999).

[75] Ali Abubakr, Al-Thaqafa al-'Arabiyya fi Nayjiriya min 'am 1804 ila 1960 'am al-Istiqlal (Beirut: n.p., 1972).

Sufis of following practices that contradicted Islam, and of using magic to dupe "idiots."[76] Gumi was a prominent figure: he had been a religious advisor to Bello and had served as Grand Khadi (chief Islamic judge) of northern Nigeria from 1962 to 1966. His anti-Sufi polemic stung. It evoked harsh responses from leading Sufis, as well as some violence. Amid these intra-Muslim tensions, Gumi's followers established the anti-Sufi organization Jama'at Izalat al-Bid'a wa-Iqamat al-Sunna (the Society for Removing Blameworthy Innovation and Establishing the Prophetic Model) in 1978. The organization, better known as Izala, institutionalized the challenge to Sufi dominance. Izala's preachers established alliances with local businessmen and Arab patrons while founding mosques and schools throughout the north.[77] In the ensuing decades, Izala and Sufis would sometimes close ranks against the perceived challenge of ascendant Christianity,[78] but in the new millennium Salafi-Sufi relations have often been tense. Anti-Sufism was not the stance that made Yusuf famous, but it was a major part of his doctrine.

As the Salafi current rose, Izala experienced schisms. Around the time of Gumi's death in 1992, Izala split into two factions, respectively based in Jos and Kaduna. The two factions had different stances on politics and theology, with the Jos faction more hardline in its anti-Sufism. Meanwhile, in the early 1990s, charismatic, well-educated members of Izala were returning home to Nigeria from Saudi Arabia, where Izala had helped them to study at the Islamic University of Medina. Some

[76] Abubakar Gumi, *Al-'Aqida al-Sahiha bi-Muwafaqat al-Shari'a* (Beirut: Dar al-'Arabiyya, 1972), 25.

[77] On Izala, see Roman Loimeier, *Islamic Reform and Political Change in Northern Nigeria* (Evanston, IL: Northwestern University Press, 1997); Kane, *Muslim Modernity*; and Ramzi Ben Amara, "The Izala Movement in Nigeria: Its Split, Relationship to Sufis and Perception of Sharia," Ph.D. dissertation, Bayreuth University, 2011.

[78] Loimeier, *Islamic Reform*.

graduates of Medina became independent preachers, reflecting their dismay at Izala's infighting, their dissatisfaction with not being given leadership roles in Izala, and their conviction that Salafism should not be confined within a formal association.

The most prominent graduate of Medina was Ja'far Adam. Along with other graduates, Adam built a mass constituency across the north. The Medina graduates worked with Izala at times but also created a network of independent mosques. The graduates served on government committees, and some took posts in universities and colleges.[79] Salafism, itself a challenge to the Muslim establishment in the north, became more decentralized in the 1990s, but also more prominent in society and major institutions.

Maiduguri became a key node in the emerging Salafi network. The implantation of Izala and the broader Salafi movement there did not occur without resistance, for Maiduguri has long been a stronghold of the Tijaniyya Sufi order.[80] Major Tijani scholars include Abubakar al-Miskin (1918–2014), Ahmad Abu al-Fath (1921/2–2003), and Ibrahim Salih (b. 1939).

In the late 1970s, the Muslim establishment of Borno, particularly the Shehu and the Tijaniyya, closed ranks against Izala. The establishment had some success in keeping Friday mosques out of Izala's control.[81] Political authorities sided with the Shehu and the Tijaniyya: Borno State's 1981 Islamic

---

[79] Alex Thurston, "Ahlussunnah: A Preaching Network from Kano to Medina and Back," in *Shaping Global Islamic Discourses: The Role of al-Azhar, al-Madina, and al-Mustafa*, edited by Masooda Bano and Keiko Sakurai, 93–116 (Edinburgh: Edinburgh University Press, 2015).

[80] Muhammad Nur Alkali, Abubakar Kawu Monguno, and Ballam Shettima Mustafa, "Overview of Islamic Actors in Northeastern Nigeria," Nigeria Research Network Working Paper no. 2, January 2012, 9–10, http://www3.qeh.ox.ac.uk/pdf /nrn/WP2Alkali.pdf.

[81] Loimeier, *Islamic Reform*, 264.

Religious Preachings Law created an Islamic Religious Preaching Board, giving the Muslim establishment the legal authority, at least on paper, to decide who could preach publicly.[82] In 1982, after a local riot by Maitatsine followers unconnected with Izala, influential voices in the state called for the outright banning of Izala. The state government refused the suggestion, citing the need to protect religious liberty.[83] Meanwhile, Sufi-dominated mosque and school networks were expanding. Both Abu al-Fath and Salih established major new mosque-school complexes in the 1980s and 1990s.[84]

Nevertheless, Salafis made inroads in Maiduguri. One important figure was Muhammad Abba Aji (1942–2009), of mixed Kanuri and Fulani heritage. Born in Maiduguri, Aji followed the hybrid educational trajectory that has marked many of Nigeria's leading Salafis, pursuing both classical Islamic studies and formal education in government colleges and universities. Aji disseminated a reformist, Salafi-leaning message through multiple channels—through the school he founded in Hausari Ward in 1974; through religious programs on state-run radio and television; as imam at the Mairi Friday Mosque; and through his Qur'anic exegesis or *tafsir*. In tafsir, he became a pioneer in rendering the Qur'an in colloquial Kanuri and Mandara, rather than in the specialized Kanembu language that many of Borno's exegetes used, and that many ordinary Kanuri Muslims did not understand. (Yusuf, for his

[82] Borno State Government, "Islamic Religious Preachings Law," 1981, reproduced in *Sharia Implementation in Northern Nigeria 1999–2006: A Sourcebook*, vol. 6, *Ulama Institutions*, edited and compiled by Philip Ostien, chapter 8, part 2 (published online, 2011: http://www.sharia-in-africa.net/media/publications/sharia-implementation-in-northern-nigeria-volume-six/Chapter%208%20Part%20II.pdf), 11–17.

[83] Borno State, *Government White Papers*, 14–15.

[84] Kyari Mohammed (Muhammad Kyari), "The Changing Responses of the Ummah to the Challenges of Western Education: Recent Trends in Maiduguri Mosques," *Al-Ijtihad: The Journal of the Islamization of Knowledge and Contemporary Issues* 5:2 (July 2005): 147–59.

part, would later speak dismissively of Kanembu.[85]) This effort of bringing Islam's core texts closer to popular audiences through vernacular languages was a hallmark of Salafism in northern Nigeria. Aji faced resistance from Sufis, especially in the late 1970s and early 1980s. Sufis sometimes blocked his access to the media.[86] But like Salafi pioneers elsewhere in northern Nigeria, Aji had the support of businessmen and professionals. These allies helped him to develop the Mairi Mosque and an associated primary and secondary school during the 1980s and 1990s.[87] By the end of his life, Aji was a prominent figure in Borno, earning tributes from Sufis and elected politicians.[88]

Yusuf would later claim to have received Aji's blessing, but the older scholar practiced a different kind of politics than Yusuf. In the aftermath of anti-Christian riots in Maiduguri during the worldwide Danish cartoon controversy of 2006, Aji expressed his sympathies for Christian victims and his hope that "Allah would exchange (what they lost) for something better."[89]

If figures such as Aji represented a first wave of Salafization in the northeast, the graduates of Medina initiated a second wave in the 1990s. After returning from Medina in 1993, Ja'far Adam began giving an annual Ramadan tafsir at the Muhammad

[85] Yusuf, "Tarihin Musulmai."

[86] Reciter Muhammad al-Barnawy blog, "Sheikh Muhammad Abba Aji Biography," 23 January 2015, http://indimialafasy.blogspot.com/2015/01/sheikh-muhammad-abba -aji-biography.html; see also Baba Goni Sheriff, "Sheikh Muhammad A. Aji: Exit of an Excellent Islamic Scholar," *Daily Trust*, 19 December 2009, http://dailytrust.com .ng/weekly/index.php/comments/8931-sheikh-muhammad-a-aji-exit-of-an-excellent -islamic-scholar; and Loimeier, *Islamic Reform*, 226.

[87] Kyari Mohammed (Muhammad Kyari), "Changing Responses," 154–55.

[88] Isa Umar Gusau, "Sheikh Abba Aji Dies in Mecca," *Daily Trust*, 7 December 2009, http://allafrica.com/stories/200912080262.html.

[89] "Hankali Ya Fara Kwanciya A Maidugurin Jihar Borno," VOA Hausa, 20 February 2006, http://www.voahausa.com/content/a-39-2006-02-20-voa1-91731074/1369983 .html.

Indimi Mosque. Although Adam was based in Kano, he had close colleagues in the northeast, such as Ali Mustafa of Maiduguri and Dr. Ibrahim Jalingo of Taraba State. By the time Muhammad Yusuf gravitated toward the Salafi movement, likely in the late 1990s, the movement possessed strong networks and mosque infrastructures in Maiduguri and beyond—infrastructures that Yusuf soon sought to both co-opt and challenge. The 1990s reshaped Maiduguri's religious field. That transformation gave Yusuf a larger platform than a comparable figure might have had in earlier decades.

The religious field was becoming more complicated throughout northern Nigeria. In the 1970s and after, alongside Salafi-Sufi rivalries and intra-Salafi competitions for influence, there was a broader rise in the diversity of Islamic religiosity in the north. Sometimes, activism took the form of fringe, violent movements. One was led by the Cameroon-born Muhammad Marwa, nicknamed "Mai Tatsine," meaning "The One Who Curses." Marwa, based on and off in Kano after 1945, preached a millenarian, "Qur'an-only" doctrine that was far outside the northern Nigerian Muslim mainstream. He exhorted his followers to abandon modern technology. His group clashed with authorities in Kano in December 1980. Between four thousand and six thousand people were killed, including Marwa himself.

Maitatsine's social base included rural migrants to northern cities, including many migrants from Niger, and possibly also Qur'an teachers and their students.[90] The movement has

[90] For a debate on this issue, see Paul Lubeck, "Islamic Protest under Semi-industrial Capitalism: 'Yan Tatsine Explained," *Africa* 55:4 (1985): 369–89; Mervyn Hiskett, "The Maitatsine Riots in Kano, 1980: An Assessment," *Journal of Religion in Africa* 17:3 (October 1987): 209–23; and Don Ohadike, "Muslim-Christian Conflict and Political Instability in Nigeria," in *Religion and National Integration in Africa:*

been described as a direct forerunner of Boko Haram, but it is more accurate to see Maitatsine as a movement with some demographic and structural similarities to Boko Haram. It is also important to stress the key theological differences between the two movements. Unlike Boko Haram, Maitatsine lacked any connection to broader trends in Islamic thought such as Salafism or jihadism.

Maitatsine had some impact in the northeast. In 1982, authorities released hundreds of prisoners held after the Kano riots. Many of them resettled in the northeast. The movement's followers rioted in the Bulumkutu suburb of Maiduguri in 1982, killing as many as 3,350 people. Maitatsine followers rioted again in Yola, Adamawa State, in 1984, killing over 700; and in Gombe in 1985, killing 100.[91] These riots were sparked by resettled sect members' conflicts both with other Muslims—including emirs and Izala—and with political authorities.[92] For decades after the riots, Maitatsine's followers and other "Qur'an-only" or "kala kato" Muslims retained a small but noticeable presence in the northeast, but they do not seem to have been strongly connected to Boko Haram.[93]

The Maitatsine riots underscored the severe crisis of authority facing the northern Muslim elite. The official tribunal

---

Islam, Christianity, and Politics in the Sudan and Nigeria, edited by John Hunwick, 101–24 (Evanston, IL: Northwestern University Press, 1992), 114

[91] Casualty figures vary, and as Niels Kastfelt points out, classifying all the violence as "Maitatsine riots" could be misleading. See Kastfelt, "Rumours of Maitatsine: A Note on Political Culture in Northern Nigeria," *African Affairs* 88:350 (January 1989): 83–90. For casualty figures, see Elizabeth Isichei, "The Maitatsine Risings in Nigeria 1980–85: A Revolt of the Disinherited," *Journal of Religion in Africa* 17:3 (October 1987): 194–208; 194; and Allan Pred and Michael Watts, *Reworking Modernity: Capitalisms and Symbolic Discontent* (New Brunswick, NJ: Rutgers University Press, 1992), 59–62.

[92] Pred and Watts, *Reworking Modernity*, 59–62.

[93] Alkali et al., "Overview," 15–16.

of inquiry into the 1980 disturbances in Kano concluded that authorities had squandered multiple opportunities between 1962 and 1980 to neutralize Marwa. "If there had been good and effective liaison between Local Authorities, Traditional Authorities, and the Police Force," the tribunal concluded, "this country would have been properly rid of him once and for all."[94] Authorities of all stripes had been intimidated by the strength of Marwa's following. Authorities' control had been weakened by unplanned urban development: the tribunal repeatedly noted authorities' timidity in challenging Marwa's illegal construction and settlements in Kano.[95]

Borno's commission of inquiry reached a similar conclusion in 1982, saying that Maiduguri's "satellite shanty towns . . . offer comfortable abodes for religious deviants such as the Tatsine followers." The commission highlighted the declining "surveillance and monitoring capabilities" of Borno's hereditary rulers and linked this trend to what the commission saw as the chaos emanating from increasingly unregulated Islamic schools.[96] Maitatsine's violence indicated the increasing space available to fringe preachers who built mass movements in the north's largest cities.

If Maitatsine attracted some urban poor, a more elite form of dissent was emerging in northern universities. The Muslim Students' Society (MSS) was founded in 1954 in Nigeria's southwest. During the late 1970s, some northern MSS branches adopted confrontational stances. In 1979, MSS members at Ahmadu Bello University (ABU) Zaria attacked a faculty club

[94] Kano State Government, *Report of the Kano Disturbances Tribunal of Inquiry*, 14 April 1981, 21.
[95] Kano State Government, *Report of the Kano Disturbances Tribunal of Inquiry*, 72.
[96] Borno State, *Government White Papers*, 3–4.

and destroyed alcohol supplies there. The Iranian Revolution of 1979 reinforced the growing conviction among some MSS members that an Islamic state was possible in Nigeria. The onetime MSS leader Ibrahim al-Zakzaky (b. 1953) broke away and created an outspoken, "politically Shi'i" group later called the Islamic Movement of Nigeria (IMN). The movement had increasing tensions with authorities over time, including a riot in the northern city of Katsina in 1991.[97] Like Izala, the IMN fragmented in the 1990s: some members remained close to al-Zakzaky, others gravitated toward the Sunni-oriented Jama'at Tajdid al-Islam, and still others joined quietist Shi'i movements. Despite the split, IMN maintained a strong presence in the northeastern cities of Potiskum and Bauchi into the 2010s.[98]

What were young men like Yusuf and Shekau to make of this atmosphere? On the one hand, movements of dissent like Maitatsine and IMN represented only a tiny percentage of northern Muslims. Most northerners were focused on their day-to-day affairs and still largely deferred to emirs and Sufi shaykhs in religious matters. On the other hand, movements of dissent clearly intimidated politicians and the police; only the military could quell the most serious uprisings. Emirs and Sufis were often on the defensive. Meanwhile, Izala was more than a fringe movement of dissent: backed by prominent shaykhs, intellectuals, politicians, and businessmen, Salafism became a mainstream option for northern Muslims.

In the 1980s and 1990s, boundaries between the movements of Islamic dissent, and loyalties to a leader, were not

---

[97] Loimeier, *Islamic Reform*, 301–2; Toyin Falola, *Violence in Nigeria: The Crisis of Religious and Secular Ideologies* (Rochester, NY: University of Rochester Press, 1998), 194–203.

[98] Alkali et al., "Overview," 13–14.

always strong. Yusuf and Shekau may have found themselves floating from one camp to another before settling on Salafism. Yusuf's own trajectory is unclear. A prominent Nigerian Salafi has claimed that Yusuf had family ties to the Maitatsine movement, as well as an allegiance to al-Zakzaky.[99] Another Nigerian scholar has stated that Yusuf was a member of al-Zakzaky's IMN, but then left the group to join Izala.[100] Other sources report that Yusuf was an official representative of Jama'at Tajdid al-Islam in Borno during the 1990s.[101] Another source says that Yusuf "either quit or was expelled from Izala" amid disputes about whether voting was legitimate for Muslims.[102] Yet another source states that Boko Haram grew out of a group of Salafi students at the University of Maiduguri in the mid-1990s.[103] Some accounts state that Yusuf was a member of Ja'far Adam's network by 1998, by which time Yusuf was building his own following.[104] Whatever the truth, by the late 1990s, Yusuf had cast his lot with the Salafi camp. He had done so at a time when tensions were rising not just within the Muslim community, but also between Muslims and Christians.

[99] Muhammad Awwal Adam "Albani" Zaria, "In An Ki Ji 2/3," undated, https://www.youtube.com/watch?v=M2q-tNpXRqM&t=302s.

[100] Ahmad Murtada, *Boko Haram in Nigeria: Its Beginnings, Principles and Activities in Nigeria*, translated by 'AbdulHaq al-Ashanti (Salafi Manhaj, 2013 [2012]), 5–6, http://download.salafimanhaj.com/pdf/SalafiManhaj_BokoHaram.pdf.

[101] Roman Loimeier finds the evidence for this claim shaky. See "Boko Haram: The Development of a Militant Religious Movement in Nigeria," *Africa Spectrum* 47: 2–3 (2012): 137–55; 148 n. 23.

[102] Marc-Antoine Pérouse de Montclos, "Nigeria's Interminable Insurgency: Addressing the Boko Haram Crisis," Chatham House, September 2014, 8, https://www.chathamhouse.org/sites/files/chathamhouse/field/field_document/20140901Boko HaramPerousedeMontclos_0.pdf.

[103] Shehu Sani, "Boko Haram (Part Two)," *Vanguard*, 1 July 2011, http://www.vanguardngr.com/2011/07/boko-haram-the-northern-nigeria-hausaland-2/.

[104] Abdul Raufu Mustapha, "Understanding Boko Haram," in *Sects and Social Disorder: Muslim Identities and Conflict in Northern Nigeria*, 147–98 (London: James Currey, 2014), 148.

Muslim-Christian Divisions in Postcolonial Nigeria

In the mid-1970s, when Yusuf and Shekau were small boys, Nigeria's military government prepared for a transition to civilian rule scheduled for 1979. Talk of unity dominated. A new constitution asserted that the "federal character" of Nigeria should pervade appointments to office. This would "ensur[e] that there shall be no predominance of persons from a few States or from a few ethnic or other sectional groups in that government or in any of its agencies."[105]

Amid efforts to build unity, division resurfaced. Meeting to draft the constitution, Muslim and Christian delegates debated whether the constitution should create a Federal Shari'a Court of Appeal. Proponents of the court thought that it would solve the problems created when northern Nigeria's state-level shari'a courts issued contradictory rulings. The court's opponents argued that it would inappropriately Islamize Nigeria's federal government. The debate ended with the removal of the Court of Appeal from the constitution, embittering some northern Muslims.[106] The debate recurred in 1987–88, with the same result. As the next chapter discusses, when northern Muslims revived the issue in 1999, they took the battle to the states, initiating the "shari'a politics" that helped birth Boko Haram.

In the 1980s and 1990s, interreligious conflicts still occurred on the national political stage. When Ibrahim Babangida quietly

[105] Federal Republic of Nigeria, 1979 Constitution, chapter 2, 14-(3).

[106] On the "shari'a debate," see David Laitin, "The Sharia Debate and the Origins of Nigeria's Second Republic," *Journal of Modern African Studies* 20:3 (September 1982): 411–30; and Philip Ostien, "An Opportunity Missed by Nigeria's Christians: The 1976–78 Sharia Debate Revisited," in *Muslim-Christian Encounters in Africa*, edited by Benjamin Soares, 223–34 (Leiden: Brill, 2006).

applied for Nigerian membership in the Organization of the Islamic Conference in 1986, his decision generated a furor among Christians once it was discovered. But in this period, Muslim-Christian conflict turned local, and violent. Some of the most severe conflicts were in northern towns and cities, especially in zones where multiple ethnic and religious communities coexisted uneasily. Such conflicts did not center on Yobe and Borno. But during their teenage years and twenties, Yusuf and Shekau would have heard about the worst episodes of Muslim-Christian violence in Nigeria's independent history.

Four incidents deserve mention. First, in March 1987, violence broke out between Muslim and Christian students at the College of Education in Kafanchan, Kaduna State, after a traveling Christian preacher allegedly disparaged the Qur'an.[107] Second, in February 1992, intercommunal clashes occurred in Zangon-Kataf, Kaduna, between Christians from the Kataf ethnic group and Muslim Hausa traders; the latter objected to a decision to move the town's main market.[108] Third, starting in 1994, there was cyclical violence in Plateau State. In Plateau, Hausa and Fulani Muslims clashed with primarily Christian ethnic groups in Jos, Plateau's capital, as well as in other parts of the state. A fourth flashpoint has been Tafawa Balewa in Bauchi State, which saw clashes in 1991, 1995, 2001,[109] and 2004.[110] These names—Kafanchan, Zangon-Kataf, Plateau, and Tafawa Balewa—were heard frequently in Yusuf and Shekau's preaching.

[107] Jibrin Ibrahim, "The Politics of Religion in Nigeria: The Parameters of the 1987 Crisis in Kaduna State," *Review of African Political Economy* 45/46 (1989): 65–82; 65.

[108] Falola, *Violence in Nigeria*, 216–17.

[109] "Nigeria: Renewed Muslim-Christian Clashes Claim Lives," IRIN, 29 August 2001, http://www.irinnews.org/report/25540/nigeria-renewed-christian-muslim-clashes -claim-lives.

[110] "Curfew in Nigerian City after Deadly Clashes," AFP, 22 February 2009, http:// reliefweb.int/report/nigeria/curfew-nigerian-city-after-deadly-clashes.

Complex factors drive these conflicts, some of which still simmer at the time of writing. Strident religious rhetoric from both Muslims and Christians contributes to violence, but more than religion is at stake. One axis of conflict is between "indigenes" (residents given preferential legal status as the supposed rightful natives of an area), and "settlers" (residents treated as newcomers no matter how many generations their families may have lived in the area). In both Plateau and Kaduna, especially southern Kaduna where towns like Kafanchan and Zangon-Kataf are located, Hausa and Fulani Muslims complain of being treated as perpetual settlers.[111] Many Christians and other non-Muslims, meanwhile, feel threatened by Hausa and Fulani immigration into their communities. Such immigration reinforces bitter memories dating to the precolonial period, when peoples in present-day Kaduna and Plateau resisted the jihad of Uthman dan Fodio. Other memories date to the colonial period, when British authorities sometimes imposed Muslim emirs on non-Muslim peoples in a form of "sub-colonialism."[112]

Against the backdrop of this contentious history, present-day political struggles activate and reinforce various identities—ethnic, economic, political, and religious. Struggles over land, markets, and political office further heighten the stakes. Especially since 1991, when the military government created eighty-nine new LGAs, competition for local political power has yielded intercommunal violence. Contestation over control of new LGAs contributed to the Zangon-Kataf riots of

---

[111] Human Rights Watch, "'Leave Everything to God': Accountability for Intercommunal Violence in Plateau and Kaduna States, Nigeria," 12 December 2013, 35–36, https://www.hrw.org/sites/default/files/reports/nigeria1213_ForUpload.pdf.

[112] Moses Ochonu, *Colonialism by Proxy: Hausa Imperial Agents and Middle Belt Consciousness in Nigeria* (Bloomington: Indiana University Press, 2014), 1–3.

1992[113] and the Jos crisis of 1994.[114] As noted above, recurring administrative reorganization by military governments made local politics more cutthroat.

The inter-religious clashes of the 1980s and 1990s were important not just because of the violence, but also because of the way the clashes passed into communities' memories. Both Muslims and Christians decried authorities' inability, or refusal, to prevent violence and enforce accountability. As Human Rights Watch wrote later,

> The response of Nigerian authorities following mass killings has been surprisingly similar through the years. During or immediately following most spates of violence, hundreds of suspects were arrested. But those arrested were often randomly rounded up, in an attempt to calm the situation, or the police or soldiers dumped suspects en masse at police stations, with weapons and any other evidence collected at the scene all lumped together, making it nearly impossible to link individual suspects to any specific crime.

No serious investigations or prosecutions would follow, leaving many victims living side-by-side with known perpetrators of violence.[115] As with the Maitatsine riots, Muslim-Christian clashes in the 1980s and 1990s undermined ordinary northerners' confidence in authorities' ability to prevent violence and enforce accountability.

Amid de facto impunity for violence, Kafanchan's 1987 clashes became "the turning point in Nigeria's relapse into intergroup strife."[116] Many Muslims perceived a religious bias in the

---

[113] Falola, *Violence in Nigeria*, 216–17.

[114] Plateau State Government, "White Paper on the Report of the Commission of Inquiry into the Riots of 12th April, 1994 in Jos Metropolis," September 2004, 5–6.

[115] Human Rights Watch, "'Leave Everything to God,'" 17.

[116] Eghosa Osaghae and Rotimi Suberu, "A History of Identities, Violence and Stability in Nigeria," Centre for Research on Inequality, Human Security and Ethnicity

state's actions: authorities enforced long detentions for Muslims connected with the violence in Kafanchan but simultaneously allowed the inflammatory Christian preacher to remain free. Feeling themselves abandoned by the state, Muslims held solidarity rallies with the Muslim victims at Kafanchan and instituted an annual commemoration of the violence.[117] Funerals, commemorations, and other conflicts became interwoven in narratives of religious grievance.

As interreligious violence reinforced the "imagined community" of Nigerian Muslims at the national level, globalization reinforced Nigerian Muslims' feelings of solidarity with Muslims elsewhere in the world. Northern Nigeria was increasingly abuzz with electronic media, especially radio. These media encouraged greater participation by Muslim scholars in informal political debates in Nigeria.[118] Reinforcing feelings of pan-Islamic solidarity were world events: the Soviet invasion of Afghanistan in 1979, the Palestinian Intifada of 1987, the outbreak of the Bosnian War in 1992, Russia's invasions of Chechnya in 1994 and 1999, the U.S.-led Gulf War of 1991 and invasions of Afghanistan in 2001 and Iraq in 2003, and media controversies such as the Danish caricatures of the Prophet Muhammad in 2006 and the film *Innocence of Muslims* in 2012. Such events reverberated inside Nigeria, often evoking protests by northern Muslims.

For some Muslims and especially for Salafis, this global picture indicated that Islam was under siege by the West and by Christianity. Ja'far Adam frequently mentioned foreign conflict

Working Paper no. 6 (January 2005), 18–19, http://www3.qeh.ox.ac.uk/pdf/crisewps/workingpaper6.pdf.

[117] Umar Birai, "Islamic Tajdid and the Political Process in Nigeria," in *Fundamentalisms and the State: Remaking Polities, Economies, and Militancy*, edited by Martin E. Marty, 184–203 (Chicago: University of Chicago Press, 1996), 189.

[118] Muhammad Sani Umar, "Education and Islamic Trends in Northern Nigeria: 1970s–1990s," *Africa Today* 48:2 (Summer 2001): 127–50.

zones in his preaching, often demonstrating detailed knowledge of the religious and political histories of those countries. Yusuf also demonstrated a grasp of Muslim history beyond Nigeria. The popularity of electronic media and the widespread feeling of global Muslim interconnectedness helped to create the atmosphere in which Yusuf preached. Yusuf could refer almost offhandedly to the Danish cartoon controversy, America's Guantanamo Bay prison, and the torture scandal at the U.S.-run Abu Ghraib prison in Iraq—and know that most of his audience would already be familiar with those events.[119] Feelings that the Muslim world was besieged also reverberated in debates over education for Muslim children—the arena where Yusuf would seek to make his mark.

Placing Hopes on Education

Returning to the story of the 1970s, was there a way out of rural poverty for boys like Yusuf and Shekau? As military rulers sought to build post–civil war unity, they upheld education as an instrument of progress.[120] The oil boom allowed the federal government to devote tremendous resources to new educational programs. Universal Primary Education, launched in 1976, saw immediate and astonishing increases in enrollment, nearing a 500 percent increase in some states.[121] Yet the increases dramatically exceeded planners' projections,[122] as did

[119] Yusuf mentions these in the undated, two-part video of his exegesis of the Qur'an's Surat al-Tawba. See https://www.youtube.com/watch?v=Y33rL_D_6pw and https://www.youtube.com/watch?v=R3NcgQv-LVM.

[120] Marg Csapo, "Universal Primary Education in Nigeria: Its Problems and Implications," *African Studies Review* 26:1 (March 1983): 91–106; 91.

[121] Csapo, "Universal Primary Education in Nigeria," 92.

[122] Mark Bray, *Universal Primary Education in Nigeria: A Study of Kano State* (London: Routledge and Kegan Paul, 1981), 82.

the program's costs. When oil revenues fell in the early 1980s, the program collapsed, leaving in its wake a dangerous combination of elevated expectations and deep disappointment.

In North Eastern State, the military administration boasted of vast budgetary increases in the education sector (from £2 million in 1968 to £3 million in 1969). Yet the administration admitted that "the almost desperate need to increase teachers education would require flexible and very rapid means of producing teachers."[123] The northeast started from a worse position even than the rest of the north: in 1960, only 8.9 percent of six- and seven-year-olds in Borno Province were enrolled in Class 1, compared with 19 percent across the entire north.[124] Borno's civilian and then military authorities tried to rapidly expand enrollment and teacher training. In Maiduguri, "primary schools had a 36% increase in pupils and a 46% increase in teachers between 1968 and 1972 . . . [but] many classes still have over 40 pupils." As of 1974, only an estimated 8,800 school-age children, out of an overall population of around 54,000 school-age children, attended primary school in Maiduguri.[125] When Universal Primary Education began, Borno witnessed a further 47 percent increase in primary school enrollment from 1975–76 to 1976–77, but only a 24.8 percent increase in the number of primary schools in the state. The pupil-teacher ratio jumped from 28:1 in 1975–76 to 38:1 in 1976–77.[126] Northeastern authorities simply could not keep up with demand.

Meanwhile, Borno's children had limited prospects for advancing through Nigeria's education system: they were taught

[123] North Eastern State of Nigeria, *North Eastern State of Nigeria*, 3; 46.
[124] Alan Peshkin, *Kanuri Schoolchildren: Education and Social Mobilization in Nigeria* (New York: Holt, Rinehart, and Winston, 1972), 153.
[125] Max Lock Group Nigeria, *Maiduguri*, 7.3.26–7.3.27.
[126] Bray, *Universal Primary Education*, 82–84.

in local languages, but schools lacked textbooks in Kanuri and in other languages less widely spoken. Students were then expected to pass examinations in English in order to attend secondary school.[127] Education often perpetuated, rather than reduced, economic inequality. Those who did graduate had trouble finding work. Across the north, the rise and fall of Universal Primary Education coincided with a period when jobs became scarcer.[128]

Boko Haram, in other words, emerged in one of the parts of Nigeria where mass government education registered its greatest failures. In 1991, around the time Yusuf and Shekau were relocating to Maiduguri, Yobe's literacy rate was the lowest in the country—32 percent of its 1.4 million people.[129] By 2006, Yobe's population was 2.3 million;[130] out of residents aged six and older, fully 70 percent had never attended school.[131] In Borno, the situation was no better. The 2006 census showed that out of a population of nearly 4.2 million,[132] 71 percent of Borno residents aged six and older had never attended school.[133] Private schools, including "Islamiyya" schools that blended Islamic studies with government-approved curricula, were an

[127] Max Lock Group Nigeria, *Maiduguri*, 7.3.26–7.3.27.

[128] Bray, *Universal Primary Education*, 130.

[129] National Population Commission of Nigeria, "1991 Population Census of the Federal Republic of Nigeria: Analytical Report at the National Level" (Abuja, 1998), 129.

[130] National Population Commission of Nigeria, *2006 Population and Housing Census—Priority Table Volume IV: Population Distribution by Age and Sex* (Abuja, April 2010), 341, http://www.population.gov.ng/images/Priority%20table%20Vol%204.pdf.

[131] National Population Commission of Nigeria, *2006 Population and Housing Census—Priority Tables (Volume 1)*, 270, http://www.population.gov.ng/images/Priority%20Tables%20Volume%20I-update.pdf.

[132] National Population Commission of Nigeria, *2006 Population and Housing Census—Priority Table Volume IV*, 70.

[133] National Population Commission of Nigeria, *2006 Population and Housing Census—Priority Tables (Volume 1)*, 243.

attractive option for many Muslim families—but the schools' fees placed them out of reach for many poor Muslim children. Not all Muslims were comfortable attending Western-style schools, moreover. Boko Haram's rejection of Western-style education did not come out of thin air. Many colonized Muslim peoples viewed Western education with suspicion. Many Muslim parents feared that colonial schools would make their children into Christians or atheists, or would otherwise destroy their children's moral and intellectual foundations.[134] In the face of widespread noncompliance, officials in both French and British West Africa sometimes took children from families by force. One Malian Muslim, decades after the event, recalled his family's anguish when he was taken to attend a French colonial school: "Even today the cries of my mother ring in my ears."[135] Similar stories occurred in colonial northern Nigeria: one Arab from present-day Borno State recalled that his father, when asked by a British officer to send one of his children to school, initially offered a slave's child, and then—when the officer refused—reluctantly offered his youngest son.[136] "Indirect Rule" rested, in part, on an understanding between the British and the emirs that most Muslim children would not have to attend Western-style schools: missionary activities would be severely restricted, and Western-style schooling would target a limited class of future administrators.

As graduates of colonial schools in northern Nigeria achieved prominence, ambivalence came to surround Western education and its products. These graduates, or 'yan boko, personified political and professional success: Abubakar Tafawa Balewa,

[134] Muhammad Sani Umar, *Islam and Colonialism: Intellectual Responses of Muslims of Northern Nigeria to British Colonial Rule* (Leiden: Brill, 2006).

[135] Louis Brenner, *Controlling Knowledge: Religion, Power and Schooling in a West African Muslim Society* (Bloomington: Indiana University Press, 2001), 75.

[136] Jonathan Owens, *Neighborhood and Ancestry*, 124.

prime minister of Nigeria from 1960 to 1966, was one such graduate, as was Ahmadu Bello. But the graduates also challenged traditional authority. In the 1950s and 1960s, northern politicians attempted to mobilize society to support Western-style schooling, even enlisting Hausa poets in the effort to "articulat[e] Islamic religious arguments that [would] help to neutralize the longstanding negative perception of western education."[137] The introduction of Western-style schooling challenged Muslim scholars' "monopoly . . . over literacy and access to positions, resources, and prestige."[138] But ordinary Muslims' antipathy toward Western-style schooling lingered, meaning that Muslim scholars throughout the twentieth century had both an incentive and an opportunity to fan the flames of anti-Western sentiment.

Perhaps because Western education can yield such powerful benefits, and because access to quality education is so limited and expensive, some northerners resent and mistrust its bearers. Western-educated politicians and technocrats have presided over a system that has stolen much of Nigeria's wealth, leaving much of the population poor. The Western-educated are still seen as outsiders to many communities. Even after the federal government created twelve new universities in 1975—several of which are in the north, including Usmanu Danfodiyo University in Sokoto and the University of Maiduguri—some Muslim northerners continued to feel disappointed with and resentful toward Western-style schooling. Public universities were beset by overcrowding, underfunding, and chronic strikes, making them unappealing for some prospective students. Meanwhile,

---

[137] Muhammad Sani Umar, "Islamic Arguments for Western Education in Northern Nigeria: Mu'azu Hadejia's Hausa Poem, *Ilmin Zaman*," *Islam et societés au sud du Sahara* 16 (2002): 85–106; 87.

[138] Umar, "Education and Islamic Trends," 129.

graduates of such institutions were sometimes viewed as unaccountable elites.

The ambivalence surrounding Western education echoed even within the universities. In a famous 1971 commencement address, the Waziri Junaidu of Sokoto, a prominent representative of the emirate system, told an audience at Ahmadu Bello University:

> Your University like all others in Nigeria is a cultural transplant whose roots lie in another tradition. . . . It is little wonder that our so-called modern elite find it easy to violate the very laws and principles which they themselves create. When your own world is put aside you feel no respect for any other.[139]

In a convocation speech at the University of Maiduguri nine years later, Liman Ciroma, an archaeologist and civil servant from an emirate family in the northeast,[140] expressed similar concerns:

> Perhaps our misfortune lies in the rapid mobility current in our society. . . . Instantly-made leaders are propelled to the positions they assume by virtue only of having completed periods in a number of educational institutions or gone through a form of election or some selective processes and emerged as having won. Seldom do they rise to the occasion of selfless service or position of responsibility.[141]

---

[139] Waziri Junaidu Bukhari, "The Relevance of the University to Our Society," in *The Relevance of Education in Our Society: Commentaries on the Acceptance Speech of Alhaji Junaidu, Wazirin Sakkwato*, edited by Haruna Salihi (Lagos: Islamic Heritage Foundation, 2006), 17–20.

[140] Liz Moloney, "Obituary: Liman Ciroma, Nigeria's First Qualified Archaeologist," *Guardian*, June 30, 2004. Available at http://www.theguardian.com/news/2004/jul/01/guardianobituaries.obituaries; accessed October 2014.

[141] Liman Ciroma, *The Impact of Modern Education and Traditional Values* (Maiduguri: University of Maiduguri, 1980), 11.

As Islamist currents gained ground within northern universities, one could even find faculty expressing harsh opinions against 'yan boko, linking postcolonial Nigeria's political failures to Western-style education. One northern Islamist wrote, "The 'educated' Nigerians emerged from colonialism dejected, mentally deranged, and schizophrenic."[142] Another intellectual argued that colonial schools had made non-Muslim northerners despise Islam. The writer added that in "a very gradual and subtle" way, such schools had led even Muslim children toward "indoctrination against Islam and the cultivation of Western tastes and culture." The writer praised Muslim parents' decisions to keep their children out of Western-style schools, during and after colonialism: "To this day, many Muslims remain apprehensive about these Western educational institutions, defying the psychological warfare waged by the Western-educated elite to break their resolve and reconcile their minds to an education that they believe is still essentially Christian."[143] Such statements did not necessarily influence Boko Haram, but they do help explain why Boko Haram attracted university dropouts and secondary school graduates.

It might seem contradictory that Yusuf's movement would attract individuals with some exposure to Western-style education. Amid Boko Haram's rise, Qur'an students have received scrutiny—Qur'an students' alleged lack of marketable skills and social ties supposedly renders them easy recruits for Boko Haram. Yet "there is no systematic evidence to support

[142] Ibrahim Sulaiman, "The Shari'ah and the 1979 Constitution," in *Islamic Law in Nigeria: Application and Teaching*, edited by S. Khalid Rashid (Lagos: Islamic Publications Bureau, 1986), 59.

[143] Usman Bugaje, "Introduction," in Ghazali Basri, *Nigeria and Shari'ah: Aspirations and Apprehensions* (Leicester: Islamic Foundation, 1994), 12.

such assertions."[144] It seems likely that Boko Haram's social base extends beyond Qur'an students—and that people with exposure to universities number among Western education's critics. Worth noting too is that standards at the University of Maiduguri declined after the mid-1980s. Key posts fell prey to corruption: for example, at the registrar's office, bribery could influence admissions. When the money supply became tighter during the Abacha era of 1993–98, corruption worsened, with faculty members putting relatives on the university staff as a means of employing their dependents. Standards fell further.[145] Students at the University of Maiduguri in the 1990s, where Boko Haram may have taken embryonic form, would have been exposed to discourses castigating Western-educated elites for the corruption in Nigeria—and they would have seen the corrosive effects of corruption firsthand. Many would have also doubted whether their degrees would actually get them jobs. Boko Haram sought to activate people's suspicions about the content of Western-style education, as well as their anger toward its fruits.

Grassroots resentment toward Western-style education may have been particularly elevated in the northeast in the 1990s and 2000s. One scholarly account from the mid-1990s characterized the situation as follows:

At the present time Arabic and Islamic education is undergoing something of a revival. This is due not only to a broader consciousness of Bornu's Islamic heritage (and a parallel phenomenon

---

[144] Hannah Hoechner, "Traditional Quranic Students (almajirai) in Nigeria: Fair Game for Unfair Accusations?," in *Boko Haram: Islamism, Politics, Security and the State in Nigeria*, edited by Marc-Antoine Pérouse de Montclos, 63–84 (Leiden: African Studies Centre, 2014), 64.

[145] Skype interview with Jonathan Owens, 8 June 2016.

may be observed in Hausaland), but to a more conscious rejection of secular education, unwittingly encouraged by the continuing decline in standards in government-sponsored education and rising school fees.[146]

This widespread dissatisfaction created opportunities for religious entrepreneurs like Yusuf.

A more direct influence on Yusuf was Salafis' mistrust of colonial and Western-style schools. In his 1972 anti-Sufi polemic, Abubakar Gumi wrote that the "enemies of Islam" had sought to "turn the children of Muslims away from learning their religion" through two tactics: first, books that, in Gumi's view, distorted Islam and were spread among Muslims by Sufis; and second, "schools to teach the destructive culture of the West."[147] Colonial authorities had first used such schools to educate "the sons of pagan infidels whose fathers walked the earth naked." The colonialists had then placed these pagans in authority over "Muslims whose minds were sleeping." The Muslims—once they "paid attention"—had sent their children to the schools. But ultimately, Muslim children became "either hunting dogs in the foreign hunters' hands, or the prey of the hunt."[148] Like the northern intellectual quoted above, Gumi voiced a dual fear that Western-style schools empowered non-Muslim northerners and that the schools corrupted Muslim children. More than three decades after Gumi wrote those words, Yusuf quoted them, approvingly, in his own manifesto.[149]

---

[146] Hamidu Bobboyi and John Hunwick, "Bornu, Wadai and Adamawa," in *Arabic Literature of Africa*, vol. 2, *Central Sudanic Africa*, edited by John Hunwick and R. S. O'Fahey (Leiden: Brill, 1995), 383–84; 383.

[147] Gumi, *Al-'Aqida*, 78.

[148] Gumi, *Al-'Aqida*, 78–79.

[149] Muhammad Yusuf, *Hadhihi 'Aqidatuna wa-Manhaj Da'watina* (Maiduguri: Maktabat al-Ghuraba' li-l-Tawzi' wa-l-Nashr, likely 2009), 83–84.

Salafi attitudes toward Western-style education are more complex than the quoted passage might suggest: Gumi himself clearly favored some Western-style education for Muslims, including his own family. Ja'far Adam would later strongly rebuke Yusuf for his "Boko Haram" message. But even Adam argued that Western-style education, "in an indirect way," had led Muslim elites in Nigeria to lose their religious orientation. Adam claimed that the Western puppet masters of Muslim elites had "striven to train our leaders to make a division in religion: religion is one thing, and worldly life is another."[150] Adam viewed Western-style education as a tool that could help Muslim societies advance, but he also viewed Western-style education as a potential vehicle for secularist brainwashing.

Yusuf picked up on that strain of Salafi discourse, as well as a broader and ambivalent discussion about Western-style education among northern Nigerian Muslims. In a sprawling city where many youth had slipped beyond the control of emirs and politicians, and where bitter memories of unresolved religious conflict circulated, Yusuf would turn his critique of Western-style education into a broader attack on Nigeria's entire political system.

Conclusion

Between 1970 and 1999, the years when Boko Haram's founders were growing up, Nigeria experienced tremendous change. After the civil war ended in 1970, authorities sought to rebuild national unity. They leveraged massive, newfound oil wealth to finance ambitious projects in development and education. Yet divisions worsened: Muslims and Christians clashed in

---

[150] Adam, "Siyasa a Nigeria."

different localities, with political reverberations throughout the country. Muslims increasingly disagreed with one another over theology and politics. Authorities reimagined Nigeria's political structure time and again, but a definitive political solution remained elusive well into Yusuf and Shekau's adult years, fueling some activists' convictions that Nigeria needed to become an Islamic state.

Amid instability during the 1970s, 1980s, and 1990s, key questions about what it meant to be a Muslim in Nigeria went unresolved. What interpretation of Islam was correct? How should Islam be represented, or not represented, in a political system that called itself secular? For some Muslim activists, these questions acquired life-or-death significance. In the absence of clear answers, it was possible for young northern Muslims like Yusuf and Shekau to develop a profound hatred for Nigeria's political system, and a willingness to advocate revolutionary alternatives. Their worldview did not reflect majority opinion among northern Muslims, but it did echo more widespread sentiments about politics and Islam. When Nigeria returned to a civilian multiparty system in 1999, this worldview gained louder expression—and was further radicalized—by the politics surrounding Islamic law, elections, and intra-Salafi tensions. The next chapter turns to the story of Boko Haram's emergence, and the contentious politics that helped birth the movement.

2

Preaching Exclusivism, Playing Politics

Boko Haram took shape in the northeastern Nigerian city of Maiduguri, Borno State, in the early 2000s. More a mosque-based community than a tightly organized movement, Boko Haram centered on the Salafi preacher Muhammad Yusuf (1970–2009). During the late 1990s or early 2000s—it is unclear precisely when—Yusuf emerged as the group's leader. He remained its rallying point even after a temporary schism in 2003–4. Yusuf was a dynamic, even chameleon-like preacher: he presented his ideas in different ways to different audiences, which helped him build a diverse audience. He was also an adaptable political actor: his willingness to compromise with secular democracy—and his enthusiasm for armed struggle—fluctuated. From his entry into public life around 2001 until his death in 2009, his career was marked by ups and downs.

This chapter argues that a shifting political context enabled and shaped Yusuf's preaching, and that aspects of his preaching shaped his political position. Yusuf's preaching revolved around a core doctrine of religious exclusivism, but his message hardened over time in response to three forces: pressures from hardliners around him, quarrels with mainstream Salafis, and conflict with his political allies. From approximately 2001 to 2006, Yusuf attempted a delicate balancing act that would avoid open breaks with any of his key partners. Yusuf sought to keep more radical voices within his fold while placating his increasingly concerned mainstream Salafi mentors. But by 2006, Yusuf was being publicly reprimanded and marginalized by the leading Salafi preacher Ja'far Mahmud Adam (1961/2–2007). By 2007, he had lost his major political backer, Borno State governor Ali Modu Sheriff (served 2003–11). By 2008, he was in open conflict with state and federal authorities. The conflict culminated in tragedy when Yusuf and his followers launched a rebellion across parts of northern Nigeria in July 2009.

Murky Beginnings

Most accounts date the emergence of Boko Haram to 2002, but Yusuf was a public figure by 2001. That year, he was selected to join Borno State's Sharia Implementation Committee,[1] an assignment discussed below. Across the north, similar committees were being created by state governors, who carefully selected appointees to represent key Muslim constituencies in their states.[2] Yusuf's selection shows that he already had stature in Borno.

Yusuf was also, by that time, known as a key protégé of Ja'far Adam—even as Adam's main representative in Maiduguri. Adam, although based in Kano, became the leading preacher at Maiduguri's Muhammad Indimi Mosque, located on Damboa Road. The mosque was a Salafi stronghold built by the oil tycoon Muhammad Indimi in the early 1990s. By supporting Adam, Indimi was joining a wider trend in late twentieth-century northern Nigeria. In the past, businessmen were typi-

---

[1] International Crisis Group, "Curbing Violence in Nigeria (II): The Boko Haram Insurgency," 3 April 2014, 7 n. 34, http://www.crisisgroup.org/~/media/Files/africa/west-africa/nigeria/216-curbing-violence-in-nigeria-ii-the-boko-haram-insurgency.pdf.

[2] Alex Thurston, "Muslim Politics and Shari'a in Kano, Nigeria," *African Affairs* 114:454 (January 2015): 28–51.

cally subordinate to wealthy and influential Sufi shaykhs; now, businessmen were becoming patrons of young Salafi preachers.[3]

From approximately 1994 to 2006 (Adam was killed in 2007), Adam delivered an annual, monthlong exegesis of the Qur'an at the Indimi Mosque during Ramadan. One of Adam's fans has recalled that "people [would] close their place of business from far and near to attend his preaching which [was] full of wisdom." The same writer wrote glowingly of the wider impact that Adam had in Maiduguri. Adam offered lectures to diverse audiences, including women, and he organized social services for prisoners.[4]

Others in Maiduguri were less enthusiastic about Adam. A prominent Sufi leader has alleged that Indimi tricked Borno's Muslim establishment. Despite Indimi's promises that "the centre was meant for all Muslims," things changed once Adam began preaching: "Adam's first tafseer during Ramadhan revolved around condemning all the Borno Ulama [scholars] and apostatizing them." Sufi scholars felt that Adam's preaching "lacked respect and tended to set the youth against established institutions." But the Indimi Mosque, owing to its advantageous location and the free meals it offered to attendees during Ramadan, soon attracted a wide youth audience.[5]

Yusuf rode Adam's coattails. The same Sufi scholar has written, "It is well known by the locals that Adam once raised the hands of [Muhammad] Yusuf and said, 'If today there are no more scholars in Borno, this man is sufficient for you as an

---

[3] Ousmane Kane, *Muslim Modernity in Postcolonial Nigeria: A Study of the Society for the Removal of Innovation and Reinstatement of Tradition* (Leiden: Brill, 2003), 92.

[4] Ali Alhaji Ibrahim, "Sheikh Ja'afar Adam: Three Years On," Gamji, 2010, http://www.gamji.com/article9000/NEWS9076.htm.

[5] Khalifa Aliyu Ahmed Abulfathi, "The Metamorphosis of Boko Haram: A Local's Perspective" (Maiduguri: Sheikh Ahmed Abulfathi Foundation, 2016), http://sheikhahmadabulfathi.org/content/metamorphosis-boko-haram-0.

Islamic guide.'" Yusuf often preached in Adam's place.[6] The initial reasons for Yusuf's positive reception among Salafis may be rooted in his command of the Qur'an. His abilities were not exceptional among Nigeria's religious specialists, but he exceeded the level of ordinary Muslims. In his lectures, Yusuf demonstrated skill and speed in on-the-spot translations of Qur'anic verses into Hausa. Yusuf could also translate Qur'anic Arabic into his native Kanuri when he lectured in that language. Yusuf may not have had the mastery of Arabic that Adam or other graduates of Saudi Arabian universities had, but Yusuf had sufficient Arabic fluency and religious learning to distinguish him among Maiduguri's young Salafis.

Another reason for his initial success may have been a curious vacuum in Maiduguri's religious field. Early on, the Indimi Mosque became a recruitment center for the Islamic University of Medina in Saudi Arabia. Many of Maiduguri's leading young Salafi preachers went to Medina as a group in the 1990s. They did not return until around 2001 or 2002—giving Yusuf, who was not selected for the university, a chance to distinguish himself in their absence. Yusuf also benefited from some youths' perception that older Salafi figures, especially Abba Aji, had "outdated thinking." But when Maiduguri's cohort of students at Medina returned home, they found that they did not like what Yusuf had been preaching in their absence.[7] At some point between 2000 and 2003, Yusuf was chased out of the Indimi Mosque.[8] Yusuf reportedly then found a temporary home at Maiduguri's Daggash Mosque. Ultimately, how-

---

[6] Abulfathi, "Metamorphosis."

[7] Muhammad Awwal Adam "Albani" Zaria, "Karen Bana 3/3," 2 August 2009, https://www.youtube.com/watch?v=d-x9ycFGC0s.

[8] Isa Umar Gusau, "Boko Haram: How It All Began," *Daily Trust*, 2 August 2009, http://www.dailytrust.com.ng/sunday/index.php/international/35-people-in-the -news/people-in-the-news/5869-boko-haram-how-it-all-began; and Mike Smith, *Boko Haram: Inside Nigeria's Unholy War* (London: I. B. Tauris, 2015), 79.

ever, he had to build his own power center. His father-in-law and patron, the Kanuri trader Baba Fugu Muhammad, helped him establish a mosque complex, the Ibn Taymiyya Markaz (Center), in Maiduguri's Railway Quarters neighborhood.[9] There may have also been an ethnic dimension to the conflicts at Indimi Mosque. Adam was ethnically Hausa, whereas Yusuf was ethnically Kanuri. Some Kanuri attendees at the mosque felt that Adam had "monopolized the platform," denying Kanuri Muslims a leadership role. Yusuf and his close companions could preach in both Kanuri and Hausa, which helped them to appeal to a core Kanuri audience while also reaching the diverse Muslim population of Maiduguri. When Yusuf left Indimi, he took some of his Kanuri followers with him.[10]

At the same time, Yusuf benefited from changes in religiosity among non-Kanuri immigrants to the city. A German anthropologist who has worked extensively in Borno's Gwoza Hills told me that there was little conversion to Islam or Christianity in that area until after Nigeria's independence in 1960. Even in the late twentieth century, seasonal migrants to Maiduguri and to the "bean rush" on the shores of Lake Chad did not convert to Islam en masse, despite close relationships with Kanuri patrons. In the early 2000s, however, a massive conversion to Islam begin in the Gwoza Hills, for reasons that remain unclear. By the mid-2000s, there were rumors of radical preachers in the hills. Young people in the area were intensely discussing topics that revolved around religious exclusivism, such as whether a young Muslim man could inherit land from

[9] Olusegun Adeniyi, *Power, Politics and Death: A Front-Row Account of Nigeria under the Late President Umaru Musa Yar'Adua* (Lagos: Kachifo, 2011), 107; see also M. Smith, *Boko Haram*, 74–77.

[10] Telephone interview with Aminu Gamawa, 2 February 2016.

his pagan father.[11] Yusuf benefited from such changes in how in-migrants thought about Islam—and, possibly, he accelerated the pace of these changes through his own preaching.

Once in control of his own mosque network, Yusuf's popularity increased. According to one senior Nigerian official's memoir,

> [Yusuf's] daring and scathing verbal attacks on the government portrayed Yusuf as a fiery and intrepid cleric and this obviously endeared him to the common people, who began to see him as a champion of the downtrodden. Members of the political elite in Maiduguri were, however, taking note, and Yusuf was considered no more than a nuisance. . . . His initial followership was largely from among secondary school students and primary school pupils who abandoned their studies. . . . As he got more followers, his power and influence also grew.[12]

Another account reads similarly:

> At first, both cleric[s] and the larger community ignore[d] the gospel as they dismissed the preacher as unknowledgeable. . . . In Bauchi, Yobe, and Borno State, many young people dropped out of school, including university students to join them, workers including highly placed administrators and tertiary institution lecturers also joined them. That was when the clerics began to fire at them with great vehemence knowing very well that it was no longer a tea party. But it was getting late then, as many youths [had] already separated from their families, while many people abandoned their jobs for the group.[13]

---

[11] Telephone interview with Gerhard Müller-Kosack, 25 May 2016.

[12] Adeniyi, *Power, Politics and Death*, 107.

[13] Shehu Sani, "Boko Haram: History, Ideas and Revolt (3)," *Vanguard*, 4 July 2011, http://www.vanguardngr.com/2011/07/boko-haram-history-ideas-and-revolt-3/.

At his Markaz, Yusuf built "an imaginary state within a state," administering private justice and delivering social services.[14] Long after his death, hagiographies of Yusuf would stress his alleged "intense love for the poor"[15]—a key constituency he sought to recruit. It is difficult to calculate the size of Yusuf's following, but judging from videos that show his mosques filled with hundreds of attendees, one might conservatively estimate that he had a core following of over five hundred people, and a wider audience of interested and sympathetic persons that might have reached ten thousand people.

Yusuf's growing influence among the masses attracted positive attention from some elites. This attention translated into political influence. One resident of Maiduguri recalled:

> Before he was killed, you should have been here on a Friday, you would think a big party was going on here. The whole area (Railway Quarters) would be lined by exotic cars as very powerful individuals came to see Yusuf. They went in cars with tinted glasses and so nobody would identify them. That is why many people believed the man was being sponsored by some very powerful individuals.[16]

Such images contrast markedly with the widely rehearsed stereotype of Boko Haram as a movement of Qur'an school students. By most informed accounts, the movement drew from a wide socioeconomic spectrum.

With a mass constituency of poor and working people, and with contacts among Maiduguri's elite, Yusuf positioned himself at a fulcrum of political influence and economic power. Yusuf's following made him attractive to people with money.

---

[14] Sani, "Boko Haram: History, Ideas and Revolt (3)."
[15] Mu'assasat al-'Urwa al-Wuthqa li-l-Intaj al-'Ilmi, *Majmu'at Khutab li-l-Imam Abi Yusuf Muhammad bin Yusuf al-Maydughari* (2015), 4.
[16] Sani, "Boko Haram: History, Ideas and Revolt (3)."

The resources he accrued through his influence enabled him to attract more followers, including by establishing businesses and loans for his followers.[17] One Maiduguri resident who was close to some young Boko Haram devotees has said,

> This guy Muhammad Yusuf, he did a wonderful job—assuming this thing [the 2009 uprising] didn't happen, that boy could have been a hero, you know. He would give [young men] money to start businesses. . . . He preached to them that idleness is not the best, so he will give them money to start businesses, those who want to go down south to learn how to slaughter cows, he [would] send them there then. . . . He gave them money to buy motorcycles, he married wives for them, you know, gave them houses. . . . They loved him so much for that.[18]

People with economic ties to Yusuf could develop considerable loyalty to him. Moreover, there was a busy schedule of activities at his mosques, including at times a daily offering of lectures. In other words, affiliating oneself with Boko Haram could become a nearly full-time lifestyle.

Yusuf was a public figure and the movement's dominant spokesman. Abubakar Shekau and other lieutenants had decidedly secondary roles. Sometimes they preached, but sometimes they did less glamorous tasks. In one early video, Shekau sits beside Yusuf, but his role is merely that of reading questions submitted by audience members for Yusuf to answer.[19]

[17] International Crisis Group, "Curbing Violence in Nigeria (II): The Boko Haram Insurgency," 12.

[18] Pulse TV interview with Aisha Wakil, 5 September 2016, https://www.youtube.com/watch?v=gb6G4y_ZTAk.

[19] Boko Haram, untitled video called simply "Film.3gp," undated, https://www.youtube.com/watch?v=xthVNq9OKD0.

But behind the scenes, matters were complicated. Yusuf was "under serious pressure from people around him."[20] From the early 2000s, Yusuf was pulled in two directions. On one side was the mainstream Salafi movement, whose role is discussed further in the next section. On the other were hardliners, including shadowy figures named Aminu Tashen-Ilimi and Muhammad Ali, as well as Shekau. The hardliners sometimes personally recruited new members who were interested in jihad.[21] One account, published years later by the leader of the Boko Haram splinter group Ansar al-Muslimin (see chapter 3) even claims that Yusuf was a "follower" of Ali, rather than the other way around, and that Ali had led a jihadist cell in Nigeria before Yusuf began his preaching career. After Ali's death, the same account continues, Yusuf "strove ardently to unite the ranks of the Mujahidin upon the truth, and condemned disunity, feuds, and bigotry."[22]

The relationship between Yusuf and the hardliners was messier than that. It seems likely that the hardliners played a part in convincing Yusuf to reject democracy, secular government, and Western-style schooling in the early 2000s. But Yusuf had limits: he reportedly balked when the hardliners made plans to leave Maiduguri.[23] Tashen-Ilimi and others "accused Yusuf of being too liberal with the ideology and, considering him to be compromised, moved out of his enclave."[24] Around 2003,

---

[20] Interview with Gamawa.

[21] Skype interview with Dr. Fatima Akilu, 1 March 2016.

[22] Abu Usamatul Ansary, "A Message from Nigeria," *Al Risalah* 4 (January 2017): 18–21; 19.

[23] Ahmad Salkida, "Boko Haram from the Beginning," Sun News Online, 18 May 2014, http://sunnewsonline.com/new/boko-haram-beginning/. Originally published as "Genesis and Consequences of Boko Haram Crisis," Kano Online, April 2013.

[24] Isa Umar Gusau, "Boko Haram: How It All Began," *Daily Trust*, 2 August 2009, http://www.dailytrust.com.ng/sunday/index.php/international/35-people-in-the-news/people-in-the-news/5869-boko-haram-how-it-all-began.

the hardliners made good on their plans to establish a separatist religious community in rural Yobe, one of the most remote areas in northern Nigeria.

It remains unclear whether Yusuf was genuinely interested in pursuing armed jihad at that time—he may have preferred to merely flirt with jihadism in his preaching. One hagiographical account foregrounds Yusuf's role in Boko Haram's emergence and stresses his jihadist credentials but acknowledges that "he did not begin his work of jihad directly, even though he announced that the greatest goal of the society was jihad."[25] Yusuf was cautious, or perhaps reluctant, about any move from preaching to fighting.

The hardliners were not just interested in strident preaching: they were committed, at the very least, to separatism and were perhaps already committed to violent jihad. When they left Maiduguri in 2003, they depicted themselves as making *hijra* (emigration), just as the Prophet Muhammad had done when leaving Mecca for Medina in 622. In Yobe, they reportedly first settled in Zaji-Biriri village in Tarmuwa Local Government Area (LGA),[26] Shekau's home LGA. They then established a commune outside the town of Kanamma, Yunusari LGA, near Nigeria's border with Niger. The group, according to Yobe State officials, included "individuals from wealthy Islamic families in Borno State, unemployed university students and friends and colleagues from other states including Ogun and Lagos."[27] Authorities in Yobe believed that the Kanamma

---

[25] "Wali Gharb Ifriqiya: Al-Shaykh Abu Mus'ab al-Barnawi," *Al-Naba'* 41 (2 August 2016): 8–9; 8, https://azelin.files.wordpress.com/2016/08/the-islamic-state-e28 09cal-nabacc84_-newsletter-4122.pdf.

[26] Shehu Sani, "Boko Haram (2)," *Vanguard*, 1 July 2011, http://www.vanguardngr .com/2011/07/boko-haram-the-northern-nigeria-hausaland-2/.

[27] United States Embassy Abuja, leaked cable 04ABUJA183, "Nigerian 'Taliban' Attacks Most Likely Not Tied to Taliban nor al-Qaida," 6 February 2004, https:// wikileaks.org/plusd/cables/04ABUJA183_a.html.

site was not a training camp but a separatist commune;[28] it reportedly consisted of "makeshift tents."[29] Group members gained a reputation for "touring villages and preaching Islam."[30] They held the larger society at arm's length but would labor on nearby farms for money.[31]

The hardliners soon came into conflict with locals. The conflict may have begun with a dispute over fishing rights,[32] or when the hardliners began conscripting local men to work in their camp. Yobe authorities reportedly approached the group, seeking to convince them to relocate. When that failed, authorities destroyed the camp.[33] After some members were arrested, others rose up in December 2003. Some sixty fighters attacked Kanamma's police station, raiding it for weapons and ammunition. They raided the town of Geidam before marching to Damaturu, Yobe's capital, where they faced stronger resistance.[34] The military then moved in and crushed the group in Geidam and Kanamma.[35]

The beliefs of the Kanamma group are hard to reconstruct. Some members had already concluded that the Nigerian state had to be overthrown: one, an engineering student who had come all the way to Kanamma from Lagos, told journalists, "Our aim is to cause serious confusion and overthrow the government of infidels headed by the crop of present politicians who have sold

[28] U.S. Embassy Abuja, "Nigerian 'Taliban' Attacks."

[29] Anna Borzello, "Tracking Down Nigeria's 'Taleban' Sect," BBC, 14 January 2004, http://news.bbc.co.uk/2/hi/africa/3393963.stm.

[30] Borzello, "Tracking Down Nigeria's 'Taleban' Sect."

[31] Sani, "Boko Haram (2)."

[32] U.S. Embassy Abuja, "Nigerian 'Taliban' Attacks"; see also Sani, "Boko Haram (2)."

[33] Borzello, "Tracking Down Nigeria's 'Taleban' Sect."

[34] Abdullahi Bego, "'Taliban' of Nigeria: Who Are They?," Weekly Trust, 3 January 2004.

[35] "Nigeria: Security Forces Kill 27 'Taliban' Militants, Says Police," IRIN, 24 September 2004, http://www.irinnews.org/report/51490/nigeria-security-forces-kill-27-taliban-militants-says-police.

us out to the West to the detriment of Islam."[36] The group may have intended to "carve out" part of rural Yobe as an Islamic state.[37]

The group's reported use of symbols associated with the Taliban—hoisting the Taliban's flag, naming sites "Afghanistan," and calling one of its leaders "Mullah Omar"—earned it the nickname "Nigerian Taliban." Some of these symbols may have been mere rumors, or misperceptions by journalists; or perhaps the hardliners were attempting to signal their sympathies for al-Qa'ida, which recognized the Taliban's Mullah Umar as Commander of the Faithful until his death in 2013. Another theory is that Boko Haram was simply trying to frighten the Nigerian security services by using the Taliban's infamous name.[38] For its part, the U.S. Embassy concluded that there was little likelihood that the Kanamma group had ties to the real Taliban or to al-Qa'ida—or, for that matter, to Maitatsine, the 1980s uprising discussed in chapter 1.[39]

After its suppression, the Kanamma group dispersed. Muhammad Ali was killed, either during the clashes in Yobe or, according to International Crisis Group, under mysterious circumstances in Kano at the guesthouse of Ja'far Adam.[40] A few members were killed by vigilantes in Damboa, Borno, in January 2004. Others were imprisoned in Damaturu, where several died in a failed prison break in June 2004.[41] Still oth-

---

[36] "Detained Nigerian Militant Pledges Islamic Struggle," Reuters, 13 January 2004.

[37] Bego, "'Taliban' of Nigeria."

[38] Muhammad Awwal Adam "Albani" Zaria, "Karen Bana 1/3," 2 August 2009, https://www.youtube.com/watch?v=z8HUJspctzk.

[39] United States Embassy Abuja, leaked cable 04ABUJA183, "Nigerian 'Taliban' Attacks Most Likely Not Tied to Taliban nor al-Qaida," 6 February 2004, https://wikileaks.org/plusd/cables/04ABUJA183_a.html.

[40] International Crisis Group, "Curbing Violence in Nigeria (II): The Boko Haram Insurgency," 23.

[41] "Timeline of Boko Haram Attacks and Related Violence," IRIN, 20 January 2012, http://www.irinnews.org/report/94691/nigeria-timeline-of-boko-haram-attacks-and-related-violence.

ers fled to the Gwoza Hills in southern Borno, clashing with authorities in September 2004.[42] The same month, violence broke out around Bama, northeastern Borno, possibly involving the Kanamma group.[43] At least five members were arrested after fleeing into Cameroon.[44] With many members who were either born in neighboring countries or whose parents were not Nigerian, the group was familiar with the communities and porous borders of the Lake Chad basin.

How closely Yusuf was involved with the Kanamma uprising is debated. Some analysts believe that he helped plan it,[45] others that he merely knew of it.[46] In any case, Yusuf feared being associated with it afterward. He left Nigeria for Saudi Arabia, where he had already made hajj and *umra* (lesser pilgrimage) several times in the early 2000s.[47] The hajj of 2004 fell in January and February, by which time the authorities had announced that they were seeking Yusuf for questioning.[48]

While in Saudi Arabia, Yusuf approached Borno State deputy governor Adamu Dibal, who facilitated his return to

[42] Adam Higazi, "Mobilisation into and against Boko Haram in North-East Nigeria," in *Collective Mobilisations in Africa*, edited by Kadya Tall, Marie-Emmanuelle Pommerolle, and Michel Cahen, 305–58 (Leiden: Brill, 2015), 306.

[43] "Nigeria Police Hunt 'Taleban,'" BBC, 22 September 2004, http://news.bbc.co.uk/2/hi/africa/3679092.stm.

[44] "Nigeria: Security Forces Kill 27 'Taliban' Militants, Says Police," IRIN, 24 September 2004, http://www.irinnews.org/report/51490/nigeria-security-forces-kill-27-taliban-militants-says-police.

[45] Higazi, "Mobilisation into and against Boko Haram," 306.

[46] Kyari Mohammed (Muhammad Kyari), "The Message and Methods of Boko Haram," in *Boko Haram: Islamism, Politics, Security and the State in Nigeria*, edited by Marc-Antoine Pérouse de Montclos, 9–32 (Leiden: African Studies Centre, 2014), 12.

[47] See the transcript and translation of Muhammad Yusuf's 30 July 2009 interrogation at https://maxsiollun.wordpress.com/2009/08/03/videos-of-boko-haram-suspects-being-interrogated-and-executed/.

[48] "Nigeria: Sudanese Arrested, Accused of Funding December Islamic Uprising," IRIN, 20 February 2004, http://www.irinnews.org/report/48684/nigeria-sudanese-arrested-accused-of-funding-december-islamic-uprising.

Nigeria,[49] which occurred by January 2005.[50] The time after his return was the high point of Yusuf's career:

> In mid 2005, he made overtures for reconciliation to the splinter group, and there was some reintegration. After this, Yusuf rose from a poor preacher to a wealthy cleric living in opulence and driving SUVs around the city, where he was hailed as a hero for his criticism of the government and his call for sharia law. His preachings—recorded on CDs—which he daily doled out, were hot cake [*sic*] in the city and beyond, selling in thousands.[51]

Yusuf's stated views on politics continued to fluctuate. In 2006, Yusuf and his Shura (Consultative) Council stated "that Islam permits them to subsist under a modern government like Nigeria but has explicitly prohibited them from joining or supporting such governments in so far as their systems, structures and institutions contain elements contradictory to core Islamic principles and beliefs."[52] The same year, Yusuf spoke to journalists about Kanamma, as well as about his own political beliefs:

> These youths studied the Koran with me and with others. Afterwards they wanted to leave the town, which they thought impure, and head for the bush, believing that Muslims who

[49] Nick Tattersall, "Nigeria Sect Planned Bomb Attack during Ramadan," Reuters, 4 August 2009, http://www.reuters.com/article/ozatp-nigeria-sect-bombing-id AFJOE57308Z20090804.

[50] Ismail Omipidan, "Why the North Is on Fire: The Inside Story," *Daily Sun*, 2 August 2009, http://www.nairaland.com/304276/why-north-fire-inside-story.

[51] Adeniyi, *Power, Politics and Death*, 108.

[52] Ahmad Salkida, "Boko Haram from the Beginning," Sun News Online, 18 May 2014, http://sunnewsonline.com/new/boko-haram-beginning/. Originally published as "Genesis and Consequences of Boko Haram Crisis," Kano Online, April 2013.

do not share their ideology are infidels. . . . I think that an Islamic system of government should be established in Nigeria, and if possible all over the world, but through dialogue.[53]

Yusuf may have been dissimulating about his true beliefs, but such statements offer insight into his strategy at the time. After the suppression of the Kanamma uprising, Yusuf sought to reintegrate some of the hardliners, and he simultaneously worked to reestablish himself as a major, quasi-mainstream voice in Maiduguri.

It is debatable how thoroughly Yusuf reabsorbed the Kanamma group. One report claimed that the "Talibans," operating out of a base in the Gwoza Hills, attacked a police station in Bama in October 2005.[54] Meanwhile, former leaders of the Kanamma group, such as Aminu Tashen-Ilimi, were living more or less openly in Maiduguri as of 2006. The attitudes they expressed on politics were much more severe than Yusuf's. Speaking to journalists that year, Tashen-Ilimi was unrepentant:

Allah, the almighty Lord, has authorised every Muslim to fight to establish an Islamic government over the world. One day it will happen in Nigeria and everywhere. . . . I'm ready to take up arms. I don't know who gave us the name Taliban, I prefer 'mujahideen'; the fighters. I only know the Taliban in Afghanistan, and I respect them and what they did very much. . . . Those who fought in Kanama [sic] and Gwoza are only Muslims who performed their holy duty.[55]

[53] Emmanuel Goujon and Aminu Abubakar, "Nigeria's 'Taliban' Plot Comeback from Hide-Outs," AFP, 11 January 2006, http://mg.co.za/article/2006–01–11-nigerias-taliban-plot-comeback-from-hideouts.

[54] Sani Mohammad, "Borno's Changing Face," Source, 20 November 2006, http://thesourceng.com/bornofacenov20.htm.

[55] Goujon and Abubakar, "Nigeria's 'Taliban.'"

Before long, Yusuf's stated willingness to coexist with secularism would fade, and so would his ability to placate both moderates and hardliners. Indeed, one source claims that by the end of his life, Yusuf's Shura Council comprised hardliners who had experience calling for and even participating in jihad in various countries.[56] In any case, by 2009, Yusuf would sound much more like Tashen-Ilimi.

Conflicts with Mainstream Salafis

During all the years of his preaching, Yusuf presented himself as a mainstream Salafi. He depicted his positions as identical to those of Saudi Arabia's religious establishment, claiming the mantle of their authority. Yet it was on these grounds that other Nigerian Salafis challenged him, rejecting his claims to speak for the Salafi movement.[57]

In a series of meetings starting in the early 2000s, mainstream Salafis presented Yusuf with textual evidence—Qur'anic verses and recorded statements and deeds of the Prophet—that they hoped would make him recant his increasingly strident preaching against Western-style education and government employment for Muslims. Confronting Yusuf were Ja'far Adam, Adam's close associate Abdulwahhab Abdullahi, the Zaria-based scholar Muhammad Awwal Adam "Albani," the Maiduguri-based scholar and Islamic University of Medina graduate Ali Mustapha, and others. According to these Salafis,

[56] Letter from Abu Muhammad al-Hawsawi et al. to Abu al-Hasan al-Rashid al-Bulaydi, 2011, reproduced in *Nasa'ih wa-Tawjihat Shar'iyya min al-Shaykh Abi al-Hasan Rashid li-Mujahidi Nayjiriya*, edited by Abu al-Nu'man Qutayba al-Shinqiti (Mu'assasat al-Andalus, April 2017), 15, https://azelin.files.wordpress.com/2017/04/shaykh-abucc84-al-hcca3asan-rashicc84d-22sharicc84ah-advice-and-guidance-for-the-mujacc84hidicc84n-of-nigeria22.pdf.

[57] See, for example, "Albani" Zaria," "Karen Bana 1/3."

they repeatedly extracted promises from Yusuf that he would recant, only to discover later that he had continued preaching in the same vein.[58]

Some of the last private meetings occurred in 2005, by which time the mainstream Salafis were already aware that Yusuf's followers were denouncing them as "government scholars."[59] By 2006, the conflict was in the open, with Adam preaching against Yusuf. The mainstream Salafis argued that Yusuf's opposition to Western-style education would retard northern Muslims' economic and political development.[60] Adam and others painted Boko Haram as agents of outside interests, including the Shi'a, Nigerian Christians, the West, and foreign jihadists.[61] These accusations reinforced Boko Haram's sense of exclusivism, making Yusuf and his core followers feel that they could no longer trust Salafis who defended Western-style education or government service. The sect was likely responsible for Adam's 2007 assassination—as discussed above, Adam may have been involved in the murder of Muhammad Ali in 2004, after the Kanamma crisis, and Boko Haram was seeking revenge.[62] Even if Adam was not involved in Ali's death, Boko Haram would have had a motive to kill him: by silencing Adam, Yusuf could remove his most effective critic and gain even more ground in his effort to become northern Nigeria's leading Salafi voice.

---

[58] "Rahotanni Na Musamman: Boko Haram," VOA Hausa, 22 July 2011, http://www.voahausa.com/content/rahotanni-na-musamman-boko-haram-126033028/1377791.html.

[59] "Albani" Zaria, "Karen Bana 1/3."

[60] Anonymous, "Popular Discourses."

[61] Ja'far Adam, "Me Ya Sa Suke Cewa Boko Haramun Ne?," undated (likely 2005–7), https://www.youtube.com/watch?v=kkNDO0e2Jf8; Adam, "Fadakarwa Game da Halalcin Boko," undated (likely 2005–7), https://www.youtube.com/watch?v=hiM1ZUhmLAU; and "Albani" Zaria, "Karen Bana 3/3."

[62] International Crisis Group, "Curbing Violence in Nigeria (II): The Boko Haram Insurgency," p. 23.

After Adam's death, the mainstream Salafi opposition to Boko Haram continued, including in the northeast. The British-educated Salafi Dr. Isa Pantami of Gombe held a videotaped debate with Yusuf around 2008, in which Yusuf is often visibly flustered.[63] In April 2009, Adam's companion Dr. Muhammad Sani Umar Rijiyar Lemo came to Maiduguri and gave a public lecture where he said that jihadist groups were ultimately ineffective when compared with Salafis who focused on *da'wa* (missionary and educational activities);[64] reading between the lines, one could detect Rijiyar Lemo's harsh critique of Yusuf. In May 2009, Izala's Dr. Muhammad Mansur Ibrahim gave a public lecture in Bauchi in which he argued that the Qur'an and the Sunna unambiguously indicated that Muslims should seek knowledge of all kinds in order to improve themselves and better the world. Ibrahim traced the origins of "anathematizing Western education" to groups he depicted as modern-day Khawarij, a rebellious, non-Sunni sect in early Islam. Naming Yusuf as well as leaders of the Kanamma uprising, Ibrahim depicted Boko Haram as Khawarij who misread and misunderstood both the Qur'an and the edicts of contemporary Salafi scholars.[65] Mainstream Salafis worked to systematically discredit Yusuf, undermine his arguments, question his sincerity, and ultimately exclude him from the Salafi movement and even from the Sunni Muslim community.

[63] "Muqabala Mallam Isa Ali Bauchi da Mallam Muhammad Yusuf Maiduguri akan Karatun Boko Haram," circa 2008, https://www.youtube.com/watch?v=h-nhmj 3faHc.

[64] Muhammad Sani Umar Rijiyar Lemo, "Kungiyoyin Jihadi (1)" and "Kungiyoyin Jihadi (2)," recorded lectures delivered in Maiduguri, April 2009.

[65] Muhammad Mansur Ibrahim, "Matsayin Karatun Boko da Aikin Gwamnati a Musulunci," lecture delivered in Bauchi, May 2009. For context on how accusations of Kharijism function in the contemporary Muslim world, see Jeffrey Kenney, *Muslim Rebels: Kharijites and the Politics of Extremism in Egypt* (New York: Oxford University Press, 2006).

Yusuf responded by reiterating his stances. His Arabic-language manifesto, likely published in early 2009, was part of this fierce intra-Salafi debate:

> When I saw some people rushing into our business and the affairs of our mission, and trying to attribute creeds to me— Allah knows that we are innocent of them—such as the Khawarij, the Shi'a, the Qur'an-only sect, or some of the other secret groups, I undertook an explanation of our creed and the method of our mission.[66]

In his own lectures, Yusuf began referring to his private meetings with other Salafis. But in Yusuf's telling, those meetings had ended in disagreement, with Yusuf standing by his position and anchoring it in global Salafism's textual universe.[67] As Yusuf used stronger and stronger language casting democracy as unbelief, he moved toward calling mainstream Salafis unbelievers. In one of his last lectures he said that Izala, the largest Salafi organization in Nigeria, represented "scholar[s] of democracy, students of Bush [almajiran Bush] . . . hypocrites."[68]

Why did Yusuf break with mainstream Nigerian Salafism— which, as discussed below, gave its adherents a great deal of flexibility on politics? Adam understood Yusuf as power hungry, motivated by "love of fame" and "lack of knowledge."[69] Some analysts have understood the conflict between Adam and

---

[66] See Muhammad Yusuf, *Hadhihi 'Aqidatuna wa-Manhaj Da'watina* (Maiduguri: Maktabat al-Ghuraba' li-l-Nashr wa-l-Tawzi', likely 2009), 4.

[67] Muhammad Yusuf, "Warware Shubuhar Malamai," audio recording circa 2008, https://www.youtube.com/watch?v=dWfv28iSEZQ;

[68] Muhammad Yusuf, "Open Letter to the Federal Government of Nigeria," 12 June 2009, https://www.youtube.com/watch?v=yU7eVc-NOyE&ebc=ANyPxKo O4D1HDV4rhgyE1XykE21Hv7cbJvuMPB4-yuDT7ixT1X8cyTEnO-Ik3iywuzVzJ1Pp HCQkvXqk3tPIP8TXRz2gVN535Q.

[69] Ja'far Adam, "Me Ya Sa Suke Cewa Boko Haramun Ne?"

Yusuf as a raw power struggle, reading Yusuf's preaching as his bid to distinguish himself in a crowded religious marketplace. Yusuf, as an otherwise junior and relatively undercredentialed Salafi preacher, lacking a degree from the Islamic University of Medina or a senior position in Izala, had an incentive to outdo his mentors in crafting strident political rhetoric.[70]

This reading explains part of the equation, but not all of it: after all, the Medina graduates have mentored and promoted some of their locally educated students and peers, such as the Kano-based Shaykh Aminu Daurawa (b. 1969). Daurawa has served as the Commander General of Kano's Hisbah Board, a state-run religious quasi–police force, since 2011. Daurawa is one of the most influential Salafis in present-day northern Nigeria as of 2017, and he is not a graduate of Medina. Yusuf had incentives to distinguish himself by adopting hardline rhetoric, but he might have benefited from patiently remaining within the mainstream Salafi fold, following a path like Daurawa's. Or he could have emulated the locally trained preacher Muhammad Kabiru Gombe, who stands out among Salafis for the harshness of his rhetoric toward Sufis and the Shi'a but who does not call for the overthrow of the Nigerian state. Another factor to consider, then, is that Yusuf backed himself into a rhetorical corner once he began to voice stridently antidemocracy and anti-Western messages: he could keep credibility with his followers or he could remain within the Salafi mainstream, but he could not do both.

For a time, Yusuf seemed convinced that he could keep all sides happy—his hardline associates, his Salafi mentors, the political authorities, and his mass of followers—by telling them different things. Adam depicted Yusuf as a deeply hypocritical man:

---

[70] Anonymous, "Popular Discourses."

This man, after he went on pilgrimage [in 2004], remained [in Saudi Arabia], saying that the security services were looking for him. By Allah, by Allah, I was among those who met with him. I went on hajj. He said he swore to Allah that everything he had been accused of in terms of his relationship with that fatwa [calling for jihad] and those youth [in Kanamma] was a lie against him. I told him, "If it's a lie against you . . . there are major government officials from Borno State here. Let's go to them and you can affirm that it's a lie against you. . . . [They said] he should write an explanation, and speak so that one might record it on tape. . . . He himself went to seek a lawyer, after he was advised, "Don't write something yourself, you may say something that breaks a law or constitutes an accusation against yourself." He went and found a lawyer—not an engineer or a doctor, one whose [Western-style] education has become obligatory [for the health of the Muslim community], but a full-blown Taghut [an idolatrous tyrant, a word Yusuf often used to describe the Nigerian state].[71]

Behind the scenes, Adam suggested, Yusuf was an unprincipled opportunist, someone willing to work with a secular lawyer to save his own skin. This account must be at least partly true, given Borno deputy governor Dibal's role in facilitating Yusuf's return to Maiduguri. Even while preaching against democracy and flirting with jihadism, Yusuf quietly made deals to protect himself and advance his career, and he tried to placate his Salafi critics.[72] Indeed, keeping channels of communication open to the Salafi mainstream helped him to stay in the good graces of elected politicians.

[71] Adam, "Me Ya Sa."

[72] Muhammad Awwal "Albani" Zaria stated that Yusuf apologized to him personally in Maiduguri after some of Yusuf's followers had insulted him. See "Albani" Zaria's lecture "Karen Bana 1/3."

But the stratagems Yusuf used to placate the various sides in 2004 no longer worked by 2006–9. With the possibility that his hardline disciples would abandon him or outflank him rhetorically as they had in 2003–4, and with relations deteriorating between him and the political authorities (events discussed below), he may have felt that the only route open to him was to intensify his message. Meanwhile, especially after Adam's murder in 2007, there was little possibility of a reconciliation between Yusuf and Adam's circle. This situation, and the cascade of denunciations from mainstream Salafis, encouraged Yusuf to fully embrace jihad. Finally, the possibility that Yusuf believed at least some of what he said cannot be ruled out. His unflappable, almost smug demeanor during his final interrogation suggests someone willing to die for his beliefs, or at least for the beliefs he had stated. Or perhaps he calculated, wrongly, that he was too influential to be killed.

Boko Haram's Doctrine, Fully Formed

What did Yusuf preach? As a starting point, it will be helpful to summarize the teachings of the wider Nigerian Salafi community, especially the teachings of Ja'far Adam. He and other graduates of Medina preached a message that was both affirmative and combative. They affirmed Salafi doctrine—scriptural literalism and a narrow definition of monotheism—and they taught texts that supported that doctrine. Simultaneously, the graduates of Medina opposed Sufism and castigated various minority sects in Nigeria, especially the Shi'a and "Qur'an-only" Muslims.[73]

---

[73] Alex Thurston, *Salafism in Nigeria: Islam, Preaching and Politics* (Cambridge: Cambridge University Press, 2016).

As an educational movement, Nigerian Salafism emphasized not only the exegesis of the Qur'an, but also the careful study of Prophetic traditions (plural *ahadith*, singular *hadith*) and the study of a narrow canon of approved theologians and jurists from across history. Yusuf participated in this educational endeavor, particularly in the field of Qur'anic exegesis. Like other Salafis, Yusuf leaned on the exegesis of Ibn Kathir (1301–73), a medieval exegete known for his literalism.[74]

In politics, Adam and his companions displayed ambivalence toward democracy and Nigeria's multiparty system. Mainstream Salafis were willing to serve in government and to support certain politicians during elections, but Adam also expressed concerns that multiparty democracy empowered Sufis and amoral politicians to repress Salafis.[75] Neither Izala nor the Medina graduates felt that Nigeria needed an armed jihad. The Medina graduates would sometimes voice admiration for jihadists but would also point to the failures of armed jihadists.[76] The path of preaching and education, Adam and his companions concluded, was preferable to armed revolution. One Salafi scholar, Muhammad Awwal Adam "Albani" Zaria, put it this way, discussing mainstream Salafis' differences with Boko Haram:

> One should know that the unbelief that is happening among the rulers of Nigeria [*kafircin da yake faruwa a tsakankanin masu mulkin Nigeria*], and the unbelief that is happening among the common people of Nigeria, and the polytheism that is happening among the rulers of Nigeria, and the polytheism that the

[74] See, for example, the undated, two-part video of Yusuf's exegesis of the Qur'an's Surat al-Tawba: https://www.youtube.com/watch?v=Y33rL_D_6pw and https://www.youtube.com/watch?v=R3NcgQv-LVM.

[75] Ja'far Adam, recorded lecture entitled "Gwagwarmaya Tsakanin Karya da Gaskiya," 15 November 2006, Kano. Recording in the author's possession.

[76] Rijiyar Lemo, "Kungiyoyin Jihadi (1)" and "Kungiyoyin Jihadi (2)."

common people of Nigeria do, and the injustice, and corruption, and any kind of trouble that is happening . . . in this country of ours—it is good for one to know that without a doubt, undeniably, we do not support even one of those things. . . . Except the issue is, what path is one going to follow to remove unbelief, injustice, trouble, and corruption?[77]

Mainstream Salafis believe that preaching nonviolently, offering advice to politicians, and conducting educational activities can bring about a moral reorientation over the long term.

In some ways, Boko Haram is indistinguishable from other Nigerian Salafis. For example, Boko Haram's members consider themselves arbiters of who is a true Muslim. Like other Salafis, Yusuf rejected other approaches to Islam, such as Sufism, and he leaned on mainstream Salafis' writings to do so.[78] Where Yusuf broke with other Nigerian Salafis was in constructing a particularly aggressive version of Salafism's religious exclusivism.

Yusuf not only advocated a singular interpretation of what he considered true Islam; he also demanded that Muslims choose, immediately, between Islam and a set of allegedly anti-Islamic practices: democracy, constitutionalism, alliances with non-Muslims, and Western-style education. Yusuf described his mission as one of purification, but, especially in the period leading up to the 2009 uprising, he added more militant language than other Nigerian Salafis used: "We call the Muslim community to correct its creed and its behaviors and its morals . . . and to give children a correct Islamic education, then to undertake jihad in the way of Allah."[79] Yusuf's stance had a

---

[77] "Albani" Zaria, "Karen Bana 1/3."
[78] Yusuf, *Hadhihi 'Aqidatuna*, 140.
[79] Yusuf, *Hadhihi 'Aqidatuna*, 5–6.

rhetorical advantage over the positions adopted by other, non-jihadist Salafis: Yusuf's message was easier to understand, and the argumentation involved fewer steps. According to Yusuf, one simply had to choose between Islam and unbelief.[80]

Yusuf's rejection of democracy and Western-style schooling became Boko Haram's two most famous ideas. Yusuf preached against these two systems from the early 2000s. He grounded his stances in a set of interrelated doctrines that he took from Salafi scholarship. Yusuf's ultimate reference point, after the Qur'an and the hadith literature, was the Damascene theologian Ahmad Ibn Taymiyya (1263–1328), a central figure in Salafi thought. Even within Salafi circles, Ibn Taymiyya's legacy can be read in different ways, but Yusuf viewed him as a moral authority who brooked no compromise in creed or in applying Islamic law.

Yusuf also drew on a corpus of contemporary Salafi thinkers, taking pains to present himself as a mainstream Salafi thinker who was simply transmitting the views of globally respected Salafi authorities. In one lecture, Yusuf claimed that he had spent years teaching core texts by key thinkers in the Salafi canon: Muhammad ibn 'Abd al-Wahhab (1703–92), the founder of the Wahhabi movement; Muhammad ibn Ibrahim Al al-Shaykh (1893–1969), Grand Mufti of Saudi Arabia; 'Abd al-'Aziz Ibn Baz (1910–99), a later Grand Mufti; and Muhammad ibn Salih al-'Uthaymin (1925–2001), another senior Saudi scholar.[81] In Yusuf's interpretation, all these scholars supported his claims. Two other authorities were particularly important

[80] One example of Yusuf's preaching about what he saw as unbelief is the video entitled "Nasiha," undated, https://www.youtube.com/watch?v=kHG6f5cWjKs.

[81] Muhammad Yusuf, "Tarihin Musulmai," undated, https://www.youtube.com/watch?v=eUQYNucjqUE. Yusuf also taught from other books, such as Al-Rahiq al-Makhtum, a biography of the Prophet Muhammad by the Indian scholar Safiur Rahman Mubarakpuri (1941–2006).

to Yusuf: the Egyptian judge Ahmad Shakir (1892–1958), who had written against secularism; and the Saudi Arabian scholar Bakr Abu Zayd (1944–2008), who had written against Western-style education.[82]

Even as Yusuf depicted himself as a mainstream Salafi, he was quietly drawing on other, explicitly jihadist texts as well. For example, Yusuf plagiarized from *Millat Ibrahim wa-Da'wat al-Anbiya' wa-l-Mursalin* (The Creed/Community of Abraham and the Call of the Prophets and Messengers), a famous text by the Palestinian Jordanian Abu Muhammad al-Maqdisi (b. 1959), the most famous living Salafi-jihadist thinker.[83] Yusuf's critics within Nigeria's Salafi movement also accused Boko Haram of being influenced by Abu Basir al-Tartusi, a Syria-born Salafi-jihadist thinker.[84]

Whatever his intellectual debts to jihadists were in private, Yusuf remained somewhat circumspect in public about his intellectual debts to jihadist thinkers: even when mentioning the intellectual godfather of jihadism, Sayyid Qutb (1906–66), in a 2009 lecture, Yusuf was careful to claim that Qutb had been praised by Muhammad Nasir al-Din al-Albani (1914–99), the twentieth-century thinker most respected by mainstream Salafis in northern Nigeria, and a decidedly non-jihadist

---

[82] On Yusuf's use of Shakir, see Alex Thurston, *Salafism in Nigeria*, chapter 8; on Yusuf's use of Abu Zayd, see Anonymous, "Popular Discourses."

[83] On al-Maqdisi, see Joas Wagemakers, *A Quietist Jihadi: The Ideology and Influence of Abu Muhammad al-Maqdisi* (Cambridge: Cambridge University Press, 2012). On Yusuf's plagiarism of al-Maqdisi, see Thurston, *Salafism in Nigeria*, chapter 7. Pages 164–65 of Yusuf's manifesto *Hadhihi 'Aqidatuna* are a condensed form of approximately pages 14–20 in al-Maqdisi's *Millat Ibrahim wa-Da'wat al-Anbiya' wa-l-Mursalin* (self-published by Minbar al-Tawhid wa-l-Jihad, 2010 [1984]). Yusuf's use of some of the exact references that al-Maqdisi cites, including precise quotations from voluminous nineteenth-century texts, are extremely unlikely to have been coincidence rather than plagiarism.

[84] Muhammad Mansur Ibrahim, "Matsayin Karatun Boko da Aikin Gwamnati a Musulunci," text of lecture delivered in Bauchi, May 2009, 7.

thinker.[85] Yusuf, in other words, tried to smuggle jihadist thought into a Salafi community that had originally been oriented more toward non-jihadist Salafism.

Yusuf invoked a set of interrelated doctrines as the religious basis for his political stances. These doctrines were *al-wala' wa-l-bara'*, *al-hukm bi-ma anzala Allah*, and *izhar al-din*. For Salafi-jihadists, the first of these, *al-wala' wa-l-bara'*, means exclusive loyalty (*al-wala'*) to those whom they consider true Muslims, and complete disavowal (*al-bara'*) of all others. Yusuf told his followers:

> What will make you a soldier of Allah first and foremost, you make a complete disavowal of every form of unbelief: the Constitution, the legislature . . . worshipping tombs, idols, whatever. You come to reject it in your speech and your body and your heart. Moreover, Allah and His Messenger and the believers, you love them in your speech and your body and your heart.[86]

Yusuf combined *al-wala' wa-l-bara'* with other notions. He held that *al-hukm bi-ghayr ma anzala Allah* or "ruling by other than what God revealed" was equivalent to polytheism—in other words, that "man-made laws" and systems such as constitutions were idols that humans established in competition with God. The true Muslim had to choose between God's laws and those of man.[87] This stance meant that the Nigerian political

---

[85] Yusuf, "Tarihin Musulmai." With this claim, Yusuf joined a global debate about the relationship between Qutb and al-Albani. See Thurston, *Salafism in Nigeria*, chapter 8.

[86] Recording of commentary by Muhammad Yusuf on *Hadhihi 'Aqidatuna*, undated (likely 2008 or 2009), https://www.youtube.com/watch?v=JWfWa2rfsKw&index=2&list=UUdXgmSgdkq3HIwFnZcYuweA.

[87] On Boko Haram's use of this last notion, see Abdulbasit Kassim, "Defining and Understanding the Religious Philosophy of Jihadi Salafism and the Ideology of Boko Haram," *Journal of Politics, Religion and Ideology* 16:2–3 (2015): 173–200.

system was permeated with unbelief, and that unbelief tainted all those who participated in mainstream Nigerian politics.

Additionally, Yusuf championed *izhar al-din* or "manifesting religion" through public action. Yusuf rejected the idea that Islam exists only "within the walls of the mosque"—he called for an activist faith focused on confronting the idolatrous, anti-Islamic tyranny (*taghut*) that oppressed the small core of supposedly pure Muslims.[88] Personal piety alone was insufficient: Muslims needed to confront the fallen society surrounding them. In lectures from the last year of his life, he urged his followers to cultivate an unshakeable piety through practices such as *qiyam al-layl* (night prayer), implying that such practices would fortify them for a coming period of armed struggle.[89] He also spoke admiringly of symbols of defiance such as the Libyan anticolonial fighter Umar al-Mukhtar (1858–1931).[90]

For Yusuf, Western-style education represented the anti-Islamic system at its worst. Yusuf condemned both the content and the effects of this type of schooling. Pedagogically, widespread teachings such as Darwinism, he said, contradicted the Qur'an. Culturally, Western-style schools led Muslim children to adopt the mannerisms of Jews and Christians. Morally, children of different genders interacted at such schools, promoting "fornication, lesbianism, homosexuality, and other [corruptions]."[91] The "Christianizing" schools of British colonialism were no different than postcolonial government schools, but the prospect of material gain blinded Muslims to the truth: "Because of love for this world, many people's hearts have been

---

[88] Yusuf, *Hadhihi 'Aqidatuna*, 73.

[89] Muhammad Yusuf, "Guzurin Mujaahidai," 28 March 2009, https://www.youtube.com/watch?v=VWCNdqwGU-M.

[90] Muhammad Yusuf, "Tafsirin Tauba 1–2," likely 2009, https://www.youtube.com/watch?v=R3NcgQv-LVM&list=PLhFjW0pebMBHvLT8mJvngjH9sRTUlmwnN.

[91] Yusuf, *Hadhihi 'Aqidatuna*, 93.

saturated with love of these schools, until they do not see in them that which contradicts [Islam's] law."[92]

Yusuf's beliefs about intra-Muslim solidarity, the rejection of democracy, and the rejection of Western-style education formed a single package. In politics, Yusuf opposed participation in secular government: "Our movement rejects work under any government that rules by something other than what God has revealed."[93] He asserted that Muslims must commit themselves completely to Islam, and especially to Islamic law. Yusuf wrote, "The shari'a of Islam is a perfect and complete shari'a. . . . It is appropriate in every time and place, globally."[94] He lamented,

> We see a state in which Muslims are living, but they refuse the Islamic shari'a in its totality, and put in its place the system of democracy. And we see people with the name 'ulama' [scholars] calling for democracy and defending it, and making ugly refutations against the people who call others to follow the law of Allah.[95]

Yusuf argued that democracy, like man-made laws, positions the people as an authority in rivalry with God. He warned that majority rule allows for agreement on an anti-Islamic error, whereas Islam demands obedience to the Qur'an and the Sunna.

From democracy, multiple evils flowed, all of them cloaked as freedom: for example, "freedom of belief" allowed for apostasy from Islam.[96] It was insufficient to condemn democracy: the true Muslim had to oppose it through *izhar al-din*, or risk

[92] Yusuf, *Hadhihi 'Aqidatuna*, 79.
[93] Yusuf, *Hadhihi 'Aqidatuna*, 108.
[94] Yusuf, *Hadhihi 'Aqidatuna*, 143.
[95] Yusuf, *Hadhihi 'Aqidatuna*, 156.
[96] Yusuf, *Hadhihi 'Aqidatuna*, 64–65.

losing his or her own faith. Democracy "is the school of the infidels: following it, having dealings with it, or using its system is unbelief."[97]

By the end of his life, Yusuf was suggesting that his movement had always been preparing for a confrontation with the unbelieving state: "If the leader commits unbelief, one must . . . change him and install Islam, if one has the power, if one has the strength." If a group lacked the strength to overthrow the ruler, Yusuf continued, one had two options: make a religious emigration, or acquire the strength.[98] The implication was that Yusuf had patiently dedicated himself to gathering that strength in the form of a mass movement built through a sustained educational, missionary project.

This telling of history, however, was Yusuf's way of streamlining and sanitizing a more complex series of events. Ironically, Yusuf's views as expressed in 2009 seem to reflect his own bitter experience with democracy—not as a critic, but as a participant.

Shari'a Politics and Boko Haram

Yusuf's vision was extreme in the northern Nigerian context, but not so extreme that it was unrecognizable. In diverse ways, most northern Muslims believe that Islam provides a framework that should shape public life. In a 2013 survey, Pew found that 71 percent of Nigerian Muslims favored an official legal role for shari'a in their country—a percentage in keeping with survey results from many other countries in Africa, the

[97] Yusuf, *Hadhihi 'Aqidatuna*, 63.
[98] Yusuf, "Tarihin Musulmai."

Middle East, and Southeast Asia.[99] What Nigerians mean by shari'a, however, can vary tremendously. Few prominent Nigerians call for a totalizing Islamic state.

Nigeria's return to democracy in 1999—and the rise of "shari'a politics" in northern states—created openings for Muslim activists to rework the relationship between politics and Islam in northern Nigeria. In this climate, Yusuf amplified and intensified some of the more mainstream ideas that were circulating among activists.

From 1999 to 2001, twelve northern Nigerian states moved to implement "full shari'a." State governments promulgated new criminal law codes. State governments expanded the power of existing shari'a courts, giving them the power to hear criminal cases; previously, such courts could rule only on Muslims' personal status issues, for example disputes over alimony. The campaign to expand shari'a was a mainstream one: shari'a implementation was led by politicians who belonged to major, non-Islamist political parties. The effort drew support from diverse constituencies, including Sufis, Salafis, and unaffiliated Muslims. Many proponents of shari'a considered it compatible with Nigeria's federal, democratic system[100]—they called for elected politicians to enforce Islamic law, rather than for a theocracy in which unelected clerics would rule.

Mainstream Salafis displayed some ambivalence about shari'a politics. The Izala movement has claimed credit for being the

---

[99] Pew Forum on Religion and Public Life, *The World's Muslims: Religion, Politics and Society* (Washington, DC: 30 April 2013), 15. The full report is available for download at http://www.pewforum.org/2013/04/30/the-worlds-muslims-religion -politics-society-beliefs-about-sharia/.

[100] Brandon Kendhammer, "The Sharia Controversy in Northern Nigeria and the Politics of Islamic Law in New and Uncertain Democracies," *Comparative Politics* 45:33 (April 2013): 291–311.

driving force behind shari'a implementation.[101] But Ja'far Adam worried that the new system would empower Sufis and "charlatans." Adam portrayed shari'a implementation as a moral test for northern Nigeria's Muslim community, and especially for Salafis, whom he hoped would guide the program.[102] Once the new system was implemented, Salafis sometimes accepted government appointments and/or publicly offered "advice" to politicians, indicating a basic acceptance of electoral politics. At the same time, Adam and others continued to express skepticism about the capacity of democracy and secularism to facilitate a moral purification of Muslim society. It was this side of Salafi discourse that Yusuf would amplify, especially after his own career as a political preacher floundered.

Political circumstances in Borno helped create conditions that made Yusuf's brand of Salafi skepticism about shari'a particularly resonant. In 1999, when Nigeria returned to civilian multiparty rule, Mala Kachalla of the All People's Party (later renamed the All Nigeria People's Party or ANPP) won election as governor of Borno. Kachalla, a prominent businessman, found much of his single term dominated by shari'a politics. After the wave of shari'a implementation began in Zamfara State in October 1999, shari'a implementation proved highly popular with northern Nigerian Muslims. Governors like Kachalla found themselves compelled to react.

---

[101] Ramzi Ben Amara, "'We Introduced Shari'a': The Izala Movement in Nigeria as Initiator of Shari'a Reimplementation in the North of the Country; Some Reflections," in *Shari'a in Africa Today: Reactions and Responses*, edited by John A. Chesworth and Franz Kogelmann, 125–46 (Leiden: Brill, 2013). See also Paul Lubeck, "Nigeria: Mapping a Shari'a Restorationist Movement," in *Shari'a Politics: Islamic Law and Society in the Modern World*, edited by Robert W. Hefner, 244–79 (Bloomington: Indiana University Press, 2011).

[102] Ja'far Adam, recorded lecture entitled "Kalubalen Shari'a," 15/16 June 2000, Kano. Recording in the author's possession.

Some Muslims in Borno soon agitated for shariʻa implementation. In late 1999, the principal of the Borno College of Legal and Islamic Studies (BOCOLIS), Umar Gajiram, created a Committee on Sensitisation on the Implementation of Sharia. He asked the Shehu of Borno for support.[103] Gajiram told a government committee that "Muslims must stand up and compel our elected representatives to accept the implementation of Sharia."[104] State-run Islamic colleges such as BOCOLIS were key players in agitation for shariʻa; BOCOLIS's peer institution in Kano was the site of important pro-shariʻa meetings during this period.[105]

Although BOCOLIS was dominated by Sufi teachers, it is worth mentioning that future founders of Boko Haram, namely Abubakar Shekau and Mamman Nur, may have been students there in 1999.[106] The intersection of educational crisis and shariʻa agitation provides critical context for understanding the emergence of Boko Haram. At the same time that Borno's education system was failing and many graduates were going unemployed, Muslim elites were promoting shariʻa as the key to societal and moral transformation. Young students at BOCOLIS received powerful pro-shariʻa messages from their institution's leaders. The more passionate among them—perhaps

[103] Tajudeen Suleiman, "Sharia at All Costs," *Tempo*, 22 December 1999, http://allafrica.com/stories/199912220127.html.

[104] Committee on Application of Sharia in Borno State, "Report of the Committee on Application of Sharia in Borno State," April 2000, reproduced in *Sharia Implementation in Northern Nigeria 1999–2006: A Sourcebook*, vol. 1, chapter 2, supplementary materials part 4 (published online in 2007, available at http://www.sharia-in-africa.net/media/publications/sharia-implementation-in-northern-nigeria/vol_2_10_chapter_2_supp_borno_pre.pdf), 18.

[105] Alex Thurston, "The Aminu Kano College of Islamic and Legal Studies."

[106] International Crisis Group, "Curbing Violence in Nigeria (II): The Boko Haram Insurgency," 19; and Emeka Okereke, "From Obscurity to Global Visibility: Periscoping Abubakar Shekau," *Counter Terrorist Trends and Analysis* 6:10 (November 2014): 17–22.

including Shekau and Nur—might have begun to feel that shariʻa was the one vehicle that could save Nigeria, and save them. Yusuf involved himself in shariʻa politics early. In the early 2000s, he became a representative for Borno in the Supreme Council for Shariʻa in Nigeria.[107] Adam, who was still Yusuf's mentor at that time, was close to the group.[108] The council, a Salafi-leaning group, was founded in 2000 and took a hardline stance on the question of shariʻa implementation in Nigeria, as well as on issues such as Muslim-Christian relations and polio vaccinations.[109] Groups such as the council were considered relatively mainstream at the time—Muhammadu Buhari spoke at the council's national convention in 2001—and Yusuf was still a part of the Salafi mainstream in Borno.

The slow course of shariʻa implementation under Governor Kachalla frustrated those Borno Muslims who perceived him as reluctant. But shariʻa implementation was administratively complex: it involved the amendment of various state laws promulgated under military governments, as well as an ambiguous dance with provisions in the Nigerian constitution that forbade the establishment of a state religion. As other northern states rushed to enforce shariʻa, Kachalla rolled out the new system slowly. He approved the Sharia Administration of Justice Law in August 2000,[110] and he officially launched shariʻa in

[107] Bayo Oladeji, Muazu Abari, Midat Joseph, and Salisu Ibrahim, "Boko Haram Picks Datti Ahmed as Mediator," *Leadership*, 14 March 2012, http://allafrica.com/stories/201203140368.html.

[108] Andrea Brigaglia, "A Contribution to the History of the Wahhabi Daʻwa in West Africa: The Career and the Murder of Shaykh Jaʻfar Mahmud Adam (Daura, ca. 1961/1962—Kano 2007)," *Islamic Africa* 3:1 (2012): 1–23; 15–17.

[109] Human Rights Watch, "The Miss World Riots: Continued Impunity for Killings in Kaduna," 22 July 2003, n. 99, https://www.hrw.org/report/2003/07/22/miss-world-riots/continued-impunity-killings-kaduna. On polio, see "Medical Laboratory Tests Find Polio Vaccines Safe," IRIN, 18 November 2003, http://www.irinnews.org/fr/node/215191.

[110] Philip Ostien, "Documentary Materials: Borno State," in *Sharia Implementation in Northern Nigeria 1999–2006: A Sourcebook*, vol. 6, *Ulama Institutions*, edited

a ceremony at Ramat Square in Maiduguri on June 1, 2001. The initial phase of implementation affected matters such as prostitution, gambling, and alcohol. Kachalla, however, delayed enforcement of offenses such as stealing and adultery, for which *hudud* penalties (corporal punishments laid down in the Qur'an) might apply.[111]

Kachalla's shari'a committees, in their composition and their output, offer insights into broader structures of religious authority and policy making in Borno. In January 2000, Kachalla established a Committee on Application of Sharia in Borno State. It included Muslim judges, prominent scholars, elected politicians, and civil servants.[112] During statewide consultations, the committee's primary interlocutors were retired Muslim judges and Sufi shaykhs from the Tijaniyya, such as Ibrahim Salih and Abubakar El-Miskin.

The committee observed that these elites "supported the application of Sharia in the State. However, they expressed the view that taking into consideration the level of ignorance, poverty and moral decadence, Sharia should be implemented gradually."[113] The committee agreed: "The implementation of the penal aspect is not feasible for now." The committee urged the governor to focus on "poverty alleviation" and "moral reorientation of the people" while gradually introducing criminal shari'a codes over a three-year period. The committee proposed a Ministry of Religious Affairs that would more systematically centralize religious authority in the state.[114] If the committee

---

and compiled by Philip Ostien, chapter 8, part 2 (published online, 2011: http://www.sharia-in-africa.net/media/publications/sharia-implementation-in-northern-nigeria-volume-six/Chapter%208%20Part%20II.pdf), 17 n. 36.

[111] Raymond Gukas, "How Borno Residents Survive Sharia," *Daily Champion*, 7 September 2002, http://allafrica.com/stories/200209090014.html.

[112] Committee on Application of Sharia in Borno State, "Report," 3.

[113] Committee on Application of Sharia in Borno State, "Report," 5.

[114] Committee on Application of Sharia in Borno State, "Report," 10–11.

was reflecting what Kachalla wanted to hear, then the charges that the governor was reluctant to pursue shari'a seem well supported. Young radicals such as Yusuf could easily form the impression that the governor and the Sufi shaykhs were taming popular pressures for shari'a implementation by slow-rolling and bureaucratizing the process. The caution of the Muslim establishment created an opening in the religious field for someone with a strident message on shari'a.

In February 2001, Kachalla inaugurated a Sharia Implementation Committee responsible for "providing the modality of implementing the Sharia in the State."[115] Yusuf was a member of the twenty-five-person committee, but like its predecessor, this group was headed by older elites: its chairman was Professor Abubakar Mustapha, vice chancellor of the University of Maiduguri, and its secretary was Bukar Yerima, the Borno State director of public prosecution.[116] This committee, too, envisioned a long time line for shari'a implementation, given that Borno suffered from widespread poverty and "educational backwardness."[117] In a poor state with a failing school system, the committee suggested, shari'a implementation needed to be carefully aligned with other policies, or it could become a punitive, unpopular system.

The trajectory of shari'a implementation in Borno—with middle-tier Muslim scholars and some Salafis initially pressuring hereditary rulers and elected politicians to apply shari'a,

[115] Sharia Implementation Committee of Borno State, "Interim Report of the Sharia Implementation Committee," 2001, reproduced in *Sharia Implementation in Northern Nigeria 1999–2006: A Sourcebook*, vol. 2, edited and compiled by Philip Ostien, supplement to chapter 2 (published online in 2007, http://www.sharia-in-africa.net/media /publications/sharia-implementation-in-northern-nigeria/vol_2_13_chapter_2_supp _borno_post.pdf), 1.

[116] "Borno Governor Inaugurates Sharia Implementation Committee," *Vanguard*, 7 February 2001, http://allafrica.com/stories/200102070274.html.

[117] Sharia Implementation Committee of Borno State, "Interim Report," 2.

and then finding the process dominated by emirs, Sufis, and academics—was repeated in other northern states.[118] Across the north, hardliners like Yusuf found some opportunities to participate in shari'a implementation, but the conversations were dominated by a Muslim gerontocracy. Nor would hardliners be satisfied with the pace that the gerontocracy and some governors recommended. Alongside Yusuf's competition with other Salafis for audiences, he found himself a very junior figure within the structure of religious authority in the state and in the emerging shari'a system. Yusuf came to the conclusion that shari'a implementation was not serious. He said later:

> The task they gave us was to investigate the judges that were in Borno, whether they were suitable for carrying out *shari'a* or not suitable for carrying out *shari'a*, and also what they were ruling at that time. We went around and we saw. Because of that, I began saying it was not *shari'a* that they were doing, according to what I know.[119]

The early Boko Haram's dissatisfaction initially centered on Kachalla, but later broadened to condemn Nigeria's secular state.

In terms of his rhetoric, Yusuf was not completely out of the mainstream in the early 2000s. It was not just Yusuf who invoked doctrines like *al-hukm bi-ma anzala Allah* (ruling by what God has revealed). As early as 2001, the Committee on Application of Sharia in Borno State had cited Qur'anic verses such as 5:44, 5:45, and 5:47 as justification for shari'a implementation. The committee quoted the Qur'an to the effect that "those who do not govern (judge) by what Allah has sent down

---

[118] Tajudeen Suleiman, "Sharia at All Costs," *Tempo*, 22 December 1999, http://allafrica.com/stories/199912220127.html.

[119] Debate between Shaykh Isa 'Ali Pantami and Muhammad Yusuf, https://www.youtube.com/watch?v=PFhYWeLWEyk.

(revealed) are: rejecters of truth, oppressors, [and] evil doers."[120] Verse 5:44 was a staple in Boko Haram's later propaganda. Moreover, even establishment Muslim voices raised concerns about the integrity of Borno's shari'a system: the committee on which Yusuf served noted that courts in the state suffered from corruption, delays, and inadequate supervision.[121]

In 2003, shari'a was a major issue in gubernatorial contests in northern states. Incumbents tended to win, often because of the advantages of incumbency, but also because of their handling of shari'a: some incumbents benefited because of their strong affirmations of commitment to shari'a implementation, while others benefited from their skillful balancing acts vis-à-vis the Muslim and Christian communities in their states. Some challengers, however, benefited from perceptions that certain incumbents were insufficiently committed to the shari'a project.[122] Three governors in Nigeria's "shari'a states" lost their reelection bids, including Kachalla.[123]

Borno's new governor was Ali Modu Sheriff, a businessman and "godfather" who had been a major figure in state politics since the early 1990s. Sheriff was allegedly Kachalla's major financial backer before the two men fell out. Sheriff also served as senator for Borno North from 1999 to 2003.[124] His election was a turning point for Boko Haram, giving Yusuf new politi-

[120] Committee on Application of Sharia in Borno State, "Report," 7.

[121] Committee on Application of Sharia in Borno State, "Report," 13.

[122] Franz Kogelmann, "The 'Sharia Factor' in Nigeria's 2003 Elections," in *Muslim-Christian Encounters in Africa*, edited by Benjamin Soares, 256–74 (Leiden: Brill, 2006), 272–73.

[123] Gunnar Weimann, *Islamic Criminal Law in Northern Nigeria: Politics, Religion, Judicial Practice* (Amsterdam: Amsterdam University Press, 2010), 90 n. 309.

[124] See Sheriff's account of this period, in which he denies all ties to Boko Haram and Muhammad Yusuf: Ali Modu Sheriff, "My Boko Haram Story," *Vanguard*, 3 September 2014, http://allafrica.com/stories/201409040368.html.

cal prominence. In order to win election, Sheriff likely made an agreement with Yusuf: Sheriff would intensify the application of shariʻa in the state and bring Yusuf's movement into his government if Yusuf would support his campaign and portray Kachalla as weak on shariʻa. This deal has been reported in credible studies,[125] and Borno attorney general Kaka Lawan has publicly accused Sheriff of playing a role in Boko Haram's genesis.[126] The circumstantial evidence for a deal is strong: this evidence includes Borno authorities' rehabilitation of Yusuf after Kanamma, discussed above; the appointment of a Boko Haram member to a ministerial post, discussed below; and Boko Haram's campaign of assassinations against Sheriff's associates in 2010–11, discussed in chapter 3.

In 2003, Borno's political environment made it important for Sheriff to enlist youth support and support from figures who opposed the political status quo. Although Sheriff sidelined Kachalla within the ANPP, Kachalla decamped to a minor party. This move meant that in the general election, Sheriff faced a three-man race against Kachalla and the People's Democratic Party's Kashim Ibrahim-Imam.

Kachalla was down but not out: as governor, he had accrued some accomplishments, especially in infrastructure development. Yet crises in the state—"shortage of water supply even within Maiduguri metropolis, closure of hospitals due to health workers' strike, [and] non-payment of workers' salary

---

[125] International Crisis Group, "Curbing Violence in Nigeria (II): The Boko Haram Insurgency," 11; Marc-Antoine Pérouse de Montclos, "Nigeria's Interminable Insurgency: Addressing the Boko Haram Crisis," Chatham House (September 2014), 32–33, https://www.chathamhouse.org/sites/files/chathamhouse/field/field_document/20140901BokoHaramPerousedeMontclos_0.pdf.

[126] Olusola Fabiyi and Chukwudi Akasike, "Sheriff Created Boko Haram, Says Borno AG," *Punch*, 25 August 2016, http://punchng.com/sheriff-created-boko-haram-says-borno-ag/.

arrears"—had outpaced Kachalla's programs. Many youth came to view Kachalla as a member of the old guard, whose administration was primarily oriented toward benefiting older businessmen and politicians.[127]

Ibrahim-Imam, meanwhile, was not to be discounted. The People's Democratic Party was the ruling party nationally. Ibrahim-Imam had strong connections to Borno's Muslim establishment; during the lead-up to the election, the Shehu of Borno gave him the traditional title Mutawalli (treasurer), making him a member of the Shehu's Emirate Council. Sheriff, for his part, appeared "not to enjoy [the] confidence" of the Shehu and other "traditional power brokers and conservative elites" in the state.[128] Sheriff had to look elsewhere for support. Leveraging his "stupendous wealth," Sheriff positioned himself as a youth-oriented populist.[129]

To the extent that they are accurate, the official election results indicate the effectiveness of Sheriff's urban-focused, youth-focused strategy: out of approximately 1.26 million votes cast, Sheriff won a strong plurality (582,240, or 46 percent). He won nineteen of Borno's twenty-seven local government areas. His most dramatic victory came in Maiduguri, where his tally of 145,620 votes exceeded the combined totals of Kachalla (70,013) and Ibrahim-Imam (40,483).[130] One in four votes for

[127] Abdullahi Bego, "Borno: Why Governor Mala Kachalla Lost to Modu Ali Sherrif [sic]," *Weekly Trust*, 26 April 2003, http://allafrica.com/stories/200304281159.html.

[128] Sadiq Abubakar and Olalekan Bilesanmi, "Borno: Kachalla, an Incumbent Demystified," *Vanguard*, 19 January 2003, http://allafrica.com/stories/200301200553.html.

[129] Bego, "Borno: Why Governor Mala Kachalla Lost."

[130] Governor's Office, Borno State, *Selected Speeches of His Excellency, Sen. (Dr.) Ali Modu Sheriff, Executive Governor, Borno State: 731 Days in Office* (Maiduguri: Political Affairs Department, Governor's Office, Borno State; printed by Spin-Ads Communications, 2005), 215–16.

Sheriff, in other words, were cast in Maiduguri. The central-ity of Maiduguri to Sheriff's victory explains why Sheriff might have eagerly courted a young, antiestablishment, urban radical like Yusuf.

Sheriff did not win on popularity alone. At both the na-tional and the state levels, Nigeria's 2003 elections were a vio-lent, cutthroat affair, tarnished by rigging and vote buying. The European Union's observation mission reported that "in a number of States . . . minimum standards for democratic elections were not met and the results of the Presidential and Gubernatorial elections in these states can hardly be consid-ered as credible."[131] Human Rights Watch stated: "In a num-ber of locations, elections simply did not take place as groups of armed thugs linked to parties and candidates intimidated and threatened voters in order to falsify results."[132] In Borno, Sheriff reportedly used a militia called ECOMOG (after the Nigerian-led peacekeeping force deployed to Liberia, Sierra Leone, and Guinea Bissau in the 1990s) to "intimidate and silence political opponents with impunity."[133]

If Sheriff used "shari'a politics" to help win the Borno State gubernatorial election in 2003, shari'a was far from the top priority for his administration as it took office. In the report prepared by his transition committee, the word "shari'a" ap-peared only a handful of times. The committee recommended that the state government "sponsor a massive awareness cam-paign on Sharia" and "set-up Sharia Courts and upper Sharia

---

[131] European Union Election Observation Mission to Nigeria, "Final Report" (2003), 37, http://eeas.europa.eu/eueom/pdf/missions/nigeria2003.pdf.

[132] Human Rights Watch, "Nigeria's 2003 Elections: The Unacknowledged Vio-lence," June 2004, 1, https://www.hrw.org/reports/2004/nigeria0604/nigeria0604.pdf.

[133] International Crisis Group, "Curbing Violence in Nigeria (II): The Boko Haram Insurgency," 11.

courts in all parts of the state."[134] Sheriff's advisers did not discuss shari'a as the cornerstone of his administration, but rather as a public relations matter and a peripheral institution of government. Among northern governors, Sheriff was not alone in campaigning on shari'a and then essentially ignoring it. In this climate, with many governors raising expectations on shari'a and then sidelining the project once in office, many ordinary Muslims came to believe that shari'a implementation had been "stage-managed" or had even been a "mockery" that did little curb elite corruption.[135]

What the transition committee's report emphasized was the impoverishment of Borno and its infrastructure, as well as the desperate straits of the state government. From the committee's recommendation that the state government should undertake "the feeding of patients in hospitals," one gains a sense of how bad the situation was.[136] The committee blamed the state government's dysfunction on the outgoing administration, but the report revealed the long-term degradation of service provision in Borno.

This degradation, as elsewhere in Nigeria, reflected chronic and severe corruption. The report listed agency after agency that had broken-down vehicles, inadequate offices, and unpaid debts. Billions of naira had gone missing or were never even deposited in the proper accounts. The "unvouchered expenditure" for the period 1999–2003 totaled nearly 7.5 bil-

---

[134] Borno State Transition Committee, *Main Report (Executive Summary) Submitted to His Excellency Senator (Dr.) Ali Modu Sheriff, Executive Governor, Borno State,* July 2003, 102.

[135] Muhammad Nur Alkali, Abubakar Kawu Monguno, and Ballama Shettima Mustafa, "Overview of Islamic Actors in Northeastern Nigeria," Nigeria Research Networking Working Paper no. 2, January 2012, 26, http://www3.qeh.ox.ac.uk/pdf/nrn /WP2Alkali.pdf.

[136] Borno State Transition Committee, *Main Report,* 91.

lion naira,[137] leaving an "empty treasury" and "heavy liability beyond imagination."[138] Systematic theft represented a direct robbery of the people of Borno: for example, "despite the colossal sum of 1.3 [billion naira] provided by the state and local governments for rural electrification . . . most of the Projects were not executed."[139] Kleptocracy and nepotism had crippled the state government, leaving critical agencies understaffed, underfunded, and demoralized.

The dangerous and tragic results of corruption were particularly visible in the education sector. The transition committee wrote, "There is a serious shortage of qualified teachers and adequate facilities for learning while the existing ones have continued to decline at an alarming rate." Funds that should have gone to building schools and hiring teachers had instead gone to the Primary Education Board, whose "reckless financial spendings" had eaten up "the colossal amount of money expended in the sub-sector."[140] The problems extended beyond the schools into wider questions of social order. The committee depicted schools as undisciplined and backward, and characterized graduates and school dropouts as threats to society: "children often leave the schools without any prospect for employment and partly because they come out with no education at all, indisciplined [sic] and unproductive at home or on the farm."[141] The committee issued a prescient warning:

> At present there appears to be a high population explosion of the youth particularly in urban centres such as Maiduguri. Many of them are used as easy tools of violence and misconduct particularly during the times of elections. Every effort

[137] Borno State Transition Committee, *Main Report*, 44.
[138] Borno State Transition Committee, *Main Report*, 119.
[139] Borno State Transition Committee, *Main Report*, 49.
[140] Borno State Transition Committee, *Main Report*, 78.
[141] Borno State Transition Committee, *Main Report*, 80.

has to be made to open up new avenues for the engagement of these young men and women in productive ventures.[142]

Given that Sheriff had, allegedly, just used such tactics in securing his own election, the committee may have been warning him that matters were reaching a boiling point. Tellingly, the committee seemed less concerned about children and youth who had never attended school than about those who had some exposure to public education—these latter youths had had their expectations raised and then dashed in a particularly severe manner. The disappointments of joblessness and broken electoral bargains could breed unrest.

Sheriff made some efforts to intensify Islamization and shari'a implementation. In September 2005, he established a Ministry of Religious Affairs and Special Education, with responsibility for some aspects of shari'a administration and preaching. Here, public relations was again a paramount concern—the new ministry had responsibility for publicizing shari'a regulations and fielding complaints about the system.[143]

The ministry is where the "deal" between Sheriff and Boko Haram may have been temporarily fulfilled. Sheriff appointed as minister a man named Buji Foi, who has been widely identified as an associate and financier of Yusuf. Foi may have even siphoned funds from the state government and given them to Yusuf, enabling Yusuf to sponsor businesses for his followers and begin to amass weapons.[144] Attempting to dissociate himself from Boko Haram years later, Sheriff would tell reporters that he brought Foi into his government because of Foi's prior local government service, rather than as part of a deal with

---

[142] Borno State Transition Committee, *Main Report*, 88.

[143] Ostien, "Documentary Materials: Borno State," 21–22.

[144] International Crisis Group, "Curbing Violence in Nigeria (II): The Boko Haram Insurgency," 12.

Yusuf.[145] But Foi's appointment was likely effected to fulfill Sheriff's compact with Yusuf.

The alliance did not last. Yusuf may have become an irritant soon after the 2003 election. As part of a campaign across the north, the Supreme Council for Shari'a in Nigeria—of which Yusuf was a member—was fanning the flames of grassroots nervousness about polio vaccination, including in Borno. One can imagine that by February 2004, when "the immunisation exercise was flagged off in Maiduguri by the wife of Governor Sheriff," the new governor might have already come to resent the influence of his state's preachers. As the northern newspaper *Daily Trust* reported:

> The Oral Polio Vaccine has been largely rejected in Maiduguri metropolitan and Jere local government areas of Borno State as parents cite fears of possible harmful effects in the vaccine. . . . *Daily Trust* checks in Maiduguri yesterday showed that many of the immunisation officers were refused entry into households to immunise children with mothers saying that their husbands had not granted them permission to let the children immunised.[146]

Whereas Kano's Ibrahim Shekarau, another newly elected pro-shari'a governor, had joined the antipolio movement, Sheriff had courted embarrassment by supporting it. Sheriff must have been aware of the Supreme Council's—and, possibly, Yusuf's—role in the matter.

Amid the unfulfilled promise of shari'a implementation, the 2007 election marked a new phase in Sheriff and Yusuf's rupture. The year 2007 was a low point in Nigerian elections. A report

[145] Sheriff, "My Boko Haram Story."

[146] Abdullahi Bego and Habiba Adamu, "Kano, Borno Shun Polio Immunisation," *Daily Trust*, 24 February 2004, http://allafrica.com/stories/200402240437.html.

by the British government stated that the ruling People's Democratic Party (PDP) had "fixed the results in advance, even for local government, in all but a handful of states as part of an intra-elite deal."[147] Borno experienced significant election-related violence in 2006–7: clashes between rival "ECOMOG" youth groups,[148] and assassination attempts on local politicians, such as the ANPP state chairman and the party's state secretary.[149] Sheriff easily won reelection, perhaps as part of the "intra-elite deal" between the national PDP and various state governors and godfathers. Despite Sheriff's continued membership in the ANPP, he cultivated ties with President Obasanjo in the lead-up to the election, as he would with Obasanjo's successor Umaru Yar'Adua afterward.[150]

Sheriff's strategy in 2007 differed from his 2003 campaign. As a challenger in 2003, he wanted the support of radicals such as Yusuf. As an incumbent four years later, it was the machinery of the party and the relationship with Abuja that counted, along with the powers of incumbency. As one analysis noted, "Sheriff though popular is also infamous for fomenting violence and for his tight grip on dissent and opposition activities."[151] Sheriff won a smashing reelection—per one tally,

[147] United Kingdom Department for International Development, "Elections in Nigeria 2007" (undated), 2, https://www.gov.uk/government/uploads/system/uploads /attachment_data/file/67655/elections-ng-2007.pdf.

[148] Hamza Idris, "ANPP Factions Clash in Maiduguri," *Daily Trust*, 30 May 2006, http://allafrica.com/stories/200605311037.html; and Abdullahi Bego, "3 Killed in Maiduguri Violence," *Daily Trust*, 19 January 2007, http://allafrica.com/stories/200701 190402.html.

[149] Sani Mohammad, "Borno's Changing Face," *Source*, 20 November 2006, http:// thesourceng.com/bornofacenov20.htm.

[150] Isa Umar Gusau, "Will Sheriff 'Capture' Yar'Adua?," *Daily Trust*, 3 November 2008, http://allafrica.com/stories/200811040965.html.

[151] United States Embassy Abuja, leaked cable 07ABUJA697, "Snapshot of Key Northern Gubernatorial Races," 12 April 2007, https://wikileaks.org/plusd/cables /07ABUJA697_a.html.

he garnered nearly 700,000 votes to little more than 300,000 for Ibrahim-Imam, who contested for a second time under the PDP banner.[152] Sheriff had improved on his 2003 tally by almost 120,000 votes. After the elections, Sheriff tightened his grip further: by early 2009, he had ensured "the near absence of a vibrant opposition" in Borno.[153]

For Boko Haram, the governor was now a traitor, even a threat. But politically, Yusuf had nowhere to turn. A brief comparison with Kano helps make the point: there, ANPP governor Ibrahim Shekarau had come to power in 2003, the same year as Sheriff, and had also promised to strengthen shariʿa. Shekarau lost the support of some of Kano's Salafis between 2005 and 2007, but those Salafis could align themselves with Shekarau's rival, the defeated governor and PDP leader Rabiu Kwankwaso, who went on to win the 2011 gubernatorial election and appoint Salafis to major posts.[154] But in Borno, Kachalla died soon after the 2007 elections, and the state PDP chapter was quite weak. With Sheriff the only game in town, Yusuf may have viewed further alliances with politicians as a dead end, perhaps perceiving that Sheriff would be able to pick his own successor in 2011 (as indeed occurred). With his relations with other Salafis openly souring, Yusuf may have felt that the best path forward was to strengthen his incendiary rhetoric, or risk being eclipsed by restless hardline associates at a time when his own political influence was threatened.

In this climate, Buji Foi resigned from Sheriff's government in 2007, reportedly over Sheriff's "failure to abide by the deal"

---

[152] "Rigged Elections: Results So Far," *Sahara Reporters*, 15 April 2007, http://saharareporters.com/2007/04/15/rigged-elections-results-so-far.

[153] Ahmad Salkida, "Different Strokes for Governor Sheriff's Second Term," *Daily Trust*, 8 February 2009, http://allafrica.com/stories/200902090506.html.

[154] Thurston, "Muslim Politics."

with Boko Haram.[155] Over the next two years Yusuf's relations with authorities deteriorated. Boko Haram now decided that when its members were arrested, it would attempt to free them by force. In April 2007, hundreds of Yusuf's followers attacked a police station in Kano, evoking a military deployment to calm the situation.[156] In November 2008, Yusuf was arrested after some of his followers attacked a police station in Maiduguri. He was accused of attempting "to infiltrate security agencies, especially the police and the State Security Service (SSS), in order to obtain arms to instigate crises within his group . . . so as to launch a full-fledged religious war in Nigeria." After he pleaded not guilty, the Abuja High Court released him on bail in January.[157] But in February 2009 and again that April, authorities arrested and deported one of Yusuf's deputies to Niger.[158] Yusuf continued to face legal proceedings in early 2009, but the SSS was disorganized, and its representative repeatedly failed to show up for the hearings.[159] Amid all these close calls with prison, Yusuf appears to have become even more convinced that some violent action was necessary.

---

[155] Obinna Anyadike, "Nigeria—the Community Turns against Boko Haram," IRIN, 11 August 2014, http://www.irinnews.org/report/100475/nigeria-the-community-turns-against-boko-haram.

[156] "Islamists Attack Nigeria Police," BBC, 17 April 2007, http://news.bbc.co.uk/2/hi/africa/6564629.stm.

[157] Hussein Yahaya and Ibraheem Fatai, "Islamic Scholar Arraigned for 'Terrorism,'" *Daily Trust*, 12 January 2009, http://allafrica.com/stories/200901130236.html.

[158] Taye Obateru, Kingsley Omonobi, Lawani Mikairu, and Daniel Idonor, "Boko Haram Leader, Yusuf, Killed," *Vanguard*, 30 July 2009, http://allafrica.com/stories/200907310003.html.

[159] Emeka Mamah, Kingsley Omonobi, and Chris Ochayi, "Northern Govs Meet, Condemn Boko Haram Crisis," *Vanguard*, 4 August 2009, http://www.vanguardngr.com/2009/08/northern-govs-meet-condemn-boko-haram-crisis/.

Heading toward Crisis

Why did Nigerian authorities not move decisively against Yusuf at this time? President Yar'Adua would later state, credibly, that the authorities had spent years tracking Boko Haram's efforts to arm itself and manufacture bombs.[160] Incompetence and distraction might help explain authorities' relative toleration of Yusuf's activities. Authorities may also have been nervous about sentencing Yusuf to a long prison term while he still enjoyed substantial popularity. Repression could have fed that popularity. As one commentator later recalled, "Yusuf was prevented from preaching in several mosques all over the North and was denied TV/Radio appearances in Borno State. But this alienation worked to his advantage as he became the superior voice among an army of unwitting youths unable to defy him."[161] Another commentator relates that when Yusuf was released after one of his arrests, "people came all the way from Kaduna, Bauchi and Kano to welcome him. There was a long motorcade from the airport as thousands of his members trooped out to lead him to his house. He came back like a hero."[162]

Throughout the first months of 2009, Yusuf continued to travel around the north, going as far as Sokoto to visit local supporters.[163] Boko Haram continued to expand: its organized

[160] United States Embassy Abuja, leaked cable 09ABUJA1392, "Nigerian Government Quashes Extremists, but Not the Root of the Problem," 29 July 2009, https://wikileaks.org/plusd/cables/09ABUJA1392_a.html.

[161] Ahmad Salkida, "Another Look at the Boko Haram Philosophy," *Premium Times*, 6 November 2012, http://www.premiumtimesng.com/opinion/106108-another-look-at-the-boko-haram-philosophy-by-ahmad-salkida.html.

[162] Shehu Sani, "Boko Haram: History, Ideas and Revolt (3)."

[163] Lawan Adamu, "The Untold Story of Kabiru Sokoto," *Daily Trust*, 13 February 2012, http://allafrica.com/stories/201202130754.html.

presence in Bauchi, where the July 2009 uprising would begin, reportedly dated only to January of that year.[164] The sect had conflict with authorities in Sokoto, Kaduna, and Bauchi; Yusuf later said that Sokoto's governor had threatened to arrest him if he entered that state.[165] By spring 2009, Boko Haram members were leaving Maiduguri for paramilitary training. A Maiduguri resident who functioned as an adoptive mother for some Boko Haram members in the Shehuri North Ward noticed that young men were disappearing and then returning with a "reserved" air. When she confronted them about their disappearances, they told her that "they went for training, how to shoot human being[s], how to kill."[166]

Tensions were building in Borno. In November 2008, Sheriff launched an antibanditry program, "Operation Flush II." With joint military and police participation, Operation Flush was officially designed to "ensure the security of lives and property of the people in the hinterlands,"[167] as well as in Maiduguri. The problem of banditry was genuine and had been a source of concern in Borno for years.[168] But Yusuf, with some cause, came to perceive Operation Flush as an anti–Boko Haram measure. After its launch, the Nigerian press reported that security personnel had achieved some success in reducing banditry—but also that the unit was causing outcry among citizens who felt

[164] Patience Ogbodo and Uduma Kalu, "Why We Hit Bauchi, Borno Says Boko Haram," *Vanguard*, 31 July 2009, http://www.vanguardngr.com/2009/07/why-we-hit-bauchi-borno-says-boko-haram/.

[165] Yusuf, "Open Letter," https://www.youtube.com/watch?v=f89PvcpWSRg.

[166] Pulse TV interview with Aisha Wakil.

[167] Abdulkareem Haruna, "We Met Borno on the Brink of Collapse—Dibal," *Daily Independent*, 24 November 2008, http://allafrica.com/stories/200811250416.html.

[168] See Borno State Transition Committee, *Main Report*, 95–96; Sani Mohammad, "Borno's Changing Face," *Source*, 20 November 2006, http://thesourceng.com/borno facenov20.htm; and Dan Borno, "Operation Flush II and Maiduguri People," 30 December 2008, http://danborno.blogspot.com/2008/12/operation-flush-ii-maiduguri-people.html.

the security forces practiced "constant harassment" against them.[169] Together with a national law requiring motorbike riders to wear helmets, Operation Flush increased tensions on Borno's roads.

In this context, Operation Flush came to target Boko Haram—even Sheriff's former commissioner of information recalls events in these terms.[170] When Operation Flush detained and then opened fire on Boko Haram members en route to a funeral procession in June 2009, the stage was set for conflict between Yusuf and the authorities.[171] Personnel at the U.S. Embassy in Abuja followed events nervously, wondering whether "the officers of Operation Flush were deliberately seeking to provoke the group."[172] If this interpretation is correct, perhaps Borno authorities felt that by provoking Yusuf into a confrontation, they might crush his movement without making him a martyr.

Yusuf certainly read events as a provocation. Perhaps to prevent hardliners from outflanking him as they had at the time of Kanamma, he now took a hard line himself. In June 2009, he delivered his "Open Letter to the Federal Government of Nigeria," a lecture that became a turning point in the crisis. Yusuf called for an uprising against the authorities in Borno and Abuja. He linked the "injustice" of the Borno State government to what he saw as a pattern of anti-Muslim violence

[169] Isa Umar Gusau and Mustapha Isah Kwara, "In Maiduguri, 'Operation Flush' Men Brutalize Residents," *Daily Trust*, 7 February 2009, http://allafrica.com/stories /200902090198.html.

[170] Lekan Bilesanmi, "Governor, Godfather in Battle for Borno," *Vanguard*, 24 August 2014, http://allafrica.com/stories/201409040368.html.

[171] Uri Friedman, "The Bike-Helmet Law That Helped Trigger an Insurgency in Nigeria," *Atlantic*, 22 May 2014, http://www.theatlantic.com/international/archive/2014 /05/the-bike-helmet-law-that-triggered-an-insurgency-in-nigeria/371301/.

[172] United States Embassy Abuja, leaked cable 09ABUJA1053, "Nigeria: Police Shoot 17 in Maiduguri, Tensions Remain High," 12 June 2009, https://www.wikileaks .org/plusd/cables/09ABUJA1053_a.html.

in Nigeria. He mentioned the Muslim-Christian clashes discussed in chapter 1: the 1987 riots in Kafanchan, Kaduna State; the 1992 killings in Zangon-Kataf, Kaduna; and cyclical violence in Plateau State, dating to 1994. Yusuf concluded: "The government of Nigeria has not been built to do justice. . . . It has been built to attack Islam and kill Muslims." Boko Haram saw Operation Flush as the latest manifestation of such persecution: "it appeared because of us." Governor Sheriff, Yusuf said, was leading a "war" against Boko Haram.[173]

As he had written when arguing for the need to oppose democracy by engaging in public activism, Yusuf now said that it was not enough to criticize the state's persecution of Muslims. "The blood of a Muslim is expensive," he said. The doctrines of *al-wala' wa-l-bara'* (loyalty to Muslims and disavowal of their enemies) and *izhar al-din* (manifesting one's religion) demanded an aggressive defense of Islam, because Islam's enemies were on the move:

> The believer will not leave his faith. Likewise, the infidel and the hypocrite will not give up his polytheism and his craftiness. Allah Most High has said, "Many of the People of the Book wish to turn you back to unbelief after you have believed" (Qur'an 2:109). . . . Meaning if you don't follow their goals, you cannot be reconciled with them. There's nothing that can allow you to get along with the infidel and the hypocrite unless you become exactly like them.[174]

Yusuf sought to activate Muslims' feelings that different groups—Christians, the state, the West—had humiliated Muslims inside Nigeria and around the world. The conflict he called for would

[173] Yusuf, "Open Letter."
[174] Yusuf, "Open Letter."

be existential and total. In his view, the true Muslims would now confront the *taghut*: the idolatrous, tyrannical secular state.

The Uprising of July 2009

After Yusuf's sermon, he and his followers began planning their uprising, but their unsophisticated planning went awry. Borno's deputy governor Adam Dibal later told journalists that Yusuf had been plotting a bombing campaign to begin in Ramadan, or late August 2009. Boko Haram accelerated its timetable after two mishaps in July: First, authorities discovered a "training camp" in Biu, Borno State,[175] where they arrested nine sect members on July 23 over alleged possession of bomb-making materials.[176] Second, Boko Haram bomb makers accidentally detonated a bomb at a safe house in Maiduguri around July 24.[177]

If some planning went into the uprising, it also revealed a deeply reactive mindset. As one Nigerian commentator wrote afterward, "The decision to choose urban Maiduguri to fight the state is mind boggling. How can any group that has decided to take on the might of the Federal Government of Nigeria decide to converge in a mosque and be sitting ducks to the fire power of the military?"[178] The hasty and sloppy execution of the uprising also casts doubt on the idea that Boko Haram was tightly linked with al-Qa'ida at the time (see chapter 3). Dibal even told the U.S. Embassy after the uprising that Boko Haram at one time had a

---

[175] Tattersall, "Nigerian Sect Planned Bomb Attack during Ramadan."
[176] Sheriff, "My Boko Haram Story."
[177] Tattersall, "Nigerian Sect Planned Bomb Attack during Ramadan."
[178] Kyari Mohammed, "Matters Arising from the *Boko Haram* Crisis," Gamji, likely 2009, http://www.gamji.com/article8000/NEWS8744.htm.

relationship with al-Qaʿida, but that al-Qaʿida had cut off its support "after deciding Yusuf was an unreliable person."[179]

Participants in the uprising expressed determination, framing events in absolutist religious rhetoric. One sect member caught in the July 23 arrests told journalists:

> We thank Allah for bringing us into this condition [arrest]. We were arrested because we made and kept these weapons in our abode to defend ourselves against the enemies of the religion. We want to ensure that Islam is the only religion from here to Spain. We believe in our leader [Muhammad Yusuf] when he told us to prepare all these things [weapons] as tools for defense because some people were coming to attack us. We believe our leader will lead us to heaven.[180]

The rhetoric of self-defense is notable: if the group's statements are to be believed, it viewed the uprising as the inevitable culmination of authorities' crackdowns on the sect, and not as an aggressive action by Yusuf.

Late July's mishaps were swiftly followed by all-out rebellion, which may have been triggered by arrests in Bauchi.[181] Boko Haram members attempted to storm police stations in multiple northeastern cities. On July 26, around seventy Boko Haram members "armed with guns and hand grenades" attacked a police station in Bauchi. Police repulsed them, killing several dozen and arresting an estimated two hundred sect members;

[179] United States Embassy Abuja, leaked cable 09ABUJA2014, "Nigeria: Borno State Residents Not Yet Recovered from Boko Haram Violence," 4 November 2009, https://wikileaks.org/plusd/cables/09ABUJA2014_a.html.

[180] Timothy Ola, "Bomb Blast Kills One in Borno . . . as Police Burst Islamic Sect Offensive," Sun, 26 July 2009, http://www.nairaland.com/301538/bomb-blast-kills-one -borno.

[181] Ibrahim Mshelizza, "Nigerian Islamic Sect Leader Killed in Detention," Reuters, 30 July 2009, http://www.reuters.com/article/us-nigeria-sect-killing-idUSTRE 56T68420090730.

arrests went well beyond just the fighters and extended to the sect's wider membership in the city.[182] In Potiskum, Yobe, a "gun battle raged for hours" around a police station; police arrested twenty-three people. A small clash occurred between Boko Haram and police in Wudil, Kano State.[183] On July 27, severe battles paralyzed Maiduguri. Boko Haram staged "a coordinated late-night assault on the state's police headquarters, police training facilities, Maiduguri prison, and two other police stations."[184] Further battles happened in Gamboru-Ngala in Borno, near the border with Cameroon—a town that would become a flashpoint later. "Heavily armed members of the sect stormed the town and went on the rampage, burning a police headquarters, a church and a customs post in the early hours of [July 27]."[185] The next day, a small contingent of Boko Haram members in Katsina attempted to burn a police station but were rebuffed. Meanwhile, the Third Armoured Division, freshly arrived from Jos, shelled Yusuf's home in Maiduguri's Railway Quarters,[186] where some sect members had "barricaded themselves in and around the house after heavy fighting with security forces."[187]

[182] Ardo Hazzad, "Nigeria Forces Kill 32 after Attack on Police Station," Reuters, 26 July 2009, http://www.reuters.com/article/us-nigeria-riots-idUSTRE56P0MA2009 0726.

[183] David Smith, "Nigerian 'Taliban' Offensive Leaves 150 Dead," Guardian, 27 July 2009, http://www.theguardian.com/world/2009/jul/27/boko-haram-nigeria-attacks.

[184] United States Embassy Abuja, leaked cable 09ABUJA1379, "Nigeria: Extremist Attacks Continue into Night," 28 July 2009, https://wikileaks.org/plusd/cables /09ABUJA1379_a.html.

[185] "Nigeria Toll Hits 65 as Police Battle Islamists," AFP, 27 July 2009, http://www .smh.com.au//breaking-news-world/nigeria-toll-hits-65-as-police-battle-islamists -20090727-dyth.html.

[186] United States Embassy Abuja, leaked cable 09ABUJA1392, "Nigerian Government Quashes Extremists, but Not the Root of the Problem," 29 July 2009, https:// wikileaks.org/plusd/cables/09ABUJA1392_a.html.

[187] "Nigerian Troops Shell Islamists," BBC, 28 July 2009, http://news.bbc.co.uk/2 /hi/africa/8172437.stm.

Once the uprising began, Yusuf discussed it on two levels. On one level, he continued to describe Boko Haram as the victim of state violence, rather than as the aggressor. "We will not agree with this kind of humiliation," he told the journalist Ahmad Salkida on July 26. Such language might have suggested that the crisis could have been resolved if the authorities left Yusuf and his followers alone. But on another level, Yusuf described the conflict as existential and spiritual: "The end of this crisis is, Kafirci [unbelief] and the kind of harassment my people are facing must stop. Democracy and the current system of education must be changed otherwise this war that is yet to start would continue for long."[188]

The bloody denouement of the crisis helped set the stage for more conflict. On July 29, security forces stormed Yusuf's compound in Maiduguri. The security forces did not locate Yusuf until the thirtieth, when he was "found hiding in a goat pen at his parents-in-law's house." Police interrogated Yusuf. Then they shot him dead—either, per the official account, because he tried to escape, or, more likely, because someone in the chain of command had decided that the way to end the Boko Haram crisis was to kill Yusuf.[189] On July 31, police also executed Yusuf's father-in-law, Baba Fugu Muhammad, as well as Buji Foi, who had been Sheriff's commissioner for religious affairs and the alleged conduit between Sheriff and Boko Haram.[190]

The decision to execute Yusuf may have received high-level approval. Years later, Sheriff, attempting to deny that he ever had a political relationship with Yusuf, stated, "I saw late Yusuf

---

[188] Ahmad Salkida, "Sect Leader Vows Revenge," *Daily Trust*, 27 July 2009, http://allafrica.com/stories/200907270879.html.

[189] "Nigeria Sect Head Dies in Custody," BBC, 31 July 2009, http://news.bbc.co.uk/2/hi/8177451.stm.

[190] Human Rights Watch, "Nigeria: Events of 2009," 2010, https://www.hrw.org/world-report/2010/country-chapters/nigeria.

for the very first and last time when he was captured by the Military after the fierce battle they had with the sect in 2009 before he was handed to the Police. As the Chief Security Officer, the Military invited me to see him in their custody."[191] This statement may reveal more than Sheriff intended: if Sheriff saw Yusuf after his capture, Sheriff may well have ordered Yusuf's extrajudicial execution.

The officers who shot Yusuf may have even had the approval of President Yar'Adua. On July 28, as the president was leaving Nigeria for a state visit to Brazil, he told journalists that he was in close touch with governors of the affected northeastern states, as well as with the security services. "I believe that the operation we are launching now," Yar'Adua said, "will be an operation that will contain them once and for all."[192] Reading between the lines, it is easy to imagine that Yar'Adua tacitly or even explicitly blessed the move to kill Yusuf. At the same time, it is possible that officers on the spot acted on their own. One Nigerian I interviewed, a medical professional from Borno, described occasions where he knew police had reacted furiously and violently to the deaths of their colleagues, without higher-level approval; he surmised that the killing of Yusuf was a spontaneous act by officers on the spot.[193]

The 2009 uprising expanded on the 2003–4 uprising around Kanamma and simultaneously prefigured aspects of the coming conflict. As a sequel to Kanamma, the 2009 uprising also concentrated on attacking police stations, although there were other targets as well, including churches. In 2009, the sect's commanders may have believed that with hundreds of fighters, as

[191] Sheriff, "My Boko Haram Story."

[192] Sam Eyoboka, Evelyn Usman, and AbdulSalam Muhammad, "Bauchi Crisis—FG in Control, Yar'Adua Assures," *Vanguard*, 28 July 2009, http://allafrica.com/stories/200907281012.html.

[193] Interview with anonymous medical professional from Borno State, February 2016.

opposed to the dozens they mobilized in 2003, they had a greater chance to overpower the police. In Bauchi, they reportedly failed to break into the armory, their likely goal.[194] Had some of the sect's early attacks in Bauchi and Potiskum succeeded, the uprising would have been even more serious.

As a forerunner of the larger conflict, the 2009 uprising had several notable features. Geographically, its scope foreshadowed Boko Haram's later range of operations: the sect's heart lay in Maiduguri, but it had a formidable presence throughout the northeast, as well as representation elsewhere in the north. Following the uprising, authorities arrested suspected Boko Haram members across the north. The arrestees included thirty-eight people in Abuja,[195] where Boko Haram would later perpetrate major attacks, and five people in Gagi village in the far northwestern state of Sokoto,[196] the hometown of Kabiru Sokoto, a man later accused of plotting Boko Haram's Christmas Day bombings in 2011. Militarily, the 2009 uprising foreshadowed the harsh tactics Nigerian security forces would use in attempting to crush the sect, including extrajudicial executions and mass arrests. In 2009, the Nigerian government believed that such tactics had ended the problem once and for all. They would soon learn otherwise.

Conclusion

Muhammad Yusuf flourished as a preacher between 2001 and 2009. With Maiduguri as his base, he built a mass following

[194] Ogbodo and Kalu, "Why We Hit Bauchi, Borno."

[195] Abdulsalam Mohammed and Patience Ogbodo, "38 Boko Haram Members Arrested in Abuja," *Vanguard*, 1 August 2009, http://www.vanguardngr.com/2009/08/boko-haram-must-not-come-to-kano-dike-warns-security-chiefs/.

[196] Eyoboka, Usman, and Muhammad, "Bauchi Crisis."

and political clout. Yet his partners—the hardliners among his lieutenants, the mainstream Salafis who had shepherded his career, and the Borno politicians who sought his support— placed irreconcilable demands on him. For a time, Yusuf could sustain a balancing act, lying to different groups about his intentions and beliefs.

As mainstream Salafis condemned him and politicians forgot him, Yusuf increasingly made the hardliners' positions his own. He condemned democracy, Western-style education, and secular constitutionalism. By the time his conflict with authorities came to a head in 2009, Yusuf was advocating a confrontational, uncompromising religious activism. Although he was killed and his movement was suppressed after the uprising of July 2009, the final incarnation of his message would become the core doctrine of the resurgent Boko Haram starting in 2010—a movement that now openly aligned itself with jihadism.

3.

"Chaos Is Worse Than Killing"

After the failure of its poorly planned 2009 uprising and the extrajudicial execution of Muhammad Yusuf, the days of Boko Haram's public preaching were over. A new phase began. It was characterized first by clandestine regrouping, and then by terrorism and guerrilla warfare.

This chapter examines Boko Haram's career as a guerrilla movement from 2010 to 2013. This period is one of the murkiest in Boko Haram's history: as the sect exploded back onto the scene, the label "Boko Haram" sometimes outpaced the sect's own actions. Nigerians and outside observers attributed diverse forms of violence and criminality to the sect, even when evidence, or lack thereof, warranted caution. Boko Haram's renewed violence also overlapped with other forms of violence and political tension in Nigeria, particularly inter-religious clashes in Plateau and Kaduna States and the north-south rivalries surrounding the ascension and election of President Goodluck Jonathan.

This chapter argues that Boko Haram's resurgence was marked by the formulation of its doctrine into a wartime ideology. Abubakar Shekau, Yusuf's successor, invoked Yusuf's ideas, adapting them to the movement's new direction. There was strong rhetorical continuity between Yusuf and Shekau, especially given Yusuf's open embrace of jihadism in the final phase of his preaching. Shekau fit Yusuf's death neatly into Boko Haram's presentation of itself as the victim of state violence, rather than as the aggressor.

But there were differences, including a hardening of Boko Haram's exclusivism, a complete abandonment of mainstream politics, and a change in rhetorical style from preaching to propaganda: Shekau distilled Yusuf's exposition of Salafi-jihadist doctrines into simplified slogans appropriate to a conflict that was simultaneously a guerrilla campaign and an information war. Shekau also sought, publicly and behind the scenes, to closely identify Boko Haram with global jihadism, especially with al-Qa'ida. Yet Shekau's headstrong leadership style alienated his potential allies.

The larger environment also facilitated Boko Haram's resurgence. In the aftermath of the 2009 uprising, authorities were overconfident and underprepared. When Boko Haram reemerged, the interaction between repression and terrorism helped to preclude any peaceful solution to the conflict. As repression mounted, Boko Haram's targets widened. The sect moved from settling scores in Borno State into a wider campaign of terrorism, and the sect spoke out more and more on national politics.

Authorities' Early Overconfidence

In August 2009, the dust was settling from Boko Haram's uprising. Yusuf was dead, as were hundreds of his followers. The movement's mosques had been raided or destroyed. Suspected members were arrested throughout the north.

Just days after the repression of the uprising, Boko Haram (or someone claiming to speak for it) promised a fearsome revenge:

> We have started a Jihad in Nigeria which no force on earth can stop. The aim is to Islamise Nigeria and ensure the rule of the

majority Muslims in the country. We will teach Nigeria a lesson, a very bitter one. . . . From the Month of August, we shall carry out series of bombing in Southern and Northern Nigerian cities, beginning with Lagos, Ibadan, Enugu and Port Harcourt. . . . We shall make the country ungovernable, kill and eliminate irresponsible political leaders of all leanings, hunt and gun down those who oppose the rule of Sharia in Nigeria and ensure that the infidel does not go unpunished.[1]

The bombing campaign, however, did not materialize. For a time, the sect lapsed into silence.

Nigerian authorities voiced confidence that by suppressing the 2009 rebellion and executing Yusuf, they had neutralized Boko Haram. When American Embassy staff visited Maiduguri in November 2009, their interlocutors—including Borno politicians and the Shehu of Borno, the region's top hereditary Muslim ruler—"overwhelmingly supported Yusuf's death, and did not appear bothered by the extrajudicial killing."[2] In public, Nigerian authorities gestured toward the possibility of accountability. On August 4, President Umaru Yar'Adua told journalists that he had "directed the [national security advisor] to carry out a post-mortem with the security agencies as a first step so that we can have a full report of what happened during the crisis, including how the leader of Boko Haram was killed."[3] But Muhammad Yusuf's killers would be identi-

[1] "Boko Haram Resurrects, Declares Total Jihad," *Vanguard*, August 14, 2009, http://www.vanguardngr.com/2009/08/boko-haram-ressurects-declares-total-jihad/.

[2] United States Embassy Abuja, leaked cable, "Nigeria: Borno State Residents Not Yet Recovered from Boko Haram Violence," November 4, 2009, https://wikileaks.org/plusd/cables/09ABUJA2014_a.html; accessed November 2015.

[3] Emma Ujah, Emeka Mamah, Kingsley Omonobi, Chioma Obinna, and Daniel Idonor, "Yar'Adua Orders Probe of Boko Haram Leaders' Killing," *Vanguard*, August 4, 2009, http://www.vanguardngr.com/2009/08/yaradua-orders-probe-of-boko-haram-leaders-killing/; accessed November 2015.

fied and prosecuted only years later, and even then the charges were eventually dropped (see chapter 4). The contrast between Yar'Adua's words and authorities' actions suggested behind-the-scenes complacency. National and local leaders concluded that the problem of Boko Haram had been solved.

Authorities made halfhearted efforts at institutional change that would prevent any similar organization from arising in the future. On August 3, Borno State governor Ali Modu Sheriff convened a meeting of Muslim leaders. He announced that his government would assemble a "preaching board . . . to ascertain that only qualified and reliable clerics would be allowed to preach in mosques and in other places." Yusuf, Sheriff said, had taken advantage of "laxity" to "foment trouble."[4] This framing, of course, obscured questions about Sheriff's relationship with Boko Haram's founder. In practice, the Borno State authorities had little will or power to regulate preaching; as of October 2009, the preaching board was yet to be inaugurated.[5] It was not until May 2010 that Boko Haram was formally banned by Sheriff's executive order.[6]

It is easy to see why authorities were lulled into overconfidence after Yusuf's death. As discussed in chapter 1, in other instances of religious violence, Nigerian authorities' playbook had been to suppress the violence, round up suspected troublemakers, and then attempt to move on. This pattern characterized responses to Maitatsine and to intercommunal clashes in Kafanchan, Zangon-Kataf, Jos, and elsewhere. The pattern had been used as recently as February 2009. When Bauchi State

[4] Nick Tattersall and Ibrahim Mshelizza, "Nigeria to Vet Clerics More Closely after Uprising," Reuters, August 3, 2009, http://af.reuters.com/article/topNews/id AFJOE5720LK20090803?sp=true; accessed November 2015.

[5] U.S. Embassy Abuja, "Nigeria: Borno State Residents."

[6] Sheriff, "My Boko Haram Story."

experienced Muslim-Christian clashes, authorities deployed soldiers and imposed a "dusk-to-dawn curfew" in affected neighborhoods. These measures, the governor's spokesman announced, were meant to ensure "a quick return of normalcy in the city."[7] The playbook often worked, at least temporarily.

After Yusuf's death, authorities in the northeast used similar language. Borno's Deputy Governor Adamu Dibal told journalists, "The entire story was Mohammed Yusuf, Mohammed Yusuf, Mohammed Yusuf. . . . Without this kingpin . . . it will be difficult for them to regroup."[8] Major Muslim scholars were comfortable with the authorities' decisions. In a February 2010 interview with Al Jazeera, the senior Tijani Sufi Shaykh Ibrahim Salih displayed a masterful understanding of Boko Haram's worldview and motivations, an understanding that might have given him pause about the efficacy of heavy-handed repression, but he refrained from criticizing the authorities. In the same interview, Salih also spoke approvingly of the use of force against violent dissident sects: Nigerians, he said, had come to feel that "nothing works with them except violence: dealing with them with reason avails nothing, because their affair is not based on reason; dealing with them gently, nicely, and mercifully also avails nothing, and is not appropriate."[9] Even Salafi leaders, such as the national chair-

[7] "Curfew in Nigerian City after Deadly Clashes," AFP, 22 February 2009, http://reliefweb.int/report/nigeria/curfew-nigerian-city-after-deadly-clashes.

[8] Nick Tattersall, "Nigeria Sect Planned Bomb Attack during Ramadan," Reuters, 4 August 2009, http://www.reuters.com/article/ozatp-nigeria-sect-bombing-id AFJOE57308Z20090804.

[9] "Ibrahim al-Husayni . . . Qatl Ittiba' Boko Haram," Al Jazeera, 18 February 2010, http://www.aljazeera.net/programs/today-interview/2010/2/18/%D8%A5%D8%A8%D8%B1%D8%A7%D9%87%D9%8A%D9%85-%D8%A7%D9%84%D8%AD%D8%B3%D9%8A%D9%86%D9%8A-%D9%82%D8%AA%D9%84-%D8%A3%D8%AA%D8%A8%D8%A7%D8%B9-%D8%A8%D9%88%D9%83%D9%88-%D8%AD%D8%B1%D8%A7%D9%85.

man of Izala's Council of Ulama (scholars), Sani Yahaya Jingir, stated that Yusuf's death was a positive development.[10]

There was some criticism of the authorities' handling of the situation, but it came mostly from middle-tier religious figures and public intellectuals. In Maiduguri, Imam Ibrahim Ahmad Abdullahi denounced the authorities for their failure to prevent the escalation of the crisis. Numerous Muslim scholars, Abdullahi told the Associated Press in August 2009, "tried to draw the attention of the government to what these people are calling for. But I don't know what is their reason is for not taking any necessary action about it, and what happened, has happened."[11]

A few Muslim intellectuals raised pointed questions about the response to Boko Haram not just by the authorities, but also by the Muslim establishment in the north, including Sufis and Izala. One harsh critique came from Kyari Mohammed of the Federal University of Technology in Adamawa State, which borders Borno. Mohammed argued, damningly and persuasively, that the uprising had revealed the gap between the 'ulama and ordinary northern Muslims. Mohammed portrayed the Muslim establishment as deeply self-interested. The establishment, Mohamed suggested, was unwilling to ask probing questions about how Boko Haram's teachings spread, and how its followers might have been reintegrated into mainstream society without bloodshed:

[10] Y'au Waziri, "Killing of Boko Haram Leader in Order—Islamic Cleric," *Leadership*, 16 August 2009, http://allafrica.com/stories/200908170389.html. See also Aliyu Tilde, "Muslims and Rule of Law in Nigeria," Gamji, likely 2009, http://www.gamji.com/tilde/tilde101.htm.

[11] "Muslim Clerics Say Authorities Ignored Warnings about Islamist Sect," Associated Press, 1 August 2009, http://www.aparchive.com/metadata/youtube/d8ef350bcd7c6fe4612062f9a30741b5.

For watching in silence we are all culpable for this avoidable carnage and mass murder. However the ulama, traditional rulers and politicians are the main accomplices. . . . The Jama'atul Nasril Islam [JNI, an elite pan-Islamic organization in Nigeria] and the Izalatul Bidi'ah wa Ikamatis Sunnah [Izala] were especially quick in condemning them and preparing them for extermination. If indeed their position is "devilish" as the JNI advertorial signed by no less a person than the Sultan of Sokoto suggests what attempts were made to reintegrate them into "mainstream" Islam. If the leadership of Boko Haram knew what they were doing, what about those who were brain-washed? A sane society would have saved and rehabilitated the victims rather lumping them all for extermination.

For Mohammed, the collusion of state authorities and 'ulama, as well as their resistance to examining the uprising's root causes, set the stage for more violence:

The next Boko Haram like uprising is a matter of when and where, and not if. . . . In swiftly dispatching Mohammed Yusuf, the state only succeeded in killing the public face of the Boko Haram movement. Thus rather than dealing with a known figure with fixed address in Mohammed Yusuf, the state has now pushed the sect underground and martyred its leadership with deleterious consequences for national security.[12]

Such predictions would prove more accurate than the authorities' conclusion that by killing Yusuf, they had effectively destroyed Boko Haram.

---

[12] Kyari Mohammed, "Matters Arising from the Boko Haram Crisis," Gamji, likely 2009, http://www.gamji.com/article8000/NEWS8744.htm.

Echoes of the 2009 Crisis

Despite the relative calm on the security front, the 2009 crisis continued to reverberate in the Nigerian and international media. In February 2010, Al Jazeera published footage that showed Nigerian security forces shooting unarmed detainees and civilians during the uprising.[13] Also in circulation was video of policemen's final interrogation of Muhammad Yusuf, which depicted the leader shirtless and wounded, but still defiant.[14] Although human rights organizations had previously been aware of the extrajudicial killings, Al Jazeera's release of the execution videos gave new weight to these organizations' accusations against the Nigerian security services. The videos sparked controversy in Borno, with the state government continuing to defend the crackdown.[15]

Another echo of the 2009 crisis was heard in court. In April 2010, a Borno State high court ruled in favor of the family of Baba Fugu Muhammad, Muhammad Yusuf's father-in-law, who had been killed by police. The judge ordered the Nigerian government to pay the family 100 million naira (approximately $667,000) in damages.[16] The presiding judge wrote unambiguously that "the extra judicial murder of the applicant's father Alhaji Baba Fugu Muhammad, by the respondents is illegal, unconstitutional and a violation of right to life as enshrined

[13] "Nigeria Killings Caught on Video," Al Jazeera, 10 February 2010, http://www.aljazeera.com/news/africa/2010/02/20102102505798741.html.

[14] The video is online at https://www.youtube.com/watch?v=ePpUvfTXY7w.

[15] Abdulkareem Haruna, "Tension in Borno over Al-Jazeera Boko Haram Video," *Daily Independent*, 13 February 2010, http://allafrica.com/stories/201002151259.html.

[16] "Nigeria Police Found Guilty in Borno Sect Clashes Case," BBC, 14 April 2010, http://news.bbc.co.uk/2/hi/africa/8620859.stm; Camilius Eboh and Randy Fabi, "Nigeria Police to Appeal Ruling in Borno Clashes Case," Reuters, 15 April 2010, http://uk.reuters.com/article/idUKLDE63E1QA.

in the constitution of the Federal Republic of Nigeria, the African charter and the universal declaration of human rights."[17] In the legal sphere as well as in the court of public opinion, a majority view was taking shape: the security services had been merciless in their response to the 2009 uprising. Many Nigerians, Muslims and Christians alike, remained comfortable with that decision. But some Muslims may have felt some sympathy toward Yusuf and his followers. The partial freedom of operation that Boko Haram would soon enjoy in Maiduguri indicated that the movement had a robust network of helpers and passive supporters, some of whom may have initially viewed Boko Haram's remnants as heroes and victims.

Efforts at accountability by the Yar'Adua administration were perfunctory, in part because the president was sick. In November 2009, Yar'Adua was flown to Saudi Arabia for medical treatment. He remained incapacitated or even comatose for the remainder of his life. As his absence dragged on, anxious political debates occurred. In February 2010, the Senate formally designated Vice President Goodluck Jonathan as acting president. In response, Yar'Adua's family and close associates arranged for the president's return to Nigeria that month, although virtually everyone outside his inner circle was still denied access to him. The crisis of authority lasted until May 2010, when Yar'Adua died and Jonathan became the undisputed president of Nigeria. Had Yar'Adua been functional in late 2009 and early 2010, it is still unlikely that his government would have sought robust accountability for the extrajudicial executions of Yusuf, Baba Fugu Muhammad,

---

[17] High Court No. 3, Maiduguri, Borno State, judgment in the case of Baba Kura Alh. Fugu vs. the President of the Federal Republic of Nigeria, the Executive Governor of Borno State, the Attorney General of the Federation, the Attorney General of Borno State, and the Inspector General of Police, 13 April 2010, https://www.hrw.org/sites/default/files/related_material/Borno%20State%20High%20Court%20Order%20-%20April%2013,%202010.pdf.

Buji Foi, and others. Given the national political crisis during this time, such accountability became not only unlikely but also virtually inconceivable.

An unrelated terrorism scare may have reinforced Nigerian authorities' feeling that they had to be tougher on jihadists: on Christmas Day 2009, a Nigerian national, Umar Farouk Abdulmutallab (b. 1986), attempted to detonate a bomb on an inbound flight to Detroit, Michigan. Abdulmutallab was restrained by other passengers and was arrested upon landing; he would be sentenced to life imprisonment in the United States in February 2012.[18] Abdulmutallab, the disaffected son of a northern Nigerian banker, was trained by al-Qa'ida's affiliate in Yemen, rather than by Boko Haram, and he had been radicalized primarily in England and Yemen, rather than solely in Nigeria.[19] Yet the incident reinforced international perceptions of Nigeria as a hotbed of terrorism.

Nigerian officials were keen to dispel negative images of their country and end the special measures. They appealed to the United States to remove Nigeria from a list of countries whose citizens faced extra screening in air travel.[20] Nigerian authorities seemed to conclude from the incident that the way

[18] United States Department of Justice, "Umar Farouk Abdulmutallab Sentenced to Life in Prison for Attempted Bombing of Flight 253 on Christmas Day 2009," 16 February 2012, http://www.justice.gov/opa/pr/umar-farouk-abdulmutallab-sen tenced-life-prison-attempted-bombing-flight-253-christmas-day.

[19] Richard Norton-Taylor and Robert Booth, "Bomber Linked to London Extremists but Radicalised in Yemen, Officials Say," *Guardian*, 30 December 2009, http://www.theguardian.com/world/2009/dec/30/detroit-plane-bomber-yemen -radicalisation; and Peter Finn, "Al-Awlaki Directed Christmas 'Underwear Bomber' Plot, Justice Department Memo Says," *Washington Post*, 10 February 2012, https:// www.washingtonpost.com/world/national-security/al-awlaki-directed-christmas -underwear-bomber-plot-justice-department-memo-says/2012/02/10/gIQArDO t4Q_story.html.

[20] "Nigeria Makes Airport Security Checks Appeal to US," BBC, 6 January 2010, http://news.bbc.co.uk/2/hi/africa/8443333.stm.

to earn international trust on security issues was to be even tougher on jihadism at home.

Had Yar'Adua and Jonathan identified and prosecuted the killers of Muhammad Yusuf, Boko Haram would likely have resurged anyway: the sect's leaders had already gone very far down the path of rejecting the Nigerian state's existence and legitimacy. Yet such measures might have reduced the sect's ability to recruit. More serious introspection on the part of Nigerian authorities about their approach to insecurity might have yielded a different approach to the next incarnation of Boko Haram. More introspection on the part of Muslim religious leaders might have better prepared them to rebut the propaganda that Boko Haram would soon begin to disseminate. As it was, when the group began its campaign of violence in 2010, authorities responded primarily with repression—a blunt tool that failed to halt the sect's momentum.

Boko Haram's Return

On the night of September 7, 2010, Boko Haram attacked the central prison in the northeastern city of Bauchi and freed an estimated 721 inmates, many of them suspected members of the sect.[21] The attack previewed patterns to come: daring surprise attacks by Boko Haram, slow responses by the security forces, and bewilderment and fear among civilian survivors. The prison break also marked a turning point for Boko Haram's fortunes. In the months after the raid, likely because of its replenished ranks, the sect carried out numerous attacks. While not as systematic as the (future) Islamic State's "Break-

---

[21] Adam Nossiter, "Prison Raid in Nigeria Releases Hundreds," *New York Times*, 8 September 2010, http://www.nytimes.com/2010/09/09/world/africa/09nigeria.html ?_r=0.

ing the Walls" campaign of 2012–13, a yearlong effort that involved eight prison breaks,[22] Boko Haram's Bauchi raid was part of the sect's structured reorganization into a jihadist, guerrilla force.

Boko Haram's initial violence in 2010–11 was local to the northeast. The group focused on assassinating enemies and attacking sites of perceived public immorality.[23] From July 2010 through the election of April 2011, Boko Haram assassinated three major categories of persons: members of the security services, Borno State politicians from the ruling All Nigeria People's Party (ANPP), and Muslim religious leaders who had publicly denounced the sect.

Assassinations were typically carried out by teams of gunmen riding motorbikes. The problem quickly became so severe that by September 2010, Borno State authorities were restricting the use of motorbikes at night.[24] Killings of policemen—and perhaps police informants as well—began over the summer of 2010, especially in the Bulumkutu, Bulabulin, and Gomari neighborhoods of Maiduguri. These were, notably, some of the neighborhoods discussed in chapter 1 as ethnically mixed, impoverished, poorly serviced, and less beholden to the Shehu and the local authorities than the city's core Kanuri neighborhoods. The pattern of violence suggests

[22] Jessica Lewis, "Al-Qaeda in Iraq Resurgent: The Breaking the Walls Campaign, Part I," Institute for the Study of War, Middle East Report 14, September 2013, http://www.understandingwar.org/sites/default/files/AQI-Resurgent-10Sept_0.pdf.

[23] Detailed timelines of Boko Haram's violence during this period can be found at "Timeline of Boko Haram Attacks and Related Violence," IRIN, 20 January 2012, http://allafrica.com/stories/201101310880.html; Freedom Onuoha, "The Audacity of the Boko Haram: Background, Analysis and Emerging Trend," *Security Journal* 25 (2012): 134–51; and Ioannis Mantzikos, "Boko Haram Attacks in Nigeria and Neighbouring Countries: A Chronology of Attacks," *Perspectives on Terrorism* 8:6 (2014), http://www.terrorismanalysts.com/pt/index.php/pot/article/view/391/html.

[24] Ndahi Marama, "Mysterious Deaths: Borno Restricts Okada Movement," *Vanguard*, 8 September 2010, http://www.vanguardngr.com/2010/09/mysterious-deaths -borno-restricts-okada-movement/.

that Boko Haram had a significant presence in the city, with well-developed networks of informers. Assassinated at their homes, at their posts, or near mosques, the victims were often known to the perpetrators.[25]

The assassinations focused on settling local scores in Borno. Boko Haram killed members of the security services because they had repressed the sect. It killed ANPP politicians because they were close to Governor Sheriff, the sect's onetime political partner who had now become its bitter enemy. The political assassinations claimed the lives of Sheriff's brother-in-law, Awana Ali Ngala, who was also a Borno ANPP state chairman;[26] Sheriff's cousin, Fanami Gubio, who was the ANPP's original gubernatorial candidate for 2011; and Sheriff's younger brother, Goni Sheriff, who died alongside Gubio.[27] Sheriff's political ally Goni Ali Modu, who was also Borno's Speaker of the Assembly, was unsuccessfully targeted in October 2010.[28] Sheriff's close friend and political ally Mustapha Flawama would be shot later, in October 2012.[29] The anti-Sheriff nature of the violence was clear.

With the religious assassinations—which killed at least six shaykhs in Maiduguri and Biu, Borno, between October 2010

[25] "Rising Fear in Borno over Mysterious Killings," *Weekly Trust*, 4 September 2010, http://www.thenigerianvoice.com/news/33698/1/rising-fear-in-borno-over-mysterious-killings.html. See also "Boko Haram: Summary of Killings," *Weekly Trust*, 16 October 2010, http://www.gbooza.com/group/crime/forum/topics/boko-haram-summary-of-killings.

[26] "Boko Haram Militants Strikes [*sic*] at the Heart of Borno Political Elite," *Sahara Reporters*, 7 October 2010, http://saharareporters.com/2010/10/07/boko-haram-militants-strikes-heart-borno-political-elite.

[27] Dauda Mbaya and Stanley Nkwocha, "Guber Candidate, 6 Others Killed," *Leadership*, 29 January 2011, http://allafrica.com/stories/201101310880.html.

[28] "Boko Haram Militants Strikes [*sic*] at the Heart of Borno Political Elite."

[29] Hamza Idris and Ronald Mutum, "Boko Haram—Sheriff under Watch, IG says," *Daily Trust*, 1 November 2012, http://allafrica.com/stories/201211010253.html.

and September 2011,[30] and wounded another[31]—Boko Haram targeted those who had directly criticized it, including Salafis. Here again it is worth underscoring the intensely personal nature of these assassinations. Boko Haram knew who its political and religious enemies were, where they lived, and why it wanted them dead. Religious rivals were seen as possible threats to Boko Haram's religious credibility, and as possible informants for the security and intelligence services.

Alongside the targeted killings of individuals in Borno, Boko Haram began attacking Christian churches and public "immoral" spaces in the north such as bars. As noted in chapters 1 and 2, northern Nigeria's history of interreligious clashes from the 1980s to the 2000s left a deep mark on the worldview and rhetoric of Muhammad Yusuf and Abubakar Shekau. As Boko Haram turned to terrorism, the sect sought not just to present itself as a victim of Christian aggression, but also to enflame Muslim-Christian tensions across Nigeria. The sect sought to generate new violence in older flashpoints, such as Plateau State, Kaduna State, and the Federal Capital Territory. Here attributing responsibility became murky: the rising specter of Boko Haram seemed to license some opportunistic criminality and intercommunal killings. On some occasions,

[30] "Nigerian Islamists Kill Cleric," AFP, 9 October 2010, http://www.nation.co.ke /news/africa/Nigerian-islamists-kill-cleric-/-/1066/1029434/-/view/printVersion /-/47p9lz/-/index.html; Njadvara Musa, "Nonviolent Muslim Cleric Killed in Nigeria," Associated Press, 13 March 2011, http://www.washingtonpost.com/wp-dyn/content /article/2011/03/13/AR2011031302923.html; Shehu Sani, "Boko Haram: History, Ideas, and Revolt (6)," *Vanguard*, 8 July 2011, http://www.vanguardngr.com/2011/07 /boko-haram-history-ideas-and-revolt-6/; "'Boko Haram' Gunmen Kill Nigerian Muslim Cleric Birkuti," BBC News, 7 June 2011, http://www.bbc.co.uk/news/world -africa-13679234; and "Islamic Cleric Shot Dead by Gunmen in Nigeria's NE," Associated Press, 5 September 2011, http://news.yahoo.com/islamic-cleric-shot-dead -gunmen-nigerias-ne-140609590.html.

[31] "Cleric Survives Boko Haram's Attack in Maiduguri," *Sahara Reporters*, 5 June 2011, http://saharareporters.com/2011/06/05/cleric-survives-boko-harams-attack-maiduguri.

Boko Haram's spokesmen seemed only too happy to take credit even for attacks the sect may not have orchestrated.

Two major waves of attacks occurred around the Christmases of 2010 and 2011. On Christmas Eve 2010, two churches in Maiduguri were attacked, and at least four bombs exploded in Jos, Plateau State,[32] targeting taverns and other sites.[33] Boko Haram claimed responsibility with an online statement, asserting that the group had begun "avenging the atrocities committed against Muslims in [Jos and Maiduguri], and the country in general."[34] Christmas 2011 saw another round of bombings targeting churches and other sites in Madalla, Niger State (near Abuja); Jos; and the towns of Damaturu and Gadaka, Yobe.[35] Other church attacks occurred in the north, along with attacks on bars and other places where Christians might gather.

As the violence dragged into 2012, the church bombings blended into Boko Haram's widening campaign of violence against civilians. This violence fueled a generalized atmosphere of panic in parts of the north. The church attacks did not spark the inter-religious war that Boko Haram desired, but some bombings did provoke waves of reprisals. For example,

[32] "Radical Islamist Sect Says It Carried Out Nigeria Church Attacks," Associated Press, 28 December 2010, http://www.theguardian.com/world/2010/dec/28/islamist-sect-responsibility-nigeria-attacks.

[33] For two accounts written by residents of Jos, see "The Dark Christmas of 2010: Bomb Blast at Angwan Rukuba and Gada Biyu," Musings of a Lost Soul, 30 December 2010, http://jinni-musingsofalostsoul.blogspot.com/2010/12/normal-0-false-false-false.html; and Carmen McCain, "Christmas Eve Bombing, Jos, Nigeria, 24 December 2010," A Tunanina, 26 December 2010, http://carmenmccain.com/2010/12/26/christmas-eve-bombing-jos-nigeria-24-december-2010/.

[34] The original website is now defunct, but the text's statement has been preserved at the Orange Tracker, http://theorangetracker.blogspot.com/2010/12/nigeria-christmas-bombings.html.

[35] "Nigeria Churches Hit by Blasts during Christmas Prayers," BBC, 25 December 2011, http://www.bbc.com/news/world-africa-16328940.

after three back-to-back blasts in Kaduna State in June 2012, Christians and Muslims clashed there. When Christians targeted mosques, Muslims responded by destroying at least one church.[36] Meanwhile, Boko Haram's rhetoric against Christianity sharpened even further. The year 2012 opened with Boko Haram demanding that all Christians leave the north.[37] After one bombing in Plateau, Boko Haram's spokesman told journalists, "Before, Christians were killing Muslims, helped by the government, so we have decided that we will continue to hunt down government agents wherever they are."[38] Such statements reflected the sect's increasing turn toward propagandistic slogans, rather than systematic exposition of doctrine.

With its assassinations and church bombings, Boko Haram initially minimized casualties among Muslim bystanders. But even by spring 2011, the group's attacks became more indiscriminate. The sect began bombing police and military targets in Maiduguri and beyond, killing more bystanders than ever before and profoundly disrupting life in Maiduguri. This change mirrored a change in the group's worldview and capabilities: as it became a more hardened guerrilla force and a more outspoken champion of hardline religious exclusivism, its willingness to cause "collateral damage" increased. By 2014, as chapter 4 discusses, Muslim civilians would themselves become a primary target of Boko Haram's violence.

[36] Alex Thurston, "Nigeria: Kaduna Bombings and Their Aftermath," Sahel Blog, 19 June 2012, https://sahelblog.wordpress.com/2012/06/19/nigeria-kaduna-bombings -and-their-aftermath/.

[37] Tim Lister, "Islamists Militants in Nigeria Warn Christians to Leave North within 3 Days," CNN, 2 January 2012, http://www.cnn.com/2012/01/02/world/africa /nigeria-sectarian-divisions/index.html.

[38] Buhari Bello, "Nigeria's Boko Haram Claims Deadly Plateau Attacks," Reuters, 10 July 2012, http://www.reuters.com/article/2012/07/10/us-nigeria-bokoharam-id USBRE8690N020120710.

Targeting Abuja

Boko Haram's attention began turning to the national stage in the spring of 2011. Some observers have speculated that Boko Haram sought to enflame north-south tensions that centered on control of the presidency, but the picture was more complicated than that. Before dealing with this complexity, it is worth reviewing the period's presidential politics.

In April 2011, Goodluck Jonathan, who had inherited the presidency upon the death of Umaru Yar'Adua in May 2010, won reelection. By winning a full term in office, Jonathan disrupted the ruling People's Democratic Party (PDP)'s internal agreement to rotate the presidency between northern and southern Nigeria every eight years—Olusegun Obasanjo, a southerner, served from 1999 to 2007, and Yar'Adua had intended to fill the northern slot from 2007 to 2015. With the rotational system unraveling, the announcement of Jonathan's 2011 victory provoked riots in several northern cities. The riots became sprees of violence against perceived PDP supporters, Christians, and others seen as outsiders,[39] echoing a history of such pogroms dating to the 1950s.

Some Nigerian conspiracy theorists have charged that dissatisfied northern elites sponsored Boko Haram in order to make the north ungovernable and derail Jonathan's presidency. The truth is likely simpler: as it gained strength in 2011, and as it faced crackdowns by the military, Boko Haram's anger toward the federal government increased along with its capacity to strike. Boko Haram did not parlay northern dissatisfaction with Jonathan into broad-based recruitment. And if

---

[39] Human Rights Watch, "Nigeria: Post-election Violence Killed 800," 16 May 2011, https://www.hrw.org/news/2011/05/16/nigeria-post-election-violence-killed-800.

Boko Haram nursed personal grievances against Jonathan, it was not because they wanted a Muslim president—after all, they rejected the entire constitutional system. Rather, Boko Haram's increasing anger against Jonathan was due to the escalating military campaign in the northeast, which involved the deployment of the Nigerian military's Joint Task Force in 2011.

Boko Haram signaled its widening range of targets by conducting two suicide bombings in Abuja in summer 2011, striking the National Police Force headquarters in June and the United Nations building in August. By late 2011, Boko Haram was committing ambitious attacks on major cities beyond Maiduguri. On November 4, Boko Haram inflicted its "highest death toll in a single day" since the 2009 uprising: the sect launched attacks in Maiduguri and Potiskum. Later that day, fighters killed over one hundred people in Damaturu, Yobe, in combined attacks on "the police state headquarters . . . as well as police housing, government buildings, banks, and at least six churches."[40] Even more spectacularly, Boko Haram exploded back into the city of Kano in January 2012, causing nearly two hundred casualties in a set of coordinated shootings and bombings.

In this atmosphere, Jonathan had to acknowledge and discuss Boko Haram's violence. Abubakar Shekau sought to make himself a debate partner to the president. Shekau increasingly mentioned Jonathan by name, fixating on the president as a symbol of what the sect opposed. After Jonathan called Boko Haram a "cancer" in a December 2011 speech in Madalla,[41] where

---

[40] Human Rights Watch, "Nigeria: Boko Haram Attacks Indefensible," 8 November 2011, https://www.hrw.org/news/2011/11/08/nigeria-boko-haram-attacks-indefensible.

[41] "Nigeria: Boko Haram est un "cancer", estime le président Goodluck Jonathan," *Jeune Afrique*, 31 December 2011, http://www.jeuneafrique.com/153015/politique/nigeria-boko-haram-est-un-cancer-estime-le-pr-sident-goodluck-jonathan/.

Boko Haram had bombed a church, Shekau responded in a video entitled "Message to President Jonathan:

> We are not a cancer. . . . The disease is unbelief, and as Allah says, "Chaos is worse than killing" (Qur'an 2:191). . . . Everyone knows democracy is unbelief, and everyone knows the Constitution is unbelief, and everyone knows that there are things Allah has forbidden in the Qur'an, and that are forbidden in countless hadiths of the Prophet, that are going on in Western schools. . . . We ourselves haven't forbidden anything, we haven't told the Muslim community to abandon anything, we simply stand on the path of truth.[42]

With such messages, Shekau sought to control the conversation about what Nigeria would be as a state and a society.

Boko Haram's strikes in Abuja in 2011, however, were more attention grabbing than its later attacks there. As chapter 4 discusses, Boko Haram's own attention would later become largely consumed by events in its own home territory, the northeast. What appeared to be a fearsome geographical expansion in 2011, then, would soon lose some of its momentum.

Ties to al-Qa'ida?

In 2011, as Boko Haram's violence and ambitions escalated, new questions surfaced about the group's capabilities and origins. How did Boko Haram become so deadly? Many analysts have surmised that Boko Haram's capacities grew dramatically around 2011–13 because it was making contact with branches of al-Qa'ida. To assess such claims, I examine three questions:

---

[42] Abubakar Shekau, "Message to President Jonathan," January 2012, https://www .youtube.com/watch?v=umkj50SUzck.

What kinds of contact occurred? What resulted from those contacts? And were al-Qaʿida and its affiliates successful in influencing Boko Haram's leadership, in particular Abubakar Shekau?

The early Boko Haram likely had limited contact with al-Qaʿida's core leadership in Afghanistan and Pakistan. Recall that in 2009, Borno State authorities privately stated that Muhammad Yusuf had received some early funding from Usama bin Laden, who had publicly called for jihad in Nigeria in audio recordings in 2000 and 2002. Borno authorities, however, also stated that such funding had ceased well before 2009, because al-Qaʿida found Yusuf "unreliable" (see chapter 2). For its part, the International Crisis Group reports that bin Laden gave around $3 million to Muhammad Ali, one of the radicals around Yusuf in the early 2000s and a leader in the Kanamma uprising of 2003–4. Bin Laden and Ali may have met in Sudan, where the former lived from 1992 to 1996 and where the latter was a student. Ali allegedly distributed most of this money to Boko Haram and Yusuf in 2002.[43] International Crisis Group's account is compatible with that of the Borno authorities—al-Qaʿida might have provided some early funding and then backed away from Boko Haram, before or after the Kanamma debacle.

A different account comes from the leader of the breakaway Boko Haram faction Ansar al-Muslimin (see below). In a 2017 article, Abu Usamatul Ansary asserted that at some unspecified time, likely in the late 1990s or early 2000s, a mentor to Muhammad Ali received "help and funding from members of al-Qaʾidah residing in the Arabian Peninsula." This mentor, however, allegedly abandoned jihadism, and Ansary wrote

[43] International Crisis Group, "Curbing Violence in Nigeria (II): The Boko Haram Insurgency," 3 April 2014, 23, http://www.crisisgroup.org/~/media/Files/africa/west-africa/nigeria/216-curbing-violence-in-nigeria-ii-the-boko-haram-insurgency.pdf.

that "it is extremely regrettable that such financial support fell into the hands of people who were opposed to Mujahidin." This account implies that al-Qaʿida's money never even reached Ali, let alone Yusuf.[44]

Another avenue of contact between al-Qaʿida and the early Boko Haram was a Nigerien national, Ibrahim Harun, who reportedly trained and fought alongside al-Qaʿida in Afghanistan and Pakistan between 2001 and 2003. Returning to West Africa in 2003, Harun then allegedly made contact with Boko Haram and attempted to plan terrorist attacks in Nigeria. Harun's plans failed spectacularly, however; an associate attempting to communicate with al-Qaʿida was arrested in Pakistan in 2004, and when Harun fled Nigeria he was arrested in Libya in 2005.[45]

During Yusuf's lifetime, contacts also occurred between al-Qaʿida's North African affiliate and people in Boko Haram's orbit. The affiliate, known as al-Qaʿida in the Islamic Maghreb (AQIM), merged with al-Qaʿida in 2006 and adopted its present name in 2007. Prior to that time, it was known as the Salafi Group for Preaching and Combat (best known by its French acronym GSPC). The GSPC was a splinter group of the main jihadist faction in Algeria's 1991–2002 civil war. The GSPC's founders formed their group to distance themselves from the heavy civilian casualties inflicted by the group's predecessor.

---

[44] Abu Usamatul Ansary, "A Message from Nigeria," *Al Risalah* 4 (January 2017): 18–21; 19.

[45] United States District Court, Eastern District of New York, "United States of America against Ibrahim Suleiman Adnan Adam Harun: Government's Memorandum of Law in Support of Motion for an Anonymous and Partly Sequestered Jury," 8 April 2016, http://www.courthousenews.com/wp-content/uploads/2017/02/Harun.pdf. For a maximalist interpretation of the significance of these contacts, see Jacob Zenn, "Before Boko Haram: A Profile of al-Qaeda's West Africa Chief Ibrahim Harun (a.k.a. Spinghul)," *Jamestown Militant Leadership Monitor*, March 2017.

After Algeria's civil war wound down, the GSPC had limited prospects for overthrowing the Algerian state. The group began to kidnap Europeans and attack military outposts in the Sahara. At some point prior to 2009, at least three Nigerian followers of Muhammad Ali lived with one of GSPC/AQIM's Saharan battalions, Tariq ibn Ziyad, named for an early Arab conqueror of North Africa and led by Algerian national Abd al-Hamid Abu Zayd (1965–2013).[46] These Nigerians, and others with jihadist connections, later pledged allegiance to Muhammad Yusuf.[47]

These three Nigerians were involved in Boko Haram's uprising in 2009. In late August 2009, just weeks after the failure of Boko Haram's mass uprising, Abu Zayd conveyed a message from Shekau to AQIM's overall emir, Abd al-Malik Droukdel. The three Nigerian jihadists—named as Abu Muhammad Amir al-Masir, Khalid al-Barnawi, and Abu Rihana (or perhaps Rayhana)—approached Abu Zayd after the failure of the uprising. Speaking on behalf of Shekau, they asked for a relationship between Boko Haram and AQIM. Specifically, they asked for regular communications (through phone, Internet, and an intermediary to be placed in Niger); weapons; money;

[46] Letter from Abd al-Hamid Abu Zayd to Abd al-Malik Droukdel, 24 August 2009, recovered at Usama bin Ladin's compound in Abbottabad, Pakistan, and released by the U.S. Office of the Director of National Intelligence on 19 January 2017, https://www.dni.gov/files/documents/ubl2017/arabic/Letter%20from%20Abdallah%20Abu%20Zayd%20%E2%80%98Abd-al-Hamid%20to%20Abu%20Mus%E2%80%99ab%20%E2%80%98Abd-al-Wadud%20(Arabic).pdf. A somewhat flawed English translation is available at https://www.dni.gov/files/documents/ubl2017/english/Letter%20from%20Abdallah%20Abu%20Zayd%20Abd-al-Hamid%20to%20Abu%20Mus%20ab%20Abd-al-Wadud.pdf. See also Ansary, "Message from Nigeria," 19.

[47] Letter from Abu Muhammad al-Hawsawi et al. to Abu al-Hasan al-Rashid al-Bulaydi, 2011, reproduced in Nasa'ih wa-Tawjihat Shar'iyya min al-Shaykh Abi al-Hasan Rashid li-Mujahidi Nayjiriya, edited by Abu al-Nu'man Qutayba al-Shinqiti (Mu'assasat al-Andalus, April 2017), 15, https://azelin.files.wordpress.com/2017/04/shaykh-abucc84-al-hcca3asan-rashicc84d-22sharicc84ah-advice-and-guidance-for-the-mujacc84hidicc84n-of-nigeria22.pdf.

the training of around two hundred fighters; and "guidance on raising jihad in the land of Nigeria."[48]

The letter indicates that prior to August 2009, AQIM had known of Boko Haram's existence and had respected the organization's leaders. Abu Zayd mentioned the names of Muhammad Yusuf and Muhammad Ali as though both Abu Zayd and Droukdel were familiar with those men's reputations, but Abu Zayd did not allude to any linkages with Yusuf or Ali beyond the three jihadists who had trained with his battalion. Nor did Abu Zayd suggest that AQIM played any role in organizing the 2009 uprising or in sponsoring Yusuf; the arsenal that Boko Haram had acquired before the uprising, much of which it still possessed afterward, had come from other sources. In fact, Abu Zayd did not even know until August 2009, when receiving his three Nigerian acquaintances, why Boko Haram had been known by that name. Abu Zayd also had little knowledge about Boko Haram's internal structure: "First of all, I asked them, 'Are you a [jihadist] organization [*tanzim*], or are you seeking to join an organization?'" The Nigerians responded that they would have to ask Shekau, who was at the time injured.[49] If AQIM was familiar with Boko Haram before 2009, it was only cursorily; there is no evidence, even in AQIM's communications with Boko Haram, of significant coordination between the two groups prior to August 2009. Publicly and privately, AQIM considered Yusuf a "martyr" and expressed condolences regarding the outcome of the 2009 uprising,[50] but AQIM did not plan the uprising.

---

[48] Abu Zayd letter, 1.

[49] Abu Zayd letter, 1.

[50] Letter from 'Abd al-Malik Droukdel to Boko Haram, September 2009, reproduced in *Nasa'ih wa-Tawjihat Shar'iyya min al-Shaykh Abi al-Hasan Rashid li-Mujahidi Nayjiriya*, edited by Abu al-Nu'man Qutayba al-Shinqiti (Mu'assasat al-Andalus, April 2017), 3, https://azelin.files.wordpress.com/2017/04/shaykh-abucc84-al-hcca3asan

There was some coordination after that point. In his letter to Droukdel, Abu Zayd said that he had told his Nigerian contacts that maintaining communications and positioning an intermediary in Niger would be "easy." He had also already explained the different training options that AQIM could offer.[51] Droukdel approved the request for training, funding, and other logistical and media support, although he advised Boko Haram not to immediately declare a jihad in Nigeria.[52] In February 2010, Droukdel publicly offered support: "We are ready to train your men [literally, 'your sons,' abna'ikum] in how to deal with weapons, and to help you however we can, whether with men, weapons, supplies, or equipment, to enable you to defend our people in Nigeria."[53] This public announcement was accompanied by some training, likely beginning in early 2010, and Droukdel authorized the disbursal of 200,000 Euros to Boko Haram in July 2010.[54] These developments had some impact on Boko Haram's resurgence. One prominent Boko Haram member has spoken of Boko Haram's "swift effort to save its imprisoned members who were captured in the first attack on the society, and also sending its soldiers to the great desert to train there."[55] In other words, the training and

-rashicc84d-22sharicc84ah-advice-and-guidance-for-the-mujacc84hidicc84n-of
-nigeria22.pdf.

[51] Abu Zayd letter, 2.

[52] Letter from Droukdel to Boko Haram, 4.

[53] "Khubara' Yahdhurun min Khatar Tahaluf (al-Qa'ida) fi al-Maghrib wa-'Taliban Nayjiriya,'" AFP/Al-Riyadh, 15 June 2010, http://www.alriyadh.com/534835. See also "Hal Tahalafat al-Qa'ida ma'a Buku Haram," Al Jazeera, 16 June 2010, http://www.aljazeera.net/news/reportsandinterviews/2010/6/16/%D9%87%D9%84-%D8%AA%D8%AD%D8%A7%D9%84%D9%81%D8%AA-%D8%A7%D9%84%D9%82%D8%A7%D8%B9%D8%AF%D8%A9-%D9%85%D8%B9-%D8%A8%D9%88%D9%83%D9%88-%D8%AD%D8%B1%D8%A7%D9%85.

[54] Nasa'ih wa-Tawjihat Shar'iyya, 6.

[55] "Wali Gharb Ifriqiya: Al-Shaykh Abu Mus'ab al-Barnawi," Al-Naba' 41 (2 August 2016): 8–9; 8, https://azelin.files.wordpress.com/2016/08/the-islamic-state-e2809cal-nabacc84_-newsletter-4122.pdf.

the funding seem to have helped Boko Haram stage its Bauchi prison break in September of that year.[56]

But did the training have a decisive effect on Boko Haram's character and trajectory? Perhaps not. The types of attacks that Boko Haram initially committed in 2010–11—its score settling in the northeast—involved simple assassinations. Shekau had conveyed to Abu Zayd and Droukdel his plan to launch a "guerrilla war [*harb al-'isabat*],"[57] a concept with which AQIM has long been familiar.[58] But it is doubtful whether AQIM influenced Boko Haram's use of tactics such as motorbike-based assassinations, a tactic rare in AQIM's own operations. The key factor enabling the success of these operations, as mentioned above, was Boko Haram fighters' personal knowledge of their victims and their whereabouts.

In terms of more complex operations, there are three kidnappings that occurred in 2011–12 in which AQIM and Boko Haram may have played varying roles: the January 2011 kidnapping by AQIM of two French tourists in Niamey, Niger, possibly with the help of Boko Haram's intermediary there;[59] the May 2011 kidnapping of two European engineers in Birnin Kebbi, northwestern Nigeria; and the January 2012 kidnapping of a German engineer in Kano, north central Nigeria. The latter two kidnappings may have been perpetrated by AQIM-

---

[56] Abdulbasit Kassim, "The Initial Source of Boko Haram Funding Explained," Medium, 16 May 2017, https://medium.com/@ak61/the-initial-source-of-boko-haram -funding-explained-1b142fd5a672.

[57] Abu Zayd letter, 2. Interestingly, the same phrase recurs in Abu Mus'ab's account of this period. The overlap suggests to me that Boko Haram consciously undertook a guerrilla strategy in 2010. See "Wali Gharb Ifriqiya," 8.

[58] "Hiwar ma'a al-Qa'id Khalid Abi Abbas—Amir al-Mintaqa al-Sahrawiyya li-l-Jama'a al-Salafiyya li-l-Da'wa wa-l-Qital," Minbar al-Tawhid wa-l-Jihad, 5 May 2006, http://www.ilmway.com/site/maqdis/MS_37048.html.

[59] "Une piste nigériane dans l'enquête sur la mort des deux otages français enlevés au Niger," RFI, 14 November 2011, http://www.rfi.fr/afrique/20111113-une-piste-nigeriane -enquete-mort-deux-otages-francais-enleves-niger.

trained Boko Haram members, possibly including the above-mentioned "Abu Muhammad" who had trained with AQIM's Tariq ibn Ziyad Battalion.[60] AQIM's media wing released a video of the German hostage in March 2012, accompanied by a statement demanding the release of an accused al-Qaʻida fundraiser held in Germany. Neither the statement nor the video mentioned Boko Haram, but the video was filmed in Kano.[61]

There has been debate about the identity of the kidnappers, particularly in the case of the Kebbi kidnapping.[62] But the more crucial point is this: all three kidnappings ended in failed rescue attempts by Western and/or local security forces. In all three cases, the hostages died, no ransoms were paid, and multiple kidnappers were killed. In no case did the kidnappers succeed in transferring the hostages to remote desert locations where they could be held until ransoms were paid. In other words, even if one assumes the maximum level of AQIM and Boko Haram involvement in each case, the combined jihadist forces achieved little. One conclusion might be that AQIM's skill at kidnapping Europeans in the Sahara— where it earned tens of millions of dollars in ransoms between 2003 and 2012[63]—transferred poorly to urban Nigeria.

[60] An "Abu Mohammed" was arrested in connection with incident. See Tim Cocks, "Nigeria Detains Five Suspects over Deadly Kidnapping," Reuters, 9 March 2012, http://www.reuters.com/article/nigeria-hostages-idINDEE8280B020120309.

[61] Both the video and the statement are available at http://jihadology.net/2012/03 /23/al-andalus-media-presents-a-new-statement-and-video-message-from-al-qaidah -in-the-islamic-maghrib-to-the-german-government-if-they-release-umm-sayf-allah -al-an%E1%B9%A3ari-then-we-will-re/.

[62] For a thoughtful account that is skeptical about AQIM and Boko Haram's involvement, see Andrew Walker, "What Is Boko Haram?," United States Institute of Peace Special Report 308 (June 2012), 10–11, http://www.usip.org/sites/default/files /SR308.pdf.

[63] Wolfram Lacher and Guido Steinberg, "Spreading Local Roots: AQIM and Its Offshoots in the Sahara," in *Jihadism in Africa: Local Causes, Regional Expansion, International Alliances*, edited by Guido Steinberg and Annette Weber, 69–84 (Berlin:

From a financial standpoint, Boko Haram's more successful kidnappings, incidents for which it claimed responsibility and received ransom payments, occurred in remote regions of northern Cameroon and began only in 2013.

The most consequential instance of AQIM's involvement with Boko Haram may have been the two suicide bombings that Boko Haram perpetrated in Abuja in summer 2011. These brazen assaults on formidable targets—the national police headquarters and the United Nations building—took planning and training. AQIM or its trainees may have contributed to the effort. AQIM had bombed the United Nations headquarters in Algiers, Algeria, in December 2007, in addition to striking numerous military installations in Algeria. Even here, however, evidence of AQIM's involvement is circumstantial. I have found no statement by AQIM or its closest Nigerian allies bragging about any involvement in the Abuja suicide bombings.[64]

Ultimately, the problem for AQIM seems to have been that Shekau was uncontrollable, and that he wanted to go in a different direction than showy terrorism far from Boko Haram's geographic stronghold in the northeast. Shekau had sent an effusive letter of thanks to AQIM in October 2010 proclaiming, "We see no difference between our group and your group,

---

Stiftung Wissenschaft und Politik, 2015), 70, https://www.swp-berlin.org/fileadmin/contents/products/research_papers/2015_RP05_sbg_web.pdf. See also Rukmini Callimachi, "Paying Ransoms, Europe Bankrolls Qaeda Terror," *New York Times*, 29 July 2014, https://www.nytimes.com/2014/07/30/world/africa/ransoming-citizens-europe-becomes-al-qaedas-patron.html?_r=0.

[64] Ansary, in his "Message from Nigeria," does not mention the Abuja bombings, nor are they mentioned in a significant piece of AQIM internal correspondence from 2012 where one subject being debated was whether the organization had succeeded or failed. Had AQIM masterminded the bombings, one might have expected the senior leadership to raise them as an example of its success. See Letter from AQIM Shura Council to the Shura Council of the Veiled Men Battalion, 3 October 2012, http://hosted.ap.org/specials/interactives/_international/_pdfs/al-qaida-belmoktar-letter-english.pdf.

and [between] our jihad and your jihad"[65]—but he remained his own man. Shekau may have been uninterested in pressing the campaign on Abuja: after August 2011, the center of gravity for the war shifted back to the northeast. Even if AQIM was thrilled by the suicide bombings in summer 2011, its closest allies within Boko Haram were having severe disagreements with Shekau, who was ordering attacks in the northeast that killed Muslim civilians by the dozens.

By autumn 2011, disaffected Boko Haram members—including some of the same individuals who had trained with AQIM prior to 2009—were complaining to AQIM about Shekau. Specifically, the disaffected members charged Shekau with expropriating money from Muslim civilians and practicing *takfir* (declaring other Muslims to be apostates) to an extent that alienated even these hardline jihadists. The disaffected members said that Shekau displayed "deviance and excess (*al-inhiraf wa-l-ghuluww*)."[66] They added that Shekau insisted on all members deferring to his absolute authority; those who dissented faced expulsion and threats of violence. AQIM became concerned, but their warnings to Shekau seem to have gone unheeded.[67]

In late 2011, the disaffected Boko Haram members decided to form a splinter group that would reject Shekau's leadership and minimize Muslim civilian casualties. The group, Ansar al-Muslimin fi Bilad al-Sudan (the Defenders of Muslims in the Lands of the Blacks, nicknamed "Ansaru"), was announced in January 2012. In its charter, the group softened Boko Haram's reading of *al-wala' wa-l-bara'* (loyalty and disavowal) and promised not to apply *takfir* (accusations of unbelief) "unless

[65] Letter from Abubakar Shekau to ʿAbd al-Hamid Abu Zayd, 7 October 2010, reproduced in *Nasa'ih wa-Tawjihat Sharʿiyya*, 8.

[66] Letter from Abu Muhammad al-Hawsawi et al., reproduced in *Nasa'ih wa-Tawjihat Sharʿiyya*, 12.

[67] *Nasa'ih wa-Tawjihat Sharʿiyya*, 10.

there is proof and unless all of the conditions of such case are existent."[68] Rather, the group said, it would target Westerners and the Nigerian state. Notably, its leader has said that Ansar al-Muslimin was formed "after consulting the Algerian brothers in the Sahara," a reference to AQIM.[69] If AQIM blessed the creation of Ansar al-Muslimin (or at least gave the disaffected Boko Haram members reason to believe they had the Islamic legal right to break with Shekau if necessary)[70], then AQIM's relationship with Shekau seems to have been short-lived—one can date it from August 2009 to January 2012—and it ended badly.

There were reports, however, that Boko Haram members trained with AQIM when AQIM and its allies controlled much of northern Mali between approximately April 2012 and January 2013.[71] Other reporting described Boko Haram fighters participating in combat in northern Mali during 2012.[72] Fliers for Ansar al-Muslimin were found in a home occupied by AQIM's infamous subcommander Mokhtar Belmokhtar (b. 1972) in Gao, Mali,[73] and at least one Ansar al-Muslimin fighter later fought with Belmokhtar's battalion.[74]

[68] English translation of the charter of Jama'at Ansar al-Muslimin fi Bilad al-Sudan, 2013, https://azelin.files.wordpress.com/2013/04/jamc481_at-ane1b9a3c481r-al-muslim c4abn-fi-bilc481d-al-sc5abdc481n-e2809cthe-charter-of-jamc481_at-ane1b9a3c481r-al -muslimc4abn-fi-bilc481d-al-sc5abdc481ne2809d.pdf.

[69] Ansary, "Message from Nigeria," 21.

[70] Letter from Abu al-Hasan al-Bulaydi to Abu Muhammad al-Hawsawi et al., 18 October 2011, reproduced in Nasa'ih wa-Tawjihat Shar'iyya, 64–65.

[71] Drew Hinshaw, "Timbuktu Training Site Shows Terrorists' Reach," Wall Street Journal, 1 February 2013, http://www.wsj.com/articles/SB10001424127887323926104578278030474477210.

[72] "Boko Haram en Renfort des Islamistes Armés dans le Nord du Mali," RFI, 10 April 2012, http://www.rfi.fr/afrique/20120410-mali-bamako-gao-tombouctou-boko -haram-ansar-dine.

[73] Jade Haméon, "Au Mali, dans la maison du djihadiste Mokhtar Belmokhtar," L'Express, 9 February 2013, http://www.lexpress.fr/actualite/monde/afrique/exclusif -au-mali-dans-la-maison-du-djihadiste-mokhtar-belmokhtar_1218712.html.

[74] Katibat al-Mulaththamin, "Malhamat al-Aba' [The Epic of the Fathers]," September 2013, http://jihadology.net/2013/09/09/new-video-message-from-katibat-al

But in assessing the extent of AQIM's training of Nigerian jihadists in Mali, one confronts several questions to which existing, publicly available evidence does not provide ready answers. If there was a breach between Shekau's Boko Haram and AQIM in January 2012, why would either side accept a training arrangement after that time—particularly if it is true, as AQIM has alleged, that by 2011–2012 Shekau was already ordering the murders of the Nigerian jihadists whom AQIM most respected?[75] Was there a reconciliation, either between Boko Haram and AQIM, or between Boko Haram and Ansar al-Muslimin, that facilitated a new training arrangement? If so, why did Ansar al-Muslimin remain harshly and publicly critical of Boko Haram for years afterward? Meanwhile, did rivalries within AQIM, particularly the well-known rivalry between Belmokhtar and Abu Zayd, map onto factional splits within Boko Haram—in other words, did Ansar al-Muslimin gravitate toward Belmokhtar while Boko Haram retained its relationship to Abu Zayd? Faced with all these questions, I think that one should not overestimate the extent and impact of any training that Nigerian jihadists may have undertaken in Mali during 2012—nor should one project coherence onto actors and events in order to generate a neat narrative about jihadist cooperation.

It is worth noting that in correspondence with AQIM senior leadership in 2012, Belmokhtar cast AQIM's entire project as a failure. He reportedly said: "Over the course of a decade, we have not seen a proper military attack, despite extraordinary financial capabilities. Our work has been limited to the routine of kidnappings, of which the mujahidin are getting bored."[76] These

---

-mulathamun-epic-battles-of-the-fathers-the-battle-of-shaykh-abd-al-%E1%B8
%A5amid-abu-zayd/.

[75] *Nasa'ih wa-Tawjihat Shar'iyya*, 10, footnote 2.

[76] Letter from AQIM Shura Council to the Shura Council of the Veiled Men Battalion, 26.

were not the words of a man excited about AQIM's prospects for expanding its jihad into Nigeria. The correspondence—Belmokhtar's letter and AQIM's response—made no mention of Nigeria, Boko Haram, or Ansar al-Muslimin. If training in Mali occurred, and if it allowed Boko Haram to begin holding territory in Nigeria in 2013, these developments do not seem to have enthused AQIM. Unlike in Mali, where Abu Zayd and Belmokhtar based themselves in key cities and where even Droukdel was sighted during the 2012 occupation,[77] no senior AQIM commander is reported to have appeared in Boko Haram's territory, even at the height of its territorial holdings in 2014–15. When the jihadist protostate in Mali collapsed in 2013, Belmokhtar headed for Libya, Abu Zayd was killed, and Droukdel remained in hiding.

Ansar al-Muslimin, meanwhile, attracted attention through its propaganda but has committed only a handful of major attacks. One of its leaders, Adam Kambar, was reported killed in 2012. Another leader—Khalid al-Barnawi, one of the early Nigerian jihadists to train with AQIM—was arrested by Nigerian authorities in April 2016.[78] The group, in short, has floundered. If AQIM fostered Ansar al-Muslimin's split with Boko Haram, AQIM backed the weaker party.

Shekau was the chief obstacle to a close and successful relationship between AQIM and Boko Haram. Authoritative and willing, even eager, to kill civilians, Shekau made a poor partner for global jihadists. This was not for lack of effort on his

[77] May Ying Welsh, "Mali: The 'Gentle' Face of al-Qaeda," Al Jazeera, 30 December 2012, http://www.aljazeera.com/indepth/spotlight/2012review/2012/12/201212281021 57169557.html.

[78] "Khalid al-Barnawi: Nigerian Islamist Group Head 'Arrested,'" BBC, 3 April 2016, http://www.bbc.com/news/world-africa-35956301. There has been speculation that Abu Usamatul Ansary and Khalid al-Barnawi are the same person, but Ansary, in his "Message from Nigeria," describes al-Barnawi as a separate person, saying, "May Allah free him and all Muslim prisoners," 21.

part. Days after Yusuf's death, a purported Boko Haram spokesman announced, "Boko Haram is just a version of the Al Qaeda which we align with and respect. We support Osama bin Laden, we shall carry out his command in Nigeria until the country is totally Islamised which is according to the wish of Allah."[79] In July 2010, as Boko Haram reemerged from the shadows, Shekau released a "Condolence Message" to al-Qaʻida's affiliate in Iraq (the forerunner of the Islamic State) over the recent deaths of two of its leaders. In the message, he greeted and praised al-Qaʻida leaders around the world and positioned himself as one of their kind.[80]

Shekau also tried to formally align Boko Haram with al-Qaʻida central. Among documents discovered at Usama bin Laden's compound in Abbottabad, Pakistan, the site of the raid that killed the al-Qaʻida leader, was a letter from Shekau to al-Qaʻida. The letter opened with an analogy describing the Muslim community as a single physical body. Shekau spoke of "the strong connection with which God has combined us and you." Shekau took pains to establish his Salafi credentials by quoting *hadith* reports cherished by Salafis, such as the statement that Muslims would be divided into seventy-three sects, of which only one would be saved. In Shekau's mind, the saved sect would be the united Salafi-jihadist community. Shekau praised al-Qaʻida:

> We have listened to your tapes and heard of your affairs—the tapes of the scholars of al-Qaʻida and its shaykhs, such as Usama bin Laden, may God protect him, and Dr. Ayman al-Zawahiri, and Abu Musʻab al-Zarqawi, may God have mercy

[79] "Boko Haram Resurrects."

[80] Abubakar Shekau, "Risalat Taʻziyya," July 2010, http://jihadology.net/2010/07/12/new-message-from-the-leader-of-buku-boko-%E1%B8%A5aram-in-nigeria-risalat-taaziyyah/. I am grateful to Abdulbasit Kassim for sharing his translation of the text, which appears in his forthcoming *Boko Haram Reader*.

on him, and others among its scholars, such as Abu Yahya al-Libi and Abu Qatada al-Filastini, may God protect them and preserve them.[81]

In addition to bin Laden, the figures named, respectively, were bin Laden's second-in-command, the Egyptian medical doctor al-Zawahiri; the Jordanian-born al-Zarqawi, leader of al-Qaʻida's unruly affiliate in Iraq, who had died in a U.S. airstrike in 2006; al-Libi, a Libyan warrior-theologian who held senior positions in al-Qaʻida until his death in 2012; and the Palestinian Jordanian al-Filastini, a major architect of Salafi-jihadist thought. In sum, Shekau evoked the leading lights of al-Qaʻida and sought to position Boko Haram as part of their community.

Yet Shekau evinced limited familiarity with al-Qaʻida. Although he mentioned Yusuf, he evoked no past relationship between Yusuf and al-Qaʻida. The second half of Shekau's letter was a series of requests:

> Now nothing remains for us except to know [al-Qaʻida's] system and its component organizations, for he who does not know the path he's on until after the journey begins will fail. . . . We want to be under one banner, but insight is necessary before that, for our religion is a religion of insight and knowledge.[82]

Shekau approached al-Qaʻida as an enthusiastic stranger—someone keen to join the organization based on its reputation and its statements, but also someone who wanted to know more about its inner workings.

[81] Letter from Abubakar Shekau to al-Qaʻida, circa 2010, published by the U.S. Office of the Director of National Intelligence (ODNI), http://www.dni.gov/files /documents/ubl2016/arabic/Arabic%20Praise%20be%20to%20God%20the%20 Lord%20of%20all%20worlds.pdf. The translation here is my own; the ODNI translation, which contains some errors and gaps, is here: http://www.dni.gov/files/docu ments/ubl2016/english/Praise%20be%20to%20God%20the%20Lord%20of%20 all%20worlds.pdf.

[82] Letter from Shekau to al-Qaʻida.

Open sources give little clue as to whether and how al-Qaʿida responded to Shekau's overture. What is known is that the process of joining al-Qaʿida is long and intricate. Since 9/11 and the U.S.-led invasion of Afghanistan, al-Qaʿida has operated partly on a franchise model, lending its name to various sympathetic groups who remain largely autonomous in their decision making. In its franchising, al-Qaʿida has used two primary approaches: mergers with preexisting groups, or expeditions by its own members.[83] Mergers, including in Africa, typically took years of contact, effort, and negotiation.

Shekau sought a merger, but al-Qaʿida may have been wary. Prior mergers had caused al-Qaʿida serious problems. The Libyan Islamic Fighting Group had contested the existence of a merger after al-Qaʿida made its public announcement, embarrassing al-Qaʿida's leadership and confusing jihadist audiences.[84] Abu Musʿab al-Zarqawi's al-Qaʿida in Iraq had joined al-Qaʿida but had then rejected the strategic directives of al-Qaʿida's leadership. Al-Zarqawi had dismissed al-Zawahiri's advice to tone down his anti-Shiʿa violence. Al-Zarqawi's successors would rebel outright against al-Qaʿida's authority in 2013–14, as the Islamic State of Iraq and Syria emerged.

Additionally, prior mergers had involved groups whose leaders were personally acquainted with al-Qaʿida's leaders and/or were veterans of Afghanistan's wars—this was the case with Somalia's Aden Hashi Farah Ayro and Ahmad Godane, and with Algeria's Mokhtar Belmokhtar. Relationships established in Afghanistan "facilitated affiliation arrangements that might have been impossible otherwise."[85] Boko Haram's leaders, in contrast, had no combat or training experience in Afghanistan. Shekau's

[83] Barak Mendelsohn, *The al-Qaeda Franchise: The Expansion of al-Qaeda and Its Consequences* (New York: Oxford University Press, 2016).

[84] Mendelsohn, *Al-Qaeda Franchise*, 85.

[85] Mendelsohn, *Al-Qaeda Franchise*, 100.

offer to al-Qaʿida might have been tempting on one level, but worrying on another: Yusuf's uprising in 2009 had ended in disaster, and Shekau was an unknown quantity. If al-Qaʿida did initiate a merger, it had every reason to proceed cautiously, as it had elsewhere, vetting Boko Haram over a period of years. If such a process did begin, it did not culminate in a public declaration of merger or affiliation—perhaps, as chapter 5 discusses, because Boko Haram switched camps to the Islamic State in 2015, but perhaps because al-Qaʿida was not fully committed to the relationship.

There is one further relationship that Boko Haram may have had within al-Qaʿida's network: a connection to al-Shabab (the Youth), a Somali militia that became affiliated with al-Qaʿida in stages between 2008 and 2012. In 2011, Nigeria's intelligence service asserted that Muhammad Yusuf's former deputy Mamman Nur, the alleged mastermind of the August 2011 suicide bombing in Abuja, had received training in Somalia, fleeing there after Boko Haram's 2009 uprising.[86] No less a figure than former Somali president Hassan Sheikh Mohamud (served 2012–17) has publicly stated that Boko Haram fighters trained with al-Shabab in Somalia.[87] A respected analyst of al-Shabab has written that the reports of training are "credible" and are "supported by Al-Shabaab and local observers in Somalia, as well as [the African Union Mission in Somalia], Boko Haram itself and the Nigerian authorities."[88] No jihadist sources of which I am aware, however, give details about any relationship that may have existed.

[86] Uduma Kalu, "How Nur, Shekau Run Boko Haram," *Vanguard*, 3 September 2011, http://www.vanguardngr.com/2011/09/how-nur-shekau-run-boko-haram/.

[87] "Nigerian Boko Haram Fighters Trained in Somalia: President," Reuters, 14 February 2016, http://www.reuters.com/article/us-somalia-boko-haram-idUSKCN0VN0MF.

[88] Stig Hansen, *Al-Shabaab in Somalia: The History and Ideology of a Militant Islamist Group, 2005–2012* (London: Hurst, 2013), 136.

A few final points are worth making about the extent and meaning of Boko Haram's transnational ties. First, many Boko Haram tactics appear self-generated, such as assassinating targets using motorbike teams, attacking cell phone towers, and kidnapping local women en masse. Boko Haram's massacres of villagers, moreover, duplicate the very tactics that AQIM's predecessor organization was formed to oppose in the context of Algeria's civil war. During its phase of territorial control, discussed in chapter 4, Boko Haram proved much cruder and more predatory than its peer organizations in Mali and Somalia. In short, much of Boko Haram's violence seems improvised, rather than directed from abroad; the patterns of the violence also correlate clearly with events on the ground in northeastern Nigeria, and not as clearly with the alleged interventions of outsiders and the foreign training. Shekau, meanwhile, was headstrong and sometimes erratic—making him an unattractive partner for AQIM's leaders, who have had trouble controlling unruly emirs and preventing schisms within their own organization;[89] and for al-Shabab's leaders, who spent much of 2013–14 conducting internal purges.[90]

Second, much of the military equipment that Boko Haram used seems to have come from the Nigerian security services, captured during raids. For example, as early as fall 2010, Borno governor Sheriff donated some forty Toyota Hilux trucks to the Nigerian military for use against Boko Haram.[91] Hilux trucks remained a staple of military patrols in the region. When later

[89] Rukmini Callimachi, "In Timbuktu, al-Qaida Left Behind a Manifesto," Associated Press, 14 February 2013, https://www.yahoo.com/news/timbuktu-al-qaida -left-behind-manifesto-173454257.html?ref=gs.

[90] Christopher Anzalone, "The Life and Death of al-Shabab Leader Ahmed Godane," *CTC Sentinel*, 29 September 2014, https://www.ctc.usma.edu/posts/the-life -and-death-of-al-shabab-leader-ahmed-godane.

[91] "Serial Killers in Borno," *Sunday Sun*, 24 October 2010, http://www.nairaland .com/537957/serial-killers-borno.

reports spoke of Boko Haram using "convoys of Hilux vehicles," it is not difficult to surmise that the sect stole the vehicles from the military.

Third, Nigerian authorities had a political incentive to portray Boko Haram as a manifestation of global jihad. When President Jonathan characterized Boko Haram as "an al-Qaʿida of West Africa,"[92] it allowed him to downplay Boko Haram's domestic political messages and present the group as completely lacking domestic support in Nigeria. From at least 2011, Nigerian authorities repeatedly emphasized the idea of Boko Haram's external jihadist connections—perhaps out of conviction and based on intelligence, but perhaps to distract attention from security force abuses and convince Western powers to provide more support for Nigeria's government.

Finally, there is an intellectual reason to question the theory that al-Qaʿida's affiliates played the decisive role in Boko Haram's transformation. That theory plays all too well into long-standing images of "African Islam" as essentially pacifist, "moderate," "tolerant," and even "unorthodox"—until and unless African Muslims encounter Arabs, whose Islam is frequently stereotyped as "rigid," "legalistic," and even "militant." Some observers who endorse these stereotypes seem almost incapable of imagining an African jihadism that does not have a shadowy Arab hand guiding it. Yet international jihadist themes were marginal in much of the sect's statements, especially between 2010 and 2013: Boko Haram's messages have mostly focused on Nigerian politics,[93] and since 2014–15 the messages have increasingly focused on Nigeria's neighbors.

---

[92] John Irish, "Nigerian President: Boko Haram Is West Africa's al Qaeda," Reuters, 17 May 2014, http://www.businessinsider.com/r-boko-haram-is-west-africas-al-qaeda-says-nigerian-president-2014-17.

[93] Benjamin Eveslage, "Clarifying Boko Haram's Transnational Intentions, Using Content Analysis of Public Statements in 2012," *Perspectives on Terrorism* 7:5 (October 2013): 47–76.

While Shekau's wild threats against Barack Obama and his scorn for Margaret Thatcher and Abraham Lincoln claimed headlines, the bulk of his more pertinent comments about Nigeria often went underanalyzed as observers fixated on the possibility of external jihadist connections. Boko Haram has been persistently attuned, above all, to the political, religious, and social theater of Borno State and the Lake Chad basin. With this in mind, we turn to examination of Boko Haram's religious and political messages under Shekau.

Boko Haram's Worldview under Abubakar Shekau

There has been intensive speculation about the internal dynamics of Boko Haram following Muhammad Yusuf's death, but reliable evidence is thin. Much speculation has focused on reported leadership struggles between two former companions of Yusuf, Abubakar Shekau (b. ca. 1969)[94] and Muhammad "Mamman" Nur (b. ca. 1976).[95] One account holds that these two men were Yusuf's chief deputies and were respectively his second- and third-in-command during the uprising of 2009.[96] Both men can be seen preaching in Boko Haram videos that likely date from the 2008–9 period.

Whatever happened between Shekau and Nur after Yusuf's death, the face of the reconstituted Boko Haram was Shekau. Throughout his time in the public eye, Shekau has been a figure of mystery; even the most basic facts of his biography

[94] United Nations Security Council, "Security Council al-Qaida Sanctions Committee Adds Abubakar Mohammed Shekau, Ansaru to Its Sanctions List," 26 June 2014, http://www.un.org/press/en/2014/sc11455.doc.htm.

[95] Uduma Kalu, "How Nur, Shekau Run Boko Haram," *Vanguard*, 3 September 2011, http://www.vanguardngr.com/2011/09/how-nur-shekau-run-boko-haram/.

[96] Kalu, "How Nur, Shekau Run Boko Haram."

are disputed. As chapter 2 discussed, Shekau was one of the hardliners around Yusuf and may have been one of the leaders at Kanamma. He was Boko Haram's second-in-command by the late 2000s and likely influenced Yusuf's move toward open jihadism. As one former Nigerian government official told me, media depictions of Shekau have been "wooden [and] one-sided," giving the impression of a psychopath—but logic dictates that "he cannot be a madman," given the fighting prowess and adaptability Boko Haram has shown under his leadership. At the same time, the former official says that those who knew Shekau have described him as "erratic" and "dogmatic," adding that he "tried to wrestle for control of the group even when Muhammad Yusuf was alive."[97]

In a video from before the 2009 uprising, Shekau can be seen echoing Yusuf's core teachings against Western-style education and democracy. Shekau's animated, harshly condemnatory, and wryly mocking style was already formed by this time. He preached that Western-style education corrupted young Muslim minds. In one sequence, he contrasted the language of Nigeria's pledge of allegiance with passages in the Qur'an, arguing that reciting the pledge was equivalent to worshipping the Nigerian state. Shekau presented democracy as *shirk* or polytheism, which is considered a profound sin in Islamic theology. Like Yusuf, Shekau invoked global Salafi authorities in an attempt to bolster this position, sitting with a pile of books and referencing specific passages for effect. Among others, Shekau cited the Saudi Arabian shaykh Muhammad ibn Salih al-Uthaymin to support the claim that democracy was "the school of unbelievers [*madhhab al-kuffar*]," and that whoever

---

[97] Skype interview with Dr. Fatima Akilu, 1 March 2016.

refused to condemn unbelief was himself an unbeliever.[98] Shekau would reiterate that message in later years: In one 2014 video, Shekau returned to his argument that the national pledge recited in government schools was tantamount to unbelief:"You are worshipping the nation," he told listeners.[99]

As Yusuf's successor, Shekau continued to invoke the dead leader's core doctrines, such as *al-wala' wa-l-bara'* (loyalty toward Islam and disavowal of Islam's enemies). If anything changed in Boko Haram's post-2009 messages, it was that Shekau intensified two themes: the sect's conviction that the state systematically victimized Nigerian Muslims, and the sect's demand that other Muslims choose sides in Boko Haram's war with the state.

Shekau fit the 2009 crackdown against Boko Haram into a larger narrative:

> Everyone knows the way in which our leader was killed. Everyone knows the kind of evil assault that was brought against our community. Beyond us, everyone knows the kind of evil that has been brought against the Muslim community of this country periodically: incidents such as Zangon Kataf. . . . These are the things that have happened without end.[100]

Zangon-Kataf, as chapter 1 discussed, was an intercommunal clash in Kaduna State in 1992. Yusuf evoked that incident in his preaching to prove that the Nigerian state was anti-Muslim. For Shekau, Boko Haram was the latest victim of state aggression: "They're fighting us for no reason, because we've said

---

[98] Abubakar Shekau, untitled video, circa 2008–9, https://www.youtube.com/watch?v=eQY4GLtzLdU.

[99] Boko Haram, "Min dunihi fa-Kiduni thumma La Tanzurun," 5 May 2014, https://www.youtube.com/watch?v=wrfWS_vL0D4.

[100] Abubakar Shekau, "Message to President Jonathan," January 2012, https://www.youtube.com/watch?v=umkj50SUzck.

we'll practice our religion, we will support our religion and stand on what God has said."[101] Like Yusuf, Shekau depicted Boko Haram as a group that did what Islam required, regardless of the consequences, rather than as a group that had brought a new doctrine—something that Islam forbids.

If Boko Haram was the victim, other Muslims were either friends or enemies. Shekau adopted broad criteria for pronouncing *takfir*, or declaring other Muslims unbelievers. "The excuse of ignorance is not taken into consideration for the greater polytheism," he said, claiming the right to kill other Muslims who supported democracy, constitutionalism, or Western-style education, even if they did so without realizing that Boko Haram proscribed these systems.[102]

Unlike Yusuf, Shekau rarely expounded his doctrine, but he invoked Salafi theology as a basis for violent exclusivism. In the video "This Is Our Creed," Shekau presented a rudimentary Salafism:

> Our creed is the creed of our Messenger, may God bless him and grant him peace. And our approach is the approach of our Messenger, may God bless him and grant him peace. . . . And his creed is the oneness of God, may He be glorified and exalted.[103]

Shekau evinced familiarity with the tenets of Salafi thought, moving through a well-known Salafi conception of *tawhid* (monotheism) as a three-fold doctrine comprising "unity of lordship," "unity of divinity," and "unity of [God's] names and

[101] Abubakar Shekau, "Sako Zuwa Ga Duniya," September 2012, https://www.youtube.com/watch?v=txUJCOKTluk&sns=em.

[102] Abubakar Shekau, "Wannan Ne Akidarmu," likely 2015, http://www.liveleak.com/view?i=d4b_1421362369.

[103] Abubakar Shekau, "Wannan Ne Akidarmu."

attributes."[104] Yusuf had also invoked this doctrine as a foundation for Boko Haram's other, more divisive ideas.[105] As the leader of a jihadist organization engaged in warfare, however, Shekau devoted more time to explaining the sect's positions on politics than to elucidating theological fundamentals. If there is a one-line distillation of Shekau's thought, it would be his interpretation of the Qur'anic verse "chaos is worse than killing [*al-fitna ashadd min al-qatl*]" (2:191). Many other Muslims read this verse as an injunction against precisely the type of rebellion that Boko Haram was mounting—as noted above, many Nigerian Muslims welcomed the killing of Yusuf precisely because they thought it would prevent further chaos. But for Shekau, the "chaos" the Qur'an condemns had already come to Nigeria in the form of a heretical system: democracy, constitutionalism, Western-style education, and so on. The only suitable response was to violently oppose that system: "Know, people of Nigeria and other places, a person is not a Muslim unless he disavows democracy and other forms of polytheistic unbelief [*shirk*]."[106]

This position echoed Yusuf's devotion to *izhar al-din*, "manifesting religion," or what Yusuf called the duty of Muslims to pursue an activist, confrontational expression of their faith. But whereas Yusuf had wavered about the need for violence during the mid-2000s, Shekau made *izhar al-din* equivalent to violence. Shekau's stance, especially when placed in the context of Nigeria's intrigue-filled politics, would make it difficult for the government and Boko Haram to find any common ground.

[104] Abubakar Shekau, "Wannan Ne Akidarmu."

[105] Muhammad Yusuf, *Hadhihi 'Aqidatuna wa-Manhaj Da'watina* (Maiduguri: Maktabat al-Ghuraba' li-l-Nashr wa-l-Tawzi', 2009), 14.

[106] "Boko Haram Declares a New Caliphate in Northern Nigeria," SaharaTV, 24 August 2014, https://www.youtube.com/watch?v=Rl4IgD—nKg.

Another challenge to making peace was fragmentation within Boko Haram and the announcement of Ansar al-Muslimin's founding in 2012. As noted above, after its string of early, high-profile attacks ended in 2013, Ansar al-Muslimin seemed to have been more a flash in the pan than a full-fledged, enduring rival for Boko Haram. Nevertheless, the breakaway group's very existence, and rumors of other factions operating mostly outside Shekau's control, cast further doubts on whether anyone could speak for Boko Haram in the unlikely event that the group ever came to the negotiating table.

Failed Efforts at Dialogue and Accountability

By early 2011, northeastern Nigeria's governors were talking about political solutions for the problem of a resurgent Boko Haram. Even before taking office on May 29, Borno's incoming governor Kashim Shettima floated the idea of amnesty for Boko Haram fighters who laid down arms—an offer the sect immediately rejected.[107] Shettima, an agricultural economist who held senior posts in Sheriff's second administration, had been handpicked by Sheriff after Boko Haram assassinated his first choice for a successor, Modu Fannami Gubio. Once in office, however, Shettima showed independence from his patron.

Other governors made overtures to the sect in 2011, seemingly out of fear for their personal safety. That year, reports emerged that Boko Haram was demanding apologies from

---

[107] See Alex Thurston, "Nigeria: An Amnesty for Boko Haram?," Sahel Blog, 12 May 2011, https://sahelblog.wordpress.com/2011/05/12/nigeria-an-amnesty-for-boko-haram/.

politicians who had participated in suppressing the 2009 uprising. In response, former Gombe governor Danjuma Goje (served 2003–11) issued a public apology. Sitting Bauchi governor Isa Yuguda (served 2007–15) followed suit, apologizing for "perceived injustices" the sect had experienced. He added the hope that his apology would "open the door to meaningful dialogue that will end hostilities and usher peace."[108] Yuguda reiterated these sentiments in a September 2011 speech, promising, "We will criminalise those that are criminals and rehabilitate those that are merely agitating for social justice by creating jobs for them."[109] Yet Boko Haram was unmoved. It remained unclear whether the sect's purported spokesmen quoted in the Nigerian press even represented the group.

As Boko Haram's violence exploded into Nigeria's national consciousness with the first Abuja bombing of June 2011, President Jonathan pursued various, mutually contradictory approaches. One effort involved more serious scrutiny of northeastern politicians, especially Sheriff, who stepped down as Borno's governor in May 2011. Sheriff was interrogated by Nigeria's intelligence agency, the Directorate of State Security, in July 2011, and was summoned to the presidential villa the next day to meet Jonathan.[110] Sheriff and two other prominent Borno politicians—Senators Ahmed Zanna and Ali Ndume—remained under scrutiny by the security services afterward,

[108] Kingsley Omonobi, "Boko Haram Kills LG Boss, 4 Others in Borno," *Vanguard*, 4 July 2011, http://www.vanguardngr.com/2011/07/boko-haram-kills-lg-boss -4-others-in-borno/; see also "Second Apology to Boko Haram, from Bauchi Gov Isa Yuguda," Safer Africa Group, 2 July 2011, https://saferafricagroup.wordpress.com /2011/07/02/second-apology-to-boko-haram-from-bauchi-gov-isa-yuguda/.

[109] Ola Ajayi, "Boko Haram Protesting Social Injustice, Says Yuguda," *Vanguard*, 20 September 2011, http://allafrica.com/stories/201109200450.html.

[110] Jide Ajani, "The Hunt for Boko Haram Members: Tracking an Unknown Enemy," *Vanguard*, 17 July 2011, http://www.vanguardngr.com/2011/07/the-hunt-for -boko-haram-members-tracking-an-unknown-enemy/.

and Ndume was not cleared of charges until 2017.[111] In the convoluted pathways of Nigerian politics, Jonathan and Sheriff would, toward the end of Jonathan's term, become allies. Sheriff even accompanied Jonathan on a trip to Chad in November 2014, where they met Chadian president Idriss Deby to discuss Boko Haram.[112] But in the initial panic of 2011, Jonathan seemed to suspect that Borno's politicians were intriguing against him, and that Boko Haram was a part of the plot.

Another effort was a legal gesture toward accountability for Muhammad Yusuf's death. In July 2011, a Federal High Court in Abuja opened a trial against five (initially seven) policemen accused of killing Yusuf. Authorities may never have seriously intended to see the case through; in December 2015, the charges were dropped.[113] The probe never implicated anyone in the upper levels of the security forces, the Borno State government, or the Yar'Adua and Jonathan administrations. In short, it was a weak effort at accountability.

Meanwhile, as complaints grew in Borno about the military presence there, the Jonathan administration made token efforts toward promoting reconciliation and finding a political solution to the conflict. In July 2011, Jonathan met with the Arewa Consultative Forum, an association of northern Nigerian elites.[114] The same month, the Committee of Borno

---

[111] Hamza Idris and Ronald Mutum, "Boko Haram—Sheriff under Watch, IG Says," *Daily Trust*, 1 November 2012, http://allafrica.com/stories/201211010253.html.

[112] "Jonathan Travels to Chad with Alleged Boko Haram Sponsor Modu Sheriff," *Premium Times*, 9 November 2014, http://www.premiumtimesng.com/news/head lines/167935-jonathan-travels-to-chad-with-alleged-boko-haram-sponsor-modu -sheriff.html.

[113] Senator Iroegbu, "Court Releases Suspected Killers of Boko Haram Leader Mohammed Yusuf," *This Day*, 21 December 2015, http://www.thisdaylive.com/articles /court-releases-suspected-killers-of-boko-haram-leader-mohammed-yusuf/228560/.

[114] Ahamefula Ogbu, "Boko Haram: Jonathan, Borno Leaders in Emergency Meeting," *This Day*, 13 July 2011, http://www.thisdaylive.com/articles/boko-haram-jonathan -borno-leaders-in-emergency-meeting/94942/.

Elders and Leaders of Thought issued a statement calling for the withdrawal of federal soldiers from their state. The elders also asked for efforts to initiate "honest and positive dialogue since [Boko Haram has] already presented their demands." The committee's statement was signed by prominent individuals, including former petroleum minister Shettima Ali Monguno (whom Boko Haram would later kidnap in 2013) and retired ambassador Usman Galtimari.[115]

At the end of July 2011, Jonathan appointed Galtimari to chair a seven-person Presidential Committee on Security Challenges in the North-East; the group included the ministers for defense, labor, and the Federal Capital Territory. Jonathan gave the committee two weeks (August 2–16) to assess the situation in the northeast and make recommendations to the government on resolving the crisis. The government initially implied that the group had a mandate to contact Boko Haram with a view to beginning negotiations.[116] This mandate was soon discarded, and the committee's preliminary report was kept confidential.[117] Galtimari told journalists that dialogue was impossible given the government's, and the committee's, lack of knowledge about Boko Haram: "We don't know the leaders of Boko Haram. Who are Boko Haram? If you don't know a man, how are you going to have reconciliation with him [*sulhu da shi*]?"[118] The government appeared reluctant

---

[115] Hamza Idris and Yahaya Ibrahim, "Maiduguri—Elders Demand End to Military Action—JTF Denies Wanton Killings," *Daily Trust*, 13 July 2011, http://allafrica.com/stories/201107131225.html.

[116] "Nigeria Panel Seeks Talks with Boko Haram," Al Jazeera, 31 July 2011, http://www.aljazeera.com/news/africa/2011/07/2011731145755671650.html.

[117] "Nigeria's Report on Islamist Sect Attacks Delayed," Reuters, 18 August 2011, http://af.reuters.com/article/idAFJOE77H0TH20110818?pageNumber=1&virtualBrandChannel=0&sp=true.

[118] "Usman Gaji Galtimari Speaking on the Mandate of the Presidential Committee on Boko Haram," *Daily Trust*, 22 November 2011, https://www.youtube.com/watch?v=Hzvs2Vk5OZo.

to pursue the political dimensions of the investigation. The committee's report was not released until May 2012.[119] Even then, it was largely buried: no public copy circulates. Private efforts to reach out to Boko Haram also stumbled. In March 2012, reports stated that the Nigerian government and Boko Haram had begun informal talks through a mediation team headed by Dr. Ibrahim Datti Ahmed, president of the Supreme Council for Shari'a in Nigeria. Ahmed was a credible mediator not only because of his general prominence, but also because, as noted in chapter 2, Muhammad Yusuf had been one of the Supreme Council's members in Borno.[120] Ahmed reportedly arranged to contact Boko Haram through Ahmad Salkida, a journalist who had known Yusuf in Maiduguri.[121] After contact was made, there seemed to be some grounds for negotiations: the sect, or someone claiming to speak for it, told Ahmed that it would cease attacks if the federal government released imprisoned sect members and guaranteed the safety of key leaders.[122] The talks broke down when Ahmed withdrew as mediator. He accused the government of betraying all parties' trust by leaking details of the negotiations to the Nigerian press.[123] After Ahmed's withdrawal,

---

[119] Theophilus Abbah, "White Paper on Insecurity: Report Links Boko Haram with London Scholar," *Daily Trust*, 3 June 2012, http://www.dailytrust.com.ng/sunday /index.php/top-stories/11938-white-paper-on-insecurity-report-links-boko-haram -with-london-scholar#AG42o27PWoIbwTWI.99.

[120] Bayo Oladeji, Muazu Abari, Midat Joseph, and Salisu Ibrahim, "Boko Haram Picks Datti Ahmed as Mediator," *Leadership*, 14 March 2012, http://allafrica.com /stories/201203140368.html.

[121] Emeka Omeihe, "Journalist Salkida as Boko Haram Negotiator," *Nation*, 2 June 2014, http://thenationonlineng.net/journalist-salkida-as-boko-haram-negotiator/.

[122] Oladeji et al., "Boko Haram Picks Datti Ahmed."

[123] Emeka Mamah, "FG, Boko Haram Talks Collapse," *Vanguard*, 19 March 2012, http://allafrica.com/stories/201203190749.html.

a purported Boko Haram spokesman announced that there would be no more negotiations.[124]

Another private effort came in August 2012. Former president Olusegun Obasanjo traveled to Maiduguri to meet the family of Baba Fugu Muhammad, Muhammad Yusuf's father-in-law, who was executed along with Yusuf during Boko Haram's 2009 uprising. Baba Fugu Muhammad's eldest son Baba Kura Alhaji Fugu agreed to meet Obasanjo. The meeting was arranged by the northern Nigerian human rights activist Shehu Sani, who had written an influential account of Boko Haram's emergence the previous year and who would be elected in 2015 as senator for Kaduna Central. Obasanjo, Sani, and others hoped that the meeting would help initiate dialogue with more flexible elements of Boko Haram. Potentially, the original followers of Yusuf constituted a distinct and more moderate element within Boko Haram. Fugu's family had some claim to speak for them. Fugu reportedly told Obasanjo that as a starting point toward talks, the government should enforce the 2010 Borno High Court decision that had awarded compensation to Fugu's family. But two days after the meeting, Boko Haram fighters assassinated Fugu as he stepped out of a press interview to answer his phone.[125] Hardline members of Boko Haram were willing to scuttle any potential dialogue.

Amid continued violence, calls for dialogue and amnesty continued to surface. In April 2013, Jonathan tried again, inaugurating a Committee on Dialogue and Peaceful Resolution of Security Challenges in the North. The committee was chaired by Kabiru Turaki, a lawyer and politician hailing from Kebbi

[124] Hamza Idris, "Boko Haram Says No More Talks with FG," *Daily Trust*, 21 March 2012, http://allafrica.com/stories/201203210120.html.

[125] Aruga Joe Omokaro and Maxwell Oditta, "Boko Haram Kills Former President's Host, Rejects Peace Move," *Moment*, 4 August 2012, http://allafrica.com/stories/201208050061.html.

State in northwestern Nigeria, who had been appointed as Jonathan's minister of special duties and inter-governmental affairs two months before. Turaki's committee was charged with exploring the possibility for implementing an amnesty for Boko Haram. The committee's prospects for success immediately suffered a blow when Ibrahim Datti Ahmed and Shehu Sani both declined to serve.[126] One source close to Boko Haram has also flatly stated that Boko Haram distrusted Turaki.[127]

Despite the committee's high profile, the idea of amnesty had little genuine support among Nigerian elites. A few prominent northerners expressed confidence that if the federal government released some prisoners and prosecuted Yusuf's killers, Boko Haram's leaders would be willing to negotiate.[128] But Jonathan gave mixed messages. Visiting Yobe in March 2013, he said that Boko Haram members would have to come forward publicly if there was going to be any possibility of amnesty[129]—a precondition the sect was unlikely to accept.

Even international human rights organizations voiced reservations: Human Rights Watch wrote an open letter to Turaki asking that any amnesty "exclude serious crimes committed in violation of international law."[130] As with Jonathan's previous committee, this one failed at brokering a dialogue with

[126] Luka Binniyat, "Boko Haram: Ahmed Datti Withdraws from Committee," *Vanguard*, 19 April 2013, http://www.vanguardngr.com/2013/04/boko-haram-ahmed-datti-withdraws-from-committee/.

[127] Pulse TV interview with Aisha Wakil, 5 September 2016, https://www.youtube.com/watch?v=gb6G4y_ZTAk.

[128] Mark Caldwell, "Nigeria Weighs Amnesty for Boko Haram Insurgents," Deutsche Welle, 5 April 2013, http://www.dw.com/en/nigeria-weighs-amnesty-for-boko-haram-insurgents/a-16724392.

[129] "Jonathan Visits Yobe, Says No Amnesty for Boko Haram," *Premium Times*, 7 March 2013, http://allafrica.com/stories/201303080501.html.

[130] Human Rights Watch, "Letter to the Committee on Dialogue and Peaceful Resolution of Security Challenges in the North," 2 July 2013, https://www.hrw.org/news/2013/07/02/letter-committee-dialogue-and-peaceful-resolution-security-challenges-north.

Boko Haram—and at changing government policy. As the next chapter discusses, even amid talk of amnesty in spring 2013, the government was preparing a pronounced escalation of its security response.

Recruiting for a Clandestine Movement

How did Boko Haram attract new recruits and sustain its morale during this period of guerrilla warfare? The best study on recruitment has come from Mercy Corps, whose researchers conducted forty-seven interviews with former Boko Haram members in northeastern Nigeria in autumn 2015. Of the interviewees, sixteen had joined before the 2009 uprising, and twenty-six afterward; in the remaining cases, Mercy Corps could not determine when they joined. Only twenty-two were ethnically Kanuri.[131]

Mercy Corps found that "there is no demographic profile of a Boko Haram member" and that recruitment "def[ied] neat categories of 'voluntary' and 'forced'."[132] In terms of religious and ideological commitment, Mercy Corps found that members who joined before the 2009 uprising were more attuned to Boko Haram's messages than those who joined later. Many of the post-2009 recruits "perceived joining Boko Haram as the least bad option to address a challenge given their circumstances." Often, questions of physical and economic survival were at stake.[133] Even among the post-2009 recruits, however, Mercy Corps encountered a significant number who professed

---

[131] Mercy Corps, "'Motivations and Empty Promises': Voices of Former Boko Haram Combatants and Nigerian Youth," April 2016, 9, https://www.mercycorps.org/sites/default/files/Motivations%20and%20Empty%20Promises_Mercy%20Corps_Full%20Report.pdf.

[132] Mercy Corps, "Motivations and Empty Promises," 11.

[133] Mercy Corps, "Motivations and Empty Promises," 12.

religious and ideological sympathy for Boko Haram as an organization ostensibly dedicated to defending Islam and overthrowing unbelieving tyrants.[134] Other findings from Mercy Corps' research indicate the importance of peers in recruitment, as well as the opportunities that Boko Haram gave young women for increasing their religious learning and social status.

Another major study, based on interviews with 119 former Boko Haram members, came to roughly equivalent conclusions. The study, undertaken by Anneli Botha and Mahdi Abdile, stressed the role of family and friends in recruiting new members, finding that peers had been involved in over 60 percent of inductions.[135] Most strikingly, Botha and Abdile found that 57 percent of former fighters cited "revenge" as a motivation for joining Boko Haram—revenge against the Nigerian state and its security forces.[136] Unfortunately, however, the study's overall utility is limited owing to its poor design. The authors appeared keen to refute a series of essentially straw man arguments—including the idea that Boko Haram members are recruited at "madrassas" by "firebrand imams," the idea that religion is the sole motive for joining the sect, and the idea that only poor people join the sect.

Although the authors put these ideas in the mouths of unnamed "peace builders" and "citizens" and then proceed to refute them, relatively few experts advocate such simplistic understandings of Boko Haram. By focusing on either identifying or debunking monocausal explanations, the authors missed a major opportunity to approach recruitment as a multifaceted

[134] Mercy Corps, "Motivations and Empty Promises," 14–15.

[135] Anneli Botha and Mahdi Abdile, "Getting behind the Profiles of Boko Haram Members and Factors Contributing to Radicalisation versus Working towards Peace," Network for Religious and Traditional Peacemakers (October 2016), 2, https://frantic.s3-eu-west-1.amazonaws.com/kua-peacemakers/2016/10/Boko_Haram_Study_Botha_Abdile_SUMMARY_disclaimer_included_2016.pdf.

[136] Botha and Abdile, "Getting behind the Profiles," 5.

process—and to offer more nuanced understandings of how religious and economic motivations might work. Joining Boko Haram is undoubtedly a complex decision, involving multiple and even conflicting motivations, contingencies, and pressures. Finally, one might question whether "revenge" is an intrinsically secular affair.

Moving beyond quantitative studies of recruitment, one should question the very category of "recruitment" itself. Boko Haram is not, it would appear, an organization in which one becomes a formal member through a carefully standardized process. A medical professional from Borno told me that in his area of the state, Boko Haram had often involved young men in its activities by first giving them a mobile phone and asking them to report on movements of key people—security forces, politicians, and so on—in their locales. Boko Haram had then drawn these young men further into its operations by paying them, and then further still by ordering them to commit a murder.[137] Whether or not these details are accurate, one can imagine that some kind of gradual process was used to recruit many sect members—a gradual process of building one's life around Muhammad Yusuf and the Markaz before 2009, or a gradual process of collaborating with Boko Haram's cells after 2009. At each step, there were inducements (financial, peer based, and religious) for involvement and disincentives (threats of exposure and violence) for backsliding.

The image of the phone-carrying, low-level supporter also suggests that the boundaries separating Boko Haram from surrounding civilians have always been fuzzy. One way to conceptualize these boundaries is the classic image of concentric circles. If Abubakar Shekau and the groups of masked men

---

[137] Interview with anonymous medical professional from Borno State, February 2016.

who surround him in propaganda videos are the core, then there are concentric circles radiating out from that core. These circles represent members and supporters with decreasing levels of involvement and commitment. The outermost circles represent so-called passive supporters, who may provide shelter and food to fighters—and who may do so more because they know those fighters personally than because they support Shekau's aims.

One challenge of understanding Boko Haram's character, and what it means to be a sect member, is the simultaneous fact of the group's tremendous capabilities for violence and its seemingly amorphous nature. On the one hand, Shekau (or someone) has amassed groups of fighters large enough to disrupt security over a considerable geographic area. On the other hand, the group often seems to function more as a collection of loosely linked cells and bands than as a tightly disciplined, hierarchical army.

Boko Haram's size is similarly hard to calculate. During its 2009 uprising, Boko Haram wreaked havoc in Maiduguri, Bauchi, and several other major cities. One might estimate its size then at over one thousand dedicated members, many of whom escaped—the estimated eleven hundred people killed in the ensuing crackdown must have included many innocent civilians. After 2009, Boko Haram must have grown, drawing in members as it became more attractive to sympathizers and harder to resist for people in the wrong place at the wrong time. In 2015, the U.S. government put the figure at four thousand to six thousand "hardcore" fighters.[138] This estimate is as good as any. The movement's peak membership may have come in 2015–16, coinciding with the phase of territorial control discussed in the

---

[138] Mark Hosenball, "Nigeria's Boko Haram Has Up to 6,000 Hardcore Militants: U.S. Officials," Reuters, 6 February 2015, http://www.reuters.com/article/us-nigeria-violence-bokoharam-idUSKBN0LA2J120150206.

next chapter. "Membership" in Boko Haram must have been an especially complicated category at that time, given the degrees of coercion brought to bear on those who found themselves living under Boko Haram rule.

Conclusion

From 2010 to 2013, Boko Haram evolved from the remnants of a once-public mass preaching movement into a hardened jihadist organization. From its early phase of prison breaks and targeted killings to its wider campaign of violence, both in the northeast and in major northern cities, Boko Haram grew from a local problem to a Nigerian one. By 2013, Nigeria faced a major security crisis.

Boko Haram also sought to reshape the religious field through violence, killing its critics, and intimidating those who remained silent. A Muslim establishment that had largely supported the 2009 crackdown found itself flummoxed, almost paralyzed—at a 2011 conference I attended in Kano, for example, the Sultan of Sokoto and others spoke of Boko Haram in vague terms as a problem of "peace-building" and "youth," appearing hesitant to even speak the group's name. Muslim scholars willing to criticize both the sect and the state were few.

Under Abubakar Shekau, Boko Haram retained the core ideas that Muhammad Yusuf had preached, especially toward the end of his life: a narrow definition of who counted as a Muslim, a confrontational attitude about faith, and a rejection of democracy, constitutionalism, and Western-style schooling. Boko Haram also entrenched Yusuf's politics of victimhood. Even as the group transitioned to terrorism, Shekau continued to present Boko Haram as victims of the Nigerian state—as a group of committed Muslims with their backs against the wall, forced to commit violence by a system that allowed believers no room to practice their religion authentically. Shekau fit Yusuf's death into this narrative of victimization and boiled Yusuf's doctrines down to simple slogans, epitomized by Shekau's favorite Qur'anic verse—"chaos is worse than killing." As the Nigerian state cracked down even further on Boko Haram in 2013, Boko Haram would inflict even greater chaos on Nigeria, carving out a massive Salafi-jihadist enclave in Borno and adjoining areas.

4.

Total War in Northeastern Nigeria

In 2013, the shape of the Boko Haram conflict shifted. Boko Haram still perpetrated regular acts of terrorism and continued to operate as a clandestine terrorist organization in some Nigerian cities. But the sect also bid openly for territorial control and showed increasing willingness to confront Nigerian forces in open battles. The conflict came to include not just conventional war, but total war.

Three main developments drove this change. First, the Nigerian military intensified its campaign against Boko Haram, placing three northeastern states (Borno, Adamawa, and Yobe) under a state of emergency for eighteen months. Second, the government sponsored the rise of civilian, quasi-official vigilantes. The vigilantes helped reduce Boko Haram's presence in northeastern cities. In so doing, they inadvertently pushed the sect into the countryside, where it found new opportunities. Third, Boko Haram exhibited growing territorial ambitions and capabilities. The sect moved from domination, extortion, and predation in northeastern towns and villages to outright control.

These developments were so interlinked that key questions are difficult to definitively answer: Did Boko Haram always strive to control territory, or was its turn to territorial conquest an attempt at self-preservation amid an intensifying crackdown? Was taking territory part of an effort to eradicate the civilian vigilantes? For their part, to what extent were the vigilantes an organic and grassroots phenomenon that acquired

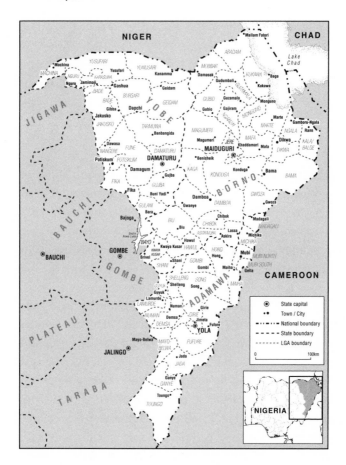

the state's backing, versus an artificial creation of the state? Were the vigilantes even a mechanism for "outsourcing" the worst human rights abuses against suspected and confirmed Boko Haram members?[1] Whatever the ultimate origin of each development, the form of war that emerged in the northeast was total: human rights violations by all sides became a core

---

[1] I thank Hilary Matfess for this phrasing.

feature of the conflict, rather than its byproduct. On the doctrinal level, Boko Haram sought to justify total war by further intensifying its exclusivist message: all civilians would now be expected to choose sides, and "enemy" Muslim civilians would be targets.

The Intensification of the Military Campaign

In spring 2013, Boko Haram appeared confident and aggressive. In March, Boko Haram staged prison breaks in quick succession in Gwoza, Borno State, and Ganye, Adamawa State,[2] freeing nearly three hundred inmates. Kidnappings and bank robberies were attributed to the group, suggesting it was poised to enjoy more funding. Boko Haram's leader Abubakar Shekau publicly rejected the idea of dialogue or peace with the Nigerian government, further embarrassing the administration of President Goodluck Jonathan.[3]

Perhaps out of frustration at Boko Haram's elusiveness, the Nigerian military's Joint Task Force (JTF) became even harsher toward civilians. Arbitrary detentions, torture, and extrajudicial killings had featured in the campaign against Boko Haram since the sect's uprising in 2009. But in late 2012, Human Rights Watch warned of "spiraling violence" in northeastern Nigeria. Researchers documented systematic abuses of civilians by

[2] "Gunmen Break Nigerian Jail, Free 170 Inmates," PM News Nigeria, 16 March 2013, http://www.pmnewsnigeria.com/2013/03/16/gunmen-break-nigerian-jail-free -170-inmates/; and "127 Prisoners Escape in Adamawa Jail Attack," Vanguard, 24 March 2013, http://www.vanguardngr.com/2013/03/127-prisoners-escape-in-nigerian -jail-attack/.

[3] Ibrahim Mshelizza, Anamesere Igboeroteonwu, and Tim Cocks, "Nigerian Islamist Leader Rejects Peace Talks in Video," Reuters, 3 March 2013, http://in.reuters .com/article/nigeria-boko-haram-idINDEE92208A20130303.

the security forces. The Nigerian government's "actions in response to [Boko Haram's] violence," they wrote, "have contravened international human rights standards and fueled further attacks."[4] In early 2013, complaints about the JTF's behavior grew louder, especially after a massacre of civilians that occurred on April 16–17, 2013, in Baga, a fishing community on the shore of Lake Chad in northeastern Borno.

The massacre was reportedly triggered when Boko Haram fighters fired at a military patrol in Baga. In reaction, soldiers rampaged through the town, killing suspected Boko Haram sympathizers and destroying homes. Afterward, senior officers downplayed the violence. Human Rights Watch, using satellite imagery, corroborated Baga residents' claims that some two thousand homes had been destroyed. Whereas the military estimated that only six civilians had died, the senator representing Baga put the toll at 220.[5]

The massacre raised broader questions about the military's behavior in the northeast. In its interim report on Baga, Nigeria's National Human Rights Commission focused on "whether the force was ultimately lawful or unlawful." The commission stated that amid disputes over casualty counts, "the impression has been created that certain thresholds or numbers of killing may be permissible as long as they are made to appear low enough. Government has not done enough to discourage this impression."[6] The commission cited deep problems in the military's conduct throughout the northeast:

[4] Human Rights Watch, "Spiraling Violence: Boko Haram Attacks and Security Force Abuses in Nigeria," October 2012, 9, https://www.hrw.org/sites/default/files/reports/nigeria1012webwcover_0.pdf.

[5] Human Rights Watch, "Nigeria: Massive Destruction, Deaths from Military Raid," 1 May 2013, https://www.hrw.org/news/2013/05/01/nigeria-massive-destruction-deaths-military-raid.

[6] National Human Rights Commission of Nigeria, "The Baga Incident and the Situation in North-East Nigeria: An Interim Assessment and Report," June 2013, 6.

The case against the JTF includes allegations of extra-judicial executions, torture, indeterminate incommunicado detention, indicating a pattern of internment without clear rules; practice that could violate the absolute prohibition in international law against enforced disappearance and against torture respectively; rape, various outrages against members of host communities and a pattern of disproportionate use of force.[7]

Excessive force, the commission suggested, was doing more harm than good. The commission warned of "a foreseeable humanitarian crisis [in] the region which could endanger the short term gains of the on-going security operations in northeast Nigeria."[8] These words accurately forecast the deterioration of the situation on both a humanitarian and a security level.

The JTF's heavy-handed tactics were not degrading Boko Haram's capacity to mount large-scale attacks. On May 8, 2013, an estimated two hundred Boko Haram fighters stormed Bama, Borno's second-largest city. They destroyed the city's police station and military barracks and freed 105 prisoners from the city's prison.[9] Perhaps the military deployments themselves had inadvertently contributed to Boko Haram's strength—whenever the sect surprised and overpowered soldiers, it gained new weaponry.

These developments compelled a response from Abuja. On May 14, 2013, President Goodluck Jonathan addressed his nation:

I hereby declare a state of emergency in Borno, Yobe, and Adamawa States. Accordingly, the Chief of Defense Staff has

[7] National Human Rights Commission, "Baga Incident," 7.
[8] National Human Rights Commission, "Baga Incident," 7.
[9] "Nigeria: 'Many Dead in Boko Haram Raid' in Borno State," BBC, 8 May 2013, http://www.bbc.com/news/world-africa-22444417.

been directed to immediately deploy more troops to those states for more effective internal security operations. The troops and other security agencies involved in these operations have orders to take all necessary actions within the ambits of their rules of engagement to put an end to the impunity of insurgents and terrorists. This will include the authority to arrest and detain suspects, the taking of possession and control of any building or structures used for terrorist purposes, the lockdown of any areas of terrorist operations, the conduct of searches and the apprehension of persons in illegal possession of weapons.[10]

Such measures were not new in Nigeria, either in general or in the specific context of the Boko Haram crisis. In January 2012, Jonathan had imposed a six-month state of emergency in sixteen local government areas in Borno, Yobe, Plateau, and Niger States, in order to combat Boko Haram as well as tamp down localized clashes in Plateau and Niger.[11] The 2013 state of emergency, however, was longer lasting and further reaching. It was renewed twice—in November 2013 and May 2014—before ending in November 2014, when the House of Representatives refused to grant Jonathan another extension.[12]

The state of emergency had a political context. It allowed Jonathan to assert greater authority over northeastern state governors, several of whom belonged to the opposition. In February 2013, the All Nigeria People's Party, which controlled Borno, Yobe, and Adamawa, had joined the emerging opposi-

[10]"Jonathan Declares State of Emergency in Borno, Yobe, Adamawa States," Channels Television, 14 May 2013, https://www.youtube.com/watch?v=3GglRw0urlw.

[11]Abdul Raufu Mustapha, "Understanding Boko Haram," in *Sects and Social Disorder: Identities and Conflict in Northern Nigeria*, edited by Abdul Raufu Mustapha, 147–98 (Suffolk: James Currey, 2014), 152.

[12]Asumpta Lattis, "Nigeria's State of Emergency 'a Failure,'" Deutsche Welle, 21 November 2014, http://www.dw.com/en/nigerias-state-of-emergency-a-failure/a-18079380.

tion coalition the All Progressives Congress (APC). Relations between Jonathan and the northeastern governors, including Borno State governor Kashima Shettima, were tense. On several occasions in 2014, Shettima publicly suggested that Boko Haram had the upper hand in the conflict. Such comments drew a harsh response from Jonathan, who at one time even threatened to withdraw the military from Borno.[13]

Much more dramatic was the conflict between Jonathan and Adamawa governor Murtala Nyako, who issued a memorandum in April 2014 entitled "On-Going Full-Fledged Genocide in Northern Nigeria." Nyako charged that official accounts of Boko Haram's violence were false. He suggested that a corrupt, unaccountable federal government was using the insurgency to assassinate critics, intimidate rivals, and provoke intercommunal conflict in the north.[14] Jonathan may have taken revenge: when Nyako was impeached by the Adamawa House of Assembly in July 2014, the national opposition accused Jonathan of having masterminded and funded the effort.[15] Alongside the state of emergency, there was an atmosphere of hostility toward northeastern politicians who criticized the federal government, the military, or the administration.

The state of emergency brought an increased military deployment. Even before the state of emergency was declared, the federal government deployed two thousand soldiers to Maiduguri and other towns in the northeast, supplementing

[13] Hussaini Monguno, "Boko Haram: Gov Shettima's Bitter Truth in Retrospect," *Desert Herald*, 30 September 2014, http://desertherald.com/boko-haram-gov-shettimas-bitter-truth-in-retrospect/.

[14] Murtala Nyako, "On-Going Full-Fledged Genocide in Northern Nigeria," Memorandum to the Northern Governors Forum, 16 April 2014. Text available at http://abusidiqu.com/going-full-fledged-genocide-northern-nigeria-gov-murtala-nyako/.

[15] Nnenna Ibeh, "APC Blames Jonathan for Nyako's Impeachment," *Premium Times*, 16 July 2014, http://www.premiumtimesng.com/news/165054-apc-blames-jonathan-for-nyakos-impeachment.html.

an estimated thirty-six hundred soldiers already there under the banner of the JTF.[16] In August 2013, the JTF would be rebranded as a new unit, the Seventh Army Division, with an estimated eight thousand total troops.[17]

On the ground, the state of emergency translated into mass arrests of young men, especially in May and June 2013. Some raids resulted in deaths on the spot. The security forces took hundreds of other men to two military prisons, Giwa Barracks in Maiduguri and Sector Alpha in Damaturu, a site also known as "Guantanamo." A select few were taken to Abuja.[18] In these prisons, suspected Boko Haram members were often tortured, sometimes to death. Other detainees died of starvation and disease.[19] By late 2014, between five thousand and ten thousand people accused of links to Boko Haram had been detained.[20]

The escalation of the war boosted Boko Haram. First, it provided Boko Haram with access to more arms. For example, in Bama Local Government Area (LGA) of Borno, 2012–13 brought not only a substantial escalation of violence, but also a series of Boko Haram raids on military and police installations.[21] Second, the state of emergency made civilians more

[16] Fund for Peace, "Conflict Bulletin: Borno State," May 2014, 2, http://library.fund forpeace.org/library/cungr1420-nigeriaconflictbulletin-borno-05a.pdf.

[17] Kingsley Omonobi, "Jonathan Creates New Army Division, Sends 8,000 Troops after Boko Haram," *Vanguard*, 18 August 2013, http://www.vanguardngr.com/2013/08 /jonathan-creates-new-army-division-sends-8000-troops-after-boko-haram/.

[18] Amnesty International, "'Welcome to Hell Fire': Torture and Other Ill Treatment in Nigeria," September 2014, 14–15, https://www.amnesty.org/en/documents /AFR44/011/2014/en/.

[19] Human Rights Watch, "Nigeria: Boko Haram Abducts Women, Recruits Children," 29 November 2013, https://www.hrw.org/news/2013/11/29/nigeria-boko-haram -abducts-women-recruits-children.

[20] Amnesty International, "'Welcome to Hell Fire,'" 14–15.

[21] Fund for Peace, "Conflict Bulletin: Borno State," 2, http://library.fundforpeace .org/library/cungr1420-nigeriaconflictbulletin-borno-05a.pdf.

isolated and vulnerable. When the authorities blacked out mobile phone communications and media access, civilians had a harder time communicating with one another. Many ordinary people were hampered by curfews and checkpoints, even as Boko Haram retained considerable freedom of movement in rural areas. "Early warning systems were crippled; schools were closed; farming virtually stopped; many markets closed; major roadways were frequently blocked; massive displacement ensued; banditry increased; and attacks and kidnappings became more commonplace."[22] Third, the heavy-handed tactics of the security forces may have boosted Boko Haram's recruitment.[23] At the very least, the security forces' behavior often alienated civilians and discouraged them from sharing important information with authorities.

Even amid escalation, Nigerian troops often had a weak presence in many northeastern towns. Sometimes, Nigerian soldiers fled when a Boko Haram attack was anticipated.[24] In one instance, nearly five hundred soldiers fled into Cameroon in August 2014 after losing ground to Boko Haram in the border town of Gamboru-Ngala.[25] After the Chibok kidnapping in April 2014 (discussed below), reports emerged that the military had received advance warning of the attack but had declined to send reinforcements to the town.[26]

---

[22] Kyle Dietrich, "When We Can't See the Enemy, Civilians Become the Enemy": Living through Nigeria's Six-Year Insurgency (Washington, DC: Center for Civilians in Conflict 2015), 3, http://civiliansinconflict.org/uploads/files/publications/Nigeria Report_Web.pdf.

[23] Dietrich, "When We Can't See the Enemy," 4.

[24] Dietrich, "When We Can't See the Enemy," 31.

[25] "Nigerian Soldiers Flee Boko Haram to Cameroon," Deutsche Welle, 26 August 2014, http://www.dw.com/en/nigerian-soldiers-flee-boko-haram-to-cameroon/a -17878610.

[26] Amnesty International, "Nigeria: Government Knew of Planned Boko Haram Kidnapping but Failed to Act," 9 May 2014, https://www.amnesty.org.uk/press-releases /nigeria-government-knew-planned-boko-haram-kidnapping-failed-act.

Some Nigerians criticized the new state of affairs. The Northern Elders Forum said that the state of emergency reflected the failure of the security forces to communicate effectively with the civilian population in the northeast.[27] Civil society activist Jibrin Ibrahim, building on their comments, wrote:

> The utility of this [military deployment and expanded powers of detention] remains doubtful especially within the context of the recent Baga debacle where over 200 citizens were allegedly murdered by security agents and thousands of houses were burnt and destroyed. The anti-community approach of security agencies has been consistently criticized by community leaders and elders such as the Borno Elders' Forum who have postulated that the path to resolution of the crisis is the withdrawal of security agencies from the states. In the last two weeks, we have been inundated with reports that the Baga Massacre has actually led to an expansion of the ranks of Boko Haram as more foot soldiers have been enlisted.[28]

These warnings were partly heeded by the government, but perhaps not in the way that civil society voices had intended. Civilian politicians and military commanders were hostile to civil society activists' and human rights groups' complaints about torture and maltreatment of civilians, but the politicians and generals were sensitive to their worsening image in the international community.

As military deployments increased and maltreatment of civilians continued, the Jonathan administration in Abuja and

---

[27] Adam Nossiter, "Nigeria's President Gives Military More Power in Struggle against Militants," *New York Times*, 15 May 2013, http://www.nytimes.com/2013/05 /16/world/africa/nigeria-military-gets-more-power-to-fight-rebels.html.

[28] Jibrin Ibrahim, "Declaration of State of Emergency on 14th May 2013: A Preliminary Assessment," Centre for Democracy Development in West Africa Blog, 15 May 2013, http://blog.cddwestafrica.org/2013/05/declaration-of-state-of-emergency -on-14th-may-2013-a-preliminary-assessment/.

Governor Kashim Shettima's administration in Maiduguri hit on a new strategy: recruiting civilian vigilantes to fight Boko Haram. In the security realm, this strategy had the advantage of activating Borno residents' real and imagined knowledge of Boko Haram's human networks, thereby increasing the government's ability to root out the sect's fighters and supporters. In the political sphere, the strategy allowed the federal and state governments to claim a newfound level of organic, grassroots popular support for the brutal campaign against Boko Haram.

The Rise of the C-JTF

The Civilian Joint Task Force or C-JTF reportedly emerged in June 2013 in Borno State,[29] one month after the state of emergency was imposed. Judging from anecdotal accounts in the Nigerian and international media, the group's social base was urban youth, including teenagers. There were also civil servants, professionals, and traders among the C-JTF's leaders. According to one account, its founder was Baba Lawal Ja'far, a "car and sheep salesman" from Maiduguri who was in his early thirties.[30]

Some youth joined for personal reasons. One vigilante explained to interviewers,

> I joined the voluntary vigilante group to make sure that all the people feeding and aiding Boko Haram were severely dealt

---

[29] Alexis Okeowo, "Inside the Vigilante Fight against Boko Haram," *New York Times Magazine*, 9 November 2014, http://www.nytimes.com/2014/11/09/magazine /inside-the-vigilante-fight-against-boko-haram.html?_r=1.

[30] Adam Nossiter, "Vigilantes Defeat Boko Haram in Its Nigerian Base," *New York Times*, 20 October 2013, http://www.nytimes.com/2013/10/21/world/africa/vigilantes -defeat-boko-haram-in-its-nigerian-base.html.

with. I want to see them arrested, captured, and made to face trial for their atrocities. It will mean a great deal of happiness and satisfaction to me because I have lost friends and persons close to me.[31]

Another motive was Boko Haram's destruction of schools: as the sect attacked schools throughout Borno and Yobe in 2012 and 2013, some youth felt that they had to choose sides. At the same time, the C-JTF's rise reinforced Boko Haram's conviction that schools were hubs for vigilantes, and that secondary school students who did not join the sect should be killed.[32]

By July 2013, the security forces and the C-JTF had largely expelled Boko Haram from Maiduguri.[33] Much of summer and fall 2013 passed without major attacks in the city. Decisive for the C-JTF was not just its numerical strength—the group soon boasted of having thousands or even tens of thousands of fighters[34]—but its fighters' ability to name and identify Boko Haram members. Local knowledge allowed the C-JTF to reduce Boko Haram's clandestine presence in Maiduguri and elsewhere. The C-JTF's presence likely had a chilling effect on Boko Haram's urban networks, fighters and passive supporters alike.[35] Even when ridiculing the C-JTF's military capabilities, Boko Haram admitted the vigilantes' intelligence-gathering

[31] Quoted in Dietrich, "When We Can't See the Enemy," 57.

[32] "Nigeria School Attacks Spur Vigilante Groups," IRIN, 27 June 2013, http://www.irinnews.org/report/98294/nigeria-school-attacks-spur-vigilante-groups. See also Monica Mark, "Nigeria's War with Boko Haram Gets a New Ground Zero," Guardian, 9 May 2013, http://www.theguardian.com/world/2013/may/09/nigeria-war-boko-haram-new-ground-zero.

[33] Human Rights Watch, "Nigeria: Boko Haram Abducts Women, Recruits Children."

[34] Obi Anyadike, "Nigeria: The Community Turns against Boko Haram," IRIN, 11 August 2014, http://www.irinnews.org/report/100475/nigeria-the-community-turns-against-boko-haram.

[35] Nossiter, "Vigilantes Defeat Boko Haram."

capabilities: "They can do nothing except guide the tyrants to the mujahidin's positions, because they are local boys."[36]

Yet the activation of the C-JTF meant that Boko Haram members now sometimes knew who had informed against them. This dynamic intensified the interpersonal dimensions of the conflict, setting the stage for cyclical reprisals between Boko Haram and the C-JTF. Even before the rise of the C-JTF, tensions over who was informing on whom had featured in the conflict. The rise of the C-JTF fueled score settling that was unrelated to the central conflict or even to membership in Boko Haram. Some civilians found themselves facing the wrath of all sides.

The degree of government sponsorship for the C-JTF has been debated: some early accounts from Borno depicted the vigilantism as a grassroots response to Boko Haram's violence against civilians. Other voices portrayed the C-JTF as an effort masterminded by the Nigerian military after the failure of its "scorched-earth policy of indiscriminate killings and burning of homes." Reports emerged of Borno residents being conscripted into C-JTF units.[37]

Soon after its formation, Borno's political authorities were openly backing the C-JTF. In September 2013, the state government launched the Borno Youth Empowerment Scheme, providing military training to an initial group of over six hundred vigilantes.[38] By late 2013, some eighteen hundred vigilantes were officially under the state government's authority. Each fighter received around $100 per month.[39] The state government did not

---

[36] "Wali Gharb Ifriqiya: Al-Shaykh Abu Mus'ab al-Barnawi," *Al-Naba'* 41 (2 August 2016): 8–9; 9, https://azelin.files.wordpress.com/2016/08/the-islamic-state-e2809 cal-nabacc84_-newsletter-4122.pdf.

[37] "Civilian Vigilante Groups Increase Dangers in Northeastern Nigeria," IRIN, 12 December 2013, http://www.irinnews.org/printreport.aspx?reportid=99320.

[38] Yusuf Alli, "Borno Retrains 632 Civilian JTF Members," *Nation*, 27 September 2013, http://thenationonlineng.net/borno-retrains-632-civilian-jtf-members/.

[39] Human Rights Watch, "Nigeria: Boko Haram Abducts Women."

arm them: vigilantes would instead arm themselves, often with aging firearms or machetes and clubs.[40]

The C-JTF and the security forces cooperated closely. Vigilantes would often capture suspected Boko Haram members and immediately turn them over to security personnel.[41] C-JTF members operated checkpoints in Maiduguri and elsewhere.[42] Soldiers and vigilantes sometimes fought side by side. After Boko Haram stormed Maiduguri's Giwa Barracks prison in March 2014, freeing many prisoners there, the military and C-JTF worked together to punish those who were recaptured. Amnesty International reported,

> As the military regained control, more than 600 people, mostly unarmed recaptured detainees, were extra-judicially executed in various locations across Maiduguri.... Eyewitnesses in Jiddari Polo, also in Maiduguri, described how members of the "Civilian Joint Task Force" rounded up freed prisoners and handed them to soldiers. More than 190 people were executed, many of whom were too frail to run.[43]

This cooperation reinforced Boko Haram's identification of the C-JTF as a bitter enemy.

Cooperation between the security forces, the C-JTF, and the political authorities did not always run smoothly. The C-JTF

[40] Obi Anyadike, "Nigeria: The Community Turns against Boko Haram," IRIN, 11 August 2014, http://www.irinnews.org/report/100475/nigeria-the-community-turns-against-boko-haram.

[41] Okeowo, "Inside the Vigilante Fight."

[42] Ashionye Ogene, "Nigerian Vigilantes Aim to Rout Boko Haram," Al Jazeera, 31 May 2014, http://www.aljazeera.com/indepth/features/2014/05/nigerian-vigilantes-aim-rout-boko-haram-2014526123758444854.html.

[43] Amnesty International, "Nigeria: War Crimes and Crimes against Humanity as Violence Escalates in North-East," 31 March 2014, https://www.amnesty.org/en/latest/news/2014/03/nigeria-war-crimes-and-crimes-against-humanity-violence-escalates-north-east/.

sometimes lynched accused Boko Haram members, even over the objections of the security forces.[44] The vigilantes also mistrusted Borno's politicians. On June 1, 2013, "hundreds" of vigilantes attacked and torched the home of Mala Othman, any ally of former governor Sheriff and the chairman of Borno's ruling All Nigeria People's Party, "accusing him of being a [Boko Haram] sponsor." The mob also attempted to burn down Sheriff's home.[45] While the C-JTF was enthusiastic about working with Governor Shettima, the vigilantes were operating in an atmosphere suffused with contentious politics and unresolved questions. It was not just Boko Haram who had a grudge against Sheriff. With the C-JTF's role in politics unclear, Nigerian civil society members and foreign analysts questioned whether the C-JTF would ultimately do more harm than good[46]—and whether it would become a tool for unscrupulous politicians, as Boko Haram had a decade earlier.

The C-JTF was closer to Shettima than to the federal government. In May 2014, as the state of emergency came up for its second six-month extension, the C-JTF called on Jonathan not to renew the measure—and asked the federal government to arm their units. A C-JTF spokesman stated:

> The Borno State government had done its best in supporting us through training and payment of our allowances which runs into millions of naira. We have structures in all the 27 local government areas and our members are highly disciplined. We

---

[44] Ibrahim Sawab, "Boko Haram Hunters Burn Another Sect Member in Maiduguri," *Daily Trust*, 27 July 2013, http://allafrica.com/stories/201307270089.html.

[45] "Civilian Vigilante Groups Increase Dangers." See also Ndahi Marama, "Youths Burn Borno ANPP Chair's House," *Vanguard*, 2 July 2013, http://www.vanguardngr.com/2013/07/youths-burn-borno-anpp-chairs-house/.

[46] See Anyadike, "Nigeria: The Community Turns against Boko Haram"; and Omar Mahmood, "Youth Vigilantes Stand Up to Boko Haram, but at a Cost," *Think Africa Press*, 28 February 2014, http://allafrica.com/stories/201403041131.html.

want arms so that we can take the fight to the insurgents in the bushes. . . . The president had once called us heroes but has never granted any financial or logistic support to our members who are risking their lives to keep the country one. We want the federal government to assist us.[47]

As the C-JTF complained of a lack of arms, the nature of the conflict continued to shift. Seeking to neutralize the C-JTF, Boko Haram increasingly turned to controlling territory in northeastern Nigeria. This control was related, intimately, to the crisis economy that had grown up around Boko Haram.

A Crisis Economy

In total, the Boko Haram crisis has represented a tremendous economic loss for northeastern Nigeria. In April 2016, Borno State governor Kashim Shettima calculated his state's losses at "almost $6 billion as a result of the insurgency."[48] The economic losses for neighboring Nigerian states, for Nigeria as a whole, and for Nigeria's neighbors are nearly incalculable.

Certain actors, however, have benefited financially from the crisis. The resulting crisis economy has been a key factor in perpetuating the violence. Boko Haram has been one major beneficiary, deriving revenues from bank robberies, extortion, kidnappings, and control of urban and rural areas. Boko Haram's extortion built on earlier patterns of rural banditry and urban criminality in northeastern Nigeria, but the scale of the

---

[47] Hamza Idris, "Civilian JTF Demands Arms, Decries Extension of Emergency," *Daily Trust*, 15 May 2014, http://allafrica.com/stories/201405160507.html.

[48] "Boko Haram-Hit Nigerian State Calls for Help to Rebuild," AFP, 19 April 2016, https://www.yahoo.com/news/boko-haram-hit-nigerian-state-calls-help-rebuild-1411 50701.html.

violence transformed local economies as never before. Boko Haram may have even directly taken over certain economic activities: In summer 2015, the Borno State government reportedly instructed traders and customers in Maiduguri not to buy fish coming from Baga, then under Boko Haram control, out of fear that sect members had begun to manage the fish trade.[49] Certain security officers and local politicians also benefited from the crisis. Sometimes, their benefit may have derived from collusion with Boko Haram. In September 2016, the military's theater commander in the northeast, Major General Lucky Irabor, accused unnamed soldiers of selling weapons and ammunition to Boko Haram.[50] Low-level Borno State politicians have been arrested on charges of aiding and abetting Boko Haram, as occurred in December 2016 when police arrested the chairman of Mafa Local Government Area for allegedly hiding a Boko Haram commander in his house.[51]

More serious profits, however, were to be made through diversions of public resources, particularly the security budget. Transparency International has stated, "During the height of the conflict, corrupt senior officers withheld ammunition and fuel from front-line soldiers, leaving them with no alternative other than to flee when attacked."[52] One Maiduguri-based

[49] Shehu Abubakar, "Something Fishy Going On in Baga," *Daily Trust*, 22 August 2015, http://www.dailytrust.com.ng/news/feature/something-fishy-going-on-in-baga /107566.html.

[50] "Nigerian Military: Some Officers Selling Arms to Boko Haram," Associated Press, 4 September 2016, http://www.voanews.com/a/nigerian-military-some-officers -selling-arms-to-boko-haram/3493038.html.

[51] Ndahi Marama, "Top Wanted Boko Haram Commander Arrested at Borno LG Chairman's House," *Vanguard*, 31 December 2016, http://www.vanguardngr.com /2016/12/top-wanted-boko-haram-commander-arrested-borno-lg-chairmans-house/.

[52] Eva Anderson and Matthew Page, "Weaponising Transparency: Defence Procurement Reform as a Counterterrorism Strategy in Nigeria," *Transparency International* (May 2017), 13, http://ti-defence.org/wp-content/uploads/2017/05/Weaponising _Transparency_Web.pdf.

Sufi shaykh has written, regarding the 2013 declaration of a state of emergency,

> The military then converted the insecurity into a lucrative business venture and purposely lacked the will to end the crisis. Both Boko Haram members and the military openly robbed, kidnapped, bombed and murdered individuals seizing their properties. The military also made profit from unjust arrest[s] of youth and demanding millions of Naira in bail money even as families were forced to declare their wards as Boko Haram members. . . . Those officers that were posted over to Maiduguri purposely deprived troops of arms and ammunitions even as the Abuja-sitting generals and officers short-changed the troops of their allocations. Officers located in Borno also pocketed allowances meant for the troops (paid by the state government), placed them on single daily meal rations while deducting the cost their allowances. These actions partly explain why the military troops turned the crisis into a profitable business since they were not catered for by the government of the day.[53]

The most serious allegation of security commanders' malfeasance has been directed at Sambo Dasuki, who served as national security advisor under President Jonathan from 2012 to 2015. In December 2015, a little more than six months after the inauguration of Jonathan's rival Buhari, Dasuki was arrested on charges of diverting more than $2 billion from the security budget. The legal proceedings against Dasuki, which were ongoing as this book went to press, have become embroiled in Nigerian partisan politics, but that does not mean that the charges are baseless.

[53] Khalifa Aliyu Ahmed Abulfathi, "The Metamorphosis of Boko Haram: A Local's Perspective" (Maiduguri: Sheikh Ahmed Abulfathi Foundation, 2016), http://sheikhahmadabulfathi.org/content/metamorphosis-boko-haram-0.

Many soldiers fighting on the front lines against Boko Haram share the perception that their superiors are corrupt. In May 2014, soldiers at Maiduguri's Maimalari Barracks opened fire on a car carrying Major General Ahmed Mohammed, "blam[ing] him for the killing of their colleagues in an ambush by suspected Boko Haram militants."[54] Three months later, a group of soldiers near Maiduguri refused to fight, saying that "the Nigerian army is not ready to fight Boko Haram" owing to a lack of weapons.[55] The mutinies—and the harsh responses commanders meted out—became international news, highlighting how corruption and inadequate resources had made the Nigerian military a shadow of what it had been in the 1990s.[56]

The combination of these trends—the economic opportunities available to whoever controlled Borno's towns and rural areas, and the weakness of a hollowed-out military—provided Boko Haram with further incentive, and opportunity, to take territorial control.

Boko Haram, the C-JTF, and Territorial Control

It is unclear when Boko Haram began to control territory in northeastern Nigeria. When President Jonathan declared a state of emergency in May 2013, he stated:

---

[54]"Nigeria Soldiers 'Fire at Army Commander in Maiduguri,'" BBC, 14 May 2014, http://www.bbc.com/news/world-africa-27417778.

[55]"Boko Haram Crisis: Nigerian Soldiers 'Mutiny over Weapons,'" BBC, 19 August 2014, http://www.bbc.com/news/world-africa-28855292.

[56]Kevin Sieff, "The Nigerian Military Is So Broken, Its Soldiers Are Refusing to Fight," *Washington Post*, 10 May 2015, https://www.washingtonpost.com/world /africa/the-nigerian-military-is-so-broken-its-soldiers-are-refusing-to-fight/2015 /05/06/d56fabac-dcae-11e4-b6d7-b9bc8acf16f7_story.html?utm_term=.2e6a3fb ec8e7.

What we are facing is not just militancy or criminality, but a rebellion, an insurgency by terrorist groups which pose a very serious threat to national unity and territorial integrity. Already, some northern parts of Borno State have been taken over by groups whose allegiance is to different flags and ideologies. These terrorists and insurgents seem determined to establish control and authority over parts of our beloved nation and to progressively overwhelm the rest of the country. In many places, they have destroyed the Nigerian flag and other symbols of state authority, and in their place hoisted strange flags suggesting the exercise of alternative sovereignty. They have attacked government buildings and facilities. They have murdered Nigerian citizens and state officials. They have set buildings ablaze and have taken women and children as hostages. These actions are marking a declaration of war and a deliberate attempt to undermine the authority of the Nigerian state.[57]

From Borno, the Northern Elders Forum said that Jonathan had exaggerated Boko Haram's degree of territorial control.[58] Yet in April 2013, the Nigerian media described at least ten of Borno's twenty-seven local government areas as "overrun" by Boko Haram. Local officials had fled to Maiduguri, leaving the sect with freedom of movement.[59] What seems clear is that by spring 2013, Boko Haram had sway over parts of Borno, but it was not until the summer of 2014 that the group

[57] "Jonathan Declares State of Emergency in Borno, Yobe, Adamawa States," Channels Television, 14 May 2013, https://www.youtube.com/watch?v=3GglRw0urlw.

[58] Adam Nossiter, "Nigeria's President Gives Military More Power in Struggle against Militants," New York Times, 15 May 2013, http://www.nytimes.com/2013/05/16/world/africa/nigeria-military-gets-more-power-to-fight-rebels.html.

[59] Yusuf Alli, "Tension as Boko Haram Grounds 10 LGs in Borno," Nation, 20 April 2013, http://thenationonlineng.net/tension-as-boko-haram-grounds-10-lgs-in-borno-2/. The ten LGAs were: Marte, Magumeri, Mobbar, Gubio, Guzamala, Abadam, Kukawa, Kaga, Nganzai, and Monguno.

would assert official territorial control over major towns. As noted above, this change reflected Boko Haram's newfound capabilities, based on its acquisition of weapons left by defeated or fleeing Nigerian soldiers; and its newfound motivations, especially its desire to destroy the C-JTF.

Boko Haram condemned the C-JTF immediately upon its formation, using ominous language that foreshadowed the widening war against civilians. In June 2013, the group's purported spokesman told journalists, "We have established that the youth in Borno and Yobe states are now against our course. They have connived with security operatives and are actively supporting the government of Nigeria in its war against us. We have also resolved to fight back."[60] The sect's long-held exclusivist conception of Islam, as well as its long-standing conviction that the state and "apostate" Muslims were colluding to fight the true vanguard of Islam, now contributed to escalating violence against civilian vigilantes and their perceived supporters. Shekau did not care that many of these targets, combatants and noncombatants alike, were Muslims; in his view, they had abandoned Islam.

In summer 2013, as the C-JTF drove Boko Haram into the northeastern countryside, the sect began to target the C-JTF and its perceived supporters. In July and August, the C-JTF sought to push beyond Maiduguri, hoping to root Boko Haram out of areas near the city. Boko Haram responded with ambushes. In late July, the sect attacked vigilantes who had come to the villages of Mainok and Dawashi.[61] In late August, it killed another two dozen vigilantes in a battle in Monguno,

[60]"Boko Haram Declares War on Borno, Yobe Youth over Vigilante Activities," *Premium Times*, 18 June 2013, http://www.premiumtimesng.com/news/139063-boko-haram-declares-war-on-borno-yobe-youth-over-vigilante-activities.html.

[61]Hamza Idris, Yahaya Ibrahim, and Ibrahim Sawab, "Boko Haram Kills 43 Borno Villagers," *Daily Trust*, 29 July 2013, http://allafrica.com/stories/201307291041.html.

thwarting the C-JTF's plan to attack the sect's camp there.[62] Boko Haram raided on towns and villages that were strongholds for the C-JTF. In Bama, Boko Haram killed fourteen vigilantes on August 25.[63]

Boko Haram often seemed to know—or to arbitrarily decide—precisely who was and was not a C-JTF member or supporter. On September 17, 2013, Boko Haram attacked Benisheikh, Borno:

> Witnesses said that based on comments from Boko Haram, many of the victims were targeted merely on the basis of where they lived: those from Maiduguri, Damaturu, and other towns in Borno and Yobe states were singled out for execution because of their perceived support for the Civilian Joint Task Force. Many of those from Kano and elsewhere were spared.[64]

Boko Haram members may have even infiltrated the C-JTF. Boko Haram also punished noncombatant civilians whom it saw as sympathetic to the C-JTF. Following the clash with vigilantes in Mainok, Boko Haram attacked the main market. Its fighters killed some two dozen people and accused villagers of having aided the C-JTF.[65] If personal networks and local knowledge helped the C-JTF identify Boko Haram members, similar assets helped Boko Haram anticipate and repel some of the C-JTF's attacks. Boko Haram's inside information may have also helped it take the offensive against the vigilantes

---

[62] Tim Cocks, "Nigeria Islamists Kill 24 Vigilantes in Ambush," Reuters, 31 August 2013, http://www.reuters.com/article/us-nigeria-violence-idUSBRE97U0FO20130831.

[63] Tim Cocks, "Nigeria Islamists Kill 14 Vigilantes in Bama Raid," Reuters, 26 August 2013, http://www.reuters.com/article/us-nigeria-violence-idUSBRE97P0PU 20130826.

[64] Human Rights Watch, "Nigeria: Boko Haram Abducts Women."

[65] Idris, Ibrahim, and Sawab, "Boko Haram Kills 43 Borno Villagers."

outside Maiduguri. Meanwhile, both forces increasingly demanded that noncombatant civilians take sides in a total war. Almost in lockstep, the decrease in violence within Maiduguri correlated with an increase in violence in other Borno LGAs, including Bama, Kaga, Biu, Gwoza, and Konduga.[66] Much violence against civilians occurred in Borno South, an ethnically and religiously diverse part of Borno.[67] Even before Boko Haram started to hold territory in those regions in summer 2014, its violence there led to a mass exodus of Christians.[68]

By the time Boko Haram attacked Giwa Barracks in March 2014, Shekau identified the C-JTF as a central enemy: "Whether you run, or you take up arms, or you put on a soldier's uniform, or you put on a police uniform, or you put on a turban. . . . What I am saying now, is that I have begun to topple you."[69] In military terms, Shekau intended the Giwa attack to bolster Boko Haram's ranks through yet another prison break. In propaganda terms, he suggested that the attack symbolized the ultimate impotence of the Nigerian military and the C-JTF against Boko Haram. Shekau bragged, "We freed a great many [literally, over 2,000] brothers . . . one of them, at the gate of the barracks, took a gun and started fighting . . . the world has changed."[70] Following the attack, Boko Haram released videos of its young fighters storming the prison.

[66] Fund for Peace, "Conflict Bulletin: Borno State," 1–2.

[67] Michael Baca, "The Tragedy of Borno State: Local Dimensions of Boko Haram's Insurgency," African Arguments, 19 December 2014, http://africanarguments.org/2014/12/19/the-tragedy-of-borno-state-local-dimensions-of-boko-harams-insurgency-by-michael-baca/.

[68] Thomas Mösch, "Why Has Borno Become a Stronghold of Terror in Nigeria?," Deutsche Welle, 15 July 2014, http://www.dw.com/en/why-has-borno-become-a-stronghold-of-terror-in-nigeria/a-17788683.

[69] Shekau, "Ma'rakat Maiduguri 2."

[70] Abubakar Shekau, "Ma'rakat Maiduguri 2," March 2014, https://www.youtube.com/watch?v=Pba8uvuf9Is.

The most infamous of Boko Haram's attacks—its kidnapping of 276 schoolgirls on the night of April 14–15, 2014—occurred in the context of this total war. At Government Secondary School in Chibok, Borno South, the teenage girls had gathered to take exams despite the general climate of insecurity. When the attack began, the girls were initially duped by Boko Haram members posing as soldiers and promising to escort them to safety. After Boko Haram loaded the girls onto trucks, a few escaped en route by grasping tree branches or fleeing during breaks. But most were driven to Boko Haram's hideouts, where they became sexual slaves and propaganda objects for the group. The incident became a national trauma for Nigeria and evoked international outcry.[71]

Chibok was part of a broader pattern. As Boko Haram attacked civilians in the northeast's villages and towns, the sect targeted boarding schools and residential colleges. In these raids, Boko Haram sometimes conscripted boys but often slaughtered them outright. This pattern occurred at Government Secondary School in Mamudo, Yobe, in July 2013;[72] at the College of Agriculture in Gujba, Yobe, in September 2013;[73] at Federal Government College in Buni Yadi, Yobe, in February 2014; and in other, smaller attacks.[74] Women, meanwhile, faced abduction and sexual slavery: by September 2013—well before

[71] It would be hard to cite all the powerful writing that the Chibok kidnapping has elicited. One title worth particular mention is Helon Habila, *The Chibok Girls: The Boko Haram Kidnappings and Islamic Militancy in Nigeria* (New York: Columbia Global Reports, 2016).

[72] Okechukwu Uwaezuoke, "Gunmen Kill 29 Boarding Students in Yobe School," *This Day*, 7 July 2013, http://www.thisdaylive.com/articles/gunmen-kill29-boarding-students-in-yobe-school/152677/.

[73] "Nigeria Attack: Students Shot Dead as They Slept," BBC, 29 September 2013, http://www.bbc.com/news/world-africa-24322683.

[74] Joe Hemba, "Nigerian Islamists Kill 59 Pupils in Boarding School Attack," Reuters, 26 February 2014, http://www.reuters.com/article/us-nigeria-violence-idUS BREA1P10M20140226.

the Chibok kidnapping—Boko Haram was regularly kidnapping groups of young women and forcing them to marry its young fighters.[75]

Such kidnappings served both material and political ends: they provided wives for potentially restless young recruits and conscripts, and they fulfilled Shekau's threat to avenge Nigerian authorities' detentions of Boko Haram members' female relatives.[76] In 2012, Shekau had said:

> They're holding our brothers in prison. They've arrested them, tortured them, and subjected them to various forms of abuse. I'm not just talking about our religious leader—now, they've started to detain our women. . . . Since you are seizing our women, you wait and see what will happen to your women.[77]

The Chibok kidnapping had strong symbolic resonance, which Shekau exploited. For both jihadists and Western governments, young women—their schooling and their bodies—symbolize visions of moral order. After Chibok, Shekau infamously proclaimed, "I seized your young women. I will sell them in the market." Seeking to internationalize the incident, he taunted Barack Obama and other world leaders. Reinforcing his personal connection to the incident, he mocked the bounty on his own head and promised to sell Jonathan and Obama as slaves.[78]

As the world's attention fixated on Chibok, the broader war continued. The sect—even more aggressively than before—claimed the exclusive right to speak for Islam in Nigeria. In

[75] Human Rights Watch, "Nigeria: Boko Haram Abducts Women."

[76] Elizabeth Pearson and Jacob Zenn, "How Nigerian Police Also Detained Women and Children as a Weapon of War," *Guardian*, 6 May 2014, http://www.the guardian.com/world/2014/may/06/how-nigerian-police-also-detained-women -and-children-as-weapon-of-war.

[77] Shekau, "Sako Zuwa Ga Duniya."

[78] Boko Haram, "Min dunihi Fa-Kiduni."

addition to killing Muslims en masse when they rejected Boko Haram, the sect brazenly attacked senior Muslim religious leaders. Increasingly after 2011, the sect targeted hereditary rulers and religious rivals, Sufis and Salafis alike. The attacks on emirs represented a move from disrespect to violence. For example, during their September 2010 prison break in Bauchi, Boko Haram members had detained the Emir of Bauchi inside the city's central mosque, rather than killing him, evincing some vestigial deference to hereditary rulers. But in spring 2011, the sect assassinated two brothers of the Shehu of Borno. Fighters made attempts on other rulers' lives: on the Shehu himself in July 2012, on the Emir of Fika in August 2012, and on the Emir of Kano Ado Bayero in January 2013.[79] These attempts failed, but in 2014, the violence against Muslim religious leaders became even more severe: Boko Haram killed the prominent Salafi shaykh Muhammad Awwal "Albani" Zaria in February, unsuccessfully targeted the leading Tijani Sufi shaykh Dahiru Usman Bauchi in July,[80] and murdered the Tijani shaykh Adam al-Nafati of Bauchi State in November.[81]

This violence was not just about silencing critics. Boko Haram was working to reshape northern Nigeria's religious field. By removing rivals, Boko Haram hoped to become the sole spokesman for Islam. After Albani Zaria's death, Shekau sent a wider message to the Muslim elite, naming and threat-

[79] Alex Thurston, "Partial List of Alleged Boko Haram Attacks on Hereditary Muslim Rulers in Northern Nigeria," Sahel Blog, 25 January 2013, https://sahelblog .wordpress.com/2013/01/25/partial-list-of-alleged-boko-haram-attacks-on-hereditary -muslim-rulers-in-northern-nigeria/.

[80] Andrea Brigaglia, "Note on Shaykh Dahiru Usman Bauchi and the July 2014 Kaduna Bombing," *Annual Review of Islam in Africa*, no. 12/1 (2013–14): 39–42.

[81] "Boko Haram Kills Scores, Islamic Cleric in Nafada," *Sun*, November 5, 2014, http://sunnewsonline.com/new/boko-haram-kills-scores-islamic-cleric-in-nafada/.

ening Izala's Sani Yahaya Jingir, several emirs, and various religious leaders in Maiduguri:

> Yahaya Jingir, the leader of *'ulama* in Jos, the leader for making Boko halal [lawful in Islam], right? We are Boko Haram, and you are Boko Halal. . . . We killed Albani Zaria. Shekau killed Albani Zaria. Tomorrow he will kill Jingir, and the day after tomorrow he will kill Dapchia [the imam of the Friday mosque in Maiduguri]. One day he will kill Wapchama [the Grand Imam of Maiduguri]. One day he will kill the Shehu of Borno and Ado Bayero. We have rebelled against you. Between us and you are hatred and ill will until you have faith in Allah.[82]

In November 2014, a Boko Haram suicide bomber attempted to kill Kano's new emir, Muhammadu Sanusi II (the former banker and Islamic scholar Sanusi Lamido Sanusi, who took the throne in June 2014).[83] When Sanusi urged Nigerians to arm themselves against Boko Haram, Shekau reacted furiously. Shekau contrasted what he called Sanusi's "religion of democracy" to Boko Haram's alleged devotion to God.[84] Such rhetoric cast the emir as an infidel.

Alongside Boko Haram's conflict with the Muslim youth who made up the bulk of the C-JTF, the sect sought to marginalize, anathematize, and kill rival religious leaders. Sometimes, the violence directly fed into Boko Haram's territorial ambitions: In May 2014, Boko Haram killed the Emir of

[82]"Za Mu Kashe Malamai da Sarakuna da 'Yan Siyasa—Boko Haram," *Aminiya*, February 21, 2014. Available at http://aminiya.com.ng/index.php/mayan-labarai/4841 -za-mu-kashe-malamai-da-sarakuna-da-yan-siyasa-boko-haram; accessed March 2014.

[83]"Nigeria Unrest: Kano Mosque Attack Kills Dozens," *BBC News*, 28 November 2014, http://www.bbc.com/news/world-africa-30250950.

[84]Abubakar Shekau, "Risala ila al-Za'im al-Musamma bi-Malik Kano," December 2014, http://www.liveleak.com/view?i=af5_1418909889.

Gwoza,[85] the town where it founded a "state" three months later.

Boko Haram's "State"

In Boko Haram's struggle with the C-JTF, a turning point came with the battle for Damboa, Borno, in June and July 2014: Boko Haram now openly held territory. This move reflected the sect's growing firepower and its desire to neutralize the C-JTF. Damboa, about fifty miles from Maiduguri, is one of Borno's major towns. The battle there lasted nearly a month, from approximately June 25 to July 18. According to a local blogger, Boko Haram drove the military out of the villages surrounding Damboa in spring 2014. Then the sect targeted the town, attacking repeatedly until soldiers and police withdrew, leaving behind an arms cache that Boko Haram confiscated. During a final assault on July 17–18, Boko Haram attacked Damboa again. It found only C-JTF there. Boko Haram fighters torched much of the town and killed dozens of residents. By the time the last C-JTF members fled on July 20, the sect had proclaimed control. According to the local blogger, the battle marked a shift: different factions of Boko Haram had united to take the town (an assertion impossible to verify through other sources). It was also, he wrote, the first time the sect had "launched a conventional operation," behaving as a military force instead of as a guerrilla group.[86] Shekau may

[85] Lanre Odo and Kwasi Kpodo, "Suspected Boko Haram Gunmen Kill Emir, Policemen in Nigeria," Reuters, 30 May 2014, http://www.reuters.com/article/2014/05/30/us-nigeria-boko-haram-kidnapping-idUSKBN0EA16220140530.

[86] Fulan Nasrullah, "24th July Nigeria SITREP (Boko Haram)," Fulan's SITREP, 24 July 2014, http://fulansitrep.com/2014/07/24/24th-july-nigeria-sitrep-boko-haram/; "Nigeria's Boko Haram Crisis: 'Many Dead' in Damboa," BBC, 18 July 2014, http://www.bbc.com/news/world-africa-28374679; Njadvara Musa, "Boko Haram Kills 60

have been brutal, but he had momentum, which helped him sustain fighters' loyalty.

In August, Shekau announced the establishment of a "state among the states of Islam" in Gwoza, Borno.[87] He harangued the C-JTF, bragging that in Damboa, "our brothers came and they are living in your houses."[88] Gwoza made a convenient headquarters: Yusuf had enjoyed a following among immigrants from Gwoza to Maiduguri, and Boko Haram retained a presence around Gwoza after his death.[89] Located in Borno South, Gwoza was emblematic of long-term social changes that may have contributed to Boko Haram's recruitment. As discussed in chapter 2, Christianity in the region dated only to the 1960s, and many Muslims there were new converts; economic competition between religious communities may have hardened some of the young Muslim converts' attitudes toward Christians.[90]

To its "state," Boko Haram soon added considerable territory in Borno and Adamawa. In September 2014, Boko Haram took Bama, the second-largest city in Borno.[91] In October, Boko Haram captured Mubi, headquarters of Adamawa's north senatorial district and the second-largest city in that state.[92]

---

in Fresh Borno Attacks," *Guardian*, 18 July 2014, http://allafrica.com/stories/2014 07210437.html; "Nigeria's Boko Haram 'Controls' Damboa in Borno," BBC, 21 July 2014, http://www.bbc.com/news/world-africa-28406645.

[87] "Boko Haram Declares a New Caliphate."

[88] "Boko Haram Declares a New Caliphate."

[89] Adam Higazi, "Mobilisation into and against Boko Haram in North-East Nigeria," in *Collective Mobilisations in Africa*, edited by Kadya Tall, Marie-Emmanuelle Pommerolle, and Michel Cahen, 305–58 (Leiden: Brill, 2015), 341–46.

[90] Mösch, "Why Has Borno Become a Stronghold of Terror in Nigeria?"

[91] "Nigeria's Boko Haram 'Seize' Bama Town in Borno," BBC, 2 September 2014, http://www.bbc.com/news/world-africa-29021037.

[92] "'Yan Boko Haram Sun Kafa Tuta a Mubi," BBC Hausa, 29 October 2014, http://www.bbc.com/hausa/news/2014/10/141029_mubi_bokoharam_flags.

Yet Boko Haram's state was heavily rural, anchored around mid-sized towns. Although Boko Haram was born in a city, many members were in-migrants to Maiduguri from rural areas. They were now operating on their home turf. Many Boko Haram members knew the northeastern countryside well: some battles occurred even in Tarmuwa, Yobe—Shekau's home LGA.[93]

Shekau averred, "Our state is ruled by the Book of God; our state establishes the Sunna of our Prophet, Muhammad."[94] Yet he showed limited interest in implementing the kind of law and order that has won other African jihadists limited popularity. When al-Shabab (the Youth) ruled southern Somalia from roughly 2009 to 2012, and when jihadists controlled northern Mali in 2012–13, those groups made efforts to implement shari'a as a comprehensive legal and social system. For its part, Boko Haram imposed a rudimentary shari'a, including *hudud* punishments (corporal penalties mentioned in the Qur'an). People who escaped told human rights investigators of incidents where Boko Haram had amputated thieves' hands and stoned an adulterer.[95] But above all, Shekau focused on war, stating, "There is nothing between us and the despots of Nigeria except jihad."[96]

[93] Hamisu Kabir Matazu, "Breaking: Babban Gida Town under Attack in Yobe," *Daily Trust*, 3 January 2015, http://dailytrust.com.ng/weekly/index.php/top-stories/18638-breaking-babagida-town-under-attack-in-yobe#j5vcZo8QZ8mQmigj.99.

[94] "Boko Haram Declares a New Caliphate."

[95] United Nations Office of the High Commissioner for Human Rights (UN OHCHR), "Report of the United Nations High Commissioner for Human Rights on Violations and Abuses Committed by Boko Haram and the Impact on Human Rights in the Affected Countries," 29 September 2015, 8, http://reliefweb.int/report/nigeria/report-united-nations-high-commissioner-human-rights-violations-and-abuses-committed.

[96] "Boko Haram Militants Display Control of Captured Towns in Northeastern Nigeria," Sahara TV, 10 November 2014, https://www.youtube.com/watch?v=7dkdFaVrCls.

Propaganda from Boko Haram–controlled territory featured battle scenes and seized military equipment,[97] but it showed no civil institutions. Perhaps, harried by several militaries, Boko Haram could not consolidate governance. Yet it is striking that the group made little effort to institutionalize Islamic courts and schools, or to distribute humanitarian relief. Boko Haram focused on destroying "social infrastructure" such as "schools, mosques, churches, prisons, hospitals, [and] markets," as a "fighting tactic to gain control over territory and prevent escapees from returning."[98] Hundreds of thousands of civilians fled.

Shekau declared that Boko Haram's state was no longer part of Nigeria; instead, it was a new territory defined by religious affiliation.[99] Creating a Salafi-jihadist enclave meant expunging Christianity. Boko Haram sought to kill or forcibly convert Christians. The sect destroyed churches and seminaries.[100]

Boko Haram made rudimentary attempts to teach its ideology. Typical is the tale of one young Christian woman. Captured by Boko Haram in Adamawa, she was forcibly converted to Islam. She was then made to spend her days praying and learning Qur'anic verses.[101]

---

[97] "Boko Haram Declares a New Caliphate."

[98] UN OHCHR, "Report . . . on Violations and Abuses," 10–11.

[99] "Boko Haram Declares a New Caliphate." For a comparative perspective on the ideological, expansionist, and irredentist aspects of jihadi "states," see Brynjar Lia, "Understanding Jihadi Proto-states," *Perspectives on Terrorism* 9:4 (2015), http://www.terrorismanalysts.com/pt/index.php/pot/article/view/441/872.

[100] Aderogba Obisesan, "Nigeria's Christians Fear Persecution from Boko Haram Rampage," AFP, 7 September 2014, http://news.yahoo.com/nigerias-christians-fear-persecution-boko-haram-rampage-131841750.html.

[101] Chika Oduah, "How I Escaped Marrying a Boko Haram Fighter," Al Jazeera, 24 March 2015, http://america.aljazeera.com/articles/2015/3/24/how-i-escaped-marrying-a-boko-haram-fighter.html.

Boko Haram presented its new territory as a haven for embattled Muslims. In one propaganda video, an unseen interviewer queried Muslim civilians about their "enjoyment" in the new state, free of "infidels."[102] Yet Boko Haram preyed on conquered populations. In 2015, when Nigerian soldiers recaptured towns, they found them devastated.[103] Continued massacres illustrated the group's willingness to kill civilians it considered infidels.

Shekau claimed to be imitating the Prophet by slaughtering "unbelievers" in northeastern communities,[104] but disaffected senior members would later accuse him of having killed civilians on the basis of whim and/or personal benefit. According to the disaffected, Shekau handed down punishments with weak scriptural justifications, killed sect members and lied about it afterward, and married women whose husbands were still alive.[105]

Boko Haram's territorial control peaked around January 2015. Fears were growing that Boko Haram would attempt to take Maiduguri itself. Its control extended from Borno South up to the shores of Lake Chad. That month, Boko Haram slaughtered as many as two thousand residents in Baga, the garrison town where Nigerian soldiers had massacred civilians nearly two years before. After the C-JTF initially repelled the sect's fighters, a larger Boko Haram force arrived—perhaps twenty vehicles and over two hundred fighters, who expelled the vigilantes, a contingent of Nigerian soldiers, and some twenty thousand civilians from Baga and nearby Doron

[102] "Boko Haram Militants Display Control of Captured Towns."

[103] Vice News, *The War against Boko Haram*, 14 April 2015, https://news.vice.com/video/the-war-against-boko-haram-full-length.

[104] "Boko Haram Declares a New Caliphate."

[105] Mamman Nur, untitled message against Abubakar Shekau, August 2016, https://www.youtube.com/watch?v=86TwFqg-Aqc.

Baga on the shores of Lake Chad.[106] In his "Message to the World on Baga," Shekau flaunted arms Boko Haram had seized and said, "Jonathan, you're in trouble. Governors of Nigeria, you're in trouble. These materials were obtained in Baga."[107] Boko Haram strove not just to defeat but to humiliate the Nigerian state.

Despite such boasts, Boko Haram's state was crumbling. Even as it accumulated territory in mid-2014, Boko Haram faced resistance from the Nigerian military. In August, Nigerian soldiers recaptured Damboa, the first major town Boko Haram had ruled.[108] Damboa remained contested through the end of 2014, with Boko Haram seeking unsuccessfully to recapture it in December.[109] The two sides traded control of other towns that autumn and winter. One such site was Chibok, where Boko Haram briefly expelled Nigerian soldiers in mid-November before the military returned in force to take back the town.[110]

In early 2015, the tide decisively turned against Boko Haram's territorial ambitions. As Nigeria and as its neighbors grew more and more nervous about Boko Haram's expansion, a loose coalition of Nigerian, Nigerien, and Chadian forces

[106] Thomas Fessy, "Boko Haram Attack: What Happened in Baga?," BBC, 2 February 2015, http://www.bbc.com/news/world-africa-30987043.

[107] Abubakar Shekau, "Message to the World on Baga," January 2015, http://jihadology.net/2015/01/21/new-video-message-from-boko-%E1%B8%A5arams-jamaat-ahl-al-sunnah-li-dawah-wa-l-jihad-imam-abu-bakr-shekau-message-to-the-world-on-baga/.

[108] Edegbe Odemwingie and Kareem Haruna, "Soldiers Recapture Damboa Town in Borno," *Leadership*, 7 August 2014, http://leadership.ng/news/380251/soldiers-recapture-damboa-town-borno.

[109] Ndahi Marama, "Over 110 Boko Haram Terrorists Killed in Damboa," *Vanguard*, 20 December 2014, http://www.vanguardngr.com/2014/12/110-boko-haram-terrorists-killed-damboa/.

[110] "Nigeria Army Says Back in Control of Chibok," Al Jazeera, 16 November 2014, http://www.aljazeera.com/news/africa/2014/11/nigeria-army-says-back-control-chibok-201411161123711739.html.

worked to recapture the sect's territory. Such moves aligned uneasily with Nigeria's electoral calendar, as Jonathan sought to reverse the perception that he had failed to respond effectively to Boko Haram.

Nigeria's 2015 Elections and Territorial Reconquest

Boko Haram became a major issue in Nigeria's 2014–15 electoral campaign. The Chibok abduction generated a well-organized protest movement, "Bring Back Our Girls." The movement attracted elite support in Nigeria; former education minister and World Bank vice president Obiageli Ezekwesili was a cofounder of the group. The movement drew support around the world, most famously when U.S. First Lady Michelle Obama tweeted a picture of herself holding up the movement's hashtag.

Although presenting itself as nonpartisan, Bring Back Our Girls was effectively a protest against the Goodluck Jonathan administration's handling of Boko Haram. The administration's response heightened the anti-incumbent mood: Jonathan accused protesters of "play[ing] politics" with the kidnapping.[111] First Lady Patience Jonathan suggested that the kidnapping was a fabrication intended to discredit her husband.[112] The kidnappings' full political impact came in the context of Boko Haram's territorial expansion: as summer and fall 2014 dragged on without recovery of the girls, many Nigerians doubted more than ever that the administration was capable of defeating Boko Haram.

---

[111] "Nigeria's Goodluck Jonathan: #BringBackOurGirls 'Political,'" BBC News, 15 July 2014, http://www.bbc.com/news/world-africa-28318259#TWEET1184698.

[112] Michelle Faul, "Nigeria First Lady Orders Arrest of Protest Leaders Calling for Return of 276 Missing Schoolgirls," Associated Press, 5 May 2014, http://www.huffingtonpost.com/2014/05/05/nigeria-first-lady-orders-arrest-of-protest-leaders_n_5265872.html.

Voters' concerns about security intersected with their anger about economic issues, especially corruption. Even as authorities released figures in early 2014 showing that Nigeria's economy was the largest in Africa, the administration was rocked by a corruption scandal. Central Bank governor Sanusi Lamido Sanusi highlighted an alleged shortfall—over $49 billion, in Sanusi's initial reckoning—in payments from the Nigerian National Petroleum Corporation to Nigeria's Federation Account. Sanusi hinted that senior administration officials were robbing Nigeria of the proceeds from its key natural resource.

Jonathan's coordinating minister for the economy Ngozi Okonjo-Iweala rejected Sanusi's claims and ordered an independent audit. Jonathan sacked Sanusi for alleged incompetence. But the administration's reputation was damaged: Sanusi, who took office in 2009, had won global acclaim for his response to the aftermath of the global economic crisis of 2007–8. Criticism from Sanusi fanned the flames of public anger. Many Nigerians felt that rapid economic growth primarily benefited the rich, and that Jonathan was only the latest in a series of Nigerian heads of state who were more interested in looting the country than in running it.

Amid public anger over insecurity and corruption, the political landscape was shifting. Many northern elites had remained under the umbrella of the ruling People's Democratic Party (PDP) through 2011, even as Jonathan disrupted the "zoning" arrangement that had rotated the presidency between north and south. But Jonathan's ambition to seek reelection in 2015 outraged some northerners. Their anger grew as Jonathan marginalized dissenters within the party. In 2013, Jonathan's allies overturned the election of Rivers State governor Rotimi Amaechi as chairman of the Nigerian Governors' Forum and suspended Amaechi from the PDP. Amaechi—a southerner—

and four northern PDP governors left the party that summer. They found a warm reception in the All Progressives' Congress (APC), a coalition of opposition parties with strength in the southwest and the north. The APC selected former military ruler and perennial opposition candidate Muhammadu Buhari as its presidential nominee.

The APC's national reach meant that although 2015 was a rematch of 2011 in terms of the principal candidates—Buhari and Jonathan—the 2015 election played out on a fundamentally different map. In 2011, Jonathan had easily defeated Buhari; the latter won only the twelve northernmost states. In 2015, Buhari stood to build a winning coalition that centered on the north and the southwest. Buhari seemed to be the type of candidate many Nigerians now wanted—a retired general, with presumed competence on security issues, but also a respected anticorruption voice, with the presumed toughness to clean up the government.

Hoping to regain credibility as commander-in-chief, Jonathan mobilized a last-minute but forceful effort to destroy Boko Haram. In early 2015, Nigerian forces began a major offensive against the sect's territory. Jonathan soon announced a postponement of the elections, from February 14 to March 28. His administration stated that the delay would give the security forces time to defeat Boko Haram. The APC protested. The well-respected Independent National Electoral Commission chairman Attahiru Jega made clear that the delay reflected the security forces' recommendation, rather than his commission's degree of readiness.[113] But amid national and international uneasiness, the delay took effect.

---

[113] "Full Text of Prof Jega's Statement on Election Postponement," *Vanguard*, 8 February 2015 (from a 7 February 2015 press conference), http://www.vanguardngr.com /2015/02/full-text-prof-jegas-statement-election-postponement/.

By mid-February, Nigerian forces were registering successes against Boko Haram. On February 16, the Nigerian military reported that it had recaptured two towns in northern Borno—Monguno and nearby Marte—using a combination of ground forces and air strikes.[114] On February 21, Nigerian forces entered Baga.[115] Around March 3, Nigerian forces retook Mafa,[116] a town on the Maiduguri-Dikwa Road, helping to break Boko Haram's partial encirclement of Maiduguri. Around March 16–17, Nigerian forces drove Boko Haram out of Goniri, Adamawa. They also expelled Boko Haram from Bama, Borno, one of the sect's largest territorial possessions.[117]

Nigeria's offensive leaned on contributions from outside the country, particularly from the militaries of Chad and Niger. These two countries, increasingly concerned that Boko Haram threatened their own security, focused on recapturing border towns. In late January 2015, Chad deployed soldiers to Cameroon to establish a base for fighting Boko Haram. Chadian forces then entered Nigeria and recaptured several border towns: Malam Fatori, Borno, on January 29,[118] and Gamboru-Ngala, Borno, on February 3. The latter town was a key node on one of Boko Haram's supply routes through

---

[114] Lanre Ola and Bate Felix, "Nigerian Troops Recapture Two Towns from Boko Haram," Reuters, 16 February 2015, http://www.reuters.com/article/us-nigeria-violence-idUSKBN0LK18S20150216.

[115] "Nierian Army Retakes Baga Town from Boko Haram," BBC, 21 February 2015, http://www.bbc.com/news/world-africa-31568055.

[116] Bukar Hussain and Aminu Abubakar, "Boko Haram Kills Scores in NE Nigeria, Militants Amass in Gwoza," AFP, 5 March 2015, http://news.yahoo.com/boko-haram-kills-68-including-children-ne-nigeria-170709581.html.

[117] "Nigeria Says It Has Ousted Boko Haram from Town of Bama," BBC, 17 March 2015, http://www.bbc.com/news/world-middle-east-31917421.

[118] "Chad Troops Drive Boko Haram Out of Nigerian Town," Al Jazeera, 30 January 2015, http://www.aljazeera.com/news/africa/2015/01/chad-troops-drive-boko-haram-nigerian-town-150130131849254.html.

Cameroon.[119] On February 17, Chadian forces reached Dikwa, Borno, which lies at the crossroads of a highway from Gamboru-Ngala to Maiduguri and another road extending from Monguno south to Cameroon's Maroua.[120] Chad would soon be joined by Niger: a joint Nigerien-Chadian offensive into Nigerian territory commenced in early March.[121] The Nigerien and Chadian forces recaptured Damasak, Borno, around March 14–15.[122]

In some towns, Boko Haram fought fiercely to defend its territory, losing hundreds of fighters. Amid the Chadian push, Boko Haram staged attacks in Biu and Gombe, highlighting its continued ability to strike even outside the borders of its crumbling state, but the sect was in retreat.[123] Elsewhere, the sect destroyed what it could and preemptively fled. Entering forces often found towns largely devoid of civilians. In Damasak, Chadian and Nigerien soldiers found a mass grave containing seventy or more bodies.[124] In Malam Fatori, an estimated thirty thousand people fled Boko Haram's initial seizure of the town, leaving behind a handful of elders, women, and children.

[119] Madjiasra Nako, "Chad Troops Enter Nigerian Town in Pursuit of Boko Haram," Reuters, 3 February 2015, http://www.reuters.com/article/us-nigeria-violence-chad-idUSKBN0L71F820150203.

[120] Adam Nossiter, "In Nigeria, Boko Haram Loses Ground to Chadians," *New York Times*, 18 February 2015, http://www.nytimes.com/2015/02/19/world/africa/nigerias-army-drives-boko-haram-from-garrison-town.html?_r=0.

[121] Madjiasra Nako and Abdoulaye Massalaki, "Chad, Niger Launch Joint Offensive against Boko Haram in Nigeria," Reuters, 8 March 2015, http://www.reuters.com/article/us-nigeria-violence-niger-idUSKBN0M40KH20150308.

[122] "Boko Haram 'Driven Out' of Northeastern Nigerian Town," Al Jazeera, 20 March 2015, http://www.aljazeera.com/news/2015/03/niger-chad-troops-nigeria-town-boko-haram-150319015134021.html.

[123] Nossiter, "In Nigeria, Boko Haram Loses Ground."

[124] "Mass Grave Found in Recaptured Nigerian Town," Al Jazeera, 21 March 2015, http://www.aljazeera.com/news/2015/03/mass-grave-recaptured-nigerian-town-150320212259942.html.

When Boko Haram finally abandoned the town in late March or early April 2015 amid the Chadian-Nigerien advance, sect members looted stores and burned homes.[125]

Ostensibly, the Lake Chad basin countries were working together under the auspices of the Multi-national Joint Task Force (see chapter 5). On the ground, however, coordination was poor. In March 2015, Chadian president Idriss Deby complained to the *New York Times* that Nigeria was a deeply unreliable counterpart: "We've been on the terrain for two months, and we haven't seen a single Nigerian soldier. There is a definite deficit of coordination, and a lack of common action." Deby stated that Chad had no desire to occupy Nigerian territory. But Nigerian forces had failed to relieve Chadian troops who were holding recaptured towns. That meant, Deby said, "All we're doing is standing in place, and it is to the advantage of Boko Haram."[126] Boko Haram even reoccupied some towns that Chadian forces had captured. In April, Chadian and Nigerien forces retook Malam Fatori, where Chad had already fought Boko Haram more than two months before.[127]

Another sign of the Nigerian military's weakness was its quiet reliance on foreign mercenaries. In 2014, Jonathan personally met with Erik Prince, the infamous founder of the now-defunct private security firm Blackwater, to hear Prince's

"$1.5 billion proposal to wipe out . . . Boko Haram."[128] Prince's proposal was rejected, but around February 2015, the administration hired Specialized Tasks, Training, Equipment and Protection (STTEP), a firm run by retired South African colonel Eeben Barlow.

Barlow angrily refuted charges that his firm was waging a "secret" or "dark" war in Nigeria. He instead presented STTEP's involvement in Nigeria as "assisting a legitimate African government that is under attack by the terrorist group known as Boko Haram." In defending his company as an African team helping an African government, Barlow, perhaps more bluntly than he had intended, pointed to the weakness of the Nigerian military and underscored why it had turned to foreign mercenaries: "Foreign armies and [private military companies] have spent considerable time in Nigeria where 'window-dressing training' has been the order of the day. But look through the window, and the room is empty."[129] STTEP's role in Nigeria went beyond training: an anonymous "senior Western diplomat" told the New York Times that the mercenaries had taken on "a major operational role," attacking Boko Haram at night and then ensuring that "the next morning the Nigerian Army rolls in and claims success."[130] Nigeria's campaign against Boko

---

[128]Matthew Cole and Jeremy Scahill, "Erik Prince in the Hot Seat," Intercept, 24 March 2016, https://theintercept.com/2016/03/24/blackwater-founder-erik-prince -under-federal-investigation/.

[129]Eeben Barlow, "Feeding the Narrative," Eeben Barlow's Military and Security Blog, 25 April 2015, http://eebenbarlowsmilitaryandsecurityblog.blogspot.com /2015/04/feeding-narrative_25.html. See also Eeben Barlow, "Updating the Nigerian Narrative," Eeben Barlow's Military and Security Blog, 31 May 2015, http:// eebenbarlowsmilitaryandsecurityblog.blogspot.com/2015/05/updating-nigerian -narrative.html.

[130]Adam Nossiter, "Mercenaries Join Nigeria's Military Campaign against Boko Haram," New York Times, 12 March 2015, http://www.nytimes.com/2015/03/13 /world/africa/nigerias-fight-against-boko-haram-gets-help-from-south-african-mer cenaries.html?_r=0.

Haram's crumbling state was calibrated toward maximum public relations effectiveness.

On March 27, the eve of the presidential vote, Nigerian forces retook Gwoza, Boko Haram's headquarters. The recapture added a crowning symbolic achievement to the campaign, but it was not a dramatic military defeat for Boko Haram. Earlier reports had indicated that Boko Haram fighters were regrouping in Gwoza, but Boko Haram declined to make a last stand there. The sect's fighters chose instead to massacre civilians in the town—including some fighters' wives, perhaps calculating that the women would slow the group down on the run, or betray it—and then melt into the countryside.[131] The announcement of Gwoza's recapture, timed for maximum political effect, did not save Jonathan. On March 28, he lost the president election to Buhari, who won twenty-one of Nigeria's thirty-six states, as well as nearly 54 percent of the vote.

Boko Haram was somewhat more attuned to the national electoral calendar in 2015 than in 2011, but its behavior still correlated most closely with events that directly affected it. Shekau's February 2015 "Message to the Leaders of the Disbelievers" made headlines for his threats against Nigeria's elections. Most of his diatribe, however, threatened Nigerien president Mahamadou Issoufou and Chadian president Idriss Deby, whose campaign to retake Boko Haram's territory was in full swing.[132] On the voting days, Boko Haram attacked polling places in the northeastern states of Bauchi and Gombe.[133]

---

[131] "Boko Haram Fighters Told to 'Kill Wives' as Troops Take Its 'HQ,'" AFP, 27 March 2015, http://news.yahoo.com/nigeria-recaptures-gwoza-boko-haram-military-114107456.html.

[132] Boko Haram, "Message to the Leaders of the Disbelievers."

[133] "Curfew in Bauchi, NE Nigeria, after Boko Haram Fighting," AFP, 29 March 2015, http://news.yahoo.com/nigerian-troops-battle-boko-haram-outside-bauchi-115230995.html; and "Eight Suspected Boko Haram Gunmen Killed in Gombe, Bauchi,"

Even in those two states, though, voting went forward largely as planned and official results were unaffected.[134] As the next chapter discusses, Boko Haram's attention was increasingly drawn to targets outside Nigeria starting in 2015. That trend reinforced the growing regionalization and even internationalization of the conflict.

After the elections, the Nigerian military and its partners continued striving to expel Boko Haram from its territory and hideouts. In April, Nigerian soldiers began a ground assault on the Sambisa Forest, a onetime game reserve west of Gwoza.[135] Covering as much as sixty thousand square kilometers, the forest had become a major refuge for Boko Haram.[136] Through 2015 and into 2016, the military continued to recapture towns. In disarray but not defeated, Boko Haram launched a wave of suicide bombings in northern cities like Maiduguri, Potiskum, Damaturu, Kano, Jos, and Zaria.

With Boko Haram's state destroyed and a new executive in office, the conflict entered a new phase by mid-2015. When Buhari took office on May 29, 2015, there were grounds for optimism about Nigeria's prospects for defeating Boko Haram. The multinational offensive had effectively destroyed the sect's state. Some towns and areas of rural Borno remained

---

Vanguard, 30 March 2015, http://www.vanguardngr.com/2015/03/eight-suspected -boko-haram-gunmen-killed-in-gombe-bauchi/.

[134] "INEC: Boko Haram Attacks Will Not Affect Bauchi Results," *This Day*, 30 March 2015, http://www.thisdaylive.com/articles/inec-boko-haram-attacks-will -not-affect-bauchi-results/205462/.

[135] "Boko Haram Crisis: Nigeria Begins Sambisa Ground Offensive," BBC, 22 April 2015, http://www.bbc.com/news/world-africa-32416155.

[136] Bodunrin Kayode, "Inside Nigeria's Sambisa Forest, the Boko Haram Hideout Where Kidnapped School Girls Are Believed to Be Held," *Guardian/ Nation*, 29 April 2014, http://www.theguardian.com/world/2014/apr/29/nigeria-sambisa-forest-boko -haram-hideout-kidnapped-school-girls-believed-to-be-held.

under the sect's sway for months to come, but the sect no longer had a defined territory that included major towns.

Upon taking office, Buhari took steps to ensure that the campaign would be guided by a sophisticated knowledge of the northeast. In June, he instructed the military to move its command headquarters to Maiduguri. In July, he appointed Borno men to two key security positions: retired major general Babagana Monguno as national security advisor, and Lieutenant General Tukur Buratai as chief of army staff. (Both men's surnames refer to localities in Borno.) The same month, the military renamed its operation against Boko Haram, choosing the title "Operation Lafiya Dole"—"Peace by Force," in the military's official translation.[137] Further operations, the new government implied, would just be mop-up efforts.

The changes at the level of personnel and messaging, however, soon confronted a grim reality: it was easier to deprive Boko Haram of territorial control than it was to prevent terrorism. Boko Haram, often deploying women and girls as suicide bombers, struck northeastern cities repeatedly: in Damaturu alone in 2015, bombings occurred in February, July, August, and October. Mosques were targeted in Maiduguri, Yola, and elsewhere. The attacks made the Buhari administration's rhetoric sound hollow: when Buhari told the BBC in December 2015 that Nigeria had "technically won the war" against Boko Haram,[138] few believed that the spate of attacks was over. According to one study, the year 2016 brought a 29 percent decline in both the number of Boko Haram's attacks

---

[137] "Army Chief in Maiduguri; Changes Code to Operation Lafiya Dole," *Vanguard*, 21 July 2015, http://www.vanguardngr.com/2015/07/army-chief-in-maiduguri-changes -code-to-operation-lafiya-dole/.

[138] "Nigeria Boko Haram: Militants 'Technically Defeated'—Buhari," BBC, 24 December 2015, http://www.bbc.com/news/world-africa-35173618.

and the casualties the group caused—but 2016 still saw nearly three hundred recorded attacks in Nigeria and the Lake Chad region.[139]

Conclusion

From 2013 to 2015, the Boko Haram crisis escalated at a dizzying pace, culminating in the sect's seizure of considerable territory in northeastern Nigeria. The Nigerian government's own actions helped to transform the conflict. By deploying more soldiers, maltreating civilians, and backing the C-JTF, the Jonathan administration inadvertently gave Boko Haram the capacity and the motivation to carve out a would-be state.

Boko Haram adapted its message of religious exclusivism and political victimhood to this new context. Presenting the C-JTF as apostate Muslims, Boko Haram tried to force civilians to choose sides. After the sect lost much of its territory in early 2015, a new phase of the conflict began. There was more assertive leadership from Abuja. But there was also a growing regionalization and internationalization of the conflict, on both a rhetorical and a military level.

[139] Omar Mahmood, "Boko Haram in 2016: A Highly Adaptable Foe," Institute for Security Studies, 7 February 2017, https://issafrica.org/iss-today/boko-haram-in -2016-a-highly-adaptable-foe.

5.

Same War, New Actors

As the Boko Haram conflict progressed, it became increasingly regionalized and to some extent internationalized. A host of new actors entered the conflict: the governments of Niger, Chad, and Cameroon, and to a much lesser extent Benin;[1] the United States, France, and the African Union; and the so-called Islamic State, of which Boko Haram became an affiliate in March 2015.

The expansion of the conflict reveals the limitations of brute force in fighting Boko Haram. Just as the rise of the Civilian Joint Task Force in northeastern Nigerian cities had the unintended consequence of increasing Boko Haram's violence in the countryside, so has the involvement of other militaries led to unintended consequences. Now, Boko Haram's violence frequently targets Nigeria's neighbors.

In response, neighboring governments have become more authoritarian, especially in regions far from their capitals, such as Niger's far southeastern Diffa region and the three northernmost regions of Cameroon. Such regions, already impoverished in comparison with others in their countries, risk being further underserved. Compounding these regions' predicament is the humanitarian disaster that Boko Haram has caused. Moreover, as International Crisis Group has warned, Boko Haram—like

---

[1] Benin participated in the May 2014 Paris summit and other anti–Boko Haram meetings and has contributed around 150 soldiers to the Multi-national Joint Task Force, but otherwise its participation has been minor. I do not discuss Benin further in this chapter.

other jihadist movements in Africa—shifted to a largely rural insurgency in 2015. Even after Boko Haram was driven from major cities, "African armies and their allies were often unable to restore security in the countryside, or even in the outskirts of some cities. Civil servants could or would not follow the military into still insecure zones, leaving vast areas run by skeleton administrations, and few, if any, public services."[2] As Nigeria and its neighbors failed to consolidate some of their military

[2] Jean-Herve Jezequel and Vincent Foucher, "Forced Out of Towns in the Sahel, Africa's Jihadists Go Rural," International Crisis Group, 11 January 2017, https://www.crisisgroup.org/africa/west-africa/mali/forced-out-towns-sahel-africas-jihadists-go-rural.

gains with political action in 2015 and 2016, Boko Haram displayed its tenacity once again.

Non-African actors have had only some effect on the trajectory of the violence on the ground. The Islamic State has intervened heavily in the propaganda sphere. The Islamic State also helped foster, or at least formalize, a schism within Boko Haram in 2016. Yet the Islamic State's military contribution has likely been quite limited.

The efforts of the United States and France have given a boost to African militaries, and perhaps a crucial one. A Boko Haram leader has alleged that Western airpower is a major factor in the success of African military efforts against Boko Haram:

> We see the airplanes of [Western] countries, fighter planes and reconnaissance planes, hovering over us densely, especially in their last campaign to expel us from the Lake Chad area and what borders it. . . . They are conducting their ruthless war through a shared operations room in Niger. If they want to launch attacks against us, the American and French forces present in Niger sent pilotless planes to observe the area. Then the joint forces undertake attacks under cover of heavy air bombardment.

Yet, the same Boko Haram leader continues, "[Western] participation is limited to the sky. They have no effective participation on the ground."[3] Meanwhile, Western powers have left the political, religious, and socioeconomic drivers of the conflict largely untouched.

All the governments involved in the crisis have continued to approach it primarily in security terms, despite some rhetoric

---

[3] "Wali Gharb Ifriqiya: Al-Shaykh Abu Mus'ab al-Barnawi," *Al-Naba'* 41 (2 August 2016): 8–9; 9, https://azelin.files.wordpress.com/2016/08/the-islamic-state-e2809cal-nabacc84_-newsletter-4122.pdf.

to the contrary. This approach has left vital questions unanswered. Will perpetrators of violence be held accountable, and if so how? Will the displaced be systematically resettled, and if so how? Will northeastern Nigeria be rebuilt, and if so how? Without thoughtful answers to these questions, the stage seems set for further uprisings.

In terms of this book's core theme—the interaction between doctrine and events—this chapter argues that after the collapse of its "state" in early 2015, Boko Haram continued down the path of making ordinary Muslims a central target. It also sought to discredit Muslim heads of state in the region. The sect's doctrine, in other words, became even more sweeping in its application. The logic of targeting Muslim civilians had been implicit in Boko Haram's messages since the time of Yusuf. In 2015, however, that tendency became even stronger—and in 2016, it evoked a backlash from within the group, generating new schisms and exacerbating older ones.

Even as Boko Haram lost even more of whatever broad-based support it originally had, the sect's expansion around Lake Chad had a distorting impact on the religious field there. Boko Haram's stark message of religious exclusivism drew new battle lines even within Muslim communities. The crisis added new tensions into the relationships between governments and ordinary Muslims, especially Salafis and youth.

The Regionalization of Rhetoric and Recruitment

Boko Haram was never confined to Nigeria. Several of its founders had family ties in the surrounding region. The early movement recruited beyond Nigeria. Regional recruitment continued, and became more systematic, after Boko Haram committed to jihadism in 2009. Recruitment seems limited in Chad, but in southeastern Niger and northern Cameroon Boko Haram found significant support.

In Niger, Boko Haram had a minor presence during the time of Muhammad Yusuf. One of Yusuf's lieutenants reportedly hailed from Kilakam, a village in the southeastern Nigerien region of Diffa.[4] By 2004, tapes of Yusuf's lectures circulated in Diffa, especially Yusuf's exegesis of the Qur'an and his commentaries on hadith collections.[5] In southern Nigerien cities, some young people, petty traders and others, liked what they heard of Yusuf's preaching. For those receptive to the message, Niger seemed gripped by what Yusuf denounced—an un-Islamic secular government, and Western-style schools where boys and girls mixed in an immoral fashion.[6] Across Niger, the 1990s and 2000s saw wide-ranging debates among Muslim intellectuals. These intellectuals were questioning the country's inheritance, from its time under French colonial rule, of concepts such as *laïcité*. That term refers to a form of secularism that denies religion a role in affairs of state and seeks to minimize religion's role in public life.[7] Boko Haram was a peripheral player in such debates, but it benefited from an atmosphere where there was some skepticism about Niger's political system.

As early as 2005, Boko Haram controlled a mosque in the town of Diffa.[8] In Diffa, some youth refused to attend school after hearing Boko Haram's messages, which spread by means

[4] Juliana Taiwo and Michael Olugbode, "Boko Haram Leader Killed," *This Day*, 31 July 2009, http://allafrica.com/stories/200907310001.html.

[5] Telephone interview with Salafi leader in Diffa, 12 June 2016.

[6] Skype interview with Ibrahim Yahaya Ibrahim, 3 February 2016.

[7] Abdoulaye Sounaye, "Ambiguous Secularism: Islam, Laïcité and the State in Niger," *Civilisations* 58:2 (2009): 41–57.

[8] Interview with Ibrahim.

of mobile phones, even in remote areas.[9] Niger was also affected by the disputes occurring between Muhammad Yusuf and rival Salafis. One Salafi leader from Diffa told me that in 2005, he traveled to Maiduguri with a group called Lajnat Shabab al-Da'wa (Youth Preaching Committee) and preached about the necessity of avoiding division within the Muslim community—a message that subtly rebuked Yusuf. At that time, Yusuf declined to rebut such arguments directly, but by 2008, Shekau was visiting Niger and debating other Salafis. Boko Haram suppressed recordings of the debates, however, likely fearing that audiences might be swayed by rival Salafis' arguments. Shekau also declined to debate Diffa's Salafis on the radio, perhaps fearing that Nigerien authorities—who more tightly control media than their Nigerian counterparts—would arrest him.[10]

Under Shekau's leadership of Boko Haram, Diffa has been a zone of both recruitment and violence. In January 2012, authorities in Diffa arrested fifteen suspected members of Boko Haram.[11] By 2014, tales of recruitment were rife: gang members told the BBC they had been paid to join the sect in Diffa.[12] Boko Haram used a mix of techniques—conscription, payment, and proselytization—to win new members. Some of its passive Nigerien supporters, meanwhile, dismissed reports of the sect's most brutal attacks as Western propaganda. They argued that Boko Haram fought in self-defense.[13]

[9] Skype interview with Abdourahmane Idrissa, 28 March 2016.
[10] Telephone interview with Salafi leader in Diffa.
[11] "Niger: Diffa Traders Hit by Nigerian Border Closure," IRIN, 20 February 2012, http://www.irinnews.org/report/94904/niger-diffa-traders-hit-by-nigerian-border -closure.
[12] Thomas Fessy, "Niger Hit by Nigeria's Boko Haram Fallout," BBC, 22 April 2014, http://www.bbc.com/news/world-africa-27111884.
[13] Interview with Ibrahim.

In Cameroon, Boko Haram also established a presence from an early point. "People were scandalized" when Yusuf was killed in 2009. Some youth had "ideological sympathy" for Boko Haram, particularly during the early phase of its terrorist violence in 2010–11. At that time, the group was targeting security forces, bars, and churches, rather than killing Muslim civilians en masse. Ordinary Muslim civilians did not yet perceive that they themselves might one day become the sect's targets.[14] In 2010, Cameroon's president, Paul Biya, privately confided to the U.S. ambassador that "he was beginning to worry about Islamic extremists infiltrating Cameroon from Nigeria and making inroads through Cameroonian mosques."[15] In 2012, Cameroonian authorities began quietly arresting suspected members. Residents of Cameroon's Far North Region reported that preachers were traveling from town to town seeking youths willing to fight in Nigeria.[16]

Cameroonian authorities have stated that Boko Haram has recruited volunteers and paid fighters in the Far North. In 2015, a Cameroonian military officer told journalists, "When you go to border villages, all you see are women and children and old people. Young [men], between the ages of 10 and 45 are no longer there. They are across the [Nigerian] border with Boko Haram militants." Between approximately 2012 and 2015, authorities said, a change had occurred in the pattern of Boko Haram's recruitment, as the sect moved from preaching to payment. Youth found themselves joining Boko Haram to

[14] Skype interview with Ahmed Khalid Ayong, 30 March 2016.

[15] United States Embassy Yaoundé, leaked cable 10YAOUNDE83, "Cameroonian President Biya Gives Ambassador Political/Economic Overview," 5 February 2010, https://wikileaks.org/plusd/cables/10YAOUNDE83_a.html.

[16] "Fears in Cameroon of Boko Haram Recruitment," IRIN, 16 April 2014, http://www.irinnews.org/report/99949/fears-in-cameroon-of-boko-haram-recruitment.

survive, as the sect's presence and rising Cameroonian military deployments pushed civilians to choose a side.[17]

With government clampdowns in Niger and Cameroon, there is less space, even in neighborhood discussion circles, for Muslim youth to discuss and debate, much less to state support for, Boko Haram. Fears of surveillance are now common in both countries.[18] At the same time, some clandestine recruitment likely continues.

Why would anyone from outside Nigeria join Boko Haram, particularly at a time when doing so means risking death? For one thing, much of Boko Haram's recruitment outside Nigeria appears to be based on money. In Diffa, the crisis collided with economic setbacks. From 2008 to 2013, China National Petroleum Corporation conducted successful explorations for oil in the Agadem block in eastern Niger, in the northern part of the Diffa region—an endeavor that created thousands of jobs for Diffa residents. By 2014, however, many of the construction projects and other projects involving unskilled labor were completed. As many as four thousand local workers were laid off. At the same time, Boko Haram's outreach was increasing. Diffa residents reported seeing young men from the region disappear, only to return three to six months later with enough money to open a store or build a house.[19]

Politics might drive some recruitment. Diffa is sparsely populated and far from Niger's capital, Niamey, leading to neglect. International Crisis Group researchers found significant resentment in Diffa toward the central government.[20] South-

[17]"No Shortage of Recruits for Boko Haram in Cameroon's Far North," 5 March 2015, IRIN, http://www.irinnews.org/feature/2015/03/05.

[18]Interview with Ibrahim; interview with Ayong.

[19]Skype interview with Mahamidou Attahirou, 28 March 2016.

[20]International Crisis Group, "The Central Sahel: A Perfect Sandstorm," 25 June 2015, 7 n. 39, http://reliefweb.int/sites/reliefweb.int/files/resources/227-the-central -sahel-a-perfect-sandstorm.pdf.

ern Diffa is also a heavily Kanuri zone, as is far northeastern Nigeria. Ethnic ties may facilitate interactions between Nigerian and Nigerien Boko Haram members—and may prevent some unaffiliated Kanuri from speaking to authorities.[21]

Religious appeals may mobilize some youth. Boko Haram has adapted its message to the regionalization of the conflict. Beginning in 2014, Shekau increasingly castigated the West. He now sought to appeal more thoroughly to international jihadist audiences. At the same time, he used international issues as a rhetorical cudgel against Lake Chad basin politicians, particularly the Muslim heads of state in Niger and Chad, Presidents Mahamadou Issoufou and Idriss Deby. The doctrines of *al-wala' wa-l-bara'* (exclusive loyalty to "true" Muslims and disavowal of non-Muslim persons and systems) and *al-hukm bi-ma anzala Allah* (ruling by what God has revealed) gave Shekau a flexible platform from which to denounce both the West and the Nigerien and Chadian presidents. In January 2015, Shekau responded to the French newspaper *Charlie Hebdo*'s cartoons of the Prophet:

> Anyone who insults our Prophet is an unbeliever. Anyone who doubts that is an unbeliever. Anyone who boasts of this is an unbeliever. O people of the world, repent to Allah Most High and if not, you will see what you see. . . . Our Lord, may He be glorified and exalted, has said, "No one rules but God" (Qur'an 12:40). And He has said, "Whoever does not rule by what God has revealed, they are the unbelievers" (5:44). And He has said, may He be glorified and exalted, "O you who believe, do not take the Jews and the Christians as allies [*awliya'*]. They are allies of one another. And whoever is an ally to

---

[21] Interview with Idrissa.

them among you, then indeed, he is one of them" (5:51). He is one of them.[22]

In another message, Shekau cast Issoufou and Deby as apostate Muslims who had violated the principle of *al-wala' wa-l-bara'* and had become creatures of the godless West. "You follow François Hollande," Shekau said. He invoked the same Qur'anic verses as in his previous message, as well as others (39:65 and 6:88) referring to the dangers of *shirk* or associating partners with God. Issoufou and Deby, Shekau continued, applied man-made laws and imported democracy from the West—systems that Shekau depicted as un-Islamic heresies. "The people of democracy are infidels, we have no doubt . . . whoever has a doubt, he is an unbeliever [as well]." Shekau offered ordinary Muslims a choice: repent and join Boko Haram, or persist in unbelief, fighting on the side of Hollande and Obama.[23]

The Lake Chad Basin: The Structure of Boko Haram's Violence

Of Nigeria's neighbors, Boko Haram attacked Cameroon first. This decision may reflect geographical considerations more than anything else: the Mandara Mountains, which run along the border between Nigeria and Cameroon, became a refuge for Boko Haram in 2004 and 2009. The Mandaras served as a refuge again in 2013, when Boko Haram was driven from

---

[22] Abubakar Shekau, "Message to the World on Baga," January 2015, http://jihadology
.net/2015/01/21/new-video-message-from-boko-%E1%B8%A5arams-jamaat-ahl-al
-sunnah-li-dawah-wa-l-jihad-imam-abu-bakr-shekau-message-to-the-world-on-baga/.

[23] Boko Haram, "A Message to the Leaders of Disbelievers," February 2015,
http://jihadology.net/2015/02/17/al-urwah-al-wuthqa-foundation-presents-a-new
-video-message-from-jamaat-ahl-al-sunnah-li-l-dawah-wa-l-jihads-boko-%E1%B8%B8
%A5aram-abu-bakr-shekau-a-message-to-the-leader/.

Maiduguri by the Civilian Joint Task Force. Long after the Nigerian army had recaptured the town of Gwoza in March 2015, Boko Haram fighters were hiding out in the Gwoza Hills and the Mandara Mountains.[24]

Proximity made Cameroon an attractive site from which to resupply and, beginning in 2013, to stage attacks for both profit and intimidation.[25] In February 2013, Boko Haram kidnapped a French family on holiday in the Far North. Two months later, the family was released, reportedly after either France or Cameroon paid a ransom of over $3 million, and after Cameroon released some imprisoned Boko Haram fighters.[26] Another kidnapping followed in May 2014, when Boko Haram snatched ten Chinese workers in Waza. In July 2014, Boko Haram attacked the northern border town of Kolofata. Fighters seized the wife of Cameroon's vice prime minister, Amadou Ali, along with the town's hereditary Muslim ruler, Lamido Seini Boukar Lamine, and fifteen other people. Both groups—the Chinese workers and the Kolofata victims—were released in October 2014,[27] possibly for a ransom of $400,000.[28]

[24] Telephone interview with Gerhard Muller-Kosack, 25 May 2016.

[25] Hans de Marie Heungoup, "Cameroon's Rising Religious Tensions," African Arguments, 8 September 2015, http://africanarguments.org/2015/09/08/cameroons -rising-religious-tensions/.

[26] "Nigeria's Boko Haram 'Got $3m Ransom' to Free Hostages," BBC, 27 April 2013, http://www.bbc.com/news/world-africa-22320077.

[27] Tansa Musa, "Boko Haram Kidnaps Wife of Cameroon's Vice PM, Kills at Least Three," Reuters, 27 July 2014, http://www.reuters.com/article/us-cameroon -violence-boko-haram-idUSKBN0FW0CQ20140727; Aaron Akinyemi, "Cameroon President Announces Release of 27 Boko Haram Hostages," *International Business Times*, 11 October 2014, http://www.ibtimes.co.uk/cameroon-president-announces -release-27-boko-haram-hostages-1469546.

[28] "Cameroon Paid Boko Haram $400K Ransom, Plus Arms and Ammunition, to Secure Release of Deputy Prime Minister's Wife, Other Hostages," *Sahara Reporters*, 11 October 2014, http://saharareporters.com/2014/10/11/cameroon-paid-boko -haram-400k-ransom-plus-arms-and-ammunition-secure-release-deputy-prime.

In early 2015, Boko Haram's violence became systematically regional. The sect began launching reprisal attacks over Niger and Chad's participation in the war inside northeastern Nigeria. As Marc-Antoine Pérouse de Montclos has pointed out, given that Boko Haram had a presence outside Nigeria from an early point, the involvement of Nigeria's neighbors in the 2015 anti–Boko Haram campaign—and the sect's increasing violence outside Nigeria—"effectively broke the mutual non-aggression pact that had prevailed until then."[29]

Niger was hard hit. In February 2015, a wave of attacks struck the Diffa Region, beginning with a raid on the border town of Bosso and continuing with a suicide bombing in the town of Diffa.[30] Following a pattern that would also play out in Cameroon and Chad, Boko Haram regularly bombed towns and raided villages in southeastern Niger. In 2015, Diffa suffered eighty attacks, followed by seventy-six attacks the next year.[31]

Boko Haram's first attack inside Chadian territory was a February 2015 raid against soldiers stationed in the village of Ngouboua on the shores of Lake Chad.[32] Summer 2015 marked the real beginning of Boko Haram's war inside Chad. Bombings struck the capital, N'Djamena, on June 15 and July 11.

---

[29] Marc-Antoine Pérouse de Montclos, "Boko Haram: Les enjeux régionaux de l'insurrection," Fondation Jean Jaures, 10 February 2015, http://www.jean-jaures.org/Publications/Notes/Boko-Haram.

[30] "Boko Haram Launches First Attack in Niger," BBC, 7 February 2015, http://www.bbc.com/news/world-africa-31162979; David Lewis, "Two Female Suicide Bombers Strike in Niger Town Diffa: Sources," Reuters, 11 February 2015, http://www.reuters.com/article/us-nigeria-violence-diffa-idUSKBN0LF1T720150211.

[31] United Nations Office for the Coordination of Humanitarian Affairs (UN OCHA), "Niger—Diffa: Key Facts and Figures (December 2016)," January 2017, http://reliefweb.int/sites/reliefweb.int/files/resources/NER_Diffa_Timeline_2501 2017.pdf.

[32] "Nigeria's Boko Haram Militants Attack Chad for First Time," BBC, 13 February 2015, http://www.bbc.com/news/world-africa-31453951.

As Chadian authorities increased security in N'Djamena, Boko Haram carried out repeated suicide bombings in western Chad: Baga Sola on October 10; Ngouboua on November 8; and Koulfoua on December 5. The bombings targeted police stations, markets, and refugee camps.

Amid the reprisal campaign, Cameroon was also a prime target. Boko Haram's attacks against Cameroonian authorities and civilians have included periodic waves of suicide bombings, beginning on July 12, 2015, with a suicide bombing in Fotokol. On July 22 and 25, major attacks occurred in Maroua. In December 2015 and January 2016, another wave of bombings hit mosques and markets in towns such as Kolofata, Bodo, and Kouyape. The attacks often involved female bombers, including adolescent girls, reflecting similar trends across the border in Nigeria. By fall 2015, Boko Haram had staged approximately 150 attacks in Cameroon, many of them involving direct clashes with the Cameroonian military.[33] By early 2016, there was a palpable economic effect in both southern Chad and northern Cameroon due to Boko Haram's attacks and raids, including raids that targeted commerce and transport.[34] By June 2016, the total of Boko Haram's attacks on Cameroon had risen to over 200,[35] and 120 recorded attacks occurred in Cameroon in 2016 alone—almost as many as in Nigeria itself (133).[36] Meanwhile, the financial costs of the

---

[33] Heungoup, "Cameroon's Rising Religious Tensions."

[34] Moki Kindzeka, "Chad Merchants Say Boko Haram Attacks Hurt Economic Activity," Voice of America, 26 January 2016, http://www.voanews.com/content/chad-merchants-fear-boko-haram-attacks-are-stagnating-economic-activity/3162937.html.

[35] Amnesty International, "Cameroon: Boko Haram Attack Brings Total Killed to Nearly 500 in a Year," 30 June 2016, https://www.amnesty.org/en/latest/news/2016/06/cameroon-boko-haram-attack-brings-total-killed-to-nearly-500-in-a-year/.

[36] Omar Mahmood, "Boko Haram in 2016: A Highly Adaptable Foe," Institute for Security Studies, 7 February 2017, https://issafrica.org/iss-today/boko-haram-in-2016-a-highly-adaptable-foe.

war on Boko Haram have been high for Chad,[37] Cameroon,[38] and Niger.[39]

Politics, Authoritarianism, and Boko Haram in the Lake Chad Region

Boko Haram has not yet caused political crises for Nigeria's neighbors to the extent that it did in Nigeria. The insecurity did not become an effective electoral cudgel for the opposition as Nigeriens and Chadians went to the polls in spring 2016 and as supporters of Cameroon's Biya called for elections to be held in 2016 instead of in 2018. Yet the war had a political impact: the crisis evoked authoritarian reactions from incumbent governments, particularly in Niger.

In Cameroon and Chad, the Boko Haram crisis has occurred amid political continuity. Cameroonian president Paul Biya took office in 1982. Since that time, Biya has blocked any political transition and kept potential successors off balance. In 1992, when pressures for democratization rose across Africa, Biya won reelection narrowly in a multiparty vote. Yet he dominated subsequent contests: official results gave Biya 93 percent of the vote in 1997, 75 percent in 2004, and 78 percent in 2011. Biya weathered multiple crises in 2008, suppressing

---

[37] Nako Madjiasra and Omer Mbadi, "Tchad: Les finances publiques plombées par Boko Haram et la chute du cours du baril de pétrole," *Jeune Afrique*, 7 November 2016, http://www.jeuneafrique.com/mag/367565/economie/tchad-finances-pub liques-plombees-boko-haram-chute-cours-baril-de-petrole/.

[38] Georges Dougueli, "Boko Haram, une guerre qui coûte cher au Cameroun," *Jeune Afrique*, 15 February 2015, http://www.jeuneafrique.com/225299/archives-thematique /boko-haram-une-guerre-qui-co-te-cher-au-cameroun/.

[39] Abdoulaye Massalaki and Makini Brice, "Niger Increases Budget on Boko Haram, 2016 Elections—Govt," Reuters, 17 September 2015, http://www.reuters.com /article/niger-budget-idUSL5N11N34Y20150917.

economically motivated riots and engineering the removal of presidential term limits.[40]

Despite continuity, Biya's long-term rule has hollowed out some of Cameroon's governing institutions, complicating the fight against Boko Haram. Even the Cameroonian military's elite Battalion d'Intervention Rapide (Rapid Intervention Battalion, BIR), the frontline force against Boko Haram, is viewed by some Cameroonians as a tool of presidential power—in 2008, the BIR was key to the suppression of protests.[41] Meanwhile, the extended political jockeying to replace Biya has made his succession "at the same time, the only taboo subject in public discussion and the only important subject in private discussion."[42]

In Cameroon, the Boko Haram crisis occasioned a crackdown that echoed the one in neighboring Nigeria. In the Far North, Amnesty International has reported, "Cameroon's authorities and security forces have committed human rights violations on a significant scale." The abuses included civilian casualties in counterterrorism operations, arbitrary detentions, torture, unfair trials, and widespread sentencing of suspects to death on flimsy evidence.[43] Amnesty implicated the BIR in many of the abuses, suggesting that the crackdown had approval at the highest levels. The International Crisis Group, for its part, found "similar concerns as Amnesty's, but when

---

[40] Randy Joe Sa'ah, "President Paul Biya: Cameroon's 'Lion Man,'" BBC, 6 November 2012, http://www.bbc.com/news/world-africa-20219549.

[41] "Rapid Intervention Unit Strays from Its Mission," IRIN, 29 August 2008, http://www.irinnews.org/report/80065/cameroon-rapid-intervention-military-unit-strays-its-mission.

[42] United States Embassy Yaoundé, leaked cable 09YAOUNDE256, "Cameroon's Justice Minister Says North Will Support Biya, but Not Another Beti or Bami," 12 March 2009, https://wikileaks.org/plusd/cables/09YAOUNDE256_a.html.

[43] Amnesty International, "Right Cause, Wrong Means: Human Rights Violated and Justice Denied in Cameroon's Fight against Boko Haram," 14 July 2016, 6. Available for download at https://www.amnesty.org/en/documents/afr17/4260/2016/en/.

speaking to a wide range of people it also found a high degree of local support for army actions in the face of Boko Haram's bewildering violence."[44] One test of Cameroon's heavy-handed approach will come in 2018, when voters return to the polls.

Like Cameroon, Chad has been ruled by one man for over two decades. President Idriss Deby took power in a 1990 rebellion. Deby has never faced a significant challenge at the ballot box—in a climate of intimidation, he easily won reelection in 1996, 2001, 2006, 2011, and 2016. But Deby nearly lost power in two major rebellions in 2006 and 2008. He survived partly owing to French military intervention against the rebels, partly owing to his rapprochement with neighboring Sudan, and partly because oil production—against the wishes of the World Bank—allowed him to vastly increase military spending.[45]

Since 2008, Deby has made himself an indispensable security partner for France and the United States. Deby volunteered Chadian forces to fight alongside France when it invaded northern Mali in 2013; Chadian soldiers saw fierce combat against jihadists, whereas other African contributors, including Mali's own forces, often avoided the deadliest fighting. In Nigeria as in Mali, Deby has sought to demonstrate that he is invaluable to the preservation of stability in Africa. This strategy brought Deby respect not just from the West, but from his African peers. When the African Union Commission needed a new chair in January 2017, thirty-nine of fifty-four African Union members ultimately backed Deby's

---

[44] Hans de Marie Heungoup, "In the Tracks of Boko Haram in Cameroon," International Crisis Group, 2 September 2016, https://www.crisisgroup.org/africa/central -africa/cameroon/tracks-boko-haram-cameroon.

[45] For more on the story of Chad, oil, and the World Bank, see Celeste Hicks, *Africa's New Oil: Power, Pipelines and Future Fortunes* (London: Zed Books, 2015).

candidate. The vote was widely seen as a sign of respect and appreciation for Chad's role in regional security.[46] Chad's prominent supporters amid the vote included Mali, Niger, and Nigeria.[47]

But Chad may be more fragile than it first appears. Chad's April 2016 elections—which Deby won handily—occurred amid an unprecedented level of protest. The trigger for the protests was the February 2016 rape of a teenage girl, allegedly by a group that included the sons of some of Deby's close associates. The incident evoked widespread anger against Deby—and France.[48] In this atmosphere, Deby's claim that only he could guarantee stability became a slogan he could deploy to reassure both Chadians and foreign partners. A proregime singer, during the 2016 campaign, could be heard on official media singing, "Idriss Deby / The great warrior of Africa / Terrorists will never again sleep peacefully / The Chadian army is on their trail."[49] By late 2016, however, Deby was facing protests from multiple segments of Chadian society, especially students and civil servants angry that their stipends and salaries were going unpaid amid budgetary austerity. Although falling global oil prices were the most important reason for

[46]"Sommet de l'UA: Moussa Faki Mahamat élu à la tête de la Commission," RFI, 31 January 2017, http://www.rfi.fr/afrique/20170130-sommet-ua-moussa-faki -mahamat-elu-tete-commission.

[47]Seidik Abba, "Union africaine: Les trois raisons de la victoire du Tchadien Moussa Faki Mahamat," Le Monde, 31 January 2017, http://www.lemonde.fr/afrique /article/2017/01/31/union-africaine-les-trois-raisons-de-la-victoire-du-tchadien -moussa-faki-mahamat_5072242_3212.html#RqIA7mfveUDqVicS.99.

[48]WATHI, "Présidentielle Tchad: Une campagne électorale marquée par des contestations et des arrestations," 6 April 2016, http://www.wathi.org/laboratoire /initiatives/election_tchad/pre-campagne/presidentielle-tchad-campagne-electorale -marquee-contestations-arrestations/#.Vwl1k1NyTC0.twitter.

[49]Fabien Offner, "Tchad: Idriss Déby justifie son pouvoir absolu au nom de la stabilité," MediaPart, 13 April 2016, https://www.mediapart.fr/journal/international /130416/tchad-idriss-deby-justifie-son-pouvoir-absolu-au-nom-de-la-stabilite?utm _source=twitter&utm_medium=social&utm_campaign=Sharing&xtor=CS3-67.

budget shortfalls, security expenditures in the fight against Boko Haram were another drain on the treasury.

In Niger, the Boko Haram conflict has occurred amid political transition. From 2009 to 2011, as the conflict was accelerating, Niger suffered an unrelated political crisis: a civilian president's unconstitutional third term bid prompted a military coup in 2010. The political crisis ended with the inauguration of President Mahamadou Issoufou in April 2011.

Issoufou inherited a bleak regional picture. To Niger's north, Libya's revolution toppled longtime ruler Muammar Qadhafi. The civil war in Libya had major repercussions for Niger, included thousands of displaced persons, economic fallout from lost remittances, and smuggling of Libyan weapons across Niger. To Niger's west, Mali unraveled in 2012, as a Tuareg nationalist uprising (the fourth since Mali's independence in 1960) gave way to a jihadist takeover of northern Malian cities. In southern Mali, junior army officers seized power in April 2012, precipitating a rocky transition to a new civilian government. In early 2013, a French-led military intervention ended jihadists' rule in northern Malian cities, but jihadism has continued to trouble Mali. A third crisis that affected Niger was domestic: Niger's population, estimated at 16.5 million in 2011, is growing rapidly, even as food production falters amid recurring droughts. In many years, Niger faces severe food emergencies. In the climate of anxiety following Mali's collapse, Niger became the Sahel region's model country in the eyes of some Western observers, but the country remained fragile.[50]

---

[50] For a discussion of Niger's relative success vis-à-vis Mali but also its enduring fragility, see Stephanie Pezard and Michael Shurkin, *Achieving Peace in Northern Mali: Past Agreements, Local Conflicts, and the Prospects for a Durable Settlement* (Santa Monica, CA: RAND, 2015), chapter 5, http://www.rand.org/content/dam/rand/pubs/research_reports/RR800/RR892/RAND_RR892.pdf.

Issoufou initially enjoyed broad goodwill in Niger. A turning point came in 2014, when Issoufou moved against the Speaker of the National Assembly, Hama Amadou (b. 1950). A veteran politician, Amadou had served as prime minister from 1995 to 1996 and from 2000 to 2007. During the 2011 elections, Amadou placed third in the first round, taking approximately 20 percent of the vote. He supported Issoufou in the second round and in return took the speakership in the new government. In August 2013, however, Amadou objected to the composition of a new "unity government" that Issoufou assembled and that Amadou saw as insufficiently representative of his own party. Amadou and his party moved into the opposition. In summer 2014, political tensions escalated. Some of Amadou's close supporters were arrested on accusations of trafficking stolen babies from Nigeria. In August, Amadou fled Niger.[51]

Subsequent events made the criminal charges against Amadou seem politically motivated. In the first round of presidential elections in February 2016, Amadou—who had returned to Niger in October 2015 to declare his candidacy, and was immediately imprisoned—emerged as the second-place candidate, forcing Issoufou into a run-off. Amadou remained in prison throughout the campaign. The final official results gave Issoufou 92.5 percent of the vote.[52]

---

[51] "Main Ally of Niger Regime Quits Ruling Coalition," AFP, 23 August 2013, http://www.capitalfm.co.ke/news/2013/08/main-ally-of-niger-regime-quits-ruling -coalition/; International Crisis Group, "Niger: Another Weak Link in the Sahel?," 19 September 2013, http://www.crisisgroup.org/~/media/Files/africa/west-africa/niger /208-niger-another-weak-link-in-the-sahel-english.pdf; Christophe Boisbouvier, "Niger: Issoufou et Amadou à couteaux tires," *Jeune Afrique*, 16 June 2014, http://www.jeunea frique.com/50501/politique/niger-issoufou-et-amadou-couteaux-tir-s/; "Niger's Hama Amadou Flees over Baby-Trafficking Scandal," BBC, 28 August 2014, http://www.bbc .com/news/world-africa-28966966.

[52] Commission Electorale Nationale Independante (Niger), "Présidentielles 2eme tour du 20 mars 2016: Résultats globaux provisoires," March 2016, http://www.ceni -niger.org/ceniProject/regions2t/map.

As the political space constricted, so did the space for human rights activism. Here, unlike in electoral politics, the most dramatic constriction was directly linked to the Boko Haram crisis. In May 2015, Nigerien authorities arrested two prominent activists, Moussa Tchangari and Nouhou Arzika, because of their criticisms of the government's response to the security and humanitarian crisis in Diffa. The two activists were quickly released, but the charges against them—"infringement of national security" and "speech intended to demoralize the troops"[53]—indicated the essentially political nature of the episode. Comments authorities gave to the media were equally sensational: Minister of the Interior Hassoumi Massaoudou said that Tchangari had "been collaborating with Boko Haram for some time, and he is actively spreading propaganda and false news in liaison with Boko Haram."[54]

The trigger for the arrests was Tchangari's visit to Diffa. Shortly before the visit, Diffa's governor had ordered inhabitants of Niger's Lake Chad islands to evacuate their homes because of insecurity. Tchangari met with village chiefs who had been detained by authorities.[55] He tweeted out photographs showing massive crowds of displaced people.[56] Tchangari's

[53] "Niger: Libération et poursuite du harcèlement judiciaire de MM. Moussa Tchangari et Nouhou Arzika," Worldwide Movement for Human Rights, 11 June 2015, https://www.fidh.org/fr/regions/afrique/niger/niger-liberation-et-poursuite-du-harcelement-judiciaire-de-mm-moussa.

[54] "Journalist Arrested for Collaborating with Boko Haram," AFP, 20 May 2015, http://www.news24.com/Africa/News/Journalist-arrested-for-collaborating-with-Boko-Haram-20150520.

[55] "Niger: Inquiétude après l'arrestation d'un membre de la société civile," RFI, 20 May 2015, http://www.rfi.fr/afrique/20150520-niger-inquietude-apres-arrestation-membre-societe-civile/?aef_campaign_date=2015-05-20&aef_campaign_ref=partage_aef&dlvrit=1448817&ns_campaign=reseaux_sociaux&ns_linkname=editorial&ns_mchannel=social&ns_source=twitter.

[56] Moussa Tchangari Twitter feed, 8 May 2015, https://twitter.com/tchangari/status/596724002174939137; and https://twitter.com/tchangari/status/596723569683537920.

organization then released a scathing report, alleging that civilian and military authorities had grossly mismanaged the evacuations of the islands. The report said that authorities left terrified civilians to flee in grueling conditions: some made long marches by foot, while others suffered in overheated, overcrowded trucks. Authorities' interrogations of civilians created "a veritable climate of fear," with little oversight to control who was identified as a suspected Boko Haram. In one problematic instance,

> Many witnesses were shocked to see that it was a fisherman of Malian origin, himself displaced from one of the islands of Lake Chad, who served as a guide to the soldiers for identifying suspect persons, under the pretext that he knew everyone. On the basis of the denunciation, many persons, notably youths from the Buduma ethnic group, were kept in the sun for hours, before being freed following the intervention of the district chief of N'guigmi.[57]

Tchangari's work embarrassed the Nigerien government. His and Arzika's arrests were part of a broader pattern of repeated interrogations and arrests of Nigerien civil society activists, including figures working in domains unrelated to the war with Boko Haram.[58] The danger is not that a massive segment of Nigerien society will be radicalized by such actions, but rather that authoritarian crackdowns on civil society will increase the trickle of youth who are sympathetic to Boko Haram. Parallel developments are affecting the religious field.

[57] Alternative Espaces Citoyens, "Déplacement forcé des populations des îles du lac Tchad au Niger," May 2015, 8, http://www.alternativeniger.net/wp-content/pdf/pdf_Rapport_sur_l%C3%A9vacuation_des_iles_du_lac_Tchad.pdf.

[58] Claire Rainfroy, "Niger: Quand la lutte contre Boko Haram menace la liberté d'expression," Jeune Afrique, 29 May 2015, http://www.jeuneafrique.com/233588/politique/niger-quand-la-lutte-contre-boko-haram-menace-la-libert-d-expression/.

The Religious Field of the Lake Chad Basin: Sufi-State Alliances, Salafi Challengers

As in Nigeria, the Boko Haram crisis is reshaping the religious field of the Lake Chad basin. The religious fields of Niger, Cameroon, and Chad are closely connected to the religious field in northern Nigeria. Many of these linkages date to Uthman dan Fodio's nineteenth-century jihad, which spread into Niger and Cameroon. Parts of Chad, meanwhile, were linked to the precolonial empire of Kanem and its successor, Bornu. Muslim scholars, like many ordinary people, have continued to cross the region's postcolonial borders: northern Nigerian cities such as Kano, Maiduguri, and Yola remain intellectual hubs for Muslims from throughout the region.

In terms of the structure of the religious field, Niger is more than 90 percent Muslim, Cameroon is over 20 percent Muslim (although northern Cameroon has a Muslim plurality of around 40 percent of the population),[59] and Chad is over 50 percent Muslim. Many Muslims in the Lake Chad basin are Sufis, especially from the Tijaniyya order: an estimated 34 percent of Nigerien Muslims are Tijanis, as are 31 percent of Cameroonian Muslims and 35 percent of Chadian Muslims.[60] Many Tijanis in the region are disciples of Maiduguri's Ibrahim Salih. His students and allies, including Chad's Grand Imam

---

[59] International Crisis Group, "Cameroon: The Threat of Religious Radicalism," 3 September 2015, 1 n. 3, http://www.crisisgroup.org/~/media/Files/africa/central -africa/229-cameroon-the-threat-of-religious-radicalism.pdf.

[60] Pew Research Center, "The World's Muslims: Unity and Diversity—Chapter 1: Religious Affiliation," 9 August 2012, http://www.pewforum.org/2012/08/09/the-worlds -muslims-unity-and-diversity-1-religious-affiliation/.

Husayn Abakar, occupy many high religious posts in Chad.[61] Salih has influence in Niger and Cameroon as well. In each country, the Sufi establishment has been a key ally for incumbent regimes, with Sufis and politicians working hand-in-glove to regulate the religious field. In Niger, under military rule from 1974 to 1991, the Association Islamique du Niger (Islamic Association of Niger), dominated by Sufis and particularly by Tijanis, regulated much religious practice and discourse. The association and its successor organization, the Conseil Islamique du Niger (Islamic Council of Niger), retained some influence even after liberalization and democratization in the 1990s and 2000s.[62] In Chad, the High Islamic Council, also known as the Supreme Council for Islamic Affairs in Chad, is a government-backed, Tijani-dominated body for regulating religious life. Its legal mandate dates to 1970, but it took its present form in 1990. Its chairman is Chad's Grand Imam Abakar, who was appointed to his position by President Deby in 1991.[63] The council was authorized to monitor schools, charities, and regional Islamic councils, and its role included "advising and even reprimanding Imams on the

[61] A video uploaded to YouTube in April 2012 shows Ibrahim Salih addressing a massive crowd in N'Djamena, and offering extensive recognition to Husayn Abakar (by name) and to the assembled representatives of the High Islamic Council. See "Muhadara li-l-Shaykh Ibrahim Salih al-Husayni fi Tshad," https://www.youtube.com/watch?v=v-v38U3wS6I. For more on "the long arm of Ibrahim Salih," see Rüdiger Seesemann, "Der lange Arm des Ibrahim Salih," in *Die islamische Welt als Netzwerk*, edited by Roman Loimeier, 135–61 (Würzburg: Erlon Verlag, 2000).

[62] Sebastian Elischer, "Autocratic Legacies and State Management of Islamic Activism in Niger," *African Affairs* 114:457 (October 2015): 577–97. See also Ousseina Alidou, *Engaging Modernity: Muslim Women and the Politics of Agency in Postcolonial Niger* (Madison: University Wisconsin Press, 2005), 151.

[63] United States Embassy N'Djamena, leaked cable 07NDJAMENA455, "Grand Imam Voices Concern over Extremists' 'New Strategy' in Chad," 4 June 2007, https://wikileaks.org/plusd/cables/07NDJAMENA455_a.html. Also see the council's home page at http://csai-tchad.org/fr/.

content of their Friday sermons."[64] As discussed below, however, the top-down management of the religious field in Niger and Chad has come under strain in recent years.

In northern Cameroon, the structure of the religious field is somewhat different, but the strains are similar. From the nineteenth century to the present, religious authority has been built on alliances between hereditary Muslim rulers (known as *lamidos* among the Fulani of northern Cameroon, and as sultans among the Bamoun in western Cameroon) and classically-trained scholars, many of whom were and are Sufis.[65] Yet the past three decades have seen change. Legal reforms from the 1970s to the 1990s, including a constitutional reform in 1996, officially made the hereditary rulers part of the state.

The advent of multiparty democracy in 1992 created political challenges for Cameroon's hereditary rulers: although President Biya dominated national politics during and after the 1992 election, local politics were competitive. Hereditary rulers could—and did—find themselves on the wrong side of local elections. In the 1992 and 1997 local elections, the lamidos of Ngaoundéré and Banyo, both in the Adamawa Region, backed Biya's party only to see it lose, even among voters in the rulers' core districts. The lamidos suffered "a veritable crisis of authority" that made them targets of voters' anger. Meanwhile, rulers who held themselves aloof from electoral politics and from the regime emerged more popular with their subjects.[66] Biya, however, continued to favor some of the

---

[64] United States Embassy N'Djamena, leaked cable 07NDJAMENA508, "Corrected Version: Islam in Southern Chad," 20 June 2007, https://wikileaks.org/plusd/cables/07NDJAMENA508_a.html.

[65] International Crisis Group, "Cameroon," 2–5.

[66] Mamoudou [no surname], "Les Lamidats de l'Adamaoua à l'épreuve du processus démocratique et du gangstérisme rural," in *De l'Adamawa à l'Adamaoua: Histoire, enjeux et perspectives pour le Nord-Cameroon*, edited by Hamadou Adama, 183–99 (Paris: L'Harmattan, 2014), 188–89.

hereditary rulers, appointing roughly a dozen of them to the Senate in 2013.[67]

A sharp rise in rural banditry in the 2000s, involving kidnappings and robbery, thrust hereditary rulers into new, unfamiliar security roles.[68] Banditry also caused some mistrust between the state and the hereditary rulers. In October 2008, Jean-Baptiste Bokam, secretary of state of Cameroon's Gendarmerie, gave a speech in Kaélé, Far North Region. He accused unnamed local chiefs of involvement with banditry.[69] The dual challenge of navigating politics and confronting crime placed the hereditary rulers in a vulnerable position at the exact time that Boko Haram was emerging.

As Sufis and hereditary rulers in the Lake Chad region face challenges, Salafism has spread, particularly through Nigeria's Izala association (see chapter 1). In Niger, merchants who participated in cross border trade helped spread Izala to cities such as Maradi.[70] Izala has a strong presence in Diffa.[71] In Diffa, the Tijaniyya—still numerically dominant and still in control of the town's central mosque[72]—is partly associated with the Fulani and therefore has less appeal for Kanuri youth, which offered an opening to Izala and Salafis.[73] Izala's

[67] Léon Koungou, *Boko Haram: Le Cameroon à l'épreuve des menaces* (Paris: L'Harmattan, 2014), 51–52.

[68] Mamoudou, "Les Lamidats," 196.

[69] Koungou, *Boko Haram*, 55.

[70] Emmanuel Gregoire, "Islam and Identity in Maradi (Niger)," in *Muslim Identity and Social Change in Sub-Saharan Africa*, edited by Louis Brenner, 106–15 (London: Hurst, 1993).

[71] Government of Niger, Ministry of the Interior and Decentralization, "Etude sur les pratiques de l'islam au Niger," April 2006, 22, https://www.liportal.de/file admin/user_upload/oeffentlich/Niger/40_gesellschaft/islamrapportprovisoire24 avril2006concorde.pdf.

[72] Interview with Attahirou.

[73] Interview with Idrissa.

Nigerian leadership has paid considerable attention to Niger,[74] organizing regular preaching events in southern Niger as part of its "National Preaching [Wa'azin Kasa]" programs.[75] Niger's Izala members are also connected to Nigeria through electronic media. Niger has witnessed a boom in private religious media since the political liberalization of the 1990s.[76] Izala also gained a strong foothold in Cameroon, especially in the southern part of the country among Hausa populations.[77] Like Nigeria, Niger and Cameroon have also seen a rise in more independent Salafi preachers claiming the generalized affiliation "Ahl al-Sunna" rather than the Izala label.[78]

Compared to its presence in Niger and Cameroon, Izala is weaker in Chad. The most prominent manifestation of Salafism there is, rather, the organization Ansar al-Sunna al-Muhammadiyya (Supporters of the Prophetic Model). Ansar al-Sunna was founded in Egypt in 1926 and has influential branches in Sudan as well. In Chad, Ansar al-Sunna was officially established in 1992. It now has branches throughout much of the country,[79] as well as an influential radio station, Al-Bayan. Ansar al-Sunna has prominent and highly educated leaders, such as its president, Dr. Ahmat Mahamat Haggar, who holds a Ph.D. from François Rabelais University in Tours,

[74] Nigerien branches of Izala include the organizations Ihya' al-Sunna and Kitab wa Sunna, whose names respectively mean "Reviving the Prophetic Model" and "the Book [i.e., the Qur'an] and the Prophetic Model."

[75] See an advertisement for one November/December 2013 event at https://www.facebook.com/permalink.php?id=1471493496408506&story_fbid=1488102308080958.

[76] Abdoulaye Sounaye, "Mobile Sunna: Islam, Small Media and Community in Niger," *Social Compass* 61:1 (March 2014): 21–29; 23.

[77] Interview with Ayong.

[78] Abdoulaye Sounaye, "Irwo Sunnance yan-no! Youth Claiming, Contesting and Transforming Salafism," *Islamic Africa* 6:1–2 (2015): 82–108.

[79] Ansar al-Sunna al-Muhammadiyya bi-Tshad Facebook page, "Ta'rif Mujaz 'an Jama'at Ansar al-Sunna al-Muhammadiyya bi-Tshad," 17 June 2013, https://www.facebook.com/permalink.php?story_fbid=325057440960694&id=300613470071758.

France;[80] and Dr. Yahya Ibrahim Khalil, a lecturer at Chad's King Faysal University.[81] The expansion of Salafism in Chad has received a boost from transnational Islamic nongovernmental organizations, many of them funded by Gulf Arab countries and private donors. Although such organizations have had an impact throughout sub-Saharan Africa, Chad is a particularly attractive destination for NGOs because of its extreme poverty. In Chad, "needs on the ground are manifold." Chad also attracts Islamic charities because "it is situated at the crossroads of Arab and Black African and Western spheres of influence, and is, therefore, strategically important."[82]

The rise of Salafism has contributed to religious fragmentation. In Niger and Cameroon, Izala's spread sparked tremendous debates over Islamic orthodoxy. These debates pitted Izala against Sufis and other Muslims, reshaping religious practice in many communities.[83] Sufis sometimes attempted to bring state resources and legitimacy to bear in these conflicts. In a series of meetings with the U.S. Embassy in 2006–7, Chad's Grand Imam Abakar privately accused Ansar al-Sunna of working with foreign Islamic charities to fund jihadism in

[80] "Hiwar ma'a Fadilat D. Haqqar Muhammad Ahmad," *Shabakat al-Miskhat al-Islamiyya*, 29 December 2003, http://www.meshkat.net/node/14454.

[81] See Khalil's Facebook page (https://ar-ar.facebook.com/people/%D8%A7%D9 %84%D8%B4%D9%8A%D8%AE-%D8%AF%D9%8A%D8%AD%D9%8A%D9%89 -%D8%A5%D8%A8%D8%B1%D8%A7%D9%87%D9%8A%D9%85-%D8%AE %D9%84%D9%8A%D9%84/100003558668618) and Twitter account (https://twitter .com/dryahyakhalil).

[82] Mayke Kaag, "Transnational Islamic NGOs in Chad: Islamic Solidarity in the Age of Neoliberalism," *Africa Today* 54:3 (Spring 2008): 3–18; 6.

[83] For an analysis of Izala-Sufi disputes in Dogondoutchi, southern Niger, see Adeline Masquelier, "Debating Muslims, Disputed Practices: Struggles for the Realization of an Alternative Moral Order in Niger," in *Civil Society and the Political Imagination in Africa: Critical Perspectives*, edited by John L. Comaroff and Jean Comaroff, 219–50 (Chicago: University of Chicago Press, 1999); on Cameroon, see International Crisis Group, "Cameroon."

Africa.[84] One of those charities, Al-Haramayn, has been accused of supporting terrorism around the world. After 9/11, the U.S. Treasury Department blacklisted different country offices of the foundation, and subsequently the entire organization (in 2008).[85] Yet there is no publicly available evidence to suggest that Ansar al-Sunna in Chad has funded or participated in terrorism. Even as Sufis attempt to block Salafism's spread, meanwhile, some of the region's most revered and influential Sufi shaykhs are dying of old age.

It is misleading to see the region's religious field in teleological terms, as an uninterrupted process of "Salafization" that will inevitably displace Sufism. Sufism remains a key form of Muslim affiliation in the region, and Sufism is expanding in some communities. But dynamic, activist, and youth-based Salafi movements (many of which are internally fragmented) are reshaping religious life in Africa, including in the Lake Chad basin.

Does this mean that Boko Haram can exploit a Salafi base to recruit? No, or least not straightforwardly: it is not necessarily the case that where Salafism goes, Boko Haram follows. As in northern Nigeria, mainstream Salafi constituencies around Lake Chad have often been among the harshest critics and foes of Boko Haram. This is true not just at the national level, but also at the local level: in Diffa,[86] and in northern Cameroon,[87] Salafis and Sufis alike have publicly denounced Boko Haram and worked to delegitimize the sect. In Chad, Ansar al-Sunna's

---

[84] United States Embassy N'Djamena, leaked cable 07NDJAMENA149, "Chad's Grand Imam Requests Help to Investigate Terrorism Financing," 15 February 2007, https://wikileaks.org/plusd/cables/07NDJAMENA149_a.html.

[85] U.S. Department of the Treasury, "Treasury Designates Al Haramain Islamic Foundation," 19 June 2008, https://www.treasury.gov/press-center/press-releases/Pages/hp1043.aspx.

[86] Interview with Attahirou.

[87] Interview with Ayong.

Haggar has publicly condemned Boko Haram: "I think that it is the duty of every Muslim, Nigerian or African, to put an end to this movement which does not represent Islam." Haggar has called for dialogue rather than military solutions to jihadism. He has positioned himself as unambiguously anti-jihadist.[88]

One effect of the Boko Haram crisis has been an increase in suspicions surrounding mainstream Salafi organizations. As the Boko Haram crisis increasingly affects Chad, old accusations against Ansar al-Sunna have taken on a new edge. In March 2015, Grand Imam Abakar took to the radio to denounce the country's Salafis as Boko Haram members and even as "unbelievers [kuffar]" who should not lead other Muslims in prayer. Local media commented that "the imam had profited from the debate on the Islamists of Boko Haram in order to settle his scores with his enemies."[89] When the governments of Chad, Niger, and Cameroon banned women from wearing the niqab (full face veil), ostensibly in reaction to suicide bombings by women (and men dressed as women), their decisions reinforced the impression that the wider Salafi community, and not just Boko Haram, were becoming targets. These policies also gestured toward the possibility that Lake Chad governments and their Sufi allies might pursue more aggressively anti-Salafi measures if the crisis worsened.

Would a crackdown on Salafis radicalize them? It is unlikely that Izala or Ansar al-Sunna leaders, or mainstream, independent Salafi preachers, would ally with Boko Haram, or would independently take up arms and call for the overthrow

---

[88] Mohamadou Houmfa, "Haggar M. Ahmat: 'Il y a un terrorisme inventé à des fins politiques, éco et commerciales,'" *La Voix*, 20 November 2012, http://www.journal dutchad.com/article.php?aid=3722.

[89] Adil Abou, "Tchad: L'Imam Hassan met de l'huile au feu," Alwihda Info, 2 March 2015, http://www.alwihdainfo.com/Tchad-L-Imam-Hassan-met-de-l-huile -au-feu_a15038.html.

of Lake Chad states. Rather, one danger is that a greater number of unaffiliated Muslim youth, surveying a fragmented and contentious religious field, would begin to gravitate toward Boko Haram instead of toward mainstream Salafism. Already, there is a pull from the "super Izala" aura that Boko Haram exudes—an effort to outdo mainstream Salafis in terms of commitment to religious purity.[90] For unaffiliated youth, seeing their governments harass mainstream Salafis might activate resentment against both camps: against governments for being authoritarian, and against mainstream Salafis for being too acquiescent.

A second danger is that preachers at the fringes of the mainstream Salafi movement would seek to capitalize on a climate of anger—as Muhammad Yusuf did in Nigeria. A significant number of youth in Niger are not ideologically jihadist, but they valorize al-Qaʿida and the Islamic State as heroic, anti-Western organizations. Hardline religious rhetoric can intersect with political and socioeconomic grievances.

One such intersection occurred during antigovernment protests in January 2015. The protests broke out in opposition strongholds such as Zinder and Agadez after President Issoufou marched in Paris in a demonstration of sympathy with the French magazine *Charlie Hebdo*, which had been attacked by gunmen proclaiming allegiance to the Islamic State. The protests in Niger, which partly targeted Christians, do not in any way indicate widespread support for Boko Haram or jihadism, but the protests did reveal considerable anger among many Nigerien youth.[91] Some religious entrepreneurs, includ-

---

[90] Interview with Idrissa.

[91] Jannik Schritt, "The 'Protests against Charlie Hebdo' in Niger: A Background Analysis," *Africa Spectrum* 50:1 (2015): 49–64.

ing Izala, are seeking to harness that anger.[92] But stoking popular anger could inadvertently open space for more radical voices to intensify antigovernment rhetoric while seeking to mobilize the same constituencies.

In this atmosphere, it would be wise for Lake Chad governments to heed the advice of the International Crisis Group, which urges governments worldwide to "disaggregate not conflate" when it comes to Muslim activists. This recommendation applies to the imperative of distinguishing between jihadists and non-jihadists, but also to the need for disaggregation within jihadist organizations: "Even [the Islamic State], its local branches and al-Qaeda affiliates . . . are not monolithic."[93] The same goes for Boko Haram.

Boko Haram and the Islamic State

Boko Haram pledged allegiance to the Islamic State in March 2015 for strategic as well as ideological reasons. The two movements have common intellectual roots: Yusuf's intellectual debt to the Palestinian Jordanian Salafi-jihadist theorist Abu Muhammad al-Maqdisi (b. 1959), a relationship I have discussed in chapter 2 and elsewhere,[94] helps contextualize Boko Haram's later affiliation to the Islamic State. Al-Maqdisi mentored Abu Mus'ab al-Zarqawi (1966–2006), who founded al-Qa'ida

[92] International Crisis Group, "The Central Sahel: A Perfect Sandstorm," 25 June 2015, 12, http://reliefweb.int/sites/reliefweb.int/files/resources/227-the-central-sahel-a-perfect-sandstorm.pdf.

[93] International Crisis Group, "Exploiting Disorder: Al-Qaeda and the Islamic State," 14 March 2016, iii, http://www.crisisgroup.org/~/media/Files/exploiting-disorder-al-qaeda-and-the-islamic-state.pdf.

[94] Alex Thurston, *Salafism in Nigeria: Islam, Preaching and Politics* (Cambridge: Cambridge University Press, 2016), chapter 7.

in Iraq, the Islamic State's predecessor organization. Although al-Maqdisi broke with al-Zarqawi and later denounced the Islamic State, it is unsurprising that Boko Haram would find much in common, theologically and politically, with the Islamic State.

The timing of the affiliation—March 2015—reflected Boko Haram's weakness. As when Somalia's al-Shabab completed its merger with al-Qa'ida in 2012,[95] Boko Haram announced its merger with the Islamic State after suffering territorial losses.[96] By hitching its wagon to the rising star of the Islamic State and its brand, Boko Haram could claim global legitimacy. Even before it joined the Islamic State, Boko Haram increasingly tailored its propaganda toward global jihadists, professionalizing its media products and emphasizing Arabic over Hausa. But with Boko Haram and the Islamic State under military pressure, it is unlikely that copious weapons, fighters, and money have flowed, or will flow, from the Middle East to the Lake Chad basin. It is also unlikely that Islamic State commanders are dictating day-to-day decisions to Boko Haram, whose attacks remain reactive to regional developments.

If weakness motivated Boko Haram's initial allegiance to the Islamic State, weakness may also have sustained the rhetorical relationship. In March 2016, a brief video appeared, featuring Shekau. The video was widely mistranslated as a call by Shekau for surrender, but really Shekau spoke of purity and jihad, reassuring the sect's followers of his survival: "Dear brothers, by God's permission, your messages have reached

[95] Al-Shabab leaders had earlier pledged allegiance to al-Qa'ida in 2008. See Nick Grace, "Shabaab Reaches Out to Al Qaeda Senior Leaders," *Long War Journal*, September 2, 2008, http://www.longwarjournal.org/archives/2008/09/shabab_reaches_out_t.php.

[96] Terje Østebø, "The Virtual Significance of Boko Haram's Pledge of Allegiance to ISIS," *Conversation*, March 19, 2015, http://theconversation.com/the-virtual-significance-of-boko-harams-pledge-of-allegiance-to-isis-38690.

me. I have heard what you have said, by God's permission. . . . This is my face, and this is my speech, and this is my message to you, to you, to you, o brothers."[97] Some commentators viewed the video as a fake "cut-and-paste job,"[98] possibly stitching together old footage of Shekau.

Whatever the truth of these claims—that Shekau was surrendering or that the video was fake—Boko Haram swiftly released a more expertly produced video featuring a veiled spokesman and footage of fighters and vehicles. The spokesman referred to Boko Haram as part of the Islamic State's "Caliphate" and to Shekau as the "governor [*wali*]" of its West Africa Province. Invoking the idea that God alone had the power to grant victory, the spokesman described the coalition opposing Boko Haram as one made up of God's enemies: apostates, the Shi'a, idol worshippers, and other alleged religious deviants. The spokesman warned: "Know: there is no agreement, there is no time for discussion, there is no surrendering, there is no peace, until you come and follow God. So long as you follow unbelief, we will rebel against you." The speaker then quoted part of Qur'anic verse 60:4, one beloved by Salafi-jihadists because of its prominence in the Salafi-jihadist reading of *al-wala' wa-l-bara'*: "Indeed, we are disassociated from you [*inna bura'u minkum*] and from whatever you worship other than Allah. We have denied you, and there has appeared between us and you enmity and hatred forever until you believe in Allah alone."[99]

[97]"Alleged Boko Haram Video Depicting Leader Shekau Surrendering," Sahara TV, 26 March 2016, https://www.youtube.com/watch?v=oefFuM4JS1c.

[98]"Nigerian Military Forensically Examines New Shekau Video," *Sahara Reporters*, 24 March 2016, http://saharareporters.com/2016/03/24/nigerian-military-forensically-examines-new-shekau-video.

[99]"New Boko Haram Video Reiterates Allegiance to ISIS," Sahara TV, 5 April 2016, https://www.youtube.com/watch?v=fQAj3Fdoqng. On the Qur'anic verse in

For a group that had suffered major reversals over the previous eighteen months and whose nominal leader was either weak or dead, the veiled spokesman's video was a remarkable piece of propaganda. The sect's claim of continued legitimacy and power rested on its invocation of core doctrines dating to the time of Yusuf (expressed in almost identical language), but also on its rhetorical relationship with the Islamic State. Boko Haram's spokesman promised, "We will put you in a situation like the situation in which the followers of the idolatrous tyrants [*taghut*] of Iraq, Syria, Libya, Khorasan [Afghanistan], and Sinai [Egypt] found themselves."[100] Invoking the "Caliphate's" victories and impact elsewhere was a useful rhetorical device when attempting to convince enemies and supporters that Boko Haram was still formidable.

Nevertheless, operational cooperation between Boko Haram and the Islamic State's central leadership still seemed weak as of spring 2016, when the video appeared. For a fuller understanding of the limits of Boko Haram's cooperation with the Islamic State, a brief comparison between Nigeria and Libya is helpful. The Islamic State has had an official presence in Libya since October 2014, drawing support from three key constituencies: Libyan fighters who had fought in Syria;[101] former loyalists of Qadhafi;[102] and local jihadists whom the Islamic State wooed away from local jihadist groups such as

---

question, see Joas Wagemakers, "Defining the Enemy: Abu Muhammad al-Maqdisi's Radical Reading of Surat al-Mumtahana," *Die Welt des Islams* 48 (2008): 348–71.

[100] "New Boko Haram Video Reiterates Allegiance to ISIS."

[101] United Nations Security Council (UNSC) Analytical Support and Monitoring Team concerning al-Qaida and Associated Individuals and Entities, "Report . . . concerning the Terrorism Threat in Libya," 19 November 2015, 7–8, http://untribune .com/wp-content/uploads/2015/12/MT-report-on-Libya-ENG.pdf.

[102] Wa'il 'Isam, " 'Al-Dawla al-Islamiyya' fi Libiya Tatallaqa Da'man min Qaba'il Kanat Mawaliya li-l-Qadhdhafi," *Al-Quds al-Arabi*, 20 February 2015, http://www .alquds.co.uk/?p=298959.

Ansar al-Shari'a (Supporters of Islamic Law), which has ties to al-Qa'ida.[103]

Despite some local support, however, the Islamic State's presence in Libya has been overseen by a series of non-Libyans personally deputized by the Islamic State's leader Abubakar al-Baghdadi.[104] The Islamic State's centralized approach to the management of its Libyan affiliate contrasts markedly with the loose relationship between the Islamic State and Boko Haram, whose leaders have remained Nigerian and whose ranks boast few visible foreign fighters (meaning, here, fighters from beyond the Lake Chad region and Nigeria).

Moreover, amid fears that the two Islamic State affiliates were working together, the Islamic State seemed keener to draw West Africans to Libya than to Nigeria, especially when Boko Haram was losing ground. In May 2016, one of the Islamic State's Libya provinces released a propaganda video entitled "From Humiliation to Glory." The video targeted West Africans, featuring testimonials from several West African fighters in Libya, including a Hausa-speaking Nigerian. The

[103] Frederic Wehrey and Ala' Alrababa'h, "Splitting the Islamists: The Islamic State's Creeping Advance in Libya," Carnegie Endowment for International Peace, 19 June 2015, http://carnegieendowment.org/syriaincrisis/?fa=60447.

[104] "Al-Baghdadi Yu'ayyin 'Wisam 'Abd al-Zubaydi' Amiran li-Da'ish fi Libiya," Al-Mjhar, 11 March 2015, http://www.almjhar.com/ar-sy/NewsView/81/89801/%D8%A7%D9%84%D8%A8%D8%BA%D8%AF%D8%A7%D8%AF%D9%8A_%D9%8A_%D8%B9%D9%8A%D9%86_%D9%88%D8%B3%D8%A7%D9%85_%D8%B9%D9%8B%D8%AF_%D8%A7%D9%84%D8%B2%D8%A8%D9%8A%D8%AF%D9%8A_%D8%A3%D9%85%D9%8A%D8%B1%D8%A7_%D9%84%D8%AF%D8%A7%D8%B9%D8%B4_%D9%81%D9%8A_%D9%84%D9%8A%D8%A8%D9%8A%D8%A7.aspx; see also "Amir Da'ish fi Libiya Shurti 'Iraqi Munshaqq Kana Rafiqan li-l-Baghdadi fi Sijnihi," Al-Masalah, 20 February 2015, http://almasalah.com/ar/NewsDetails.aspx?NewsID=47815; and "Interview with Abul-Mughirah al-Qahtani," Dabiq 11 (Dhu al-Qada 1436/September 2015), 62, http://www.clarionproject.org/docs/Issue%2011%20-%20From%20the%20battle%20of%20Al-Ahzab%20to%20the%20war%20of%20coalitions.pdf.

video urged West Africans to come to Libya and made no mention of Boko Haram.[105]

Additionally, doctrinal differences between Boko Haram and the Islamic State remain: Boko Haram is less millenarian than its new patron. Rather than preparing for apocalypse,[106] Boko Haram looks to purge the Lake Chad region of alleged unbelief. Boko Haram's posture toward other Sunni Muslims is harsher than that of the Islamic State. The latter has committed unspeakable violence against civilians, but has also built alliances with Sunni constituencies in Iraq and Syria, and has need of some popular support. Boko Haram, under Shekau, antagonized almost the entire spectrum of Muslims in its region, committing atrocities that likely foreclose the possibility of collaboration with any other sizeable Muslim constituency, save other jihadist groups.

In 2016, the Islamic State either fostered or endorsed a schism within Boko Haram, siding against Shekau. Echoing developments in 2011–12, when al-Qa'ida in the Islamic Maghreb supported the creation of Boko Haram splinter group Ansar al-Muslimin (see chapter 3), the Islamic State had apparently found Shekau too difficult to work with. In August 2016, an Islamic State newsletter published an interview with Abu Mus'ab al-Barnawi, who is widely suspected to be Muhammad Yusuf's son Habib. The Islamic State, referring to al-Barnawi as the "governor [*wali*]" of West Africa, effectively demoted Shekau.

---

[105] Islamic State Tripolitania Province (Wilayat Tarabulus), "Min al-Dhill ila-'Izza," May 2016, available at http://jihadology.net/2016/05/29/new-video-message-from-the-islamic-state-from-humiliation-to-glory-wilayat-%E1%B9%ADarabulus/.

[106] On the Islamic State's millenarianism, see William McCants, *The ISIS Apocalypse: The History, Strategy, and Doomsday Vision of the Islamic State* (New York: St. Martin's, 2015).

In the interview, al-Barnawi referred to Shekau only once and did so respectfully, describing Shekau's leadership in the period after Yusuf's death:

> They began combat operations on the ground, and the society passed through many stages and developments in its jihadist journey. Among the stages through which it passed are: its swift effort to save its imprisoned members who were captured in the first attack on the society, and also sending its soldiers to the great desert to train there, and also its transition to the stage of guerrilla war to the stage of consolidation and the extension of control. The most prominent of those developments was the historic development that completely startled the world, and that was the announcement of its allegiance to the Caliph of the Muslims, [Abubakr al-Baghdadi] may God protect him.

Yet al-Barnawi made implicit criticisms of Shekau and distanced Boko Haram from violence against Muslim civilians. The key exchange in the interview relied on certain readings of jihadist doctrine about whether Muslim civilians living under an "infidel" system had themselves become unbelievers or not. Al-Barnawi, breaking with Shekau, said that such civilians were effectively innocent until proven guilty. He told the interview, "The [Islamic] State has forbidden targeting the mass of people who belong to Islam, and it is innocent of that action. Everyone who does this, does it for himself, not in the name of the Caliphate—may God strengthen it—and it does not claim responsibility for this kind of thing."[107] Al-Barnawi suggested that Boko Haram would focus, going forward, on attacking the state and Christians.

---

[107] "Wali Gharb Ifriqiya," 9.

If the official elevation of al-Barnawi was polite, the ensuing war of words between Shekau and al-Barnawi's camp was not. Days after the publication of the Islamic State's interview with al-Barnawi, Shekau released an audio message addressed to the Islamic State's Abubakar al-Baghdadi. Shekau stated his differences with al-Barnawi regarding the issue of unbelief, arguing that Muslims who displayed no signs of enmity toward the "idolatrous tyrant [al-taghut]" were unbelievers, whereas al-Barnawi disagreed. Shekau said that he had appealed to al-Baghdadi for a ruling, with as many as seven messages, one of them ten pages long. "I sent you many messages to the effect that their creed is false, because their creed is the creed of irja' . . . but I received no response."[108]

With the accusation of irja', Shekau referred to an early Muslim theological school, the Murji'a, who held that Muslims should delay judgment of whether grave sinners had become unbelievers, because only God could judge. Salafis regard the Murji'a as theological deviants, and accusations of irja' are common in intra-Salafi debates.[109] Shekau was trying to convince al-Baghdadi that he, Shekau, was the true Salafi, and that al-Barnawi had left the fold.

Al-Barnawi's camp fired back with an even more hostile message. Their audio recording ran over eighty minutes. They may have originally intended it to circulate only among Boko Haram members, but it soon appeared on YouTube. In the recording, Muhammad Yusuf's companion Mamman Nur castigated and threatened Shekau. Nur recounted numerous incidents in which, he claimed, Shekau had abused his position for personal gain and had twisted scripture to justify violence

---

[108] Abubakar Shekau, untitled audio message, 4 August 2016, https://www.youtube.com/watch?v=chIBAwlKf0k.

[109] Daniel Lav, *Radical Islam and the Revival of Medieval Theology* (Cambridge: Cambridge University Press, 2012).

against his opponents and those who stood in his way. Nur threatened to kill Shekau: "Now, inside his house, we have our own people, whom he does not know, but if he touches us, they will touch him there." Nur further explained that it was he and al-Barnawi who had complained about Shekau to al-Baghdadi, suggesting that they were the ones managing the relationship.[110] The Nigerian press speculated that Nur had merely elevated the younger al-Barnawi as the face of the Islamic State–endorsed Boko Haram, but that Nur himself was effectively in charge. Whatever the case, the two factions soon clashed in different localities in Borno.[111]

Within this intra–Boko Haram conflict, the Islamic State had become a potent symbol, and perhaps a key player. Both sides appealed to al-Baghdadi. Perhaps each leader's connections to the central organization afforded him some protection from the others, who might threaten but not actually kill a sort of "made man," to use a mafia analogy. Yet the Islamic State's influence also appeared to widen existing fractures within the organization. These fractures reflected a personality conflict centered on Shekau, but also a theological and strategic disagreement centering on the treatment of Muslim civilians. One could certainly interpret the Islamic State's designation of al-Barnawi as a sign of its profound influence over Boko Haram, but one could also interpret the same event—as I do—as a sign of further weakness within a badly divided and somewhat demoralized organization. By supporting al-Barnawi's side, the Islamic State had ensured that even more of Boko Haram's violence would be directed against itself.

[110] Mamman Nur, "Fallasa," 5 August 2016, https://www.youtube.com/watch?v=86 TwFqg-Aqc.

[111] Hamza Idris, "Shekau vs. Barnawi: The Battle for Boko Haram's Soul," *Daily Trust*, 11 September 2016, http://www.dailytrust.com.ng/news/news/shekau-vs-barnawi -the-battle-for-boko-haram-s-soul/162159.html.

War on Terror Context

If Boko Haram seeks to embed itself in the global jihadist scene, it has also long been deeply embedded in another international context: that of the "Global War on Terror." This "war" comprises both a set of conflicts and a set of political assumptions. After the 9/11 attacks, American authorities made consequential decisions to treat jihadist terrorism as a form of war, rather than crime; to treat jihadism as a moral evil rather than a political perspective; and to subordinate concerns about human rights to the perceived imperative of eliminating jihadists and securing "the homeland." Such approaches to security were not entirely new—some approaches were familiar from the Cold War and other contexts—but the War on Terror gave new discursive, legal, and policy freedoms to states confronting jihadism or alleged jihadism.[112]

During the War on Terror, U.S. policy makers have often looked the other way when their counterterrorism partners suppress domestic dissent, violate human rights, and shrink the space available to journalists and human rights activists. In Africa, the ruling regimes in Ethiopia, Uganda, and other counterterrorism partners have racked up absurdly high margins in elections and have suppressed dissent, even branding peaceful dissidents and journalists as terrorists—and Washington appears unfazed. In April 2016, before electoral results had even been released in Chad, then U.S. ambassador to the

---

[112] For an analysis of how "expert" views on terrorism evolved from the 1970s to the post-9/11 era, see Lisa Stampnitzky, *Disciplining Terror: How Experts Invented "Terrorism"* (New York: Cambridge University Press, 2014). For an analysis of how the War on Terror expanded state power in Morocco, see Ann Wainscott, *Bureaucratizing Islam: Morocco and the War on Terror* (New York: Cambridge University Press, 2017).

United Nations Samantha Power announced a trip to Nigeria, Cameroon, and Chad to discuss the anti–Boko Haram effort, implicitly legitimating Deby. At times, the United States appears to consider strongmen such as Chad's Deby and Cameroon's Biya more reliable than Nigeria's (semi)democratically elected leaders. And although Niger is more of a democracy than Chad or Cameroon, the United States looked the other way when Issoufou harassed human rights activists and manipulated Niger's electoral playing field in 2015–16.

Under Issoufou, Niger has been at the forefront of a trend toward securitization in Africa, and particularly the Sahel. Despite several terrorist attacks inside Niger between 2011 and 2013, Niger's relative stability made it an attractive partner for the United States, which established two bases there for unarmed drones.[113] As the threat Boko Haram posed to Niger grew, the United States' role there increased. By 2015, there was a small team of around twenty U.S. Special Forces in Diffa. The soldiers had a mandate to provide security for anti-Boko Haram community leaders. The soldiers also supported a Pentagon-funded nonprofit group, Spirit of America. The nonprofit group provided nonmilitary equipment to Nigerien soldiers and helped organize anti–Boko Haram efforts, such as meetings of community leaders.[114] Such efforts offered mutual benefits to Washington and Niamey: Washington could pursue the style of military expansionism that has come to characterize the post–Iraq War world (quiet Special Forces

[113] Craig Whitlock, "Pentagon Set to Open Second Drone Base in Niger as It Expands Operations in Africa," *Washington Post*, 1 September 2014, https://www.washingtonpost.com/world/national-security/pentagon-set-to-open-second-drone-base-in-niger-as-it-expands-operations-in-africa/2014/08/31/365489c4-2eb8-11e4-994d-202962a9150c_story.html.

[114] Warren Strobel, "Exclusive: In Niger, U.S. Soldiers Quietly Help Build Wall against Boko Haram," Reuters, 18 September 2015, http://www.reuters.com/article/us-usa-niger-boko-haram-idUSKCN0RI0C020150918.

deployments,[115] and an ostensible focus on development and community-building rather than war), while Niamey received a boost in both military and political terms.

Nigeria's status in the War on Terror has been complicated. From Washington's perspective, Nigeria is not Egypt—a pillar of U.S. geostrategy, and therefore a country whose military regimes are nearly immune to criticism. But neither is Nigeria like Ethiopia—a less important country in Washington's eyes, and one viewed almost exclusively in security terms. This kind of in-between status means that Nigeria has multifaceted importance to the international community and the global economy—importance due not just to security and stability concerns, but also to oil production, investment, and peacekeeping operations. At the same time, Washington and Europe do not consider Nigeria's governments off-limits when it comes to criticism. U.S. policy makers and their European counterparts have sometimes been more outspoken about democracy and human rights issues in Nigeria than elsewhere in Africa, particularly during Nigeria's contentious 2006–7 political succession process.[116]

Nigeria has also been subject to stricter regulations on U.S. military aid than have countries that U.S. policy makers consider more strategically central, such as Egypt. Washington regularly exempts Egypt from having to meet basic thresholds

[115] Souad Mekhennet and Missy Ryan, "Outside the Wire: How U.S. Special Operations Troops Secretly Help Foreign Forces Target Terrorists," *Washington Post*, 16 April 2016, https://www.washingtonpost.com/world/national-security/outside-the-wire-how-us-special-operations-troops-secretly-help-foreign-forces-target-terrorists/2016/04/16/a9c1a7d0-0327-11e6-b823-707c79ce3504_story.html?postshare=4401461017547366&tid=ss_tw.

[116] "Signs of Obasanjo Third-Term Bid Stir Already Boiling Pot," IRIN, 17 March 2006, http://www.irinnews.org/report/58473/nigeria-signs-obasanjo-third-term-bid-stir-already-boiling-pot; and Lydia Polgreen, "Governing Party Wins in Nigeria, but Many Claim Fraud," *New York Times*, 24 April 2007, http://www.nytimes.com/2007/04/24/world/africa/24nigeria.html?_r=0.

of democracy, press freedom, and freedom of association, thresholds on which military aid is ostensibly dependent.[117] The Obama administration took pains to avoid calling Egypt's 2013 military coup what it was. Instead, Washington characterized the Egyptian takeover as an effort at "restoring democracy"—language intended to avoid triggering the suspension of aid that must follow a military coup. For Nigeria, however, American policy makers largely deferred to strict interpretations of laws on foreign assistance during the early part of the Boko Haram crisis. American policy makers repeatedly insisted that military aid to Nigeria was constrained by the Leahy Amendment, which prohibits military assistance to foreign military units credibly accused of involvement in gross violations of human rights. This policy and legal decision remained strictly enforced through the 2014 Chibok kidnapping, after which time Washington began seeking workarounds that would allow more training, intelligence-sharing, and other anti–Boko Haram activities (see below). In sum, for much of the Boko Haram crisis Nigeria was not treated as an unimpeachable American ally in the War on Terror, but rather as a country that could be criticized and to which aid could be partly limited.

Nevertheless, the War on Terror context has helped to ensure that a military approach remains the dominant element of the international and Nigerian domestic response to Boko Haram. First, the War on Terror has helped make the idea of a political solution anathema to most policy makers, Nigerian, American, and European alike. A turning point in the securitization of the Boko Haram crisis came in 2013, when,

[117] See, for example, Secretary of State John Kerry's May 2015 letter to Congress requesting a waiver for Egypt from legal provisions that would limit military aid: http://graphics8.nytimes.com/packages/pdf/international/2015/egyptwaiver.pdf.

in quick succession, the Nigerian, British, and American governments declared Boko Haram to be a terrorist group[118]—a group, in other words, legally removed from the sphere of legitimate political interaction.

It is worth noting that many Nigerians were deeply offended by the fact there was any debate at all in the United States over whether to designate Boko Haram a "Foreign Terrorist Organization." Some Nigerians felt that the debate indicated that Americans were not taking Boko Haram seriously. Yet the issue was not whether Boko Haram was violent and dangerous, but rather whether Boko Haram should be placed into a legal category that would reduce the chances of involving the sect in negotiations.

On the ground, the three governments' proclamations had limited effect: Nigeria's decision to formally ban Boko Haram and subject its members to provisions in the 2011 Terrorism Prevention Act served to formalize, legally, the existing state of affairs. London's and Washington's declarations are primarily intended to freeze assets and prohibit support for designated terrorist groups. But Boko Haram (and its breakaway faction Ansar al-Muslimin, which was included in the designations) had no major financial assets in the West, nor did the groups have any open supporters or members there. The declarations' real effect was primarily discursive: coming on the heels of the Nigerian government's failed dialogue initia-

---

[118] See Central Bank of Nigeria, "Terrorism Prevention Proscription Order Notice, 2013," 10 June 2013, http://www.cenbank.org/out/2013/fprd/terrorism%20(prevention) %20(proscription%20order)%20notice,%202013.pdf; United Kingdom Home Office, "Proscribed Terrorist Organisations" (2015), https://www.gov.uk/government/uploads /system/uploads/attachment_data/file/472956/Proscription-update-20151030.pdf; and United States Department of State, "Terrorist Designations of Boko Haram and Ansaru," 13 November 2013, http://www.state.gov/r/pa/prs/ps/2013/11/217509.htm. Nigeria's designation came in May 2013, the UK's in July 2013, and the United States' in November 2013.

tives (see chapter 3), the declarations reinforced the idea that only military solutions were viable.

Second, the War on Terror has facilitated Nigerian security forces' abuses against civilians and Boko Haram members. Nigerian military commanders have often publicly dismissed reporting by Human Rights Watch, Amnesty International, and other human rights organizations. For example, in June 2015, Ministry of Defence spokesman General Chris Olukolade responded to an Amnesty report on security forces' human rights abuses. Olukolade not only denied that the report was accurate, he also presented Amnesty as a covert supporter of Boko Haram:

> It is curious that a body that has never been able to seriously condemn terror in Nigeria now claims to have done an extensive research with the aim of discrediting the nation's effort at curtailing terror. It is clear that Amnesty International becomes more active in presenting distractive allegations whenever the terrorists are losing ground in the battle. It is very unfortunate that Amnesty International has used this report to further confirm its questionable interest in the counterterrorism effort in Nigeria.[119]

The War on Terror has given Nigerian military and political hardliners a set of rhetorical tools with which they can easily rebut and undermine criticism: Boko Haram or "the terrorists" are depicted as purely evil, Nigeria's government is presented as a heroic participant in a global struggle, and all critics are cast as either deliberately or unwittingly proterrorist. Although the United States and other Western powers have publicly criticized Nigerian human rights abuses, actions speak louder than

[119] Madu Onuorah, "Anger in Military over Amnesty Report," *Guardian*, 8 June 2015, http://www.ngrguardiannews.com/2015/06/anger-in-military-over-amnesty-report/.

words—Nigerian abuses have slowed, but not blocked, the intensification of military cooperation between Nigeria and the West.

Third, then, the War on Terror context meant that when the Boko Haram conflict began to clearly exceed Nigeria's capacity to manage it, the United States and Western European powers helped to further militarize the response. After the Chibok kidnapping, the United States provided intelligence assistance in the form of unmanned aerial surveillance drones. In October 2015, as it was becoming clear that the Nigerian-Chadian-Nigerien assault on Boko Haram's protostate had not destroyed the sect, the United States dispatched some three hundred armed soldiers to Cameroon to support "airborne intelligence, surveillance and reconnaissance operations."[120] By February 2016, a new drone base—in Maroua, Far North, Cameroon—was "fully operational, hosting a fleet of four Gray Eagle drones, a successor to the original Predator." U.S. Special Forces have also deepened their preexisting training relationship with Cameroon's Rapid Intervention Battalion, or BIR.[121] In early 2016, the Pentagon began moving forward with plans to deploy "small dozens" of Special Forces to Maiduguri, in noncombat, advisory roles; British special forces were already deployed to the city.[122]

[120] White House, "Press Briefing by Press Secretary Josh Earnest, 10/14/2015," 14 October 2015, https://www.whitehouse.gov/the-press-office/2015/10/14/press -briefing-press-secretary-josh-earnest-10142015.

[121] Joshua Hammer, "Hunting Boko Haram: The U.S. Extends Its Drone War Deeper into Africa with Secretive Base," Intercept, 25 February 2016, https://the intercept.com/2016/02/25/us-extends-drone-war-deeper-into-africa-with-secretive -base/. This relationship dates to at least 2013. See Scott Rawlinson, "Silent Warrior Strengthens Partner Development," AFRICOM, 23 April 2013,.

[122] Eric Schmitt and Dionne Searcey, "U.S. Plans to Help Nigeria in War on Boko Haram Terrorists," New York Times, 25 February 2016, http://www.nytimes.com /2016/02/26/world/africa/us-plans-to-help-nigeria-in-war-on-boko-haram-terror ists.html?_r=0.

There have been bumps on the road to greater security cooperation, including an extended dispute in 2014 between Abuja and Washington concerning military helicopter sales that the United States refused to approve for Nigeria. But the overall trend has been for the United States and Western European powers to intensify the militarization of the crisis. In 2016, Washington moved to intensify its security assistance to Nigeria, including by moving to approve the sale of light attack aircraft (executive approval would come under U.S. president Donald Trump in April 2017) and by deploying new military advisors to Nigeria.[123] The election of Buhari played a role in fueling U.S. policy changes, but that reflected Washington's confidence in Buhari as a counterterrorism partner rather than a definitive embrace of accountability and transparency by Nigerian authorities. As Amnesty International wrote in March 2016:

> [The] announcement that the US plans to deploy military advisors to assist the Nigerian government fight Boko Haram and is considering restarting the training of an infantry battalion, despite the lack of investigation by Nigerian authorities in to possible war crimes and possible crimes against humanity by the Nigerian military should raise alarm bells. In the absence of concrete action to investigate possible atrocities the Obama administration risks giving its seal of approval to impunity.[124]

[123] Helene Cooper and Dionne Searcey, "After Years of Distrust, U.S. Military Reconciles with Nigeria to Fight Boko Haram," *New York Times*, 15 May 2016, https://www.nytimes.com/2016/05/16/world/africa/boko-haram-nigeria-us-arms-sales-war planes.html.

[124] Adotei Akwei, "Turning a Blind Eye on Impunity in Nigeria," Amnesty International Blog, 2 March 2016, http://blog.amnestyusa.org/africa/turing-a-blind-eye -on-impunity-in-nigeria/.

The longer and more violent the conflict becomes, the more the United States and European powers are willing to compartmentalize their concerns about human rights violations by Nigeria's government—and the governments of neighboring countries. This approach does not directly feed recruitment to Boko Haram, in my view, but it does mirror, in disturbing ways, the regionalization and internationalization of the sect's rhetoric.

The West's aversion to negotiating with jihadists, however, has not prevented Nigerian governments from doing so. Indeed, Buhari's efforts to negotiate with Boko Haram appear more serious than the committees created by Jonathan, although Buhari reportedly balked at Boko Haram's demands for a five million euro ransom for the Chibok girls.[125] In October 2016, the Buhari administration—reportedly through the International Committee of the Red Cross and the government of Switzerland—negotiated the release of twenty-one Chibok girls, possibly in exchange for some Boko Haram prisoners and a (smaller) ransom payment.[126] Another group of eighty-two Chibok girls was released in May 2017. On both occasions, the girls' liberation drew significant acclaim within Nigeria, indicating that neither the country's leaders nor its peoples had fully subscribed to the militarized, antipolitical mindset of the War on Terror.

---

[125] John Paden describes some of these efforts in *Muhammadu Buhari: The Challenges of Leadership in Nigeria* (Berkeley, CA: Roaring Forties, 2016), 105 and 178.

[126] "Nigeria's Chibok Schoolgirls Freed in Boko Haram Deal," BBC, 13 October 2016, http://www.bbc.com/news/world-africa-37641101; and Michelle Faul, "Reports: Chibok Girls Swapped for Detainees, Ransom or Both?," Associated Press, 14 October 2016, http://bigstory.ap.org/article/2b598a8335a94d20b29e2befa1dc29ee /reports-chibok-girls-swapped-detainees-ransom-or-both.

France and the African Union

There are two other key international actors involved in the conflict: France and the African Union (AU). With the increasing spillover of the Boko Haram crisis into Nigeria's Francophone African neighbors, France has taken a leadership role in encouraging regional responses to the crisis. French president François Hollande, who served 2012–17, pursued an interventionist foreign policy in Africa, most dramatically with the French-led campaign in northern Mali in 2013 but also, to a lesser extent, with regard to Boko Haram. In May 2014, Hollande held a summit for the heads of state of Nigeria, Niger, Cameroon, Chad, and Benin, along with senior diplomats from the United States, the United Kingdom, and the European Union. The African participants at the summit resolved to launch joint patrols on a bilateral basis and to share intelligence bilaterally and multilaterally. The non-African participants pledged to increase funds for socioeconomic development and to intensify sanctions against Boko Haram and Ansar al-Muslimin.[127] Exchanges of visits have reinforced France's visibility and influence in the fight against Boko Haram: Hollande headed to Niger and Chad in July 2014 (after having visited Nigeria that February), and he hosted Nigeria's Buhari in September 2015.[128]

The AU has sought to play a coordinating role in Lake Chad basin countries' fight against Boko Haram. After international

[127] French Presidency/Élysée, "Conclusions du 'Sommet de Paris pour la sécurité au Nigeria,'" 17 May 2014, http://www.elysee.fr/declarations/article/conclusions-du-sommet-de-paris-pour-la-securite-au-nigeria/.

[128] Embassy of France in Abuja, "Official Visit to France of the President of Nigeria," 18 September 2015, http://www.ambafrance-ng.org/Official-Visit-to-France-of-the-president-of-Nigeria.

concern about Boko Haram's violence escalated through 2014, the AU's Peace and Security Council authorized a twelve-month deployment of the Multi-national Joint Task Force (MNJTF) in January 2015. The MNJTF, originally created in the 1990s to fight banditry around Lake Chad, received a mandate from the AU to combat Boko Haram, protect civilians, and assist in humanitarian and stabilization operations in the region.[129] The force—initially envisioned as comprising seventy-five hundred troops, and later as having up to nine thousand—remained more notional than real into 2016, and it functioned partly as a rebranding of existing national deployments rather than as a truly integrated regional force. One assessment of the MNJTF from September 2016 concluded that the force was "gradually gaining ground" but conceded that it "still struggles to demonstrate its effectiveness."[130] The problems in coordination between Nigeria and its neighbors, as discussed in chapter 4, have continued despite the MNJTF framework.

The Humanitarian Toll of Boko Haram

One major element of the regionalization and internationalization of Boko Haram's violence is a complex humanitarian emergency that spans the Lake Chad basin—northeastern Nigeria, southeastern Niger, southwestern Chad, and northern

[129] African Union Peace and Security Council, "Report of the Chairperson of the Commission on the Implementation of Communiqué PSC/AHG/COMM.2 (CDLXXXIV) on the Boko Haram Terrorist Group and on Other Related International Efforts," 3 March 2015, http://www.peaceau.org/uploads/psc-489-rpt-boko -haram-03-03-2015.pdf.

[130] William Assanvo, Ella Jeannine Abatan, and Wendyam Sawadogo, "Assessing the Multinational Joint Task Force against Boko Haram," Institute for Security Studies, West Africa Report, no. 19 (September 2016), 1, https://issafrica.s3.amazonaws .com/site/uploads/war19.pdf.

Cameroon. This emergency involves not only massive displacement of ordinary people, but also a hunger crisis and severe disruption of planting and harvest cycles. Such developments set the stage for years of increased economic hardship in the region. Another, equally important long-term effect of the emergency will be the micropolitics of reintegration as the displaced head home: whether and how victims and killers make peace, or do not make peace, will shape life in the region for years to come.

Boko Haram's violence forced people to flee their homes from an early point, but the mass displacement crisis began in 2014,[131] amid Boko Haram's bid for territorial control and its war with the Civilian Joint Task Force. By January 2016, the overall emergency affected nearly half of the twenty million people in the Lake Chad basin. The conflict had displaced at least 2.8 million people, including 2.2 million who remained inside Nigeria,[132] of whom 1.4 million were in Borno State.[133] The numbers were little better in January 2017: the crisis affected an estimated 11 million people, 7 million of whom faced food insecurity. Some 2.3 million people were still displaced.[134]

[131] International Organization for Migration, "Displacement Tracking Matrix, Round VIII Report," February 2016, 4, http://nigeria.iom.int/sites/default/files/dtm /01_IOM%20DTM%20Nigeria_Round%20VIII%20Report_20160229.pdf.

[132] United Nations Office for the Coordination of Humanitarian Affairs (UN OCHA)—Lake Chad Basin, "Humanitarian Needs and Overview," January 2016, http://reliefweb.int/sites/reliefweb.int/files/resources/OCHA%20Lake%20Chad%20 Basin%20Needs%20&%20Response%20Overview%20Jan%202016_0.pdf?utm_con tent=bufferc0a88&utm_medium=social&utm_source=twitter.com&utm_campaign =buffer.

[133] Internal Displacement Monitoring Centre, "Nigeria IDP Figures Analysis," 2016, http://www.internal-displacement.org/sub-saharan-africa/nigeria/figures-analysis.

[134] United Nations Office for the Coordination of Humanitarian Affairs (UN OCHA), "2017 Humanitarian Needs and Requirement Overview: Lake Chad Basin Emergency," January 2017, 1–3, http://reliefweb.int/sites/reliefweb.int/files/resources /LCB_HNRO_2017_0.pdf.

Individual cities in northeastern Nigeria faced tremendous burdens: Maiduguri hosted half a million displaced by January 2015,[135] and "hundreds" were still arriving a year later.[136] In February 2016, Maiduguri Metropolitan Council Local Government Area (LGA) held an estimated 824,234 displaced individuals, while the surrounding Jere LGA hosted 489,205.[137] Yola, Adamawa, received 400,000 displaced persons by the end of 2014, more than doubling its normal population.[138] Conditions outside major urban centers were even worse: as of January 2016, "camps sheltering people in the tens of thousands in several locations—in Dikwa and reportedly Ngala—remained unreached by the international humanitarian community."[139] An estimated 80 percent of the displaced sought shelter outside of camps, staying with friends, relatives, and wider communities.[140]

As Boko Haram's violence spread to Nigeria's neighbors, the displacement crisis worsened in those countries as well. By January 2016, the number of displaced stood at nearly

[135] Kareem Haruna, "Maiduguri, a Troubled Capital City Overtaken by IDPs," *Leadership*, 11 January 2015, http://leadership.ng/features/401050/maiduguri-troubled -capital-city-overtaken-idps.

[136] International Organization for Migration, "Nigeria Emergency Operations: Situation Report," January 2016, 1, https://www.iom.int/sites/default/files/situation _reports/file/IOM-Nigeria-Emergency-Operations-Sitrep-Jan2016.pdf.

[137] International Organization for Migration, "Displacement Tracking Matrix, Round VIII Report," February 2016, 3, http://nigeria.iom.int/sites/default/files/dtm /01_IOM%20DTM%20Nigeria_Round%20VIII%20Report_20160229.pdf.

[138] Karen Attiah, "Nigeria's Worrisome Humanitarian Situation Demands More Attention," *Washington Post*, 13 November 2015, https://www.washingtonpost.com /blogs/post-partisan/wp/2015/11/13/nigerias-worrisome-humanitarian-situation -demands-more-attention/.

[139] International Organization for Migration, "Nigeria Emergency Operations: Situation Report," January 2016, 1.

[140] United Nations Office for the Coordination of Humanitarian Affairs (UN OCHA)—Lake Chad Basin, "Humanitarian Brief: An Overlooked Crisis in an Overlooked Region," October 2015, 1, http://reliefweb.int/sites/reliefweb.int/files/resources /Chad_Basin_Boko_Haram_v2.pdf.

320,000 in Niger, over 254,000 in Cameroon, and approximately 61,000 in Chad.[141] A year later, the figures were over 300,000 in Niger, around 200,000 in Cameroon, and over 129,000 in Chad.[142] Many of the displaced came from Lake Chad: in 2015, a combination of Boko Haram attacks and military-led "evacuations" emptied many islands and lakeside villages of inhabitants.[143] As in Nigeria, civilian populations in neighboring countries experienced a heavy burden as they hosted the displaced: in Cameroon's Far North, the World Food Program estimated in April 2015 that only 45,000 out of an estimated 200,000 total displaced lived in official camps, leaving the rest to seek shelter with local communities.[144] The United Nations established official refugee camps, most notably Minawao in the Far North, which opened in July 2013. Two years later, the population at Minawao had reached nearly 45,000, straining the camp's original intended capacity of 30,000.[145] Commerce in northern Cameroon declined, and various groups—especially economic migrants and refugees, who were now formally required to produce official identity documents—came under greater scrutiny from authorities.[146]

The displacement crisis was compounded by a food emergency. Boko Haram's predations against civilians intersected

[141] International Organization for Migration, "Nigeria Emergency Operations: Situation Report," January 2016, 3.

[142] UN OCHA, "2017 Humanitarian Needs and Requirement Overview: Lake Chad Basin Emergency."

[143] Mark Doyle, "Lake Chad: New Violence, New Displacement," UNHCR, 24 September 2015, http://www.unhcr.org/560405546.html.

[144] World Food Program, "Boko Haram Violence Inflicts More Suffering on Already Vulnerable Communities in Cameroon's Far North Region," 29 April 2015, https://www.wfp.org/stories/funding-shortages-threaten-cameroon-food-security.

[145] "Nigerian Refugees Move from Volatile Border Zone in Cameroon," UNHCR, 21 July 2015, http://www.unhcr.org/55ae61746.html.

[146] Monde Nfor, "Cameroon Pays High Price for Joining Boko Haram Fight," IRIN, 31 July 2015, http://www.irinnews.org/analysis/2015/07/31.

with preexisting drivers of food insecurity in the region: increasingly sporadic rainfall, desertification, cattle rustling, and population growth.[147] By fall 2015, 4.6 million people in Nigeria and 850,000 in nearby areas of Niger, Chad, and Cameroon needed humanitarian assistance.[148] In early 2016, the Famine Early Warning Systems Network classified most of Borno and eastern Yobe as "crisis" zones for hunger and classified remaining parts of Borno, Yobe, and Adamawa as "stressed."[149] Ironically, the humanitarian emergency may have begun to undermine Boko Haram by early 2016. Reports emerged that some "hungry" Boko Haram members were surrendering to the military in northeastern Nigeria,[150] while other sect members were beginning to raid northern Cameroonian villages for food.[151]

In the context of the complex emergency, the displaced have been caught between multiple forces, leading to repeated displacements and creating conditions for further violence. Around 60 percent of displaced families have had to flee multiple times.[152] Flight was not easy: nearly 55 percent of the displaced inside Nigeria were children, almost half of whom were under the age of five, and the average displaced household

---

[147] Mbom Sixtus, "Boko Haram Is Losing, but So Is Food Production," IRIN, 11 March 2016, https://www.irinnews.org/news/2016/03/11/boko-haram-losing-so-food-production.

[148] UN OCHA—Lake Chad Basin, "Humanitarian Brief: An Overlooked Crisis," 3.

[149] Famine Early Warning Systems Network, "Food Security Outlook: Conflict in the Lake Chad Region Continues to Impact Livelihood Activities and Food Access," February 2016, http://www.fews.net/west-africa/nigeria/food-security-outlook/february-2016.

[150] "76 Hungry Boko Haram Members Surrender to Nigerian Military," Associated Press, 2 March 2016, http://www.voanews.com/content/hungry-boko-haram-members-surrender-to-nigerian-military/3216234.html?platform=hootsuite.

[151] Dionne Searcey, "Boko Haram Falls Victim to a Food Crisis It Created," *New York Times*, 4 March 2016, http://mobile.nytimes.com/2016/03/05/world/africa/boko-haram-food-crisis.html?smid=tw-share&_r=0&referer=https://t.co/s4n698ywQy.

[152] IRIN, "Lost in the City," http://newirin.irinnews.org/lost-in-the-city/.

comprised seven persons.[153] In camps, life became precarious. Camps attracted the suspicion of authorities who feared that recruitment was occurring there or that Boko Haram would target the sites. Attacks indeed occurred: one of the most dramatic was a suicide bombing by two women at a camp in Dikwa, Borno, in February 2016.

By late 2015, Nigerian authorities were pressuring the displaced to return home, perhaps out of budgetary concerns but likely also for political reasons: to have a large and enduring displaced population in Maiduguri and elsewhere revealed, to both domestic and foreign audiences, that the authorities did not yet fully control the countryside.[154] After the Nigerian military announced the opening of three major roads in Borno in February 2016, Nigerian authorities increased the pressure on the displaced to go home, in part because of mounting concerns that if Borno farmers did not plant crops in time, the hunger crisis would escalate.[155] Nigeria's neighbors also pushed the displaced to return home. In August 2015, Cameroonian authorities deported some fifteen thousand Nigerians, citing security concerns.[156]

Humanitarian workers complained that the Nigerian government was moving too quickly and that conditions in the Borno and Adamawa countryside were not yet secure. Most displaced persons said they did not feel safe going back

[153] International Organization for Migration, "Displacement Tracking Matrix, Round VIII Report," February 2016, 1, http://nigeria.iom.int/sites/default/files/dtm /01_IOM%20DTM%20Nigeria_Round%20VIII%20Report_20160229.pdf.

[154] Sylvestre Tetchiada, "Nigerians Who Fled Boko Haram Forced Home," IRIN, 21 August 2015, http://www.irinnews.org/report/101900/nigerians-who-fled-boko -haram-forced-home.

[155] Obi Anyadike, "Go Home, Nigerian Government Tells Boko Haram Victims," IRIN, 9 March 2016, http://www.irinnews.org/news/2016/03/09/go-home-nigerian -government-tells-boko-haram-victims.

[156] Tetchiada, "Nigerians Who Fled Boko Haram Forced Home."

home.[157] When they did return home, violence would often
follow. A *Washington Post* reporter who visited Madagali,
Adamawa, interviewed locals who described Boko Haram's
continued presence in the area, its assaults on towns, and its
theft of food and aid supplies.[158]

Equally profound challenges surrounded issues of reconciliation and reintegration for both perpetrators and victims
of violence. Unless one expects the Nigerian security forces to
achieve the impossible task of identifying all past and present Boko Haram members and either prosecuting or killing
them, then the region will be home to thousands of perpetrators of violence for decades. These include people who killed,
robbed, or raped their neighbors. As people return home,
they may find strangers living in their homes or on their land.
Many people may live with devastating uncertainty, questioning whether unknown former Boko Haram members dwell
near them, whether lost family members are alive or dead,
and whether they can be truly safe again. When interviewing
civilians in northeastern Nigeria, human rights organizations
have found some support for the idea of reconciliation at both
the national and local levels—in part because civilians have so
little trust in the legal system and fear being targeted if they
report Boko Haram members to the authorities.[159]

At the federal level, "deradicalization" programs have been
in effect since around 2013, but there are real questions about
the seriousness of such efforts: the director of the program

---

[157] "Nigeria Says 'Go Home', but Is It Safe from Boko Haram?," IRIN, 17 November 2015, http://www.irinnews.org/feature/2015/11/17.

[158] Attiah, "Nigeria's Worrisome Humanitarian Situation."

[159] Kyle Dietrich, *"When We Can't See the Enemy, Civilians Become the Enemy":
Living through Nigeria's Six-Year Insurgency* (Washington, DC: Center for Civilians in
Conflict, 2015), 64, http://civiliansinconflict.org/uploads/files/publications/Nigeria
Report_Web.pdf.

under Goodluck Jonathan, Dr. Fatima Akilu, was abruptly fired in October 2015, after Muhammadu Buhari took office. A form of the program continued under Dr. Ferdinand Ikwang, attempting to convince imprisoned Boko Haram members to renounce violence and exposing them to alternative interpretations of Islam. But the numbers involved in the programs have been small, the funding has been low, and both program administrators and many northeastern civilians feel that "there can be no reintegration for the most hardcore Boko Haram." In 2015, Ikwang voiced plans to use halfway houses to reintegrate reformed sect members while keeping them under surveillance, but the program's long-term viability is in question.[160] Meanwhile, the Nigerian government's continued emphasis on military approaches to Boko Haram suggests the pessimistic conclusion that despite the seemingly sincere intentions of those government workers involved in deradicalization, senior politicians and military officers may view the programs primarily as public relations props to placate Western governments (who themselves also emphasize the military aspect, despite rhetoric to the contrary). Whatever reintegration occurs may be locally managed, ad hoc, and incomplete.

Local efforts at deradicalization are highly sensitive and vulnerable, not just to Boko Haram's violence but to government suspicion. In August 2016, the Nigerian Army declared three persons wanted because of their contacts with Boko Haram: Aisha Wakil, a lawyer who knew some Boko Haram members from her time living in Maiduguri, and who had served on one of Jonathan's committees; Ahmad Salkida, a journalist who had known Muhammad Yusuf; and Ahmed Bolori, a young Maiduguri man who ran an NGO, Exit Lanes,

---

[160] Obi Anyadike, "The Road to Redemption? Unmaking Nigeria's Boko Haram," IRIN, 1 October 2015, http://newirin.irinnews.org/boko-haram-road-to-redemption/.

that sought to prevent radicalization. After reporting for questioning, the three were soon released, but the episode highlighted the military's distrust of anyone who pursued dialogue with Boko Haram outside approved federal channels. When I interviewed Bolori in January 2017, however, he remained committed to the idea that "soft measures" would be more efficient and effective in ending the crisis than military means alone.[161] I agree with him.

Conclusion

The regionalization of the Boko Haram crisis brought three significant costs to Nigeria's neighbors Niger, Cameroon, and Chad. First, there is the impact of the violence itself, in terms of lives lost, property destroyed, and territory contested. Second, there is the humanitarian crisis, involving millions of people displaced, and even more facing hunger and starvation. Finally, there are the long-term uncertainties about how the crisis will affect politics and society in these countries, where political and civil society space is relatively closed, including compared with Nigeria. One important question concerns how Boko Haram's presence will affect the religious field in the Lake Chad basin, and how Muslims will relate to one another and to their states as the crisis drags on.

Regionalization has been accompanied by a significant internationalization of the crisis. While the violence has not spilled beyond the Lake Chad region and Nigeria, the crisis has drawn the attention of diverse actors. The United States and European powers, particularly France, perceive opportunities to extend their military and political influence over

---

[161] Skype interview with Ahmed Bolori, 9 January 2017.

African governments during the "War on Terror." The Islamic State perceives an opportunity to create an affiliated enclave in West Africa, albeit one under looser control than its affiliates in Libya and elsewhere in the Middle East. The internationalization of the crisis heightens its unpredictability: as more actors become involved, the potential for unintended consequences grows. Boko Haram, for its part, now applies its divisive and exclusivist rhetoric not just inside Nigeria, but toward all Muslims around Lake Chad, from heads of state to ordinary people.

Conclusion

▶▶▶▶▶▶▶▶▶▶▶▶▶▶

From 2003 to the present, Boko Haram has inflicted violence on governments and civilians, many of them Muslims. This book has argued that the violence is largely driven by mutually reinforcing interactions between religious trends, including Boko Haram's own worldview, and its political environment. Boko Haram's initial worldview coalesced in the early 2000s amid several trends: the rise of "shari'a politics" in Fourth Republic Nigeria, the competition for leadership within northern Nigeria's Salafi movement, generational changes in the religious field, unresolved patterns of intercommunal violence and failures to enforce accountability, and rising socioeconomic discontentment in the north. Boko Haram's worldview hardened in the ensuing years owing to internal debates within the movement, as well as the movement's ruptures with former allies, including the Salafi shaykh Ja'far Adam and Borno State governor Ali Modu Sheriff. Matters headed for a crisis in 2009 as tensions with authorities culminated in a mass uprising by Boko Haram.

In the aftermath of the uprising, Boko Haram's worldview hardened still further, as the movement transformed from a controversial preaching community into a violent clandestine group. Further changes to Boko Haram's worldview occurred as the group rose in power as a guerrilla force, experienced a backlash in its home state of Borno, and turned to widespread territorial conquest and civilian massacres as a means of neutralizing the backlash. The collapse of Boko Haram's protostate and the military involvement of Nigeria's neighbors then regionalized the crisis, with Boko Haram targeting Nigeria's neighbors both militarily and rhetorically.

)22   ̣hout the crisis, Boko Haram has deployed a doctrine
      ̣ous exclusivism to claim legitimacy for its message. It
    presented itself both as the victim of other actors' aggres-
̣.ɔns and as a righteous vanguard fighting for the purity of
Islam. The interplay of doctrine and events means that there
is no easy way out of the crisis. Boko Haram represents an ugly
paradox: its ideas have limited appeal but significant staying
power. The group can be crushed militarily, yet state violence
fuels its narrative of victimhood.

How can Boko Haram be stopped? The conventional wisdom, often repeated in Washington and sometimes in Abuja,
is that a combination of military operations and socioeconomic
development can solve the problem. Military operations can
kill the hardcore Boko Haram members. Socioeconomic development can assuage the grievances of "moderates" and sympathizers, while simultaneously preventing the emergence of
other militant groups in northeastern Nigeria or the Lake Chad
basin. Or so the argument runs.

In my view, this solution appeals to its proponents because
it deploys an "antipolitics" that attempts to eliminate the messi-
ness of politics from understandings of both the causes of and
solutions for the crisis. As Jacob Mundy has eloquently written,

> Some of today's most prevalent forms of international con-
> flict management—the economic prevention and regulation
> of civil wars, global preemptive counterterrorism doctrine,
> the use of military force to interrupt mass atrocities, and the
> rectification of war-torn societies through truth commissions
> and other forms of transitional justice—arise out of depoliti-
> cized understandings of late warfare.[1]

---

[1] Jacob Mundy, *Imaginative Geographies of Algerian Violence: Conflict Science, Conflict Management, Antipolitics* (Stanford, CA: Stanford University Press, 2015), 9.

No durable solution can be found to Boko Haram, in my view, until politics is brought back into view and confronted. What political complaints does the sect have, and in what ways are these complaints irreducible to economic deprivation? What political decisions are necessary for ending the conflict—who will be the winners and losers? Will arrested Boko Haram members face trials, or be enrolled into deradicalization programs? Will there be reconciliation between perpetrators of violence and their victims? Will the Nigerian government compensate those whom it has victimized, or unfairly detained, or whose family members it has executed? Will Muhammad Yusuf's killers face another, more serious trial? Will Ali Modu Sheriff stand trial?

The answers to these questions cannot all be determined through some impersonal, technocratic process—there is no singular "right" answer to any question. Rather, all the answers constitute political decisions that will make some people happy and other people unhappy. And if authorities do not answer those questions, their silence in itself will supply one of the possible answers. Silence and "moving on" have tragic legacies in Nigeria: history has passed a negative verdict about Nigerian authorities' deployment of such strategies after crises in Kaduna, Plateau, and Borno, from the 1980s to the present.

Yet such history suggests that the Boko Haram crisis may end with a drawn-out, agonizing process of sporadic violence and entrenched impunity, rather than with a crescendo of accountability and reconciliation. Business as usual, I believe, would set the stage for future violence in northern Nigeria and the Lake Chad basin. In 2009, Muhammad Yusuf recalled the tragedies of 1987 in Kafanchan and 1992 in Zangon-Kataf, invoking them to argue that the Nigerian state victimized Muslims, and that Muslims had no choice but to respond through violence. It is not difficult to imagine a successor to Yusuf, in

2029 or 2039, invoking the memory of Boko Haram to make a similar argument.

At some point, then, authorities will have to bring politics back in. Among other implications, this will mean trying to talk to Boko Haram. Most attempts to dialogue with Boko Haram have so far failed, but this does not mean that the government of Nigeria, or governments of neighboring countries, should abandon the effort. As this book has shown, Boko Haram is dynamic, and past failures nevertheless offer a few slivers of hope: certain credible interlocutors like Shehu Sani (now a senator) and Ibrahim Datti Ahmed have made contact with the group, and grassroots organizers in Maiduguri, such as Ahmed Bolori, are pursuing community-based deradicalization efforts. The releases of some Chibok girls in 2016 and 2017 show that dialogue can bear some fruit.

International Crisis Group notes that around the world, "opportunities to engage [jihadists] in ways that might have de-escalated violence . . . have been lost," including with Boko Haram. Yet, Crisis Group continues, "although policymakers can entertain no illusions about the nature of the [Islamic State] and al-Qaeda top commands, opportunities to open unofficial, discreet lines of communication, through community leaders, non-state mediators or others, are usually worth pursuing, particularly on issues of humanitarian concern."[2] Boko Haram and Lake Chad governments are unlikely to reach agreement on the question of the region's political future—but dialogue could peel away some less hardened members of the group, allow for negotiations on prisoner exchanges, or bring to light new, and actionable, paths to decreasing the violence.

[2] International Crisis Group, "Exploiting Disorder: Al-Qaeda and the Islamic State," 14 March 2016, iv, http://www.crisisgroup.org/~/media/Files/exploiting-disorder-al-qaeda-and-the-islamic-state.pdf.

In the absence of political responses to the conflict, Boko Haram might follow a trajectory similar to its jihadist peers in Africa: al-Qaʿida in the Islamic Maghreb (AQIM) and Somalia's al-Shabab. AQIM was not always a predatory, transnational group blending criminality and jihadism: its genealogy reaches back to Algeria's civil war in the 1990s, when the Armed Islamic Group (French acronym GIA) initially enjoyed significant popular support. The GIA marginalized itself through its involvement in massacres of Algerian civilians, and the Algerian government marginalized the GIA by extending amnesties to more mainstream Islamist resistance movements and by targeting the GIA's leaders. A breakaway faction of the GIA, however, went on to become AQIM, troubling Saharan and Sahelian countries from 2003 to the present through kidnappings and attacks, and benefiting opportunistically, albeit briefly, from Mali's 2012–13 collapse.

If Boko Haram follows a similar path, it could cultivate a career inside and outside Nigeria, as a mobile jihadist gang, for years to come. It is tempting to argue that Shekau's faction of Boko Haram, like the GIA, will destroy itself, and that al-Barnawi's faction will linger on as an AQIM-like terrorist group, but analogies should be stretched only so far—and unlike in Algeria, there is no mainstream Islamist armed faction within the conflict.

Al-Shabab, like Boko Haram, controlled and then lost significant territory. In al-Shabab's case, territorial loses sparked multiple changes within al-Shabab: an internal purge of senior leaders in 2014, a focus on staging spectacular terrorist attacks in neighboring Kenya (as revenge for Kenya's military presence inside Somalia), and a kind of time-biding strategy of attacking African Union peacekeepers in Somalia but also trying to outlast them. Al-Shabab appeared weaker in 2016 than it did in October 2011, when the African Union said it had expelled the movement from its last stronghold in Somalia's capital, Mogadishu; but in 2017, al-Shabab also appears more tenacious than ever. When the funding and patience for African Union peacekeepers runs out, al-Shabab may be poised for a comeback.

If Boko Haram follows al-Shabab's path, it could remain a thorn in Nigeria's side over the long term, poised to renew control over parts of the northeast. Boko Haram could simultaneously remain a long-term threat to Nigeria's neighbors, deploying small teams of terrorists to inflict massive civilian casualties and embarrass governments. Both the "AQIM" and "al-Shabab" scenarios suggest that security measures alone cannot defeat Boko Haram, and that economic development is insufficient: reading news stories trumpeting Maiduguri's renaissance in 2016,[3] I was grimly reminded of similar stories about Mogadishu—stories whose publication was frequently followed, weeks or even days later, by fresh terrorist attacks in the city.

I invoke these scenarios not to enjoin pessimism but to insist on the need for a long-term, fine-grained approach to understanding the Boko Haram crisis and to devising solutions for it. In this book, I have tried to show the value of this long-term perspective, one that looks far back into the past for answers about why the sect emerged when and where it did, and why its violence has continued despite a massive security crackdown and significant political change, including positive developments like the competitive 2015 election in Nigeria. An understanding of the complexity of Nigeria's recent past, I hope, can assist in the effort to meet the challenges of the country's equally complex future.

[3] For one example, see Eromo Egbejule, "Defiance on the Dancefloor: Clubbing in the Birthplace of Boko Haram," *Guardian*, 27 September 2016, https://www.the guardian.com/world/2016/sep/27/clubbing-birthplace-boko-haram-maiduguri-nigeria.

Selected Bibliography

▶▶▶▶▶▶▶▶▶▶▶▶▶▶▶▶▶▶▶▶▶▶▶▶▶▶▶▶▶

Books, Articles, and Reports

Abubakr, Ali. *Al-Thaqafa al-'Arabiyya fi Nayjiriya min 'Am 1804 ila 1960 'Am al-Istiqlal.* Beirut: n.p., 1972.

Abulfathi, Khalifa Aliyu Ahmed. "The Metamorphosis of Boko Haram: A Local's Perspective." Maiduguri: Sheikh Ahmed Abulfathi Foundation, 2016.

Achebe, Chinua. *The Trouble with Nigeria.* Oxford: Heinemann, 1983.

Adams, Paul. "State(s) of Crisis: Sub-national Government in Nigeria." Africa Research Institute Briefing Note 1602 (March 2016).

Adeniyi, Olusegun. *Power, Politics and Death: A Front-Row Account of Nigeria under the Late President Umaru Musa Yar'Adua.* Lagos: Kachifo, 2011.

Adesoji, Abimbola. "Between Maitatsine and Boko Haram: Islamic Fundamentalism and the Response of the Nigerian State." *Africa Today* 57:4 (Summer 2011): 99–119.

Afsaruddin, Asma. *Striving in the Path of God: Jihad and Martyrdom in Islamic Thought.* Oxford: Oxford University Press, 2013.

Akwei, Adotei. "Turning a Blind Eye on Impunity in Nigeria." Amnesty International Blog. 2 March 2016, http://blog.amnestyusa.org/africa/turing-a-blind-eye-on-impunity-in-nigeria/.

Alapiki, Henry. "State Creation in Nigeria: Failed Approaches to National Integration and Local Autonomy." *African Studies Review* 48:3 (December 2005): 49–65.

Alexander, Boyd. *From the Niger to the Nile.* Vol. 1. New York: Longmans, Green, 1907.

Ali, Baba Gana Kachalla. *A History of Yerwa since 1907.* Vol. 1. Maiduguri: n.p., 2005.

Alidou, Ousseina. *Engaging Modernity: Muslim Women and the Politics of Agency in Postcolonial Niger.* Madison: University Wisconsin Press, 2005.

Alkali, Muhammad Nur, Abubakar Kawu Monguno, and Ballama Shettima Mustafa. "Overview of Islamic Actors in Northeastern Nigeria." Nigeria Research Network Working Paper no. 2 (January 2012).

Alternative Espaces Citoyens. "Déplacement forcé des populations des îles du lac Tchad au Niger." May 2015.

Aluko, Benjamin. "Political Finance-Related Corruption and Its Implication for Governance and Peace-Building in Nigeria." Wilson Center Africa Program, Research Paper no. 16 (February 2017).

Aluko, T.K.O. "An Evaluation of the Effects of the National Economic Empowerment and Development Strategy (Needs) on Poverty Reduction in Nigeria." In *Nigeria's Democratic Experience in the Fourth Republic since 1999: Policies and Politics*, edited by A. Sat Obiyan and Kunle Amuwo, 360–79. Lanham, MD: University Press of America, 2013.

Amnesty International. "Cameroon: Boko Haram Attack Brings Total Killed to Nearly 500 in a Year." 30 June 2016.

———. "Nigeria: Government Knew of Planned Boko Haram Kidnapping but Failed to Act." 9 May 2014.

———. "Nigeria: War Crimes and Crimes against Humanity as Violence Escalates in North-East." 31 March 2014.

———. "Right Cause, Wrong Means: Human Rights Violated and Justice Denied in Cameroon's Fight against Boko Haram." 14 July 2016.

———. " 'Welcome to Hell Fire': Torture and Other Ill Treatment in Nigeria." September 2014.

Anonymous. "The Popular Discourses of Salafi Radicalism and Salafi Counter-radicalism in Nigeria: A Case Study of Boko Haram." *Journal of Religion in Africa* 42:2 (2012): 118–44.

Anzalone, Christopher. "The Life and Death of al-Shabab Leader Ahmed Godane." *CTC Sentinel*. 29 September 2014.

Asad, Talal. "The Idea of an Anthropology of Islam." Georgetown University Center for Contemporary Arab Studies, Occasional Papers Series, 1986.

Assanvo, William, Ella Jeannine Abatan, and Wendyam Sawadogo. "Assessing the Multinational Joint Task Force against Boko Haram." Institute for Security Studies, West Africa Report, no. 19 (September 2016).

Bano, Masooda. *The Rational Believer: Choices and Decisions in the Madrasas of Pakistan*. Ithaca, NY: Cornell University Press, 2012.

Bargery, G. P. *A Hausa-English Dictionary and English-Hausa Vocabulary*. 2nd impression. London: Oxford University Press, 1951 [1934].

Barkindo, Atta. "How Boko Haram Exploits History and Memory." Africa Research Institute. 4 October 2016.

Ben Amara, Ramzi. "The Izala Movement in Nigeria: Its Split, Relationship to Sufis and Perception of Shari'a Re-implementation." Ph.D. dissertation, Bayreuth University, 2011.

———. " 'We Introduced Shari'a': The Izala Movement in Nigeria as Initiator of Shari'a Reimplementation in the North of the Country; Some Reflections." In *Shari'a in Africa Today: Reactions and Responses*, edited by John A. Chesworth and Franz Kogelmann, 125–46. Leiden: Brill, 2013.

Birai, Umar. "Islamic Tajdid and the Political Process in Nigeria." In *Fundamentalisms and the State: Remaking Polities, Economies, and Militancy*, edited by Martin E. Marty, 184–203. Chicago: University of Chicago Press, 1996.

Blench, Roger. "An Atlas of Nigerian Languages." 3rd ed. Cambridge: Roger Blench, 3 December 2012.

Bloom, Mia, and Hilary Matfess. "Women as Symbols and Swords in Boko Haram's Terror." *PRISM* 6:1 (March 2016), http://cco.ndu.edu/Portals /96/Documents/prism/prism_6-1/Women%20as%20Symbols%20and%20 Swords.pdf.

Bobboyi, Hamidu, and John Hunwick. "Bornu, Wadai and Adamawa." In *Arabic Literature of Africa*, vol. 2, *Central Sudanic Africa*, edited by John Hunwick and R. S. O'Fahey, 383–84. Leiden: Brill, 1995.

Bonner, Michael. *Jihad in Islamic History: Doctrines and Practice*. Princeton, NJ: Princeton University Press, 2006.

Botha, Anneli, and Mahdi Abdile. "Getting behind the Profiles of Boko Haram Members and Factors Contributing to Radicalisation versus Working towards Peace." Network for Religious and Traditional Peacemakers. October 2016.

Bourdieu, Pierre. "Genesis and Structure of the Religious Field." *Comparative Social Research* 13 (1991): 1–43.

Bukhari, Waziri Junaidu. "The Relevance of the University to Our Society." In *The Relevance of Education in Our Society: Commentaries on the Acceptance Speech of Alhaji Junaidu, Wazirin Sakkwato*, edited by Haruna Salihi, 17–20. Lagos: Islamic Heritage Foundation, 2006.

Bray, Mark. *Universal Primary Education in Nigeria: A Study of Kano State*. London: Routledge and Kegan Paul, 1981.

Brenner, Louis. *Controlling Knowledge: Religion, Power and Schooling in a West African Muslim Society*. Bloomington: Indiana University Press, 2001.

Brigaglia, Andrea. "A Contribution to the History of the Wahhabi Da'wa in West Africa: The Career and the Murder of Shaykh Ja'far Mahmoud Adam (Daura, ca. 1961/1962—Kano 2007)." *Islamic Africa* 3:1 (Spring 2012): 1–23.

———. "Note on Shaykh Dahiru Usman Bauchi and the July 2014 Kaduna Bombing." *Annual Review of Islam in Africa* 12:1 (2013–14): 39–42.

Bugaje, Usman. "Introduction." In Ghazali Basri, *Nigeria and Shari'ah: Aspirations and Apprehensions*. Leicester: Islamic Foundation, 1994.

Ciroma, Liman. *The Impact of Modern Education and Traditional Values*. Maiduguri: University of Maiduguri, 1980.

Cohen, Ronald. "The Analysis of Conflict in Hierarchical Systems: An Example from Kanuri Political Organization." *Anthropologica* 4:1 (1962): 87–120.

———. *The Kanuri of Bornu*. New York: Holt, Rinehart, and Winston, 1967.

Cole, Juan. "Today's Top 7 Myths about Daesh/ISIL." Informed Comment, 17 February 2015, http://www.juancole.com/2015/02/todays-about-daesh .html.

Comolli, Virginia. *Boko Haram: Nigeria's Islamist Insurgency*. London: Hurst, 2015.

Csapo, Marg. "Universal Primary Education in Nigeria: Its Problems and Implications." *African Studies Review* 26:1 (March 1983): 91–106.

Cyffer, Norbert. "Maiduguri and the Kanuri Language." In *From Bulamari to Yerwa to Metropolitan Maiduguri: Interdisciplinary Studies on the Capital of Borno State, Nigeria*, edited by Rupert Kawka, 117–25. Köln: Rüdiger Köppe Verlag, 2002.

Dietrich, Kyle. *"When We Can't See the Enemy, Civilians Become the Enemy": Living through Nigeria's Six-Year Insurgency*. Washington, DC: Center for Civilians in Conflict, 2015.

Easton, David. *A Framework for Political Analysis*. Upper Saddle River, NJ: Prentice Hall, 1965.

Eickelman, Dale, and James Piscatori. *Muslim Politics*. 2nd ed. Princeton, NJ: Princeton University Press, 2004.

Elischer, Sebastian. "Autocratic Legacies and State Management of Islamic Activism in Niger." *African Affairs* 114:457 (October 2015): 577–97.

Eveslage, Benjamin. "Clarifying Boko Haram's Transnational Intentions, Using Content Analysis of Public Statements in 2012." *Perspectives on Terrorism* 7:5 (October 2013): 47–76.

Falola, Toyin. *Violence in Nigeria: The Crisis of Religious and Secular Ideologies*. Rochester, NY: University of Rochester Press, 1998.

Falola, Toyin, and Matthew M. Heaton. *A History of Nigeria*. Cambridge: Cambridge University Press, 2008.

Francis, Paul, et al. *State, Community and Local Development in Nigeria*. Washington, DC: World Bank, 1996.

Fund for Peace. "Conflict Bulletin: Borno State." May 2014.

Gowon, Yakubu. "The Dawn of National Reconciliation." Speech broadcast 15 January 1970.

Gregoire, Emmanuel. "Islam and Identity in Maradi (Niger)." In *Muslim Identity and Social Change in Sub-Saharan Africa*, edited by Louis Brenner, 106–15. London: Hurst, 1993.

Gumi, Abubakar. *Al-'Aqida al-Sahiha bi-Muwafaqat al-Shari'a*. Beirut: Dar al-'Arabiyya, 1972.

Habila, Helon. *The Chibok Girls: The Boko Haram Kidnappings and Islamic Militancy in Nigeria*. New York: Columbia Global Reports, 2016.

Hamid, Shadi. "Does ISIS Really Have Nothing to Do with Islam? Islamic Apologetics Carry Serious Risks." *Washington Post*. 18 November 2015, https://www.washingtonpost.com/news/acts-of-faith/wp/2015/11/18/does-isis-really-have-nothing-to-do-with-islam-islamic-apologetics-carry-serious-risks/.

Hansen, Stig. *Al-Shabaab in Somalia: The History and Ideology of a Militant Islamist Group, 2005–2012.* London: Hurst, 2013.

Hare, John Neville. "How Northern Nigeria's Violent History Explains Boko Haram." *National Geographic,* 14 March 2015, http://news.nationalgeo graphic.com/2015/03/150314-boko-haram-nigeria-borno-rabih-abubakar -shekau/.

Haykel, Bernard. "On the Nature of Salafi Thought and Activism." In *Global Salafism: Islam's New Religious Movement,* edited by Roel Meijer, 33–57. New York: Columbia University Press, 2009.

Heck, Paul. "*Jihad* Revisited." *Journal of Religious Ethics* 32:1 (March 2004): 95–128.

Hegghammer, Thomas, and Stéphane Lacroix. "Rejectionist Islamism in Saudi Arabia: The Story of Juhayman al-'Utaybi Revisited." *International Journal of Middle East Studies* 39:1 (February 2007): 103–22.

Heungoup, Hans de Marie. "In the Tracks of Boko Haram in Cameroon." International Crisis Group. 2 September 2016.

Hicks, Celeste. *Africa's New Oil: Power, Pipelines and Future Fortunes.* London: Zed Books, 2015.

Higazi, Adam. "Mobilisation into and against Boko Haram in North-East Nigeria." In *Collective Mobilisations in Africa,* edited by Kadya Tall, Marie-Emmanuelle Pommerolle, and Michel Cahen, 305–58. Leiden: Brill, 2015.

Hiskett, Mervyn. "The Maitatsine Riots in Kano, 1980: An Assessment." *Journal of Religion in Africa* 17:3 (October 1987): 209–23.

Hoechner, Hannah. "Traditional Quranic Students (almajirai) in Nigeria: Fair Game for Unfair Accusations?" In *Boko Haram: Islamism, Politics, Security and the State in Nigeria,* edited by Marc-Antoine Pérouse de Montclos, 63–84. Leiden: African Studies Centre, 2014.

Human Rights Watch. "'Everyone's in on the Game': Corruption and Human Rights Abuses by the Nigeria Police Force." August 2010.

———. "'Leave Everything to God': Accountability for Inter-communal Violence in Plateau and Kaduna States, Nigeria." 12 December 2013.

———. "Letter to the Committee on Dialogue and Peaceful Resolution of Security Challenges in the North." 2 July 2013.

———. "The Miss World Riots: Continued Impunity for Killings in Kaduna." 22 July 2003.

———. "Nigeria: Boko Haram Abducts Women, Recruits Children." 29 November 2013.

———. "Nigeria: Boko Haram Attacks Indefensible." 8 November 2011.

———. "Nigeria: Events of 2009." 2010.

———. "Nigeria: Massive Destruction, Deaths from Military Raid." 1 May 2013.

Human Rights Watch. "Nigeria: Post-election Violence Killed 800." 16 May 2011.

———. "Nigeria's 2003 Elections: The Unacknowledged Violence." June 2004.

———. "Spiraling Violence: Boko Haram Attacks and Security Force Abuses in Nigeria." October 2012.

Ibrahim, Jibrin. "Declaration of State of Emergency on 14th May 2013: A Preliminary Assessment." Centre for Democracy Development in West Africa Blog. 15 May 2013, http://blog.cddwestafrica.org/2013/05/decla ration-of-state-of-emergency-on-14th-may-2013-a-preliminary-assessment/.

———. "The Politics of Religion in Nigeria: The Parameters of the 1987 Crisis in Kaduna State." *Review of African Political Economy* 45/46 (1989): 65–82.

Internal Displacement Monitoring Centre. "Nigeria IDP Figures Analysis." 2016.

International Crisis Group. "Cameroon: The Threat of Religious Radicalism." 3 September 2015.

———. "Curbing Violence in Nigeria (II): The Boko Haram Insurgency." 3 April 2014.

———. "The Central Sahel: A Perfect Sandstorm." 25 June 2015.

———. "Exploiting Disorder: Al-Qaeda and the Islamic State." 14 March 2016.

———. "Niger: Another Weak Link in the Sahel?" 19 September 2013.

International Organization for Migration. "Displacement Tracking Matrix, Round VIII Report." February 2016.

———. "Nigeria Emergency Operations: Situation Report." January 2016.

Isichei, Elizabeth. "The Maitatsine Risings in Nigeria 1980–85: A Revolt of the Disinherited." *Journal of Religion in Africa* 17:3 (October 1987): 194–208.

Jalal, Ayesha. *Partisans of Allah: Jihad in South Asia*. Cambridge, MA: Harvard University Press, 2010.

Jezequel, Jean-Herve, and Vincent Foucher. "Forced Out of Towns in the Sahel, Africa's Jihadists Go Rural." International Crisis Group. 11 January 2017.

Joseph, Richard. *Democracy and Prebendal Politics in Nigeria: The Rise and Fall of the Second Republic*. Cambridge: Cambridge University Press, 1987.

Kaag, Mayke. "Transnational Islamic NGOs in Chad: Islamic Solidarity in the Age of Neoliberalism." *Africa Today* 54:3 (Spring 2008): 3–18.

Kane, Ousmane. *Muslim Modernity in Postcolonial Nigeria: A Study of the Society for the Removal of Innovation and Reinstatement of Tradition*. Leiden: Brill, 2003.

Kaplan, Seth. "How Inequality Fuels Boko Haram." *Foreign Affairs*, 5 February 2015.

Kassim, Abdulbasit. "Defining and Understanding the Religious Philosophy of Jihadi Salafism and the Ideology of Boko Haram." *Journal of Politics, Religion and Ideology* 16:2–3 (2015): 173–200.

Kastfelt, Niels. "Rumours of Maitatsine: A Note on Political Culture in Northern Nigeria." *African Affairs* 88:350 (January 1989): 83–90.

Kawka, Rupert. "The Physiognomic Structure of Maiduguri." In *From Bulamari to Yerwa to Metropolitan Maiduguri: Interdisciplinary Studies on the Capital of Borno State, Nigeria*, edited by Rupert Kawka, 33–64. Köln: Rüdiger Köppe Verlag, 2002.

————. "Social Status and Urban Structure in Yerwa." In *From Bulamari to Yerwa*, 159–187.

Kendhammer, Brandon. "The Sharia Controversy in Northern Nigeria and the Politics of Islamic Law in New and Uncertain Democracies." *Comparative Politics* 45:33 (April 2013): 291–311.

Kenney, Jeffrey. *Muslim Rebels: Kharijites and the Politics of Extremism in Egypt*. New York: Oxford University Press, 2006.

Kogelmann, Franz. "The 'Sharia Factor' in Nigeria's 2003 Elections." In *Muslim-Christian Encounters in Africa*, edited by Benjamin Soares, 256–74. Leiden: Brill, 2006.

Koungou, Léon. *Boko Haram: Le Cameroon à l'épreuve des menaces*. Paris: L'Harmattan, 2014.

Lacher, Wolfram, and Guido Steinberg. "Spreading Local Roots: AQIM and Its Offshoots in the Sahara." In *Jihadism in Africa: Local Causes, Regional Expansion, International Alliances*, edited by Guido Steinberg and Annette Weber, 69–84. Berlin: Stiftung Wissenschaft und Politik, 2015.

Lacroix, Stéphane. "Between Revolution and Apoliticism: Nasir al-Din al-Albani and His Impact on the Shaping of Contemporary Salafism." In *Global Salafism*, ed. Meijer, 58–80.

Laitin, David. "The Sharia Debate and the Origins of Nigeria's Second Republic." *Journal of Modern African Studies* 20:3 (September 1982): 411–30.

Lasswell, Harold. *Politics: Who Gets What, When, How*. New York: Whittlesey House, 1936.

Last, Murray. "From Dissent to Dissidence: The Genesis and Development of Reformist Islamic Groups in Northern Nigeria." In *Sects and Social Disorder: Muslim Identities and Conflict in Northern Nigeria*, edited by Abdul Raufu Mustapha, 18–53. Suffolk: James Currey, 2014.

————. "The Search for Security in Muslim Northern Nigeria." *Africa* 78:1 (February 2008): 41–63.

Lauzière, Henri. *The Making of Salafism: Islamic Reform in the Twentieth Century*. New York: Columbia University Press, 2015.

Lav, Daniel. *Radical Islam and the Revival of Medieval Theology*. Cambridge: Cambridge University Press, 2012.

LeVan, Carl. *Dictators and Democracy in African Development: The Political Economy of Good Governance in Nigeria*. Cambridge: Cambridge University Press, 2014.

Lewis, Jessica. "Al-Qaeda in Iraq Resurgent: The Breaking the Walls Campaign, Part I." Institute for the Study of War, Middle East Report 14. September 2013.

Lewis, Peter. "From Prebendalism to Predation: The Political Economy of Decline in Nigeria." *Journal of Modern African Studies* 34:1 (March 1996): 79–103.

Lia, Brynjar. "Understanding Jihadi Proto-states." *Perspectives on Terrorism* 9:4 (2015), http://www.terrorismanalysts.com/pt/index.php/pot/article/view/441/872.

Loimeier, Roman. "Boko Haram: The Development of a Militant Religious Movement in Nigeria." *Africa Spectrum* 47:2–3 (2012): 137–55.

———. *Islamic Reform and Political Change in Northern Nigeria*. Evanston, IL: Northwestern University Press, 1997.

Lubeck, Paul. "Islamic Protest under Semi-industrial Capitalism: 'Yan Tatsine Explained." *Africa* 55:4 (1985): 369–89.

———. "Nigeria: Mapping a Shari'a Restorationist Movement." In *Shari'a Politics: Islamic Law and Society in the Modern World*, edited by Robert Hefner, 244–79. Bloomington: Indiana University Press, 2011.

Mahmood, Omar. "Boko Haram in 2016: A Highly Adaptable Foe." Institute for Security Studies. 7 February 2017.

Mamoudou [no surname]."Les Lamidats de l'Adamaoua à l'épreuve du processus démocratique et du gangstérisme rural." In *De l'Adamawa à l'Adamaoua: Histoire, enjeux et perspectives pour le Nord-Cameroon*, edited by Hamadou Adama, 183–99. Paris: L'Harmattan, 2014.

Mantzikos, Ioannis. "Boko Haram Attacks in Nigeria and Neighbouring Countries: A Chronology of Attacks." *Perspectives on Terrorism* 8:6 (2014), http://www.terrorismanalysts.com/pt/index.php/pot/article/view/391/html.

Masquelier, Adeline. "Debating Muslims, Disputed Practices: Struggles for the Realization of an Alternative Moral Order in Niger." In *Civil Society and the Political Imagination in Africa: Critical Perspectives*, edited by John L. Comaroff and Jean Comaroff, 219–50. Chicago: University of Chicago Press, 1999.

Max Lock Group Nigeria. *Maiduguri: Surveys and Planning Reports for Borno, Bauchi and Gongola State Governments*. Max Lock Group Nigeria, 1976.

———. *Potiskum: Surveys and Planning Reports*. Max Lock Group Nigeria, 1976.

McCants, William. *The ISIS Apocalypse: The History, Strategy, and Doomsday Vision of the Islamic State*. New York: St. Martin's, 2015.

———. "Trump's Misdiagnosis of the Jihadist Threat." Brookings Institution Markaz Blog. 11 November 2016, https://www.brookings.edu/blog/markaz/2016/11/11/trumps-misdiagnosis-of-the-jihadist-threat/.

Mendelsohn, Barak. *The al-Qaeda Franchise: The Expansion of al-Qaeda and Its Consequences.* New York: Oxford University Press, 2016.

Mercy Corps. "Motivations and Empty Promises: Voices of Former Boko Haram Combatants and Nigerian Youth." April 2016.

Mohammed, Kyari (Muhammad Kyari). "The Changing Responses of the Ummah to the Challenges of Western Education: Recent Trends in Maiduguri Mosques." *Al-Ijtihad: The Journal of the Islamization of Knowledge and Contemporary Issues* 5:2 (July 2005): 147–59.

———. "The Message and Methods of Boko Haram." In *Boko Haram: Islamism, Politics, Security and the State in Nigeria,* edited by Marc-Antoine Pérouse de Montclos, 9–32. Ibadan, Nigeria: French Institute for Research in Africa, 2014.

Mundy, Jacob. *Imaginative Geographies of Algerian Violence: Conflict Science, Conflict Management, Antipolitics.* Stanford, CA: Stanford University Press, 2015.

Murtada, Ahmad. "Jama'at 'Boko Haram': Nash'atuha wa-Mabadi'uha wa-A'maluha fi Nayjiriya." *Qira'at Ifriqiyya,* 13 November 2012.

Mustapha, Abdul Raufu. "Understanding Boko Haram." In *Sects and Social Disorder: Muslim Identities and Conflict in Northern Nigeria,* edited by Abdul Raufu Mustapha, 147–98. Suffolk: James Currey, 2014.

Mustapha, Abdullahi. "Introduction." In *On the Political Future of Nigeria,* edited by Ibraheem Sulaiman and Siraj Abdulkarim. Zaria: Hudahuda, 1988.

Newman, Paul. "The Etymology of Hausa *Boko*." Mega-Chad Research Network, 2013.

Ochonu, Moses. *Colonialism by Proxy: Hausa Imperial Agents and Middle Belt Consciousness in Nigeria.* Bloomington: Indiana University Press, 2014.

Ohadike, Don. "Muslim-Christian Conflict and Political Instability in Nigeria." In *Religion and National Integration in Africa: Islam, Christianity, and Politics in the Sudan and Nigeria,* edited by John Hunwick, 101–24. Evanston, IL: Northwestern University Press, 1992.

Okereke, Emeka. "From Obscurity to Global Visibility: Periscoping Abubakar Shekau." *Counter Terrorist Trends and Analysis* 6:10 (November 2014): 17–22.

Onuoha, Freedom. "The Audacity of the Boko Haram: Background, Analysis and Emerging Trend." *Security Journal* 25 (2012): 134–51.

Osaghae, Eghosa, and Rotimi Suberu. "A History of Identities, Violence and Stability in Nigeria." Centre for Research on Inequality, Human Security and Ethnicity Working Paper no. 6 (January 2005).

Østebø, Terje. *Localising Salafism: Religious Change among Oromo Muslims in Bale, Ethiopia*. Leiden: Brill, 2012.

Ostien, Philip. "Documentary Materials: Borno State." In *Sharia Implementation in Northern Nigeria 1999–2006: A Sourcebook*, vol. 6, *Ulama Institutions*, edited and compiled by Philip Ostien, chapter 8, part 2. Published online, 2011, http://www.sharia-in-africa.net/media/publications/sharia-implementation-in-northern-nigeria-volume-six/Chapter%208%20Part%20II.pdf.

———. "An Opportunity Missed by Nigeria's Christians: The 1976–78 Sharia Debate Revisited." In *Muslim-Christian Encounters in Africa*, edited by Benjamin Soares, 223–34. Leiden: Brill, 2006.

Othman, Shehu. "Classes, Crises, and Coup: The Demise of Shagari's Regime." *African Affairs* 83:333 (October 1984): 441–61.

Owens, Jonathan. *Neighborhood and Ancestry: Variation in the Spoken Arabic of Maiduguri, Nigeria*. Philadelphia: J. Benjamins, 1998.

Paden, John. *Muhammadu Buhari: The Challenges of Leadership in Nigeria*. Berkeley, CA: Roaring Forties, 2016.

———. *Religion and Political Culture in Kano*. Berkeley: University of California Press, 1973.

Pérouse de Montclos, Marc-Antoine. "Boko Haram: Les enjeux régionaux de l'insurrection." Fondation Jean Jaures. 10 February 2015.

———. "Nigeria's Interminable Insurgency: Addressing the Boko Haram Crisis." Chatham House, September 2014.

Peshkin, Alan. *Kanuri Schoolchildren: Education and Social Mobilization in Nigeria*. New York: Holt, Rinehart, and Winston, 1972.

Pew Forum on Religion and Public Life. *The World's Muslims: Religion, Politics and Society*. Washington, DC: Pew, 30 April 2013.

Pezard, Stephanie, and Michael Shurkin. *Achieving Peace in Northern Mali: Past Agreements, Local Conflicts, and the Prospects for a Durable Settlement*. Santa Monica, CA: RAND, 2015.

Pred, Allan, and Michael Watts. *Reworking Modernity: Capitalisms and Symbolic Discontent*. New Brunswick, NJ: Rutgers University Press, 1992.

Renard, John. "Al-Jihad al-Akbar: Notes on a Theme in Islamic Spirituality." *Muslim World* 78:3–4 (October 1988): 225–42.

Reno, William. *Warlord Politics and African States*. Boulder: Lynne Rienner, 1999.

The Resettlement of Gwoza Hill Peoples. Maiduguri: Department of Geography, Borno State Advanced Teachers College, November 1982.

Reynolds, Jonathan. *The Time of Politics (Zaminin Siyasa): Islam and the Politics of Legitimacy in Northern Nigeria, 1950–1966*. Bethesda, MD: International Scholars, 1999.

Schritt, Jannik. "The 'Protests against Charlie Hebdo' in Niger: A Background Analysis." *Africa Spectrum* 50:1 (2015): 49–64.

Seesemann, Rüdiger. "Der lange Arm des Ibrahim Salih." In *Die islamische Welt als Netzwerk*, edited by Roman Loimeier, 135–61. Würzburg: Erlon Verlag, 2000.

Siollun, Max. *Oil, Politics and Violence: Nigeria's Military Coup Culture (1966–1976)*. New York: Algora, 2009.

Smith, Daniel Jordan. *A Culture of Corruption: Everyday Deception and Popular Discontent in Nigeria*. Princeton, NJ: Princeton University Press, 2006.

Smith, Mike. *Boko Haram: Inside Nigeria's Unholy War*. London: I. B. Tauris, 2015.

Sounaye, Abdoulaye. "Ambiguous Secularism: Islam, Laïcité and the State in Niger." *Civilisations* 58:2 (2009): 41–57.

———. "Irwo Sunnance yan-no! Youth Claiming, Contesting and Transforming Salafism." *Islamic Africa* 6:1–2 (2015): 82–108.

———. "Mobile Sunna: Islam, Small Media and Community in Niger." *Social Compass* 61:1 (March 2014): 21–29.

Stampnitzky, Lisa. *Disciplining Terror: How Experts Invented "Terrorism."* New York: Cambridge University Press, 2014.

Suberu, Rotimi. "The Struggle for New States in Nigeria, 1976–1990." *African Affairs* 90:361 (October 1991): 499–522.

Sulaiman, Ibrahim. "The Shari'ah and the 1979 Constitution." In *Islamic Law in Nigeria: Application and Teaching*, edited by S. Khalid Rashid, 52–74. Lagos: Islamic Publications Bureau, 1986.

Tamuno, Tekena. "The Nigeria Police Force and Public Security and Safety." In *Security, Crime and Segregation in West African Cities since the 19th Century*, edited by Laurent Fouchard and Isaac Albert, 119–40. Paris: Karthala, 2003.

Thurston, Alexander. "Ahlussunnah: A Preaching Network from Kano to Medina and Back." In *Shaping Global Islamic Discourses: The Role of al-Azhar, al-Madina, and al-Mustafa*, edited by Masooda Bano and Keiko Sakurai, 93–116. Edinburgh: Edinburgh University Press, 2015.

———. "The Aminu Kano College of Islamic and Legal Studies: A Site for the Renegotiation of Islamic Law and Authority in Kano, Nigeria." In *Muslim Institutions of Higher Learning in Postcolonial Africa*, edited by Mbaye Lo and Muhammed Haron, 247–64. New York: Palgrave, 2015.

———. " 'The Disease Is Unbelief': Boko Haram's Religious and Political Worldview." Brookings Institution Project on U.S. Relations with the Muslim World, Analysis Paper no. 22. January 2016.

———. "Muslim Politics and Shari'a in Kano, Nigeria." *African Affairs* 114: 454 (January 2015): 28–51.

Thurston, Alexander. *Salafism in Nigeria: Islam, Preaching and Politics.* Cambridge: Cambridge University Press, 2016.

Umar, Muhammad Sani. "Education and Islamic Trends in Northern Nigeria: 1970s–1990s." *Africa Today* 48:2 (Summer 2001): 127–50.

———. *Islam and Colonialism: Intellectual Responses of Muslims of Northern Nigeria to British Colonial Rule.* Leiden: Brill, 2006.

———. "Islamic Arguments for Western Education in Northern Nigeria: Mu'azu Hadejia's Hausa Poem, *Ilmin Zaman.*" *Islam et societés au sud du Sahara* 16 (2002): 85–106.

Usman, Zainab. "The Successes and Failures of Economic Reform in Nigeria's Post-military Political Settlement." University of Oxford Global Economic Governance Programme Working Paper 115 (March 2016).

Varin, Caroline. *Boko Haram and the War on Terror.* Santa Barbara, CA: Praeger, 2016.

Vaughan, Olufemi. *Nigerian Chiefs: Traditional Power in Modern Politics, 1890s–1990s.* Rochester, NY: University of Rochester Press, 2006.

Wagemakers, Joas. "Defining the Enemy: Abu Muhammad al-Maqdisi's Radical Reading of Surat al-Mumtahana." *Die Welt des Islams* 48 (2008): 348–71.

———. *A Quietist Jihadi: The Ideology and Influence of Abu Muhammad al-Maqdisi.* Cambridge: Cambridge University Press, 2012.

Wainscott, Ann. *Bureaucratizing Islam: Morocco and the War on Terror.* New York: Cambridge University Press, 2017.

Walker, Andrew. *"Eat the Heart of the Infidel": The Harrowing of Nigeria and the Rise of Boko Haram.* London: Hurst, 2016.

———. "What Is Boko Haram?" United States Institute of Peace Special Report 308 (June 2012).

WATHI. "Présidentielle Tchad: Une campagne électorale marquée par des contestations et des arrestations." 6 April 2016.

Watts, Michael. *Silent Violence: Food, Famine and Peasantry in Northern Nigeria.* Athens: University of Georgia Press, 2013 [1983].

Wehrey, Frederic, and Ala' Alrababa'h. "Splitting the Islamists: The Islamic State's Creeping Advance in Libya." Carnegie Endowment for International Peace. 19 June 2015.

Weimann, Gunnar. *Islamic Criminal Law in Northern Nigeria: Politics, Religion, Judicial Practice.* Amsterdam: Amsterdam University Press, 2010.

Wiktorowicz, Quintan. "Anatomy of the Salafi Movement." *Studies in Conflict and Terrorism* 29:3 (2006): 207–39.

Yakubu, Mahmood. *An Aristocracy in Political Crisis: The End of Indirect Rule and the Emergence of Party Politics in the Emirates of Northern Nigeria.* Aldershot, UK: Avebury, 1996.

Yusuf, Shehu Tijjani. "Stealing from the Railways: Blacksmiths, Colonialism, and Innovation in Northern Nigeria." In *Transforming Innovations in Africa: Explorative Studies on Appropriation in African Societies*, edited by Jan-Bart Gewald, André Leliveld, and Iva Peša, 275–96. Leiden: Brill, 2012.

Zenn, Jacob. "Exposing and Defeating Boko Haram: Why the West Must Unite to Help Nigeria Defeat Terrorism." Bow Group, July 2014.

———."Nigerian al-Qaedaism." *Current Trends in Islamist Ideology*. 14 March 2014, http://www.theguardian.com/world/2014/may/06/how-nigerian-police-also-detained-women-and-children-as-weapon-of-war.

Documents from Governments and Multilateral Organizations

African Union Peace and Security Council. "Report of the Chairperson of the Commission on the Implementation of Communiqué PSC/AHG/COMM.2 (CDLXXXIV) on the Boko Haram Terrorist Group and on Other Related International Efforts." 3 March 2015.

Annual Report for Northern Nigeria, 1907–8.

Borno State Government. *Government White Papers on the Report of the Commission of Inquiry into the Religious Disturbances in Bulum-Kutu Area of Maiduguri between the 26th–29th October, 1982*. Maiduguri: Borno State Government, 1982.

———. "Islamic Religious Preachings Law." 1981. Reproduced in *Sharia Implementation in Northern Nigeria 1999–2006: A Sourcebook*, vol. 6, *Ulama Institutions*, edited and compiled by Philip Ostien, chapter 8, part 2, 11–17. Published online, 2011, http://www.sharia-in-africa.net/media/publications/sharia-implementation-in-northern-nigeria-volume-six/Chapter%208%20Part%20II.pdf.

———. *Local Govt. Reforms and You*. Maiduguri: Information Division, Military Governor's Office; printed by Baraka Press Limited, 1977.

Borno State Transition Committee. *Main Report (Executive Summary) Submitted to His Excellency Senator (Dr.) Ali Modu Sheriff, Executive Governor, Borno State*. July 2003.

Central Bank of Nigeria. "Terrorism Prevention Proscription Order Notice, 2013." 10 June 2013.

Committee on Application of Sharia in Borno State. "Report of the Committee on Application of Sharia in Borno State." April 2000. Reproduced in *Sharia Implementation in Northern Nigeria 1999–2006: A Sourcebook*, vol. 1, chapter 2, supplementary materials part 4, edited by Philip Ostien. Published online, 2007, http://www.sharia-in-africa.net/media/publications

/sharia-implementation-in-northern-nigeria/vol_2_10_chapter_2_supp
_borno_pre.pdf.

European Union Election Observation Mission to Nigeria. "Final Report."
2003.

Federal Republic of Nigeria. 1979 Constitution.

French Presidency/Élysée. "Conclusions du 'Sommet de Paris pour la sécurité au Nigeria.'" 17 May 2014.

Government of Niger, Ministry of the Interior and Decentralization. "Etude
sur les pratiques de l'islam au Niger." April 2006.

Governor's Office, Borno State. *Selected Speeches of His Excellency,
Sen. (Dr.) Ali Modu Sheriff, Executive Governor, Borno State: 731 Days
in Office.* Maiduguri: Political Affairs Department, Governor's Office,
Borno State; printed by Spin-Ads Communications, 2005.

High Court No. 3, Maiduguri, Borno State. Judgment in the case of Baba
Kura Alh. Fugu vs. the President of the Federal Republic of Nigeria, the
Executive Governor of Borno State, the Attorney General of the Federa-
tion, the Attorney General of Borno State, and the Inspector General of
Police. 13 April 2010.

Kano State Government. *Report of the Kano Disturbances Tribunal of Inquiry.* 14 April 1981.

National Bureau of Statistics (Nigeria). *2011 Annual Socio-economic Report.*
2011.

National Human Rights Commission of Nigeria. "The Baga Incident and the
Situation in North-East Nigeria: An Interim Assessment and Report."
June 2013.

National Population Commission of Nigeria. "1991 Population Census of
the Federal Republic of Nigeria: Analytical Report at the National Level."
Abuja, 1998.

———. *2006 Population and Housing Census.* Abuja, April 2010.

———. "Nigeria 2008 Demographic and Health Survey: Key Findings."
2009. North Eastern State of Nigeria. *The North Eastern State of Nigeria.*
Zaria: Gaskiya, 1968.

Nyako, Murtala. "On-Going Full-Fledged Genocide in Northern Nigeria."
Memorandum to the Northern Governors Forum. 16 April 2014.

Plateau State Government. "White Paper on the Report of the Commission
of Inquiry into the Riots of 12th April, 1994 in Jos Metropolis." September 2004.

Sharia Implementation Committee of Borno State. "Interim Report of the
Sharia Implementation Committee." 2001. Reproduced in *Sharia Imple-
mentation in Northern Nigeria 1999–2006: A Sourcebook*, vol. 2, *Ulama
Institutions*, edited and compiled by Philip Ostien, supplement to chap-

ter 2. Published online, 2011, http://www.sharia-in-africa.net/media/pub
lications/sharia-implementation-in-northern-nigeria/vol_2_13_chapter
_2_supp_borno_post.pdf.

United Kingdom Department for International Development. "Elections in
Nigeria 2007." Undated.

United Kingdom Home Office. "Proscribed Terrorist Organisations" (2015).

United Nations Department of Economic and Social Affairs/Population Division. "World Population Prospects: The 2015 Revision, Key Findings and
Advance Tables." 2015.

United Nations Office for the Coordination of Humanitarian Affairs (UN
OCHA). "2017 Humanitarian Needs and Requirement Overview: Lake
Chad Basin Emergency." January 2017.

———. "Niger—Diffa: Key Facts and Figures (December 2016)." January
2017.

United Nations Office for the Coordination of Humanitarian Affairs (UN
OCHA)—Lake Chad Basin. "Humanitarian Brief: An Overlooked Crisis in
an Overlooked Region." October 2015.

———. "Humanitarian Needs and Overview." January 2016.

United Nations Office of the High Commissioner for Human Rights (UN
OHCHR). "Report of the United Nations High Commissioner for Human Rights on Violations and Abuses Committed by Boko Haram and
the Impact on Human Rights in the Affected Countries." 29 September
2015.

United Nations Security Council. "Security Council al-Qaida Sanctions Committee Adds Abubakar Mohammed Shekau, Ansaru to Its Sanctions List."
26 June 2014.

United Nations Security Council (UNSC) Analytical Support and Monitoring Team concerning al-Qaida and Associated Individuals and Entities.
"Report . . . concerning the Terrorism Threat in Libya." 19 November
2015.

United States Central Intelligence Agency. "The World Factbook—Nigeria."

United States Department of Justice. "Umar Farouk Abdulmutallab Sentenced to Life in Prison for Attempted Bombing of Flight 253 on Christmas Day 2009." 16 February 2012.

United States Department of State. "Terrorist Designations of Boko Haram
and Ansaru." 13 November 2013.

United States District Court, Eastern District of New York, "United States of
America against Ibrahim Suleiman Adnan Adam Harun: Government's
Memorandum of Law in Support of Motion for an Anonymous and Partly
Sequestered Jury," 8 April 2016, http://www.courthousenews.com/wp-con
tent/uploads/2017/02/Harun.pdf.

United States Embassy Abuja. Leaked cable 04ABUJA183. "Nigerian 'Taliban' Attacks Most Likely Not Tied to Taliban nor al-Qaida." 6 February 2004.

———. Leaked cable 07ABUJA697. "Snapshot of Key Northern Gubernatorial Races." 12 April 2007.

———. Leaked cable 09ABUJA1053. "Nigeria: Police Shoot 17 in Maiduguri, Tensions Remain High." 12 June 2009.

———. Leaked cable 09ABUJA1379. "Nigeria: Extremist Attacks Continue into Night." 28 July 2009.

———. Leaked cable 09ABUJA1392. "Nigerian Government Quashes Extremists, but Not the Root of the Problem." 29 July 2009.

———. Leaked cable 09ABUJA2014. "Nigeria: Borno State Residents Not Yet Recovered from Boko Haram Violence." 4 November 2009.

United States Embassy N'Djamena. Leaked cable 07NDJAMENA149. "Chad's Grand Imam Requests Help to Investigate Terrorism Financing." 15 February 2007.

———. Leaked cable 07NDJAMENA455. "Grand Imam Voices Concern over Extremists' 'New Strategy' in Chad." 4 June 2007.

———. Leaked cable 07NDJAMENA508. "Corrected Version: Islam in Southern Chad." 20 June 2007.

United States Embassy Yaoundé. Leaked cable 09YAOUNDE256. "Cameroon's Justice Minister Says North Will Support Biya, but Not Another Beti or Bami." 12 March 2009.

———. Leaked cable 10YAOUNDE83. "Cameroonian President Biya Gives Ambassador Political/Economic Overview." 5 February 2010.

Newspapers, Online News Sources, and Blogs

African Arguments
Agence France-Presse (AFP)
Al Jazeera
Al-Quds al-Arabi
Alwihda Info
Aminiya
Associated Press
Atlantic
BBC
Channels Television
Conversation
Daily Champion
Daily Independent

Daily Trust
Dan Borno
Desert Herald
Deutsche Welle
Eeben Barlow's Military and Security Blog
L'Express
Fulan's SITREP
Gamji
Guardian
Intercept
International Business Times
IRIN
Jeune Afrique
Kano Online
Leadership
Long War Journal
Al-Masalah
Al-Mjhar
MediaPart
Moment
Le Monde
Musings of a Lost Soul
Nation
New York Times
Orange Tracker
PM News Nigeria
Premium Times
Pulse TV
Punch
Radio France Internationale (RFI)
Reciter Muhammad al-Barnawy
Reuters
Sahara Reporters
Sahel Blog
Source
Sun
Sunday Sun
Sun News Online
Tempo
Think Africa Press
This Day
A Tunanina

Vanguard
Vice News
Voice of America
La Voix
Wall Street Journal
Washington Post
Weekly Trust

Jihadi Videos and Audio Recordings

Boko Haram. "Boko Haram Declares a New Caliphate in Northern Nigeria." 24 August 2014. Available at https://www.youtube.com/watch?v=Rl4IgD—nKg.

———. "Boko Haram Militants Display Control of Captured Towns in Northeastern Nigeria." 10 November 2014. Available at https://www.youtube.com/watch?v=7dkdFaVrCls.

———. "A Message to the Leaders of Disbelievers." February 2015. Available at http://jihadology.net/2015/02/17/al-urwah-al-wuthqa-foundation-presents-a-new-video-message-from-jamaat-ahl-al-sunnah-li-l-dawah-wa-l-jihads-boko-%E1%B8%A5aram-abu-bakr-shekau-a-message-to-the-leader/.

———. "Min dunihi fa-Kiduni thumma La Tanzurun." 5 May 2014. Available at https://www.youtube.com/watch?v=wrfWSvL0D4.

———. "New Boko Haram Video Reiterates Allegiance to ISIS." 5 April 2016. Available at https://www.youtube.com/watch?v=fQAj3Fdoqng.

Islamic State Tripolitania Province (Wilayat Tarabulus). "Min al-Dhill ila-ʿIzza." May 2016. Available at http://jihadology.net/2016/05/29/new-video-message-from-the-islamic-state-from-humiliation-to-glory-wilayat-%E1%B9%ADarabulus/.

Katibat al-Mulaththamin. "Malhamat al-Aba.ʾ" September 2013. Available at http://jihadology.net/2013/09/09/new-video-message-from-katibat-al-mulathamun-epic-battles-of-the-fathers-the-battle-of-shaykh-abd-al-%E1%B8%A5amid-abu-zayd/.

Nur, Muhammad (Mamman). "Fallasa." August 2016. Available at https://www.youtube.com/watch?v=86TwFqg-Aqc.

Shekau, Abubakar. "Alleged Boko Haram Video Depicting Leader Shekau Surrendering." March 2016. Available at https://www.youtube.com/watch?v=oefFuM4JS1c.

———. "Maʿrakat Maiduguri 2." March 2014. Available at https://www.youtube.com/watch?v=Pba8uvuf9Is.

———. "Message to President Jonathan." January 2012. Available at https://www.youtube.com/watch?v=umkj50SUzck.

———. "Message to the World on Baga." January 2015. Available at http://jihadology.net/2015/01/21/new-video-message-from-boko-%E1%B8%A5arams-jamaat-ahl-al-sunnah-li-dawah-wa-l-jihad-imam-abu-bakr-shekau-message-to-the-world-on-baga/.

———. "Sako Zuwa Ga Duniya." September 2012. Available at https://www.youtube.com/watch?v=txUJCOKTIuk&sns=em.

———. Untitled audio message. 4 August 2016. Available at https://www.youtube.com/watch?v=chIBAwlKf0k.

———. Untitled video. Undated, likely 2008–9. Available at https://www.youtube.com/watch?v=eQY4GLtzLdU.

———. "Wannan Ne Akidarmu." Undated, likely 2015. Available at http://www.liveleak.com/view?i=d4b1421362369.

Yusuf, Muhammad. "Film.3gp." Undated. Available at https://www.youtube.com/watch?v=xthVNq9OKD0.

———. "Guzurin Mujaahidai." 28 March 2009. Available at https://www.youtube.com/watch?v=VWCNdqwGU-M.

———. Hadhihi 'Aqidatuna (untitled audio commentary). Undated (likely 2008 or 2009). Available at https://www.youtube.com/watch?v=JWfWa2rfsKw&index=2&list=UUdXgmSgdkq3HIwFnZcYuweA.

———. "Nasiha." Undated. Available at https://www.youtube.com/watch?v=kHG6f5cWjKs.

———. "Open Letter to the Federal Government of Nigeria." 12 June 2009. Available at https://www.youtube.com/watch?v=f89PvcpWSRg.

———. Police interrogation video (untitled). 30 July 2009. Available at https://www.youtube.com/watch?v=ePpUvfTXY7w.

———. "Tafsirin Tauba." Undated. Part 1 available at https://www.youtube.com/watch?v=Y33rLD6pw; part two available at https://www.youtube.com/watch?v=R3NcgQv-LVM.

———. "Tarihin Musulmai." Likely 2009. Available at https://www.youtube.com/watch?v=eUQYNucjqUE.

———. "Warware Shubuhar Malamai." Audio recording circa 2008. Available at https://www.youtube.com/watch?v=dWfv28iSEZQ.

Written Jihadi Sources

Abu Zayd, Abd al-Hamid. Letter to Abd al-Malik Droukdel. 24 August 2009. Recovered at Usama bin Ladin's compound in Abbottabad, Pakistan and released by the U.S. Office of the Director of National Intelligence on 19 January 2017.

Al-Bulaydi, Abu al-Hasan. *Nasa'ih wa-Tawjihat Shar'iyya min al-Shaykh Abi al-Hasan Rashid li-Mujahidi Nayjiriya*, edited by Abu al-Nu'man Qutayba al-Shinqiti. Mu'assasat al-Andalus, April 2017. Available at: https://azelin.files.wordpress.com/2017/04/shaykh-abucc84-al-hcca3asan-rashicc84d-22sharicc84ah-advice-and-guidance-for-the-mujacc84hidicc84n-of-nigeria22.pdf.

Al-Qaida in the Islamic Maghreb (AQIM) Shura Council. Letter to the Shura Council of the Veiled Men Battalion. 3 October 2012. Recovered by the Associated Press in Timbuktu, Mali in 2013.

Ansary, Abu Usamatul. "A Message from Nigeria," *Al Risalah* 4 (January 2017): 18–21.

"Hiwar ma'a al-Qa'id Khalid Abi Abbas—Amir al-Mintaqa al-Sahrawiyya li-l-Jama'a al-Salafiyya li-l-Da'wa wa-l-Qital." Minbar al-Tawhid wa-l-Jihad. 5 May 2006.

Islamic State. "The Bay'ah from West Africa," *Dabiq* 8 (Jumada II 1437/April 2015): 14–16.

———. "Foreword." *Dabiq* 8 (Jumada II 1437/April 2015): 3–6.

———. "Interview with Abul-Mughirah al-Qahtani," *Dabiq* 11 (Dhu al-Qada 1436/September 2015).

———. "Wali Gharb Ifriqiya: Al-Shaykh Abu Mus'ab al-Barnawi." *Al-Naba'* 41 (2 August 2016): 8–9.

Jama'at Ansar al-Muslimin fi Bilad al-Sudan. Charter. 2012.

Shekau, Abubakar. Letter to al-Qa'ida. Circa 2010. Recovered at Usama bin Ladin's compound in Abbottabad, Pakistan and released by the U.S. Office of the Director of National Intelligence on 1 March 2016.

———. "Risalat Ta'ziyya." July 2010.

Yusuf, Muhammad. *Hadhihi 'Aqidatuna wa-Manhaj Da'watina*. Maiduguri: Maktabat al-Ghuraba', likely 2009.

———. *Majmu'at Khutab li-l-Imam Abi Yusuf Muhammad bin Yusuf al-Maydughari*. Mu'assasat al-'Urwa al-Wuthqa li-l-Intaj al-'Ilmi, 2015.

Videos, Recordings, and Unpublished Documents by Nigerian Salafis (non–Boko Haram)

Adam, Ja'far Mahmud. "Fadakarwa Game da Halalcin Boko." Undated (likely 2005–7). Available at https://www.youtube.com/watch?v=hiM1ZUhmLAU.

———. "Gwagwarmaya Tsakanin Karya da Gaskiya." Recorded lecture. 15 November 2006.

———. "Kalubalen Sharia." Recorded Lecture. 15/16 June 2000.

———. "Me Ya Sa Suke Cewa Boko Haramun Ne?" Undated (likely 2005–7). Available at https://www.youtube.com/watch?v=kkNDO0e2Jf8.

————. "Siyasa a Nigeria." Recorded lecture. 2003.

"Albani" Zaria, Muhammad Awwal Adam. "In An Ki Ji 2/3." Undated. Available at https://www.youtube.com/watch?v=M2q-tNpXRqM&t=302s.

————. "Karen Bana." 2 August 2009. Part 1 available at https://www.youtube.com/watch?v=z8HUJspctzk. Part 3 available at https://www.youtube.com/watch?v=d-x9ycFGC0s.

Ibrahim, Muhammad Mansur. "Matsayin Karatun Boko da Aikin Gwamnati a Musulunci." Text of a lecture delivered in Bauchi. May 2009.

Pantami, Isa Ali (Isa Ali Bauchi). Debate with Muhammad Yusuf. Undated, likely 2008. Available at https://www.youtube.com/watch?v=h-nhmj3faHc.

Rijiyar Lemo, Muhammad Sani Umar. "Kungiyoyin Jihadi." Parts 1 and 2. Recorded lecture. April 2009.

Interviews

Akilu, Fatima. Skype. 1 March 2016.

Attahirou, Mahamidou. Skype. 28 March 2016.

Ayong, Ahmed Khalid. Skype. 30 March 2016.

Bolori, Ahmed. Skype. 9 January 2017.

Gamawa, Aminu. Telephone. 2 February 2016.

Ibrahim, Ibrahim Yahaya. Skype. 3 February 2016.

Idrissa, Abdourahmane. Skype. 28 March 2016.

Medical professional from Borno State (anonymous). February 2016.

Müller-Kosack, Gerhard. Telephone. 25 May 2016.

Owens, Jonathan. Skype. 8 June 2016.

Salafi leader in Diffa, Niger (anonymous). Telephone. 12 June 2016.

Index

▶▶▶▶▶▶▶

PRINCETON STUDIES IN MUSLIM POLITICS